INTRODUCING THE BIBLE

Volume 2

The New Testament

Edited by

John C. Brunt

Douglas R. Clark

pericope, p. 234

Mon, May 1
12-1:30
Herb cooking
RMH outpatient
center
(4th floor)

University Press of America, Inc.
Lanham • New York • London

Copyright © 1997 by
University Press of America,® Inc.
4720 Boston Way
Lanham, Maryland 20706

12 Hid's Copse Rd.
Cummor Hill, Oxford OX2 9JJ

Library of Congress Cataloging-in-Publication Data

Introducing the Bible / edited by John C. Brunt, Douglas R. Clark.
p.   cm.
Includes bibliographical references.
Contents: v. 2. The New Testament.
1. Bible--Introductions. I. Brunt, John. II. Clark, Douglas R.
BS475.2.I533   1997   220.6'l--dc21   96-47215 CIP

ISBN 0-7618-0631-8 (v. 2 : cloth: alk. ppr.)
ISBN 0-7618-0632-6 (v. 2 : pbk: alk. ppr.)

⊖™ The paper used in this publication meets the minimum
requirements of American National Standard for information
Sciences—Permanence of Paper for Printed Library Materials,
ANSI Z39.48—1984

Dedication ─────────────────────────────────────

With deepest gratitude for his gentle Christian way, his unstinting insistence on reading the Bible on its own terms and his friendship as teacher and colleague, we dedicate *Introducing the Bible* to:

J. PAUL GROVE
Professor Emeritus
School of Theology
Walla Walla College

Table of Contents ────────────────────────────

Table of Illustrations

List of Abbreviations ――――――――――――

Gen	Genesis	Dan	Daniel
Exod	Exodus	Hos	Hosea
Lev	Leviticus	Joel	Joel
Num	Numbers	Amos	Amos
Deut	Deuteronomy	Obad	Obadiah
Josh	Joshua	Jon	Jonah
Judg	Judges	Mic	Micah
Ruth	Ruth	Nah	Nahum
1 Sam	First Samuel	Hab	Habakkuk
	(=1 Kingdoms)	Zeph	Zephaniah
2 Sam	Second Samuel	Hag	Haggai
	(=2 Kingdoms)	Zech	Zechariah
1 Kgs	First Kings	Mal	Malachi
	(=3 Kingdoms)		
2 Kgs	Second Kings	Tob	Tobit
	(=4 Kingdoms)	Jdt	Judith
1 Chr	First Chronicles	Add Esth	Additions to Esther
2 Chr	Second Chronicles	Wis	Wisdom of Solomon
Ezra	Ezra	Sir	Sirach (=Ecclesiasticus)
Neh	Nehemiah	Bar	Baruch
Esth	Esther	1 Esdr	First Esdras
Job	Job	2 Esdr	Second Esdras
Ps(s)	Psalms		(2 Esdr 1-2= 5 Ezra)
Prov	Proverbs		(2 Esdr 3-14=4 Ezra)
Eccl	Ecclesiastes		(2 Esdr 15-16=6 Ezra)
Song	Song of Songs	Ep Jer	Epistle of Jeremiah
Isa	Isaiah	Pr Azar	Prayer of Azariah
Jer	Jeremiah	Sus	Susanna
Lam	Lamentations	Bel	Bel and the Dragon
Ezek	Ezekiel	1 Macc	First Maccabes

2 Macc	Second Maccabes	*H.E.*	*Historia Ecclesiastica*
3 Macc	Third Maccabes		*(Ecclesiastical History)* by
4 Macc	Fourth Maccabes		Eusebinus
Pr Man	Prayer of Manasseh	LXX	Septuagint=Greek Old
			Testament
Matt	Matthew	MT	Masoretic Text=Hebrew
Mark	Mark		Bible
Luke	Luke	vs(s)	verse(s)
John	John		
Acts	Acts		
Rom	Romans		
1 Cor	First Corinthians		
2 Cor	Second Corinthians		
Gal	Galatians		
Eph	Ephesians		
Phil	Philippians		
Col	Colossians		
1 Thess	First Thessalonians		
2 Thess	Second Thessalonians		
1 Tim	First Timothy		
2 Tim	Second Timothy		
Titus	Titus		
Phlm	Philemon		
Heb	Hebrews		
Jas	James		
1 Pet	First Peter		
2 Pet	Second Peter		
1 John	First John		
2 John	Second John		
3 John	Third John		
Jude	Jude		
Rev	Revelation		

ANET	*Ancient Near Eastern Texts Relating to the Old Testament*, ed. by James B. Pritchard
B.C.E.	Before the Common Era (=B.C.)
C.E.	The Common Era (=A.D.)
ch(s)	chapter(s)
DSS	Dead Sea Scrolls

Foreword ————————————————————

Introducing the Bible is written by a dozen or so Bible teachers, all of whom have either worked together or are well acquainted with each other. Even so, it reveals significant differences in style, approach and perspective. Furthermore, all the writers have taught undergraduate religion courses at some point in their careers and are here offering glimpses into the ways they approach the Bible and its interpretation in the lecture room. A cursory reading of the chapters will reveal that they provide a series of introductions to significant topics surrounding the Bible and to the individual books of the Old and New Testaments.

By this novel approach the authors draw attention to their wish that the reader will focus not upon a particular orientation or "school of thought" in this Introduction, but on the task of teaching the Bible to students in college as well as to adults, who may not have given the Scriptures much thought or who may have become intimidated by the academic discussion of them. Recent popular essays on the Bible in the news magazines have raised Bible readers' curiosity about the historicity of the Bible stories, about the teachings of Jesus, about the apocalypse, the end of the world, and about human origins. Other news stories have revealed the shocking results of religious fanaticism fueled by unexamined Bible texts, and without the benefit of ethical and moral standards.

This calls for an ever renewed attention to the history of the Scriptures, the story of the Bible, the setting and background of its books and the teaching of its writings. The Bible is sacred to Jews and Christians, preserved as a witness to the God of creation and redemption, to his Christ and to the life and faith of his church. It is the expressed hope of the many writers of this introduction that its readers will examine the Bible anew and with new understanding.

Niels-Erik Andreasen
Andrews University

Acknowledgements ————————————————————

A number of people have contributed significantly to bringing this introduction into being and they deserve our highest accolades and our most sincere gratitude. The authors have dedicated long hours to the task of producing articles and chapters which speak from the heart as well as the head. We commend them.

Other individuals read the manuscript or portions of it, paying close attention to details of punctuation, grammar, style, readability, content, and issues of faith. These include Donna Evans, a secondary educator; Linda Veverka, former secretary for the School of Theology at Walla Walla College; and Cheryl Weis, current secretary for the School of Theology along with two Walla Walla College seniors, Tina Batten and Mindy Rodenberg. It is especially to Tina and Mindy that we owe a singular debt of gratitude for their months of intense, steady labor with anxious editors, pressing deadlines and recalcitrant computers. Their copy-editing and work with charts, illustration boxes and indices were indispensable. Our thanks as well to Michelle Harris and Helen Hudson of the University Press of America who always proved helpful and gracious.

We are also deeply grateful to Leanne Heaton Culver, a graduate of Walla Walla College, for the drawings which appear throughout and grace the two volumes and which consistently and creatively capture well the biblical stories and books we introduce. The maps were computer-generated by Robert Carr, a current student at Walla Walla College, and Dale Chapman, graphic designer for the Office of College Relations at Walla Walla College and also a graduate of Walla Walla College, and reflect careful attention to detail, scale and texture. In addition, we are indebted to the Administration and Faculty Development Committee of Walla Walla College which funded two faculty research grants for this project.

Although this two-volume set could not have appeared without the people mentioned above, people to whom we are eternally grateful, we take full responsibility for the contents of the volumes.

Introduction to the Set

Since the time of the Reformation in Protestantism, and at least since Vatican II in Catholicism, the church has emphasized that the Bible should belong to the people. It should serve as a source of inspiration and a foundation for faith. Yet, in an age of specialization, when the average person is often intimidated by the scholar, the Bible can appear to be formidable, foreign territory. How are ordinary people, non-specialists, to work their way through the many kinds of literature, from poems to letters, and prophetic oracles to genealogies, and make sense of it all? And when the scholars, who supposedly know, disagree about so many things, how can the casual reader have confidence?

This two-volume work is designed as a map to help non-specialists enter the world of the Bible for themselves. The work provides important background material, charts and maps that will help the reader feel more at home with the world of the Bible. Most of the work, however, is devoted to articles that introduce each of the books of the Bible, so that the reader can then read and study the biblical books with more information and less fear.

These volumes attempt to take seriously both up-to-date scholarship and an affirming faith stance. The goal is a theologically balanced approach, with attention to traditional concerns of introduction, as well as a focus on issues of relevance and practical religious value in the study and interpretation of Scripture. We have tried to avoid the polemic tone of some of the more conservative introductions, as well as the more speculative and value-free perspectives of more progressive readings.

To accomplish these goals, we have divided each chapter relating to a biblical book into several categories. The first is a brief overview of the book. The second section treats background concerns, matters of authorship, dating, historical background, and helpful archaeological material when it is relevant. The third section focuses on literary considerations. What kind of literature are we reading when we enter this book? What are the literary devices that the author uses to communicate with the readers?

The fourth section focuses on the message of the book. It begins with a brief outline, and then discusses major concerns and themes. Obviously, a book cannot be reduced to a simple propositional message, especially if the book is rich in story and poetry. But there were concerns that drove the writer to write, and here we try to analyze those concerns. The next section treats the value and

relevance of the book for today. How might we bridge the gulf of centuries and hear this book, given our time and place in the world?

The final two sections give opportunity for additional study. The first offers questions and issues for discussion and reflection. These are especially helpful when the book is used in an academic class or a group study setting. The final section lists further reading on the individual biblical books. These readings include commentaries and other monographs that will help the reader.

Because the chapters are written by a variety of authors, there will not always be total consistency of opinion on every detail. The editors have chosen to let the authors speak for themselves and to allow the readers to see that legitimate differences in viewpoint exist among equally committed scholars.

A target audience for this book is the undergraduate college or university student. In fact, all of the authors either have taught or are teaching undergraduate religion courses in biblical studies in a college or university setting. We hope, however, that many church members and even pastors will find this introduction helpful. To add to the usefulness of the book we have included maps, charts, chronological and genealogical tables, a glossary, indices, and even a set of charcoal drawings commissioned especially for this project. We hope thereby to provide an academically, devotionally and aesthetically significant contribution to the study of the Bible.

Our real hope, however, is that you will not only enjoy these two introductory volumes, but that they will help you appreciate and benefit from your study of the Bible.

John C. Brunt
Douglas R. Clark

Chapter 1

The First Century Greco-Roman World
John C. Brunt

HISTORY AND POLITICS

In order to understand the makeup of first century cultural, political and social life it is necessary to go back at least four centuries to the conquests of Alexander the Great. He set out from Macedonia (Northern Greece) and conquered most of the Mediterranean world to the east as far as Palestine, Egypt, and even the borders of India.

His goal was not only political. He had been tutored by the philosopher Aristotle and wanted to bring about a fusion of cultures that would unite the world under the banner of Greek thinking and ways of life. But in actual fact much of the world that he conquered was already appreciative of and open to Greek culture. It was considered the wave of the future. Many were anxious to jump on this bandwagon. To understand the attitude you might think of the way people around the world today are anxious to drink Coke, eat Big Macs, wear blue jeans and listen to rock and roll.

Alexander died, however, before he could consolidate a united empire. He was only thirty-two years old when he died in 323 B.C.E. His kingdom was divided among his generals who soon began fighting with each other so that the vision of a united political empire was not realized. But he did help to bring about a remarkable degree of cultural unity around the Mediterranean. Greek became the common language and Greek thinking and customs influenced the entire area, including Palestine. This phenomenon is known as "Hellenism," a culture that prevailed over the next several centuries.

The political unification of this part of the world had to wait for the Romans. In the second and first centuries B.C.E. Rome conquered most of the Mediterranean world. But Rome herself had been strongly influenced by Hellenism so that the cultural change was not a drastic one. Throughout the first century Greek language and thought prevailed. Yet Roman rule did bring

1

significant changes in certain ways of life. The Romans were more pragmatic and technically oriented so that with them came increased mobility, communications and urbanization. For example, the empire was covered with roads, and all of them really did lead to Rome. Trade increased, people both traveled more and moved more, and the old Greek system of closely knit city-states gave way to large cities and transient populations.

The political conquests of Rome were also welcomed by many. The previous years had been a time of turmoil and uncertainty. The *pax Romana* or peace of Rome that enabled people to live and move about the empire was a benefit that many appreciated. In addition, Rome was willing to give a significant degree of self-governance to its conquered people as long as they were willing to cooperate.

Toward the end of the first century B.C.E. the desire for stability in Rome enabled Octavian, who took the name Augustus, to take unprecedented power for himself, and the Roman Republic gave way to the Empire with a ruling emperor. Augustus ruled from 31 B.C.E. to 14 C.E. In spite of his power, he ruled with a sensitivity and diplomatic skill that unfortunately was sorely lacking in some of those who followed him, such as Caligula (37-41, whom the Roman historian Suetonius, who lived from about 69 to 140, called a "monster"[1]) and Nero (54-68). Both of these emperors abused their power and ruled with terror.

ECONOMIC LIFE

In the first century Greco-Roman world wide disparities existed in economic conditions. In rural agrarian environments there were wealthy absentee landlords who ruled over the modern equivalents of sharecroppers. In the cities there were the extremely rich as well as those who were almost totally dependent on Roman welfare for their existence. In between were skilled tradesmen and government workers of various types who made up a middle class that varied in size in different parts of the empire.

Throughout the empire, but especially in Rome the number of slaves was high. It is estimated that in the city of Rome as much as a third of the population, between 200,000 and 300,000 were slaves.[2] People originally became slaves through debt, piracy, and primarily war. Generation after generation was born into slavery. The status of slaves varied greatly, however. Some were highly educated and trusted tutors who had considerable status and power in the household, while others were severely mistreated, exploited, and even abused sexually.

For the most part the institution of slavery was simply assumed as part of the social order, although the Stoic and Cynic teachers (see below) argued that slaves should be treated humanely, and some even went so far as to challenge the idea of slavery.

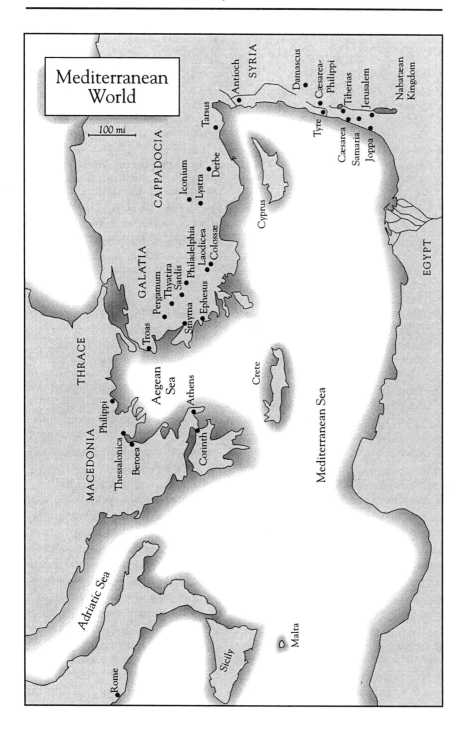

Mediterranean
World

100 mi

The following excerpts from the moral letters of Seneca show how Stoic teachers argued that slaves should be treated with respect, but also demonstrates how slaves were often mistreated by the rich who lived in wanton luxury.

I am glad to learn, through those who come from you, that you live on friendly terms with your slaves. This befits a sensible and well-educated man like yourself. 'They are slaves,' people declare. Nay, rather they are men. 'Slaves!' No, comrades. 'Slaves!' No, they are unpretentious friends. 'Slaves!' No, they are our fellow-slaves, if one reflects that Fortune has equal rights over slaves and free men alike.[3]

When we recline at a banquet, one slave mops up the disgorged food, another crouches beneath the table and gathers up the left-overs of the tipsy guests. Another carves the priceless game birds; with unerring strokes and skilled hand he cuts choice morsels along the breast or the rump. Hapless fellow, to live only for the purpose of cutting fat capons correctly—unless, indeed, the other man is still more unhappy than he, who teaches this art for pleasure's sake, rather than he who learns it because he must. Another, who serves the wine, must dress like a woman and wrestle with his advancing years; he cannot get away from his boyhood; he is dragged back to it; and though he has already acquired a soldier's figure, he is kept beardless by having his hair smoothed away or plucked out by the roots, and he must remain awake throughout the night, dividing his time between his master's drunkenness and his lust; in the chamber he must be a man, at the feast a boy .... With slaves like these the master cannot bear to dine; he would think it beneath his dignity to associate with his slave at the same table! Heaven forfend![4]

In protest against the conspicuous luxury of the upper classes many of the teachers of the day advocated an ideal of freely chosen poverty. Wearing a threadbare coat and eating barley cakes became a symbol of this lifestyle, although for some the poverty was more pretense than reality.

One large class of people in the first century empire was that of freedmen, former slaves who had gained their freedom. This could be accomplished in a number of ways. Some were allowed to earn money and buy their freedom. Others were set free in their master's wills. The freed slave often participated in a service at the temple or shrine of one of the gods where the slave was symbolically sold to the god and received freedom. This class of former slaves became so large and powerful that the emperors felt the need to placate them by giving them official functions in the emperor cult (to be discussed below).

One significant feature of economic and social life in the empire was the prevalence of craft and trade associations. Workers in a particular trade or profession, as well as trade partners would form guilds or associations that not only allowed them to pool their resources to meet emergencies, but also provided the primary groups for social life and fellowship.

Another significant factor in economic life was trade. With the increased mobility and travel that Rome provided there was a constant flow of trade across the empire. The following list in Rev 18 gives a good idea of the kind of items that were transported, traded and sold:

> The merchants of the earth will weep and mourn over her because no one buys their cargoes any more—cargoes of gold, silver, precious stones and pearls; fine linen, purple, silk and scarlet cloth; every sort of citron wood, and articles of every kind made of ivory, costly wood, bronze, iron and marble; cargoes of cinnamon and spice, of incense, myrrh and frankincense, of wine and olive oil, of fine flour and wheat; cattle and sheep; horses and carriages; and bodies and souls of men (Rev 18:11-13, NIV).

INTELLECTUAL AND RELIGIOUS LIFE

Several attitudes prevailed in the Hellenistic age that seriously affected what people sought in the philosophies and religions of the day. The breakdown of the city-states and the rise of large urban centers had produced the kind of "lonely crowd" phenomenon that we have experienced in the twentieth century. This contributed to a sense of powerlessness and lack of control over one's life that in turn led to a strong emphasis on fate. Astrology, which had been around for some time, became more popular and many were convinced that all of life was pre-determined by fate. Many were also led, however, to seek ways of overcoming fate.

Increased trade and communication also led to a spirit of both tolerance and a blending of various religious traditions (known as "syncretism"). Teachers emphasized that the various nations and cultures of the empire really worshiped the same gods, but merely gave them different names. Almost all of the Greek and Roman gods were paired into equivalents, so that Zeus equaled Jupiter, etc. The same person could worship at the temples and shrines of various gods and cults without showing disloyalty to any of them, and beliefs and practices from a variety of religious traditions could be formed into new combinations. All of this made it very difficult for the Hellenistic world to understand the exclusive devotion that Jews and Christians gave to their God.

By the first century the traditional pantheon of gods, with their stately temples in Greece and Rome, had lost most of their power in the popular mind. Many attended their services much more out of a sense of civic pride and tradition than a personal religious devotion. These gods were not really thought to be very powerful against the forces of fate. Therefore the majority of the populace looked to other philosophies and religions to interpret their world and give their lives meaning.

Some turned to the popular philosophies of the day such as Epicureanism, Platonism, Stoicism, and Cynicism. In Athens Paul confronted both Stoics and Epicureans (Acts 17:18). The latter followed the teachings of Epicurus (342-270

B.C.E.) by withdrawing from public life and enjoying a private fellowship. Because of their unabashed devotion to the principle of pleasure they have been derided as hedonists, but in actuality their idea of pleasure was very austere and devoid of dissipation.

The most popular philosophy in the first century was Stoicism. Although when begun by Zeno (336-263 B.C.E.) it had a strong metaphysical and cosmological emphasis, by the first century its main emphasis was ethics. It emphasized bringing one's life into harmony with nature and the rational principle of the universe. On a practical level it stressed an attitude of detachment and self-sufficiency that remained content with life as it was and sought to change only that which was changeable. This stance was one way of coming to terms with fate. Rather than being overtaken by the inevitable, the Stoic fortified the mind to accept whatever came. For example, the Stoic philosopher Epictetus (ca. 55-135) says:

> Whenever you grow attached to something, do not act as though it were one of those things that cannot be taken away, but as though it were something like a jar or a crystal goblet, so that when it breaks you will remember what it was like, and not be troubled. So too in life; if you kiss your child, your brother, your friend, never allow your fancy free rein, nor your exuberant spirits to go as far as they like, but hold them back, stop them, just like those who stand behind generals when they ride in triumph, and keep reminding them that they are mortal. In such fashion do you too remind yourself that the object of your love is mortal....
>
> Furthermore, at the very moment when you are taking delight in something, call to mind the opposite impressions. What harm is there if you whisper to yourself, at the very moment you are kissing your child, and say, 'To-morrow you die'?[5]

Cynicism was similar, but was more iconoclastic and anti-social. Cynic teachers took pride in offending the populace by breaking social convention. The teachers of both the Stoics and Cynics taught on the street corners and in the marketplaces and were often supported financially by both patrons and hearers.

In the religious realm some of the most popular alternatives to the traditional gods were the mystery religions. These religions were devoted to gods and goddesses such as Adonis, Cybele, Attis, Mithras, and the most popular, Isis and Serapis. Cults developed around each of these deities that stressed secret initiation and various rituals of devotion. We know very little about most of these cults because the ancients really did try to keep their practices secret. In order to give an idea of what these cults were like we will focus on the Isis cult.

We know more about the Isis cult because of the writer Apuleius who wrote a fanciful tale about a golden ass that nevertheless chronicles his own devotion to the cult.[6] This cult was based on the goddess of Egypt. Devotees worshiped daily at shrines and participated in yearly festivals. Priests, who lived according to strict rules of dress and diet, led out in the rituals. In return for their devotion to Isis, she was said to be able to help her worshipers by protecting (especially seagoers), healing, aiding in romance, and even granting immortality. What is more, Isis could control fate.

In Apuleius' tale he is turned into a donkey by dabbling in magic and is eventually rescued through the intervention of Isis. He is finally initiated into the secrets of the cult. The goddess tells him to prepare for initiation which includes receiving certain books written in unknown characters from the secret place of the temple, engaging in baths and ritual purifications, and a ten day fast where he must not eat any meat or drink any wine. Then he describes the actual experience of initiation only in brief terms by saying:

> Thou shalt understand that I approached near unto hell, even to the gates of Proserpine, and after that I was ravished throughout all the elements, I returned to my proper place: about midnight I saw the sun brightly shine, I saw likewise the gods celestial and the gods infernal, before whom I presented myself and worshipped them. Behold now have I told thee, which although thou hast heard, yet it is necessary that thou conceal it; wherefore this only will I tell, which may be declared without offence for the understanding of the profane.[7]

Most of these foreign cults offended the sensitivities of the Roman aristocracy, but they were very popular with the masses because they gave a sense of personal religious experience no longer found in the worship of the more traditional temples.

Another foreign religious influence that gained some followers in the Greco-Roman world was Judaism. Many people were attracted by its monotheism and high ethical ideals. Some actually converted to Judaism, but more attended the synagogue services without becoming proselytes or converts, for the price of full conversion was high. It included both circumcision and often bearing the burden of anti-Jewish sentiments. The so-called God-fearers that we meet in Acts may have been these Gentiles who were attracted to Judaism without becoming proselytes.

A new religious and political phenomenon in the first century was the rise of the emperor cult. Augustus was diplomatic enough not to claim divine honors in Rome, but in the east, where the concept of divine kingship was traditional, he played on the concept. After his death he was proclaimed divine. Later in the first century emperors began to claim divine honors during their lifetime. Temples dedicated to emperor worship were dedicated in the east, and by the time of Domitian at the end of the first century the Roman historian Suetonius says:

> Just as arrogantly he began a letter, which his procurators were to circulate, with the words: 'Our Lord God instructs you to do this!' and 'Lord God' became his regular title both in writing and conversation. Images dedicated to Domitian in the Capitol had to be of either gold or silver, and not below a certain weight.[8]

The book of Revelation was probably written during Domitian's reign (81-96), and the persecution described there was probably because of the early Christians' refusal to participate in the worship of the emperor and the adoration of his statues. Most of the populace, on the other hand, could go through the motions of such worship with little or no actual religious stake in the process, since they were used to worshiping a number of different deities anyway.

magic

Finally we should mention the large role played by magic and superstition in first century life. There were, for example, formulas and incantations for all kinds of purposes from healing to love to athletic victory. Often these formulas would include long nonsense words heaped together with the names of all the gods one could muster to rally as much power as possible. The following example, which refrains from invoking the names of specific gods and using nonsense phrases, is nevertheless vivid. It is a curse that someone inscribed on a thin lead tablet against a charioteer.

> I conjure you up, holy beings and holy names; join in aiding this spell, and bind, enchant, thwart, strike, overturn, conspire against, destroy, kill break Eucherius, the charioteer, and all his horses tomorrow in the circus in Rome. May he not leave the barriers well; may he not make the turns well; may he not win any prizes; and if he has pressed someone hard, may he not come off the victor; and if he follows someone from behind, may he not overtake him; but may he meet with an accident; may he be bound; may he be broken; may he be dragged along by your power, in the morning and afternoon races. Now! Now! Quickly! Quickly![9]

Unfortunately we have no record of how Eucherius fared at the circus the next day!

FAMILY AND EVERYDAY LIFE

One of our major sources for knowledge of common life in the first century Greco-Roman world is a large body of letters and other pieces of paper that have been discovered beginning around the end of the last century in Egypt where the dry climate preserved them. These documents were not for publication but were the common everyday pieces of paper one might find in a wastebasket. They included official contracts, letters, wills, shopping lists, etc. From them we gain knowledge of both the language and customs of common first-century people.

The first century household usually consisted of a group larger than our typical immediate family. Often extended family were included along with slaves. Houses were built around an open courtyard surrounded by a covered walkway with access to other rooms such as bedrooms, dining room and kitchen.[10]

Governance within the household was essentially patriarchal, although in some places women had gained many rights by the first century. In fact, marriage by mutual consent rather than parental arrangement was becoming popular. The following excerpt from a 13 B.C.E. marriage contract shows what duties were expected of husband and wife:

> And from now Apollonius son of Ptolemaeus shall furnish to Thermion as his wedded wife all necessaries and clothing in proportion to his means and shall not ill-treat her nor cast her out nor bring in another wife, or he shall straightway forfeit the dowry increased by half, with right of execution upon both the person of Apollonius son of Ptolemaeus and all his property as if by legal decision, and Thermion shall fulfil her duties towards her husband and their common life and shall not absent herself from the house for a night or a day without the consent of Apollonius son of Ptolemaeus nor dishonour nor injure their common home nor consort with another man, or she again if guilty of any of these actions shall, after trial, be deprived of the dowry, and in addition the transgressing party shall be liable to the prescribed fine.[11]

The writer and moralist Plutarch (ca. 50-120) wrote an essay giving advice to brides and grooms that also gives us some insight into marital life.[12] He maintains that the woman should be subordinate, but the man should exercise his control with good will:

> So it is with women also; if they subordinate themselves to their husbands, they are commended, but if they want to have control, they cut a sorrier figure than the subjects of their control. And control ought to be exercised by the man over the woman, not as the owner has control over a piece of property, but, as the soul controls the body, by entering into her feelings and being knit to her through good will.[13]

But as Plutarch gives specifics it is clear that by today's standards this "good will" leaves much to be desired. For example, the women is to be visible only with husband and is to hide herself away when he is not present. She is to give way to his leadership and preferences and is to have no feelings of her own. In matters of property, she is to recognize that the estate belongs to her husband even if she has contributed the larger share at the time of their marriage. With regard to religion, she is to serve the same gods as her husband. Finally, while she is always to remain sexually faithful to her husband, she is to be pleased if her husband shares his debauchery with a mistress instead of her.

This latter point raises the topic of first-century attitudes toward sexual morality. Some moralists like Musonius Rufus held to strict standards in this regard. He says:

> Men who are not wantons or immoral are bound to consider sexual intercourse justified only when it occurs in marriage and is indulged in for the purpose of begetting children, since that is lawful, but unjust and unlawful when it is mere pleasure-seeking, even in marriage.[14]

It was more common to find much more equivocation in this matter and the kind of double standard we find in Plutarch above. Epictetus, for example, advocates sexual relations only within marriage, but then advises that if a man cannot handle that he should limit himself to a licensed prostitute.[15] Such prostitutes were readily available in numerous brothels. In addition, sacral prostitution was still practiced in many of the temples of the Greco-Roman gods and the mystery cults.

Few families reared more than two boys or one girl. Abortion was practiced, but the most common method for controlling family size was infanticide. Especially female infants were often simply taken to the trash heap and left. Often these infants were "rescued" and reared for prostitution.

Divorce was common and could be initiated by the woman in Roman society by the first century. Urbanization and the breakdown of the extended family network of the city-state contributed to the breakdown of marriage.

In addition to life in the household and place of worship there were numerous other attractions in the first century that occupied the time and energy of the populace. Young men went to school and studied language, music, rhetoric, philosophy and physical training. Every city had its gymnasium for physical training, and in the larger cities there were stadiums for athletic contests, including boxing, wrestling, jumping, running, and discus throwing to name but a few. Theaters and amphitheaters provided plays and circuses, and hippodromes featured horse and chariot races.

Perhaps the most popular public place, however, was the public bath. It epitomized the luxury and accomplishments of Rome and the Roman lifestyle. Therefore we close this brief look at the first century Greco-Roman world with a description of a public bath recorded by Lucian.

> On entering, one is received into a public hall of good size, with ample accommodations for servants and attendants. On the left are the lounging rooms, also of just the right sort for a bath, attractive, brightly lighted retreats. Then, besides them, a hall, larger than need be for the purposes of a bath, but necessary for the reception of richer persons. Next, capacious locker rooms to undress in, on each side, with a very high and brilliantly lighted hall between them, in which are three swimming pools of cold water; it is finished in Laconian marble, and has two statues of white marble....
>
> On leaving this hall, you come into another which is slightly warmed instead of meeting you at once with fierce heat; it is oblong, and has an apse on each side. Next to it, on the right, is a very bright hall, nicely fitted up for massage, which has on each side an entrance decorated with Phrygian marble, and receives those who come in from the exercising floor. Then near this is another hall, the most beautiful in the world, in which one can stand or sit with comfort, linger without danger and stroll about with profit.... Next comes the hot corridor, faced with Numidian marble. The hall beyond it is very beautiful, full of abundant light and aglow with color like that of purple hangings. It contains three hot tubs.[16]

In subsequent chapters we will have opportunity to see how a knowledge of this world illuminates our understanding of the New Testament.

FURTHER READING

Barrett, Charles K.
1987   *The New Testament Background: Selected Documents.* Revised ed. New York: Harper and Row.

Ferguson, Everett
1987   *Backgrounds of Early Christianity.* Grand Rapids, MI: Eerdmans.

Fox, Robin Lane
1973   *Alexander the Great.* New York: Penguin.

Green, Peter
1991   *Alexander of Macedon, 356-323 B.C.: A Historical Biography.* Berkely: University of California Press.

Koester, Helmut
1982   *Introduction to the New Testament; Volume One: History, Culture, and Religion of the Hellenistic Age.* (Hermeneia Foundations and Facets). Philadelphia: Fortress.

Lewis, Naphtali and Meyer Reinhold, Eds.
1955   *Roman Civilization; Sourcebook II: The Empire.* New York: Harper and Row.

Lohse, Eduard
1976   *The New Testament Environment.* John E. Steely, Trans. Nashville: Abingdon.

MacMullen, Ramsay
1974   *Roman Social Relations: 50 B.C. to A.D. 284.*   New Haven: Yale University Press.

Malherbe, Abraham J.
1986   *Moral Exhortation, A Greco-Roman Sourcebook.* (Library of Early Christianity). Philadelphia: Westminster.

Meeks, Wayne A.
1986   *The Moral World of the First Christians.* (Library of Early Christianity). Philadelphia: Westminster.

Stephens, William H.
1987   *The New Testament World in Pictures.* Paula A. Savage, designer. Nashville: Broadman.

Tarn, William W.
1952   *Hellenistic Civilisation.* Rev. ed. by the author and G.T. Griffith. New York: World.

Yamauchi, Edwin
1981   *Harper's World of the New Testament.* San Francisco: Harper and Row.

ENDNOTES

1. Suetonius, *The Twelve Caesars*, Penguin Classics, Trans. Robert Graves (New York: Penguin, 1957), p 159.
2. Helmut Koester, *Introduction to the New Testament, Volume One: History, Culture, and Religion of the Hellenistic Age*, Hermeneia Foundations and Facets (Philadelphia: Fortress, 1982), p 60.
3. Seneca, *Ad Lucilium Epistulae Morales*, 3 vols. Trans. Richard M. Gummere, Loeb Classical Library, (New York: G.P. Putnam's Sons, 1925) Epistle XLVII, vol. 1, pp 301-303.
4. Ibid., p 305.
5. *Arrians Discourses of Epictetus*, 2 vols., Trans. W.A. Oldfather, Loeb Classical Library (New York: G.P. Putnam's Sons, 1928), Book III, vol. 2, pp 211-213.
6. Lucius Apuleius, *The Golden Ass*, trans. William Adlington, ed. with intro. by Harry Schnur (New York: Collier Books, 1962).
7. Ibid., p 276-277.
8. Suetonius, p 304.
9. IGRR, Vol. I, No.117, quoted in *Roman Civilization; Sourcebook II: The Empire*, Ed. Naphtali Lewis and Meyer Reinhold, (New York: Harper and Row, 1955), p 570.
10. For pictures see William H. Stephens, *The New Testament World in Pictures* (Nashville: Broadman, 1987), pp 102-119.
11. Quoted in C.K. Barrett, *The New Testament Background: Selected Documents* (New York: Harper and Row, 1956), pp 37-38.
12. Plutarch, "Advice to Bride and Groom" in *Moralia*, trans. Frank Cole Babbitt, et. al., 15 vols., Loeb Classical Library (Cambridge, MA: Harvard University Press, 1927), vol. 2, pp 299-243.
13. Ibid., p 323.
14. Musonius Rufus, Fragment 12, quoted in Abraham J. Malherbe, *Moral Exhortation, A Greco-Roman Sourcebook*, Library of Early Christianity (Philadelphia: Westminster, 1986), p 153.
15. Epictetus, vol. 2, p 519.
16. Lucius, quoted in *Roman Civilization*, pp 227-228.

Chapter 2

The First Century Jewish World

John C. Brunt

Within the larger Greco-Roman world that we have just described was a significant and distinctive group known as the Jews. They were significant because of their large numbers and their influence. They were distinctive because of their unique devotion to one God and their lifestyle. By the time of the first century, the majority of the Jews were scattered throughout the Greco-Roman world, especially in the large cities of the empire. These Jews who lived outside Palestine were known as Jews of the Diaspora, or dispersion. But even for these Jews, the center of their religion was Jerusalem, with its temple. Those Jews who lived in Palestine, however, were no longer independent, but found their land occupied by Roman military forces.

HISTORY AND POLITICS

In order to understand this situation, we must understand something of the political history in the several centuries preceding the time of Jesus and the New Testament. In the previous chapter we discussed the conquests of Alexander the Great. After his death his kingdom was divided up among his generals. Seleucus controlled Syria, to the north of Palestine; Ptolemy controlled Egypt, to the south. The Jews were caught in the middle. Both Syria and Egypt wanted to control Palestine because of its strategic location. Since the land to the east is desert, and the Mediterranean Sea is on the west, Palestine is crucial to north/south travel and trade around the Mediterranean. For decades control of Palestine seesawed back and forth between Syria and Egypt. Upper class families of the Jews aligned themselves with one or the other. Thus when Syria was in control, those families who were aligned with Egypt often found it more comfortable to leave, and many went to Alexandria. On the other hand, when Egypt was in control, Syria-backers among the Jews fled to Antioch. Both of these cities developed large Jewish populations.

First- and Second-century C.E. Leaders and Events

Date	Roman Emperors	Procurators/Governors	The Herods	Other Events
10 BCE	Augustus 12 BCE-14 CE		Herod the Great 37-4 BCE	Birth of Jesus ca. 5 BCE
0 CE			Archelaus 4 BCE-6 CE (Judea, Idumea, Samaria)	
10	Tiberius 14-37		Herod Antipas 4 BCE-39 CE (Galilee, Perea)	
20		Pontius Pilate 26-36	Herod Philip 4 BCE-34 CE (Transjordan)	
30	Caligula 37-41		Co-regents	Crucifixion, Resurrection, & Ascension of Jesus ca. 31
40	Claudius 41-54		Herod Agrippa I 41-44	
50		Felix 52-60	Herod Agrippa II 50-early 90s	Jerusalem Council 49
60	Nero 54-68	Festus 60-62		
70	Vespasian 69-79			Destruction of Jerusalem 70
80	Titus 79-81			
90	Domitian 81-117			
100				
110				
120	Hadrian 117-138			

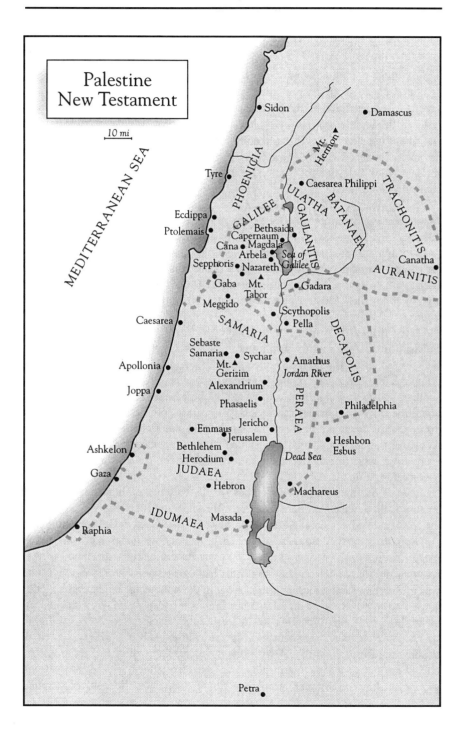

Palestine
New Testament

10 mi

MEDITERRANEAN SEA

Sidon

Damascus

PHOENICIA

Mt. Hermon

Tyre

Caesarea Philippi

TRACHONITIS

Ecdippa

GALILEE

ULATHA

BATANAEA

Ptolemais

Bethsaida

Capernaum

GAULANITIS

Cana Magdala

Arbela

Sea of

Canatha

Sepphoris Nazareth

Galilee

AURANITIS

Gaba Mt.

Tabor

Gadara

Meggido

Caesarea

SAMARIA

Scythopolis

Pella

DECAPOLIS

Sebaste

Samaria Sychar

Mt.

Amathus

Apollonia

Gerizim

Jordan River

Joppa

Alexandrium

Phasaelis

PERAEA

Philadelphia

Emmaus

Jericho

Jerusalem

Heshbon

Ashkelon

Bethlehem

Herodium

Dead Sea

Esbus

Gaza

JUDAEA

Hebron

Machareus

IDUMAEA Masada

Raphia

Petra

(handwritten margin note: Maccabean rule)

Finally in the second century B.C.E. Syria gained control and one of her leaders, Antiochus IV (known as Antiochus Epiphanes) took over the Jewish temple and attempted to end the Jews' distinctive religious devotion. He instituted Pagan sacrifices and even sacrificed pigs on the Jewish altars. In the year 164, the Jews, led by the Maccabee family, overcame the Syrian forces and restored the temple. By 140 they had set up an independent Jewish state that was about the size of David's kingdom. This independent rule was short-lived, however, for in 63 B.C.E. the Roman general Pompey came and defeated the Jews and took Palestine for Rome. From that time on, Roman occupation forces controlled Palestine.

(handwritten margin note: Herod)

In the year 40 B.C.E. the Romans named Herod the Great as King of the Jews. He was an Idumean (descendants of Esau) who became known for his intensive and impressive building activity and his cruelty whenever he felt his throne might be threatened. After his death his sons ruled sections of Palestine for several decades, always under firm Roman control. In Judea, the southern portion of Palestine, however, beginning in 6 C.E. Rome sent procurators or governors to rule. Most of these were not good administrators and contributed to unrest.

(handwritten margin note: Acts)

Jews reacted in various ways to this series of events. In other words, Judaism of the first century was by no means monolithic. There were various sects or parties of Jews whose beliefs, practices and expectations differed. One thing can be said of all of these groups, however. All were in one way or another, and to varying degrees, affected by the broader Hellenistic culture. At one time it was popular for scholars to speak of Hellenistic Judaism as distinguished from the Judaism in Palestine in the first century. Today we recognize that all of Judaism was Hellenistic to one extent or another. In fact, even those who overtly reacted against the broader Hellenistic culture were nevertheless influenced by it.

(handwritten margin note: Josephus)

One of our most important sources for the varieties of Judaism in the first century is the Jewish historian, Josephus. He was a Jewish military officer when the Jews revolted against the Romans in 66 C.E. He fought in Galilee, and when the Roman general Vespasian was clearly gaining the upper hand, Josephus predicted he would become emperor. Vespasian did, and by the time the war was over in 70 and Vespasian's son Titus had carried out the victory, Josephus was in Rome in such good favor that he sat in the reviewing stands watching the Jewish captives. He lived on for another couple of decades and wrote the history of the Jewish people, including the history of the war itself.[1]

Although he is a major source, he is not without his biases. He was anxious to show the Romans that the Jewish revolt was not the will of the majority, but only the result of a few Jewish hotheads. He also tended to paint the various groups of Jews in Roman terms, describing them as philosophical schools.

Nevertheless, we are dependent upon Josephus for much important knowledge about first century Judaism.

VARIETIES OF JUDAISM

The first group of Jews we shall attempt to describe are those of the Diaspora. This includes all Jews who lived outside of Palestine. They were scattered throughout the cities of the Roman Empire from Alexandria in Egypt to Antioch in Syria, all the way to Rome itself.

Jews living in the empire faced the inevitable tension between belonging to the broader society and maintaining their distinctive ideals and practices. Naturally different Diaspora Jews made different decisions with regard to this tension. In general, however, they tended to live together in a certain sector of town so that they could have their own courts, hospitals, meat markets and schools to avoid contact with idolatry. Since they had been granted the status of a legal religion by Julius Caesar they were allowed these privileges. In addition, they were not forced to participate in military service.

Life for Diaspora Jews centered around the synagogue. The synagogue was a meeting place where Jews met for school during the week and for worship on the Sabbath. In the synagogue the service focused on the reading of the law and the prophets, a short homily or sermon, and the singing of praises. There were no sacrifices in the synagogues. Jews only carried out animal sacrifices at the temple in Jerusalem (the temple will be described below). Many Jews of the Diaspora made pilgrimages to Jerusalem for the major feasts. Some would look forward to such a pilgrimage as a once in a lifetime experience, but every day religious experience centered around the local synagogue.

In order to facilitate an understanding of scripture, the Old Testament, which was written in Hebrew, was translated into Greek. This translation was known as the Septuagint (abbreviated LXX).

One of the most important writers of the Jewish Diaspora is Philo (20 B.C.E.–ca. 50 C.E.).[2] He lived in Alexandria in Egypt and was schooled in philosophy. He was anxious to see Jews retain their practices and wrote with deep concern about Jews who forsook Sabbath observance, abstinence from pork, etc. Yet Philo also wanted to show that Jews were a part of the broader Greek culture which he affirmed. He was especially influenced by the philosophy of Plato. Using the method of allegorization he sought to show that the Old Testament taught the same truths as the Greek philosophers. His writings show the tension of Diaspora Judaism between retaining a distinctive religious devotion and belonging to the popular culture of the day.

The Gentiles who surrounded these Diaspora Jews reacted to them in different ways. On the one hand there are many evidences of anti-Semitism, including outlandish rumors about the Jews. Popular rumor included stories about Jews worshiping the head of an ass in their holy place, or even of Jews kidnapping a Gentile, fattening him up and sacrificing him on their altar in Jerusalem.[3]

On the other hand, many Gentiles were attracted to the monotheistic faith and the high ethical ideals of the Jews. A number even joined them in worship at the synagogue. Some converted to Judaism and were known as "proselytes;" many others avoided the inconvenience of circumcision and other rituals necessary for proselytes and instead worshiped with Jews without actually converting. These Gentiles were known as God-fearers or God-worshipers. We will see when we study Acts that they were a significant part of Paul's ministry.

The other groups of Jews that we survey were all part of Palestinian Judaism. The first of these groups was the Sadducees. They were the upper class or ruling class of Jews. Most of the Sanhedrin, the ruling council of Jews, were Sadducees. Rome allowed a considerable degree of self-governance in this council. The upper class priests were Sadducees as well; in fact, the High Priest always came from this group.

The Sadducees largely controlled the temple with its services and economic benefits. Jews from Palestine and the entire empire came to the temple for the major feasts: Passover, Pentecost, Tabernacles and Dedication. The population of Jerusalem swelled several times at these feasts. Most travelers had to purchase animals for sacrifice as well as change money into money that was acceptable to the priests. This provided a strong economic advantage to those who controlled the temple. It was, in modern terms, a "tourist attraction" with a tourism intensified by religious devotion.

It is hardly surprising that in both the social and religious world the Sadducees tended to be for the status quo. They did not accept more recent teaching such as the oral tradition that the Pharisees espoused. They accepted only the five books of Moses, and they were not anxious to overthrow Rome. After all, they were doing very well.

In fact, recent excavations under the old city of Jerusalem have unearthed large homes that are believed to have been those of Sadducees. These homes were built on terraces overlooking the temple. Some were as large as two and a half thousand square feet, built on four levels with the latest in art work and pottery from Rome.

The Jerusalem temple, which the Sadducees controlled, was truly a spectacular place. Herod the Great had begun its restoration more than a decade before the birth of Jesus, and it continued until the 60's C.E. The actual temple itself was made of white marble and decorated with much gold and other precious materials. Only priests were allowed in the temple itself, but surrounding the building were large courtyards: the inner court open only to Jews, the outer court open to Gentiles as well. This area was really the heart of Jerusalem and the center of Judaism. All Jews who could worshiped there and considered it their own, but it was the Sadducees who controlled it and benefited economically from it.

Pharisees

The Pharisees placed some members on the Sanhedrin. They were probably not has rich and powerful, however, as Sadducees, although they had more popularity among the populace. Their lives centered around synagogues in Palestine. They had developed a large body of oral tradition that served to interpret the law and to build a hedge around the law to keep them from even coming close to breaking it. There seems to have been a certain anti-priestly stance in their organization. Many Old Testament laws specified the ritual purity that the priest who ministered in the temple had to uphold. Pharisees sought to be as ritually pure as the priest in the temple every time they sat down to a meal. Thus the majority of their laws had to do with ritual purity, especially in dietary matters. They were strict in their observance of the law, and yet they allowed for exceptions and concessions which were spelled out in their body of oral tradition. They genuinely attempted to be reasonable in their observance, but these exceptions for various cases tended to lead them down a road of casuistry that became burdensome.

The Pharisees were by no means the most strict in their observance of the *Essenes* law, however. The Essenes represented a sectarian group of Jews that would not even worship at the temple in Jerusalem because they saw it as corrupt. Instead, they separated themselves from Jewish society and attempted to live communally in a strict fellowship that would prepare the way for the coming of two messiahs, one kingly and one priestly, who would overthrow the Romans and restore proper temple worship in Jerusalem.

The ruins that have been found at Qumran, near the northwest corner of the *Qumran* Dead Sea, were probably some kind of Essene headquarters. This group adhered to the teachings of an earlier "teacher of righteousness" whose name we do not know. Whereas Jesus told the Pharisees that they were willing to lift an animal out of a pit on Sabbath, these Jewish sectarians would not permit such an act.

We know about these sectarians not only from Josephus' description, but also from their own writings found among the Dead Sea Scrolls (DSS). Apparently when Roman forces advanced in the 60's, these Jews hid their writings in caves. There they remained for almost nineteen hundred years until they were discovered by Bedouin shepherds in 1946. In fact, a number of caves in the area eventually yielded scrolls.

These scrolls are of two types. The Jewish sectarians had copies of the Old Testament itself. At least parts of every Old Testament book but Esther have been found among the discovered scrolls. These Biblical manuscripts have been extremely important, since they are the oldest copies of the Hebrew Old Testament that exist today, almost a thousand years older than previous manuscripts.

In addition to copies of the Bible, these Jewish sectarians had their own writings that gave the rules for their community as well as their expectations about the future.[4] One of the scrolls even spells out in precise detail the war that will occur when the Messiah leads them to battle against the Romans, while another, with equal precision, details the way temple services will be carried out once they are in control.

Zealots

Another group of first century Palestinian Jews was the Zealots. Unlike the Sadducees, these Jews did not participate in the economic advantages of the society. That fact, along with their strong belief that Palestine was the chosen, promised land given by God, led them to attempt to overthrow the Romans. The Zealots were probably not a single, organized party, but a collection of would-be leaders who initiated revolutionary activity here and there throughout the early part of the first century. Finally in 66, various bands of revolutionaries, some of them competing with each other, began a full-scale revolt against Rome. It took several years, but Rome came and defeated the Jews in 70. They destroyed the temple, and just as Jesus had predicted, not one stone was left on another. A small group of Jewish Zealots held out on the top of Masada, a large boat-shaped mountain next to the Dead Sea, which Herod the Great had fortified as his hiding place in case of a coup, and remained there until the Romans built a siege ramp and were just about to defeat them in the year 73. Rather than be taken captive by the Romans, this group of almost 1,000 Jews committed suicide.

Most Zealot activity throughout the first century consisted of small bands of men, living in caves, robbing merchant trains to gain money to fund the revolution, and overcoming Roman soldiers whenever they had the opportunity.

Common people

The final group of Jews is not really a group at all but a designation for the common people. They were known as the *Am-Ha-Aretz*. They were too poor to worry about all of the observances of parties like the Pharisees. Their main concern was food on the table for the next day. This does not mean, however, that they were secular. Many had deep religious convictions and practiced their faith with much devotion. Those who lived in rural villages were the least affected by the Hellenistic culture, whereas those who lived in cities were naturally more affected. For example, by the first century the city of Jerusalem already had a Roman theater, a hippodrome for horse and chariot racing and a gymnasium for Greek athletic events.

wisdom lit.

In addition to these specific groups we should mention two kinds of Jewish literature from this period that cannot necessarily be identified with any specific group. The first is literature in the wisdom tradition. We already find this type of writing in the Old Testament in books such as Proverbs, but the tradition continued. For example, about a century before Christ's birth a work called *Ecclesiasticus* or *The Wisdom of Ben Sirach* gave practical advice on everything from religion to ethics to etiquette. The content of such writings points to upper class authorship. Another popular kind of literature was "apocalyptic," which carried on the tradition of Daniel in talking about the end of the world with vivid symbolism.

Life in all of these groups would have been quite different from our culture today. Some of the most significant differences would have come in the roles that man and women played in society. School was only for boys. Women married early. Marriages were arranged by the parents, and often the girl would be engaged between the ages of ten and twelve, and married a year and a half to two years later—between ages twelve and fourteen. Young men were older when they married. Once a woman was married, she would hardly be seen in public without her husband, except for certain activities the women of the village participated in such as gathering water. Only the male could initiate divorce.

[margin notes: only / men / could / divorce]

Also different was the degree of privacy that people enjoyed. Homes were much smaller, and most families would sleep together in one room. When a son was married, another room would be built on the house, and the son would bring his bride to live at his parents' residence. Cooking was done in a common outdoor courtyard that several homes shared.

In the year 70, when the Romans defeated the Jews, most of the various parties of Jews that we have mentioned came to an end. The Zealots were clearly defeated in a bloody war. The Essenes at Qumran also lost their lives. The Sadducees no longer had the temple and its advantages. At that point it was Pharisaic Judaism that became normative for the entire community. Schools of scribes codified the oral tradition and made Judaism into a religion of scripture and tradition. These traditions were eventually codified in the *Mishnah*[5] around the end of the second century and later elaborated on in the *Talmud*. Probably much of what we find in the Mishnah was already operative as oral tradition among the Pharisees in Jesus' day, but there is no way of proving this with any particular teaching.

As this process of codifying Judaism into a more monolithic religion took place toward the end of the first century, sharper lines of distinction were drawn between Jews and Christians. The earliest Christians all considered themselves to be Jews. This was even true for Paul, the apostle to the Gentiles. But as Christianity spread to more and more Gentiles, and as Judaism drew its boundaries more sharply, the distinction became apparent. By the time we come to the gospel of John, for example, we see this clear separation. In fact, about this time Jews introduced into their synagogue service a curse on Christians so that they would not be able to worship in the synagogues as Jews.

[margin notes: lines / drawn / between / Xians + / Jews]

But even as Christianity became a separate religion, distinct from Judaism, it carried with it a host of lasting influences from its Jewish roots, from its earliest Scripture, the LXX, to its forms of worship, which were largely patterned after the synagogue service.

FURTHER READING

Barrett, C.K.
  1987   *The New Testament Background: Selected Documents.* Revised ed.
          New York: Harper and Row.
Danby, Herbert
  1944   *The Mishnah.* London: Oxford University Press.
Ferguson, Everett
  1987   *Backgrounds of Early Christianity.* Grand Rapids, MI.: Eerdmans.
Jeremias, Joachim
  1969   *Jerusalem in the Time of Jesus.* Philadelphia: Fortress.
Josephus
          The History of the Jews and *Jewish Wars.* Trans. by H.St.J.
          Thackeray, R. Marcus, and L.H. Feldman. (Loeb Classics, 9 vols.).
          New York: G.P. Putnam's Sons.
Koester, Helmut
  1982   *Introduction to the New Testament; Volume One: History, Culture,
          and Religion of the Hellenistic Age.* (Hermeneia Foundations and
          Facets). Philadelphia: Fortress.
Lohse, Eduard
  1976   *The New Testament Environment.* Trans. by John E. Steely.
          Nashville: Abingdon.
Philo
          Trans. by F.H. Colson and G.H. Whitaker. (Loeb Classics, 10 vols.).
          Cambridge, MA: Harvard University Press.
Stern, Menahem
  1976   *Greek and Latin Authors on Jews and Judaism: vol. 1, From
          Herodotus to Plutarch.* Jerusalem: The Academy of Sciences and
          Humanities.
Vermes, Geza
  1975   *The Dead Sea Scrolls in English,* Second ed. Baltimore: Penguin.
Yamauchi, Edwin
  1981   *Harper's World of the New Testament.* San Francisco: Harper and
          Row.

ENDNOTES

1. His two major works are *The History of the Jews* and *Jewish Wars.* See *Josephus,*
Trans. by H.St.J. Thackeray, R. Marcus, and L.H. Feldman, Loeb Classics, 9 vols. (New
York: G.P. Putnam's Sons, 1926-1965).
2. For his writings see *Philo,* Trans. by F.H. Colson and G.H. Whitaker, Loeb Classics,
10 vols. (Cambridge, MA: Harvard University Press, 1929ff).

3. For a collection of these stories see Menahem Stern, *Greek and Latin Authors on Jews and Judaism*: Vol. 1, *From Herodotus to Plutarch* Jerusalem: The Academy of Sciences and Humanities, 1976).

4. For a collection of these writings see Geza Vermes, *The Dead Sea Scrolls in English*, second ed. (Baltimore: Penguin Books, 1975).

5. Herbert Danby, *The Mishnah* (London: Oxford University Press, 1933, 1944).

Chapter 3
The History of the Text and Canon
Sakae Kubo

THE HISTORY OF THE TEXT
What is New Testament textual criticism?
Textual criticism is the scientific study of the manuscripts of the New Testament which uses valid principles to determine which manuscripts and readings of manuscripts best reflect the original text of Scripture as it came from the hand of the author. We shall say more about these principles later.

The materials for textual criticism
When the New Testament was written, papyrus was the material on which the scribes wrote. Papyrus was used from the 18th century B.C.E. up to the seventh century C.E. Parchment came to be used in the second and third centuries C.E. and became the predominant medium from 650 C.E. to the 14th century when paper took its place. This means that ordinarily a papyrus manuscript will be older than a parchment one, but since there is some overlapping of their time of use, it is not an absolute rule.

At the time of the New Testament, writing consisted of uncials letters which were capitals. There were no separations between words and no punctuation marks. Until one became used to this way of writing and familiar with vocabulary, it would be difficult to read. Even when one became familiar with the vocabulary, in certain cases the reading could be ambiguous. Not until the ninth century was punctuation used, and it was not until the eleventh century that words were separated.

Minuscule writing, which replaced the uncials, began in the ninth century. This is equivalent to our small letters and script form of writing. Minuscules made writing much faster and also saved space, which was important because of the cost of parchment. Another way of saving the cost of material was to take an old manuscript which was no longer used, scrape the letters, and rewrite over them. This kind of manuscript was called a (palimpsest) and there are biblical manuscripts of this sort. The most famous is Codex Ephraemi, in which the biblical text, unfortunately, is the original writing. The distinction in writing (uncial and minuscule) also indicates that ordinarily an uncial manuscript is older than a minuscule.

The manuscripts first used for textual criticism are the Greek manuscripts. These include the most ancient manuscripts, those written on papyri, numbering almost one hundred.[1] Several important groups of papyrus manuscripts have been discovered. The first of these is the Chester Beatty Papyri, published 1933-36, which included P^{45} (The Gospels and Acts), P^{46} (Pauline Epistles), and P^{47} (Revelation). The second group of important papyri manuscripts consists of the Bodmer Papyri, published between 1956-61. These include P^{66} (John), P^{72} (1 and 2 Peter and Jude), P^{73} (Matthew), P^{74} (Acts and Catholics), P^{75} (Luke and John). Not included in these but important because of its early date (about 125 C.E.) is P^{52}. Next come the 266 uncials. The most important of these are Codex Vaticanus (B) and Sinaiticus (ℵ). Next in importance come Alexandrinus (A), Ephraemi (C) and Bezae (D).

The minuscule manuscripts dating from the ninth century on, number, in the words of the Alands, "2,785, and many others." Some of these manuscripts may possess a good text, but the vast majority of them reflect the late text of the Middle Ages whose quality is considered the poorest.

Another group of Greek manuscripts are the lectionaries. These were readings taken from the New Testament and were assigned to be read on certain designated days throughout the year. These texts do not carry the same importance as the actual biblical manuscripts discussed above in determining the original writing of the author.

Because the church fathers often quote from Scripture or allude to it, their writings need to be examined as well. They also help us to assign certain types of readings to a specific time and place.

Besides the Greek manuscripts, the early versions or translations of the New Testament need to be considered, because some of these translations reflect a text that is earlier than many of the manuscripts that we have. The important early versions are the Old Latin, the Old Syriac, the Vulgate, the Syriac, and the Coptic. Of lesser importance are the Armenian, Georgian, Ethiopic, Arabic and Gothic versions.

Principles of textual criticism

How does one go about determining the original writing of the New Testament with such a welter of material to examine? Let us look at how people went about doing this. As long as there were only individual manuscripts to look at or use, one simply used the manuscript at one's disposal and made no evaluation, since no differences were indicated. However, when more than one manuscript was examined, and these were not identical, a decision had to be made and some principle had to be used as the basis for this decision. When the first Greek printed text was published by Erasmus in 1516, he had to decide which text he would publish if there were differences. However, he had a limited number of manuscripts at his disposal, and the science of textual criticism had not even begun. He only had late medieval manuscripts, and in most cases they were very similar in their readings so that no decision needed to be made.

Once this text was printed, it was revered more so than printed material today, and being convenient and accessible it was difficult to dislodge, even when something better was discovered. This printed text came to be known as the Textus Receptus or received text. When better readings were discovered, they were added in the margin or on the bottom of the page, but did not displace the text itself.

Johann Bengel (1725) was the first to enunciate principles which we consider valid today. He began to classify manuscripts into different text types, as the Asiatic (the majority) and the African (fewer but earlier and better). Thus he began to weigh manuscripts rather than count them. He also stated the principle that a difficult reading is to be preferred over an easy one, i.e., the scribe would have a tendency to remove difficulties in a text rather than create them. Griesbach (1745-1812) refined the work of Bengel and Semler (1764), the latter having added a third classification, the Western. Griesbach's work was significant and laid the groundwork for that of Westcott and Hort (1881), who used one of the principles of Griesbach in selecting readings, i.e., that the reading of the text type is to be selected rather than the reading of a single manuscript. They did this after they determined that a certain text type (they called it the Neutral) was the best text type. They moved away from making decisions on individual readings based on individual manuscripts because they felt it was too subjective. The reading of the group removes the possibility of selecting a weak reading of a particular manuscript even if it may be the best manuscript in the group.

On the basis of conflation, where a reading of one manuscript is combined with a reading from another manuscript, Westcott and Hort determined which group of manuscripts was superior. In studying these conflated readings they found that the Syrian manuscripts (Byzantine or Koine) tended to conflate readings found in the Western and Neutral manuscripts. By examining closely and comparing the readings of the Western text with those of the Neutral, they concluded that the latter was more reliable. Readings not found in the Neutral, Western, or Syrian texts were considered Alexandrian. Their classification, Neutral, was soon changed to Alexandrian by other text critics, who did not believe in the distinction they made between the Neutral and Alexandrian readings.

B.H. Streeter (1924) added another text type, Eastern, which included the Caesarean and the Old Syriac. The significance of Streeter's classification is his principle of location, thus called local text theory. He sought to explain the relationship between the texts on the basis of their geographical proximity to each other. However, what is significant for our purpose is that Streeter felt that while the Alexandrian text might be the best, the possibility for the preservation of the pure text in other localities was present as well as the possibility of the corruption of any local text, including the Alexandrian. If important variants already existed in the third century in all of these localities, no objective means can determine the genuine reading. One must rely upon one's insight, judgment and common sense.

Guenther Zuntz (1946) pushed further Streeter's view that there is no objective means to determine the text. He felt that every reading within a given manuscript must be determined on its own merits without regard ultimately to its relationship to a group of documents. He, however, protested the term "subjective" applied to his method and affirmed:

> The convergence of arguments drawn from the distribution of the evidence, the dependence of one reading upon the other, the known habits and typical faults of scribes, the characteristic proclivities of interpolators, the development of the language, the stylistic peculiarities of the writer, the context of the passage in question—these, and still other factors combined can yield a certainty which is no whit inferior to that of the conclusions drawn from a Euclidean axiom.[2]

Major text-types and their characteristics

We have seen above how the different classifications of text-types developed. Today four text-types are recognized, although some questions are raised regarding one of them. These are the Alexandrian, the Western, the Byzantine and the Caesarean.

1. *Alexandrian*

This text is generally regarded as superior to all the others. The text shows the marks of skillful editors. The representatives of this text are P^{66}, P^{75}, P^{72}, B and ℵ, going back to the second century at least. It is characterized by a short text as compared to the Byzantine and especially the Western.

2. *Byzantine*

The majority of manuscripts fall under this classification. They are characterized by lucidity and completeness, fewer omissions, harmonization and interpolations.

3. *Western*

Codex D is its leading representative. It is characterized by interesting additions and significant omissions and harmonizations. Some scholars consider it superior to the Alexandrian text, but they are a small minority. The Western text has some interesting readings, which in some cases appear primitive but not authentic. Some scholars have explained these readings as due to the fact that they were in the source document but the compiler did not use them. Some attribute their presence to oral tradition. Even those who may find some authentic readings in the Western text are not too confident of its overall reliability.

4. *Caesarean*

This text is characterized by its distinctive mixture of Western and Alexandrian readings. It lacks a homogeneous character, attributable to the fact that the differences are due to a textual process rather than a common origin.

One cannot expect to become a text critic by reading this article, but one can grasp some of the basic ideas such as that the earliest manuscripts, because they are closest to the time of the writers of the New Testament, would generally be better than later manuscripts. In addition, the shorter reading is more often the original than longer readings, since scribes had a tendency to add rather than subtract. In a similar way, the most difficult reading is often the original, since scribes tended to try to make the difficult simple. The reading that best explains the origin of other readings is also to be preferred.

This is an important issue to consider in the debate concerning the King James Version (KJV) and newer versions. The KJV was based on later manuscripts, whereas most modern versions are based on earlier manuscripts that had not yet been discovered in 1611 when the KJV was translated. Sometimes the majority text argument is used to say that the KJV is better, but we have seen that this argument does not hold. We have to weigh rather than count manuscripts. The inferior quality of the majority text has been shown by its more full text, its lucidity, its conflation and harmonization.

We must also consider the reason why there are more manuscripts of this inferior text-type. When the New Testament first came to be written, it was written on papyrus, a material that does not last as well as parchment. Because the church was poor, it could not afford to produce many copies. Also, because it had a longer period through which it had to survive, the chances of an earlier manuscript (second century) surviving are much smaller than say a fourteenth century manuscript. When one considers the fragile nature of the material, the longer time it had to survive, and the smaller number of manuscripts, it is a wonder that there are as many extant early manuscripts as there are and that they are as well preserved as they are. On the other hand, the majority text manuscripts were written very late, in greater numbers, and on durable parchment. One can see that the majority text argument is not a sound one at all. Along with this, when we consider the principles of text criticism already

Major Greek Manuscripts of the New Testament

Symbol	Manuscript	Date	Part of NT Preserved in Manuscript
א	Sinaiticus	ca. 325	Almost complete
A	Alexandrinus	5th Century	Missing most of Matthew and a few other passages
B	Vaticanus	ca. 325	Missing 1 Tim - Philemon and from Heb 9:14 to end
C	Ephraemi Rescriptus	5th Century	Most of New Testament but missing many pages
D	Baeza	5th Century	Gospels - Acts, missing some pages
P^{45}	Chester Beatly Papyrus	3rd Century	Sections of Gospels and Acts
P^{46}	Chester Beatly Papyrus	ca. 200	Sections of Paul's letters
P^{47}	Chester Beatly Papyrus	3rd Century	Sections of Revelation
P^{52}	Rylands Fragment	ca. 115-125	John 18:31-33, 37-38
P^{66}	Bodmer Papyrus	ca. 200	Most of the Gospel of John
P^{72}	Bodmer Papyrus	3rd - 4th Century	1 & 2 Peter and Jude
P^{73}	Bodmer Papyrus	7th Century	Matthew
P^{74}	Bodmer Papyrus	7th Century	Acts and General Epistles
P^{75}	Bodmer Papyrus	3rd Century	Luke - John
P^{90}	Bodmer Papyrus	2nd Century	John 18:36-19:7

enunciated, and the fact that the more the manuscript goes through the process of copying the more we find some type of addition or changes creeping in, it is hardly possible for us to favor the majority text.

THE HISTORY OF THE CANON

The New Testament did not descend to us from heaven neatly packaged, all twenty-seven books in the order that we find them in our Bibles. This was not true of the Old Testament anymore than the New, although the period when the New Testament books were written was considerably shorter than that of the Old Testament books. There are some other interesting differences between them. When the New Testament was written, the Old Testament canon was more or less complete. At any rate a good part of it had canonical significance. One would think that this would make it much more difficult for the New Testament books to reach canonical status. However, while there was Moses in the Old Testament, there was One greater than Moses in the New. For the Christians Jesus Christ was a dominating figure whose life, teaching, and significance had overshadowed everything else, even the Old Testament, so that what was written about him and because of him had great importance.   *church's*

What is obvious from a reading of the New Testament is that the church's *canon :* canon was the Old Testament. The Gospel of Matthew relates the life of Christ *OT* as a fulfillment of the Old Testament. Paul and other writers of the New Testament quote the Old Testament as authoritative (Rom 3:4; 1 Cor 1:19).

In that kind of context one would not expect the New Testament writings to have canonical status immediately. Paul's letters to the churches would hardly have been considered canonical when he wrote them. For the disciples and followers of Jesus who were his contemporaries, the written Gospels would not be as significant as for later Christians, since they were eyewitnesses of his life. They had witnessed his life and had heard his teachings. This oral tradition from those who lived with him would be of more value at this time than anything written about him.

The apocalyptic and eschatological climate in which the early disciples lived was also not conducive to the development of a New Testament canon. Because there were eyewitnesses who would surely live until the end, no canon was needed.

We have to remember, too, that the early followers probably were not literary people. They had limited education and means. Christian communities were relatively isolated from one another. While communication took place, it would take some time. Universal acceptance could not easily be gained in that context.

The need for a canon only arose when the apostles began to pass away and the oral tradition became confused and contradictory. Those who taught differently from the oral tradition would accelerate the need for a canon by which to judge between true and false teaching. So the development of the canon was a gradual one.

In the New Testament itself, as we look back from our vantage point, we can see the beginnings, the earliest steps, toward a canon. The letters of Paul were apparently being read and, in some cases at least, exchanged among different church groups (1 Thess 5:27; Col 4:16). The Book of Revelation was also being read (Rev 1:3). An interesting passage is 2 Pet 3:16, which seems to indicate that Paul's writings were considered on the same level as the Old Testament. People who date this in the middle of the second century would not consider this as witness of early acceptance of Paul's writings. It could also mean simply that they distort Paul's writings, as they do in the Old Testament, without necessarily placing them on the same level, i.e., if the latter was a common occurrence, it is natural to compare what is being done with Paul's writings to it.

Another interesting aspect within the New Testament is the fact that later writers sometimes use an earlier writer. For example, it is generally assumed that Matthew and Luke are dependent on Mark for some of their material. Second Peter is also based on Jude. Could it be that at this point this is a recognition of some kind of status for Mark?

Paul frequently (1 Cor 11:23-25; 15:3-7; 7:10-11; 9:14) refers to traditions regarding what Jesus did and said. He obviously did not have the written Gospels. This reflects that period when oral traditions or written traditions which have not been preserved prevailed. Acts 20:35 quotes an agrapha, a saying of Jesus which we do not find in the Gospels. There were most likely others which were not transmitted in the writings which we have.

The Apostolic Fathers, the earliest noncanonical writers of the church whose writings have been preserved, witness further to the gradual development of the canon. The Old Testament is clearly canonical, but while some writings of the New Testament are referred to, there is no clear-cut indication of their canonical authority. They were still living in that period when oral tradition was valued highly. This is clear in Papias in his *Exegeses of the Dominical Oracles*, quoted in Eusebius, *H.E.* 3, 39, 3-4. The *Didache* makes reference to Matthew and alludes to Luke and John. Papias knew Matthew, Mark, John, 1 John and 1 Peter. Hermas alludes to Hebrews, John, Matthew, Mark, and Ephesians. Clement of Rome knew and alludes to Matthew, Luke, Ephesians, Romans, 1 Corinthians, Galatians, Philippians, Hebrews. *Second Clement* alludes to Matthew, Luke, Romans, 1 Corinthians, Galatians, Ephesians, Philippians, Hebrews and perhaps James and 1 Peter. While the Old Testament is definitely scripture, some Gospel books are also considered as scripture, but not Paul's writings.

Ignatius of Antioch probably knew a collection of Pauline epistles and two or three Gospels, but he did not regard any of them as Scripture. Polycarp of

Smyrna knew at least eight Pauline letters: 1 Peter, *1 Clement*, 1 or 2 John, Hebrews, the *Letters of Ignatius* and perhaps the Gospel of Matthew. However, none of these he considered as Scripture. The writer of the *Epistle of Barnabas* knew Matthew, probably the Gospel of John, and may have known the Pastoral Epistles. What we have in the Apostolic Fathers is some knowledge of the New Testament writings, but they are not definitely quoted as Scripture as the Old Testament was. This is still a time when the oral tradition was highly valued, and therefore the written word was not as important as it was later.

Paul wrote his letters to seven churches and to three individuals in Greece, Asia Minor, and Italy. We indicated earlier that Col 3:16 mentioned an exchange of his letters among some of the churches. Clement of Rome knew some of his letters, and Ignatius and Polycarp probably knew all the letters to the churches, while the latter knew also 1 and 2 Timothy and Hebrews. Marcion's canon included Galatians, 1 and 2 Corinthians, Romans, 1 and 2 Thessalonians, Ephesians, Colossians, Philemon and Philippians. Omitted from the list are 1 and 2 Timothy, Titus and Hebrews. The Muratorian Canon omits Hebrews but includes all the rest. Irenaeus lists all except Philemon, Titus and Hebrews.

Justin Martyr (ca. 150 C.E.) knew and quoted all four Gospels. Tatian (ca. 170 C.E.) composed the *Diatesseron*, a harmony of the four Gospels. Irenaeus of Lyons (ca. 180 C.E.) placed the Gospels in the following chronological order: Matthew, Mark, Luke and John. He also sought to justify the fact that there were four Gospels.

Thus by the middle of the second century the letters of Paul and the four Gospels had been formed into collections and accepted. The other major writings were also generally accepted. The process was a gradual one as different churches to whom Paul had written, valuing their own letter, would discover that he had also written to other churches. This could very well have begun during Paul's lifetime but would be accelerated after his death. One theory puts the development of the collection at Corinth, since the Corinthian letters are placed at the beginning of the collection in the Muratorian Canon and Tertullian. Goodspeed's ingenious though unlikely theory places the collection after the publication of Acts (ca. 85 C.E.), before which the letters were virtually neglected and forgotten. According to Goodspeed, Onesimus sought out the other letters Paul had written (he already had Colossians and Philemon). As an introduction to this collection, Onesimus wrote Ephesians based on Colossians and other Pauline letters.

By the end of the second century all the books of the New Testament were generally accepted except for the Catholic Epistles, Hebrews and Revelation. Irenaeus included 1 Peter, 1 and 2 John, and Revelation, but omitted the rest, i.e., 2 Peter, 3 John and Hebrews. The Muratorian Fragment omitted Hebrews, 1 and 2 Peter, one of the Johannine epistles, and James, but included an *Apocalypse of*

Peter and the *Wisdom of Solomon*. Tertullian omitted Hebrews, James, 2 and 3 John and 2 Peter. Clement of Alexandria omitted from his list James, 2 Peter and 3 John, but included some apocryphal and pseudepigraphal writings and apostolic fathers. Origen omitted 2 and 3 John and 2 Peter. Eusebius listed three groups: the acknowledged writings (the four Gospels, Acts, Pauline Epistles, 1 John, 1 Peter and perhaps Revelation), the disputed writings (James, Jude, 2 Peter, 2 and 3 John), rejected writings (*Gospel of Peter*, *Gospel of Thomas*, *Gospel of Matthias* and other gospels, *Acts of Andrew*, *Acts of John* and others). He also, under disputed writings, had a classification of spurious writings (*Acts of Paul*, *Shepherd of Hermas*, *Revelations of Peter*, *Epistle of Barnabas*, *Didache* and perhaps the Revelation of John and the Gospel of Hebrews). Notice his wavering regarding the Revelation which he places under both acknowledged and spurious books.

Here is the picture at the end of the second century. The basic nucleus of the New Testament was established. The book of Hebrews in the West, the two shorter epistles of John, the second epistle of Peter, the epistles of James, Jude and the Revelation were not yet unanimously received. On the other hand, especially at Alexandria there was a tendency to have a few other books which are not found in our present canon, i.e., *Shepherd of Hermas*, *Epistle of Barnabas*, *Didache*, *1 Clement* and the *Revelation of Peter*.

The problem of Hebrews was the question of its authorship, not its contents, and the minor Catholic epistles lack of acceptance was because of their lack of use. According to Grant, the problem of Hebrews was overcome at Alexandria because the Christians there knew that *1 Clement* used it and it was in harmony with Christian thinking. James had reflections of the Gospels, Jude proved helpful against the heretics, and 2 Peter was connected with 1 Peter (2 Pet 3:1). 2 and 3 John were similar in style and content with 1 John.[3]

At any rate the first canonical list identical to ours came forth in the year 367 C.E. in Athanasius' *Easter Letter*. Jerome's Vulgate no doubt exerted a great influence in fixing the canon to its present limits. The conciliar pronouncements (Hippo, 393, and Carthage, 397) helped further to establish the present canon.

Since the fourth century, especially during the Reformation period, questions have arisen regarding the authorship and quality of Hebrews, and with the authority of James, Jude, 2 Peter, and Revelation.

In recent days quite a bit of discussion has centered on the canon, focusing on the kinds of questions raised during the time of the Reformation, but going beyond to other questions as well. Luther's principle of a canon within a canon, although outside the scope of this discussion, is one of the issues that continues to be debated.

FURTHER READING

Filson, Floyd V.
1937   *Which Books Belong in the Bible?* Philadelphia: Westminster.
Gamble, Harry Y.
1985   *The New Testament Canon: Its Making and Meaning.* Philadelphia: Fortress.
Greenlee, J. Harold
1964   *Introduction to New Testament Textual Criticism.* Grand Rapids, MI: Eerdmans.
Metzger, Bruce M.
1987   *The Canon of the New Testament.* New York: Oxford University Press.
1964   *The Text of the New Testament.* New York: Oxford University Press.
Reumann, John H.P.
1965   *The Romance of Bible Scripts and Scholars.* Englewood Cliffs, NJ: Prentice-Hall.
Souter, Alexander
1954   *The Text and Canon of the New Testament.* Rev. ed. Naperville, IL: Allenson.

ENDNOTES

1. This and other totals of manuscripts are taken from Kurt Aland and Barbara Aland, *The Text of the New Testament* (Grand Rapids, MI: Eerdmans, 1987).
2. Guenther Zuntz, *The Text of the Epistles: A Disquisition upon the Corpus Paulinum* (London, 1953), p 13.
3. Robert Grant, *The Formation of the New Testament*, p 182.

Chapter 4

Letters in Hellenistic Society

Bruce C. Johanson

WHAT IS A LETTER?

What a letter is would seem to be fairly obvious and hardly in need of careful definition. However, since the letter has been used for many purposes, from simple personal contacts to apocalyptic revelations, it is necessary to try to arrive at a basic idea of its essential character. A natural inclination is to define it in terms of its most frequent and wide-spread use to contact distant associates, to pass on or request information of personal interest, or simply to mediate a personal sense of presence that negotiates an ongoing relationship. This, however, does not entirely explain the use of letters that consist of philosophical essays, biographies and autobiographies, and even an entire apocalypse.

It would seem that the best way to arrive at an adequate definition is to ask for the most general features that persist in all of these different types of communication. In this regard it may be observed that the most general function of the letter would be to provide verbal communication between two parties by means of writing when circumstances have made it either infeasible or undesirable to do so by a personal, oral encounter. In other words, the letter should be understood basically as a surrogate for oral communication. This would exclude such works as dictionaries, encyclopedias, textbooks, etc., which would not naturally qualify as appropriate oral communications.

But what about philosophical essays, apocalypses, etc.? It seems fair to say that an appropriate or acceptable use of the letter as a form for such types of communication may find relative constraints in terms of the length of the material, the type of content to be mediated, and above all, a type of social role of the author that can naturally accommodate the communication of a sense of personal interest and presence, or at least the fiction of personal interest and presence. Different cultural traditions will, of course, apply such constraints

37

more widely or more narrowly in relation to the needs of different communication situations.

BACKGROUNDS

Due to the moister climate in the Northern parts of the Mediterranean world and the fragility of materials used, e.g., waxed wooden tablets and sheets of papyrus imported from Egypt, we do not have anything near the abundance of letter remains like those found in the Near East and in Egypt. This has made it very difficult to achieve an accurate knowledge of the early development and use of letters in Greece and Rome. The sources available are largely references to letters or the incorporation of letters in other documents preserved by a process of copying down through the ages, i.e. plays, histories, treatises, etc. On the other hand, the dry climate of Egypt has helped to preserve hundreds of letters from ca. 300 B.C.E. to 400 C.E. While most of these were written on papyrus, there are also a few on leather. By contrast, there is an abundance of preserved letters on clay tablets from the Sumarian, Assyrian and Babylonian cultures that reach back to the third millennium B.C.E.

The advance of literacy in the sixth and fifth centuries B.C.E. in Greece contributed to the growth of the use of letters to replace oral communication by a messenger person. However, at that early period letters were used primarily for serious, sensitive or sinister messages where secrecy was important.[1] As far as we are able to tell, this development makes its appearance in the Roman world from around 200 B.C.E.[2] As literacy increased further, letter-writing became more common, but only at certain social levels and only for long-distance communication due to some pressing need.[3] At the first stage of education during Hellenistic times, young boys learned basically to read and write. Letter-writing was probably a part of the secondary stage of education before they went on to the third stage at which rhetoric was the primary focus. It was most likely learned by imitation of models rather than from a set of comprehensive rules and theory.[4]

Apart from letters sent by government dignitaries or by the wealthy who could use a servant as carrier, there was a great deal of uncertainty in the delivery of letters. For the common person letters had to be entrusted for the most part to strangers. If they were fortunate, a travelling acquaintance or friend could be counted on. Travel was also hazardous. Whether by sea or by land there was danger from pirates and robbers, shipwreck, or illness of the carrier. In fact, we hear a fair amount of frustration in ancient correspondence over this dilemma.[5] As Roman power expanded, the problem was somewhat alleviated by better roads and safer travel due to the reduction of robbers and pirates.

GRECO-ROMAN LETTER CONVENTIONS

Starting around 100 B.C.E. handbooks on letter-writing and theory began to appear. They generally viewed letters as a surrogate for actual dialogue, to be composed as real communications rather than technical treatises, and as needing to be concise, clear and appropriate to the circumstances.[6] However, as may be expected, what was preached by some was not always practiced by others. We find in Hellenistic letters most of the spectrum of private and public verbal communication. There are the so-called "documentary letters" that have been divided into the subordinate genres of family correspondence, letters of introduction and recommendation, letters of petition, and memoranda.[7] Other genres include business letters, official letters used to carry out administrative purposes, public letters used to try to influence political opinion or policy, pseudonymous letters, and letter-essays containing scientific or philosophical teaching, moral exhortation, biographies, etc.[8]

Several of these categories certainly included technical contents and hardly conformed to the norm of being concise. Also, the various categories cover a spectrum that shades off from the non-literary to the literary, with the bulk of documentary and business letters belonging to the non-literary side. While it may be useful for descriptive purposes to make a distinction between the ordinary *letter* in contrast to the more literary *epistle*, the differences are fairly fluid in many instances such as the letters of Cicero, Pliny the Younger, Seneca, etc.[9] Another distinction that may be made is the one between real and apparent letters. The former would be defined by concretely specified senders and recipients and by messages with only immediate, practical, and personal concerns. The latter would be defined as writings intended for a non-specified audience with more universal concerns placed within the framework of a letter so as to create the fiction of a letter. This distinction, however, also begins to break down when real letters, even business letters, written by Cicero, among others, were intentionally written with wider, non-specific audiences of posterity in mind. As a consequence, they were preserved for their lasting value in both thought and literary excellence, quite apart from their immediate practical purposes and specific addressees.

In the case of letter-essays, we find an essay placed within the framework of a brief prescript (e.g. X to Y, greeting) and a closing "goodbye".[10] The latter is often omitted. What made the letter an attractive framework for philosophical teaching, moral exhortation, biography, etc., was most probably its capacity to generate a sense of the writer's personal presence and interest in whoever the reader may be. Such a phenomenon was possibly one of the contributing causes of the prevalence of pseudonymous letters. A more tangible cause, however, seems to have been the imitation of the style and thought of literary or rhetorical masters as part of school exercises.[11] Another important, contributing cause appears to have been the desire on the part of a disciple to honor a deceased teacher by preserving and even extending his teachings. In this instance, the consciousness of belonging to a particular tradition apparently gave the practice its sense of legitimacy.[12] However we may understand the phenomenon of pseudepigraphy, it led to a great number of pseudonymous letters attributed to Plato, Socrates, and various Stoic and Cynic philosophers.[13]

Samples of the practice of pseudepigraphy are to be seen in early Christian literature. Examples among the apostolic fathers are *The Epistle of Barnabas* and *The Second Epistle of Clement to the Corinthians*.[14] *The Letter of Peter to Philip* is an example in Christian gnostic literature.[15] Examples of much later works are *The Epistle to the Laodiceans*, the apocryphal letters between Seneca and Paul, and the *Epistle of Titus* created to variously satisfy curiosity or support a particular concern.[16] In the New Testament, the letters that have been most widely questioned by modern scholarship as being pseudonymous are 1 Timothy, 2 Timothy, Titus, 1 Peter, and especially 2 Peter and Jude. Ephesians, Colossians and 2 Thessalonians are strongly debated, but the evidence against Pauline authorship is not decisive. On the other hand, both Hebrews and 1 John are actually anonymous. The author of 2 and 3 John is virtually anonymous in view of the cryptic reference to him as the "Elder". As for James, there is no explanation regarding which James we are dealing with (see the respective chapters on each of these books).

Non-literary letters in the Greco-Roman tradition were by far the most numerous and the most stereotyped in formulation. Evidence for this comes primarily from papyri preserved in Egypt, as mentioned above. Such letters have been characterized in general by three basic functions: to express or maintain a friendly relationship, to mediate the writer's presence, and to facilitate dialogic communication.[17] The large majority are very brief. Their basic structure may be outlined as follows:

1. *The Letter Opening*:[18] This consists of a prescript which identifies the sender and the recipient and expresses a greeting. The most common formula is, e.g., "Apion to Gaius, greeting." Less common are the formulations "To Gaius, greeting. Apion" or "To Gaius from Apion." The latter of these two is frequent in letters of petition or application.

2. *The Letter Body*: An opening wish or prayer for good health and/or other sentiments of good will, or in the event of strained relations, an expression of surprise or displeasure is most usual at this point.[19] It is followed by the message part of the letter which, depending on its character and purpose, will contain various expressions of disclosure, petition, appeal, injunction, joy, astonishment, compliance or hearing/learning, etc. All of these serve introductory, transitional or terminal functions as the author moves from one topic to the next.[20] At the close of this part greetings are often extended to

others apart from the addressee. An additional wish or prayer for the addressee's good health may be included.

3. *The Letter Closing*:[21] Here we usually find a final "goodbye" or equivalent expression. Sometimes the date was given. Also, in the event of the use of a secretary or professional letter-writer, an illiteracy formula or an authenticating subscription from the sender was sometimes added before or after the "goodbye" in writing identifiable as a second hand.[22]

An address was placed on the back of the letter, e.g. "To Apion from Gaius." Sometimes this was accompanied by more detailed instructions of where to find the recipient. The following are typical examples of such letters. The former is a letter of introduction from the second century B.C.E. The latter is a family letter from the second century C.E. They illustrate how little conventions changed over a long period of time. The italicized words and phrases, as well as the transliterated Greek, gives one an idea of some of the typical expressions used in such letters.

> Polycrates to Philoxenus, *greeting* (*chairein*). If you are well and things are going agreeably well for you, it would be just as we desire. *We* ourselves *are in health* (*hugiainomen*). Regarding the things we wanted, we have sent Glaucias, who is one of us, to you to personally consult with you. Therefore, please listen to him and instruct him about things for which he has come. Above all, take care of yourself, that *you may be in health* (*hugiaineīs*). *Goodbye* (*errōso*). The 29th year, Phamenoth....
> (Addressed on the back) To Philoxenus.[23]

> Irenaeus to Apolinarius my brother, *many greetings* (*polla chairein*). *I pray* (*euchomai*) always that *you may be in health* (*hugienen*), just as *I* myself *am in health* (*hugienō*) . *I want you to know* (*ginōskein de thelō*) that I reached land on the sixth of the month of Epeiph and finished unloading my ship on the 18th of the same month. I went up to Rome on the 25th of the same month and, as God willed, the place welcomed us. We keep waiting every day for our discharge, so until today none of those in the corn business has been released. *I send greetings* (*aspazomai*) to your wife, to Serenus, and by name to all those who love you. *Goodbye* (*errōso*) Mesore 9.
> (Addressed on the back) To Apolinarius from Irenaeus his brother.[24]

The next letter illustrates how a writer could leave many usual conventions out or creatively improvise on them according to circumstances and inclination. It is written in poor Greek by a young, quite disgruntled son to his father.

> Theon to Theon my father, *greeting* (*chairein*). A fine thing you did! You didn't take me away with you to the city! If you don't want to take me with you to Alexandria, I certainly won't write you a letter, or speak to you, or *wish you health* (*huigenō*) If you should go to Alexandria, I won't hold your hand beside you or greet you again from now on. If you don't wish to take me, that's what will happen! My mother said to Archelaus, "He upsets me. Take him away!" But, a fine thing you did! You sent me gifts! Big ones! Like tiny

wild peas! They fooled us there, on the 12th, when you sailed. Therefore, send for me, *I urge (parakalo̅)* you. If you don't send (for me), I won't eat, I won't drink! That's for sure! *I pray (euchomai)* that you may be in health. Tubi 18. (Addressed on the back) Deliver to Theon from Theon his son.[25]

Another example is provided by a letter of consolation in which typical conventions are changed to suit the occasion, i.e. the change of greeting, the absence of a health-wish at the opening or closing, and the absence of greetings at the end. The closing consists of a simple admonition to mutual comfort (cf. 1 Thess 4:18) with a "farewell" expression.

> Irene to Taonnophris and Philo, *good courage (eupsuchein)*. I grieved and wept as much over the blessed one as I wept over Didymas. I and all who were with me, Epaphroditus and Thermouthion and Philion and Apollonius and Plantas, did all that was appropriate. But for all that, there is nothing anyone can do in proportion to such things. Comfort, therefore, one another. *Farewell (eu prattete)*. Hathyr 1.
> (Addressed on the back) To Taonnophris and Philo.[26]

Very often a person who used a secretary would write the closing salutation or some part of the closing in his or her own hand-writing. In the following letter from 50 C.E. the hand-writing changes for the closing salutation and the date.

> Mystarion to his own Stotoetis, many greetings. I sent to you my Blastus about wooden forks for my olive orchards. See now that you do not detain him. For you know how I need him every hour. (*In another hand-writing*) Goodbye. The 11th year of Tiberius Claudius Caesar Augustus Germanicus Imperator, in the month Sebastus 15.
> (Addressed on the back *in the first hand-writing*) To Stotoetis, chief priest, at the island ....[27]

SOME ARAMAIC LETTER CONVENTIONS

Besides letters in Greek, there are letters in Aramaic preserved in Egypt on papyrus and leather which date from the last couple of centuries B.C.E. into the first century C.E. The following outline gives an overview of their structure and phraseology:[28]

1. *The Letter Opening*: There are five different ways of expressing the identity of the sender and the recipient: a) "To X, your servant/brother/son, Y," b) "To X, from Y," c) "From X, to Y," d) "X to Y," and e) "To X." Following this there is either a short or an extended expression of greeting using "peace" (*shalom*) or a verb of "blessing". In a few instance there is only *shalom* like the Greek "greeting" (*chairein*). Some official letters leave out the greeting altogether. In some letters there is a secondary greeting in which greetings are sent to others known to the sender and recipient.

2. *The Letter Body*: The initial greetings are often followed by the expression "and now." This is used not only to introduce the message part of the letter as a whole, but also to demarcate transitions between subsections in the message part.

3. *The Letter Closing*: Only two phrases appear to be formulaic at the close of these letters. They both include the expression *shalom*: a) "I have sent this letter for your peace of mind," b) "Be at peace!" Toward the end of the more official letters, one often finds a reference to the secretary who drafted the letter and the scribe who copied it or took dictation. A date is sometimes added.

The address on the outside of the letter usually took the form of "To X." On official letters it took the form "From X, to Y."

PAUL AS LETTER WRITER

Even if we did not have the specific information that Paul was a Pharisee of high education under Gamaliel (Acts 22:3), we could have inferred his Jewishness from the contents and the manner of scriptural interpretation in his letters alone. At the same time, his close familiarity with Hellenism is evident from his native use of Koine Greek, even though it has somewhat of a semitic accent. It should come as no surprise to find the influences of literary traditions from both these worlds influencing and enriching his writing. In fact, the Jewish milieu of his time was fairly heavily influenced by Hellenism, even in Judea. *familiar* ~

Paul was well-acquainted with Hellenistic letter conventions. He even *Hellenistic* mentions a particular genre, the letter of recommendation (1 Cor 16:3; 2 Cor 3:1-*conventions* 2). As a letter writer, however, he was far from a rigid imitator of the current conventions. While he used many of the customary phrases and formulas of the Greek documentary letters, we find him creatively adapting them to the Christian message and the particular situations he addressed. We know that he made use *used a* of a secretary. There is the explicit reference in Rom 16:22 where Tertius refers *secretary* to himself as the secretary. There are also clear examples of authenticating subscriptions in 1 Cor 16:21, Gal 6:11, Col 4:18, 2 Thess 3:17 and Phlm 19, apparently added by Paul in his own handwriting.[29] These all imply the use of a secretary. Furthermore, the general uniformity of language and style in most of his letters suggests that his dictation was followed quiet closely by those who wrote for him. Only Ephesians and Colossians show a heavier, somewhat different style and vocabulary, particularly in the introductory parts. These and the following observations on his letter-writing are based on Romans, 1 and 2 Corinthians, Galatians, Ephesians, Philippians, Colossians, 1 and 2 Thessalonians and Philemon. The Pastorals, which differ greatly in language, style and theological expression, do not appear to be directly authored by Paul and are therefore not used as primary sources here.

Due in part to improved travel conditions in the Roman empire in the first century C.E., but even more to reliable delivery by fellow Christian carriers, Paul's attitude to the letter as a secure and effective form of communication is very positive. This appears to have given him the confidence to put in a great deal of time and energy to write at length.[30] In fact, according to 2 Cor 10:10, Paul's letters were so undeniably powerful that even his detractors had to concede it.

PAUL'S USE OF GRECO-ROMAN LETTER CONVENTIONS

With regard to the letter opening or prescript, Paul uses the usual "X to Y, greeting" formula, but with some significant differences. First of all, the most striking difference is his replacement of the usual "greeting" (*chairein*) by "grace to you and peace" (*charis humin kai eirēnē*). There seems to be an intentional play on similar sounding consonants in the replacement of *chairein* by *charis*. For Paul "grace" was a one-word designation for the whole gospel. As for the addition of "peace," this probably was influenced both by the Aramaic letter tradition in which *shalom* was a typical part of the greeting and also by the special meaning "peace" obtains in the gospel (Phil 4:7; Eph 2:14; Col 1:20). First Thess 1:1 has the shortest greeting formulation just mentioned. All the other letters elaborate the greeting by adding *"from God our Father and the Lord Jesus Christ,"* except for Col 1:2 which has only *"from God our Father."* Secondly, apart from official or legal letters involving political or religious dignitaries, we find relatively few elaborations attached to the sender and/or the addressee's names in Greco-Roman letters. Paul always adds a theological elaboration to one or the other or to both. He usually qualifies himself as an "apostle" and/or "servant" of Jesus Christ. In Gal 1:1 he elaborates on his apostolic status and in Rom 1:1-6 the elaboration on his apostleship grows into a miniature statement of the gospel before he comes to the identification of the addressees. With regard to the addressee part, the shortest prescript in 1 Thess 1:1 makes the following elaboration: "to the church of the Thessalonians *in God the Father and the Lord Jesus Christ.*" In Gal 1:2b-5 the elaboration after "To the churches of Galatia" turns into a miniature statement of the Gospel closed by a doxology and "amen."

The particularly extended elaborations in the prescripts of Galatians and Romans are quite apparently motivated by persuasive strategies. In Galatia, some persons had cast doubt on Paul's apostolic authority in an effort to assert a gospel that included Jewish observances of the Torah. Paul's elaborations both assert his apostolic commission through Jesus Christ and allude to the freedom that the gospel brings. Both topics get extensive treatment in the letter. As for Romans, the argumentation in chs 9-11 indicates some sort of tension between

Jewish and Gentile Christians. Not only was Paul committed to reconciliation between the two communities, but he also wanted to use the Roman church as a springboard for mission to Spain (Rom 15:20-33). Consequently, the very traditional expression of the gospel-in-a-nutshell in Rom 1:1-6 was probably intended to establish his credentials and to hold the attention of those who might be suspicious of his theology.

Before moving on to the message part of Paul's letters, we need to make one *an* more observation. Much like Seneca, Paul adopts the familiar stance of a Greco-*authority* Roman authority figure in his self-presentation by dramatizing the effect of his *figure* teaching on his addressees (e.g., 1 Cor 4:14-21, 2 Cor 3:1-3, 10:7-12, Eph 3:2-3, Gal 4:12-20).[31] While this is true, it is not the whole picture. In only Romans and Ephesians do we find Paul alone as sender in the prescript. In the Thessalonian letters he includes Silvanus and Timothy. In 2 Corinthians, Philippians, Colossians and Philemon he includes Timothy. In 1 Corinthians he *but* *includes* includes Sosthenes. In Galatians he includes "all the members of God's family *community* who are with me." This indicates that, in spite of the tenacious defenses of his authoritative status as apostle (Rom 1:1-6; 2 Cor 10-12; Gal 1:1-2:14) and as spiritual father (1 Cor 4:14-21), his letters were not exclusively extensions of his apostolic authority, but were also vehicles of Christian community. Even his letter to the individual Philemon included several other specifically named persons together with the whole church in his house (Phlm 1a-2). *Message:*

Turning now to the message part of Paul's letters, instead of the usual health *thanksgiving* wish, we find extended thanksgiving and prayer reports (Rom 1:8-12; 1 Cor 1:4- *and* 9; Phil 1:3-11; Col 1:3-14; 1 Thess 1:2-10; 2:13-14; 3:9-10; 2 Thess 1:3-12; *prayer* 2:13-15; Phlm 4-7), elaborate introductory blessings (2 Cor 1:3-7; Eph 1:3-14) *report,* and an introductory passage expressing displeasure opened by a formula of ironical surprise (Gal 1:6-10). In Ephesians the blessing section is extended further by a thanksgiving and prayer report in 1:15-23. The instances in 1 and 2 Thessalonians are somewhat different from the other letters. In the former the thanksgiving and prayer report extends over half the letter (1 Thess 1-3). In the latter the initial thanksgiving and prayer report (2 Thess 1:3-12) is renewed in 2:13-15. In between is sandwiched a section of corrective instruction (2:1-12). Also, the wording in 2 Thessalonians differs. It has "We must always give thanks," whereas in all the other instances Paul writes "I/we give thanks."

While there are some brief instances of thanksgiving and/or prayer reports for the addressee's health and well-being in Greco-Roman letters, there are very few instances that compare with Paul's elaborate formulations. Basically he has turned them into what would function as *exordia* (introductions) in speeches. They serve to appeal to the addressees' goodwill, to enhance the author's credibility, and very often to indicate the purposes and/or topics to be developed in the letter. As expressions of warmth and goodwill, they generally reflect good current relations with the community addressed.

The introductory blessing paragraphs in 1 Corinthians and especially Ephesians tend to be more formal and reflect less personal warmth. This is probably no accident, since Paul's relations with the Corinthian church appear to be particularly strained in the second letter. Also, the more formal opening would suit Ephesians, if it was originally intended as a circular letter. In support of this view, the oldest manuscripts do not have "in Ephesus" in the prescript at all. Also, the lack of personal familiarity expressed in Eph 1:15 and 3:2 suits a wider audience than Ephesus alone where Paul worked for close to three years (Acts 19). In the case of Galatians, the replacement of a thanksgiving and prayer report by an expression of surprise and censure suits Paul's unhappy relation to those churches, as is evident from the rest of that letter.

It is customary to describe the message part of Paul's letters as generally divided into a theological section followed by a section of moral and/or practical admonition. It is important not to oversimplify this, because one clearly finds admonitions mingled with theological exposition and theological expositions intermingled with moral and practical admonitions. The division referred to here is one in which one or the other tends to be predominant. Such a two-part formation finds no clear parallel in Hellenistic letter conventions. It is found in Romans, Galatians, Ephesians, Colossians, and 1 Thessalonians. The moral and/or practical hortatory sections begin in Rom 12:1, Gal 4:12, Eph 4:1, Col 3:1, and 1 Thess 4:1. Some of these open with expressions of petition typically used in Hellenistic letters. One finds *parakalō* , "I urge," "I exhort" (Rom 12:1 and Eph 4:1), *parakalō* together with *erōtaō*, "I request," I "ask" (1 Thess 4:1), and *deomai*, "I beg," "I implore" (Gal 4:12). Such expressions are basically signals of transition to an exhortatory, imperatival mode of expression, and do not become specialized formulas to identify what follows as entirely a section of moral exhortation. This may be illustrated by 1 Cor 1:10, 2 Cor 10:1, and 2 Thess 2:1 where *parakalō* opens other kinds of admonitions, some of which develop into theological expositions. In the case of Col 3:1 there is no request formula. The shift to exhortation is simply marked by the content and the predominant use of the imperative mood.

The following letters do not easily conform to the above-mentioned two-part division.

First Corinthians first addresses the problem of factions in 1:10-4:21. Then in chs 5-15 we find fairly clearly demarcated sections of theological exposition and instruction mingled with exhortation on various issues in the Corinthian church. From ch 7 on, Paul responds to questions posed in a letter from the Corinthian church. Shifts from one topic to the next are often marked by "now concerning" (*peri de*), e.g. in 7:1, 25; 8:1; 12:1, 16:1, or by an expression of disclosure "I want you to know" (*gnōrizō de humin*) in 15:1 (RSV). Second Corinthians is possibly a compilation of letters by Paul. Chapters 1-7 basically expound on the nature and authenticity of Paul's ministry supported by theological expositions. Chapters 8-9 deal with the Jerusalem collection. The rest of the letter is a defense of Paul's integrity and apostleship. Some of the major transitions are marked by typical expressions of transition used in the Hellenistic letter tradition, namely, disclosure statements (1:8; 8:1), the topical marker "now concerning" (8:1 RSV), and expressions of request (10:1, 2). Philippians is also a possible compilation of Pauline letters. One finds a concatenation of theological exposition, moral exhortation and practical or personal notices and admonitions. Only a couple of instances of typical letter phraseology, a disclosure (1:12) and a request (4:2) expression, are found at transitional points in the message part.

While the predominating types of contents in Paul's letters are the theological expositions and the ethical/practical implications of the gospel, we also find a fair representation of themes that are typical of the documentary letters in the Hellenistic papyri.[32] The most common themes in the papyri are the writing and exchange of letters, health, and business, with other such themes as domestic events, visit talk, and government affairs not far behind.[33] Since the gospel touched all aspects of life, these themes are usually blended in with Paul's theological or ethical materials. At the end of the message part of Paul's letters, he tends to introduce, commend or simply refer to the person or persons who will carry or accompany the carrier of the letter (Rom 16:1-2, Eph 6:21-22, Col 4:7-9, and possibly 1 Cor 17-18). This can occur at the beginning or end of Hellenistic letters in general. One of the anomalies that suggests a compilation of letters in Philippians is that such notices and commendations occur in the middle of the letter in 2:19-30. Furthermore, they are followed in Phil 3:1 by what could easily be the conclusion of a letter, especially when a genuine alternative translation of "rejoice (*chairete*) in the Lord" may be "farewell in the Lord" (cf. 2 Cor 13:11: *chairete* = goodbye). In general, Paul also follows the typical Hellenistic letter convention of sending greetings (*aspazomai*). Romans 16:1-24 is the longest example of this. Other instances are 1 Cor 16:19-20, 2 Cor 13:13, Phil 4:21-22, Col 4:10-15, 1 Thess 5:26, and Phlm 23-24. Another closing convention is his frequent use of the authenticating subscription already mentioned above.

As for the letter closing, the typical "goodbye" (*errōso* or *eutuxei*) is replaced by a benediction of grace: "The grace of the Lord Jesus Christ be with you" (1 Cor 16:23; 1 Thess 5:28; "all of you" in 2 Thess 3:18) or "be with your spirit" (Gal 6:18; Phil 4:23; Phlm 25). In keeping with its more general, impersonal tone as a whole, Ephesians has "Grace (be) with all who have an undying love for our Lord Jesus Christ" (6:24). Second Cor 13:13 has a trinitarian formulation: "The grace of the Lord Jesus Christ, the love of God, and the communion of the Holy Spirit (be) with all of you." The ending of Romans is too complicated to go into here. One indication of its complication is to be seen in a benediction of peace in 15:33 and a benediction of grace located in 16:20b between closing admonitions and a resumption of greetings. The doxology in 16:25-27 closes the letter.

Finally, since we have no (autographs) of Paul's letters, we have no idea of whether dates were appended. Nor do we know how or if an address was placed on the back of each scroll. The titles that we have on all the letters in the New Testament are added later in manuscripts by copyists. They are very brief in earlier manuscripts and get more elaborate in later ones. There are also concluding notices added at the end of the copied manuscripts. These have been included in the KJV.

NON-EPISTOLARY CONVENTIONS IN PAUL'S LETTERS

There are many features in Paul's letters which are obviously not from the Greco-Roman letter tradition. A significant number of these make Paul's letters particularly suited to be read in the community at worship. We have already noted the changed greeting of "grace and peace" and the closing benediction of grace. Also, the thanksgiving/prayer reports and the blessing paragraphs resonate with the language of worship. In the Old Testament and in subsequent Jewish literature, expressions of praise, thanksgiving and blessing are all interchangeable in what are called "thanksgiving psalms" (e.g., Ps 9; 106; and the *Psalms of Thanksgiving* from Qumran, 1QH ii.20; vii.6).

Besides these, it is possible to see sermon-like features in Paul's letters. A probable background for the two-part division in the above-mentioned letters is to be found in Old Testament and intertestamental Jewish speeches.[34] If we look at speeches in the Old Testament at a fairly high level of generality, we find that the covenant speech in, e.g., Deut 1-4 and Josh 24, has a long narrative recollection of salvation history followed by exhortation to be faithful to God and keep his commandments. The pattern is also found in the farewell or testament speech in Josh 23. The same holds true for testament speeches in intertestamental Jewish literature (e.g., *Jubilees* 21; *Testaments of the Twelve Patriarchs*). However, at this later time the narrative, recollective section tends to become overshadowed by theological exposition, and the exhortation section focuses more on specifically moral admonitions, especially in the *Testaments of the Twelve Patriarchs*.

Other worship appropriate features in Paul's letters are to be seen in his frequent use of doxologies with a concluding "amen" (Rom 1:25; 9:5; 11:36; Gal 1:5; Eph 3:21; Phil 4:20) and wish-prayers (Rom 15:5-6; 13; Col 1:11-12; 1 Thess 3:11-13; 5:23-24; 2 Thess 2:16; 3:5, 16) to bring certain sections of his discourse to a close. These observations suggest that, with regard to background traditions, Paul's letters have been shaped not only by Hellenistic letter conventions but also by Jewish worship conventions.[35] With regard to their immediate situational contexts, they have been shaped to be read in Christian worship. Where else would the congregations to which they were addressed most likely hear them read (see 1 Thess 5:27)?

Unfortunately, we do not have any independent examples of the synagogue sermon preserved apart from the one reported by Luke in Acts 13:12-41. It is referred to in 13:15 as a "word of exhortation" (*logos paraklēseōs*, cf. Heb 13:22). This has been shown to have a section of examples from Israel's salvation history, a conclusion drawn from them, followed by an exhortation.[36] The exhortation, however, is to belief and acceptance of the gospel rather than exhortation to continued commitment and moral behavior. This, however, is probably an adaptation of what Paul knew his synagogue audience was used to hearing. When one compares the Old Testament speeches to Paul's synagogue sermon in Acts 13, it certainly supports seeing Old Testament speeches as an influencing background, both for his sermon and for several of his letters.

Paul also draws on other non-epistolary conventions. In the exhortation sections of Ephesians and Colossians we find household admonitions (Eph 5:21-6:9, Col 3:18-4:1) that do not naturally belong to the letter tradition of antiquity, but to the exhortation (*paraenesis*) of many of the Greco-Roman moral philosophers. A striking difference, though, is that instead of addressing husbands, fathers, and masters first or exclusively, Paul addresses the wives, children and slaves first, and often calls for reciprocity in the relationships he prescribes.[37] He seldom uses a traditional form or formula without bending it and reshaping it to conform to his own particular communicative purposes and to the gospel. We find him using a multitude of other non-epistolary forms, formulas and types of materials: the use of stereotyped catalogues of vices and virtues typical of classical literature (e.g., Rom 1:29-31/Gal 5:22-23); early Christian catechetical or teaching materials formed on the analogy of the Old Testament. Holiness Code (e.g., 1 Thess 4:1-9); confessional formulas (e.g., Rom 10:9); hymnic materials (e.g., Phil 2:6-11, Col 1:15-20); autobiographical materials (e.g., Gal 1:11-2:14); apocalyptic materials (e.g., 2 Thess 2:1-12); diatribe, which is typical of Greek moral philosophers in which the speaker/writer confronts and debates with an imaginary addressee in order to instruct an audience (e.g., Gal 3:1-9, Rom 2:17-24); midrash, which is typical of Jewish interpretive methodology in which scripture is cited and commented upon, e.g., by analogy, typology, allegory, etc. (e.g., Gal 3:16; 4:21-31, 2 Cor 3:4-18); and finally, many features of Greco-Roman rhetoric in terms of strategies of invention and arrangement, persuasive techniques and stylistic devices.[38]

APPROACHES TO ANALYZING THE STRUCTURE OF A PAULINE LETTER

Galatians as a case study

How a text is formulated has an important bearing on understanding its message. If we are able clearly to identify an introductory paragraph, we would be able to conclude that, although it may signal the theme or themes to be dealt with, the primary message of the communication will be in the subsequent section or sections and not in the introduction itself. To give another example, it is most important not to isolate the theological exposition of righteousness by faith rather than works in Rom 1-8 from Rom 9-11 where Paul addresses the tensions between Jewish and Gentile Christians. Those who have done such an isolated reading have been led to understand chs 1-8 purely in terms of personal, individual salvation and to ignore the corporate dimension. When the theology in chs 1-8 is connected to chs 9-11 as a basis for corporate unity between two groups at odds with each other, the corporate dimension of salvation is able to come to light. This brings about a major difference in our understanding of what the primary message and communicative purpose is in Romans. In other words, communicative connections integral to the message of a text exist, not just between sentences, but also among paragraphs and the larger sections of a text. Consequently, it is important that our analysis of the structure of a text be as accurate and faithful to the text as possible.

letter form ?

The diversity of materials incorporated into Paul's letters indicate that a simple use of the typical formulas of request, disclosure, etc., cannot serve as the primary indicators of the structure of the letter body. The contents are far richer than that of the brief private letters with which he shares many such formulas and other features, as brought out above. Some scholars, however, have been so impressed by these correspondences that they have used them to determine the basic outline when analyzing the structure of any one of his letters. Galatians may be taken as a case in point. First of all, there is the prescript (1:1-5) which identifies the sender and recipients and expresses a greeting. Then there are the censure formula "I am astonished that ..." (1:6), the request formula "I beg you ..." (4:12) and the subscription (6:11-17). On the basis of the censure formula and the request formula, a simple two-part structure of the body of Galatians is suggested between the salutation and the subscription:

1:1-5	Salutation
1:6-4:11	Rebuke Section, with inclusion of autobiographical details and theological arguments
4:12-6:10	Request Section, with the inclusion of personal, scriptural, and ethical appeals
6:11-18	Subscription[39]

By way of critique, "rebuke" hardly captures the purpose of 1:11-2:14 where Paul clearly is appealing to the Galatians regarding his personal integrity and authority. Nor does it reflect the purpose of 2:15-4:11 where he persuades them regarding faith as the basis of salvation rather than works of the law. Instead, "rebuke" is an adequate indicator of what he does in 1:6-10. What comes after are sections that have different communicative functions. The same applies to "request" in 4:12. It is only one among other indicators of "appeal" that Paul makes for the Galatians to stick to his gospel. Furthermore, it certainly is not adequate as a description of the moral exhortation found in 5:13-6:10.

In the last few decades an appreciation has grown for the relevance of *rhetoric: persuasive strategy* Greco-Roman rhetoric for analyzing the dynamics of Paul's persuasive strategies and how these impacted the structures of the letters he wrote. The highly argumentative character of Galatians in particular has invited some to look to Greco-Roman rhetoric as a key to analyzing its structure, especially in terms of the judicial genre of speech developed for use in courts of law. The rhetorical approach has the advantage of being better able to establish not only structural units, but also show how these units of text function in relation to each other and towards the addressees in achieving persuasion. In the judicial genre of speech the *exordium* (introduction) typically serves to evoke good will, to establish the credibility of the speaker, and to define the central issues. The *narratio* (narration) provides background or facts that are relevant to the case. The *propositio* (proposition) presents points of agreement and disagreement and the basic issue to be argued. The *probatio* (confirmation) develops the main arguments. The *refutatio* (refutation) rebuts the opponent's arguments, and the *peroratio* (conclusion) summarizes the case and tries to evoke sympathy for a favorable decision. H.D. Betz, who sees the letter as a defense of Paul's gospel of justification by faith rather than by works, has applied this to Galatians.[40] While recognizing that not all the above-mentioned features are in evidence, he finds the following correspondences within an epistolary framework:

1:1-5	Epistolary Prescript
1:6-11	*Exordium*
1:12-2:14	*Narratio*
2:15-21	*Propositio*
3:1-4:31	*Probatio*
5:1-6:10	*Exhortatio*
6:11-18	*Peroratio* within an Epistolary Postscript

Although this approach is certainly useful in observing some important features, it falls short in making sense of others. One can immediately see that the *exhortatio* is not a part of the conventions of a defense speech. Also, a careful reading of his commentary shows that he is able to find in 1:6-11 and 1:12-2:14 and 2:15-21 all kinds of rhetorical devices and strategies typical of

Greco-Roman defense speeches, but hardly any for what he regards as the argumentation in 3:1-4:31. Here Paul argues, not in a Greco-Roman, but in a typical Jewish-Rabbinical fashion. Furthermore, the fact that astute practitioners of analysis based on Greco-Roman rhetoric strongly differ among themselves over whether Galatians belongs to the judicial genre or the deliberative genre must raise a warning flag about the level of Paul's self-conscious use of Greco-Roman rhetoric when writing this letter. In spite of observing this disagreement on genre, B.L. Mack himself simply refines the rhetorical analysis of Galatians once more in terms of the judicial type of speech without showing how 5:1-6:10 is integrated with the overall "judicial" strategy of persuasion.[41] It is here that the features of the Old Testament covenant and testament speeches noted above help to make sense of the transitions from narrative/theological sections to exhortatory sections which urge allegiance to the salvation history that has been narrated and/or theologically argued and which also urge the consequent patterns of behavior.

It is questionable whether the three genres of Greco-Roman speeches are at all appropriate when trying to categorize any of Paul's letters. Judicial speeches were designed for court situations. Deliberative speeches were designed for the political arena. And the so-called epideictic speech was designed to laud or blame persons, values, etc. It became the catch-all for any type of speech which did not fit the first two contexts. Each of these genres would, therefore, have their own particular functions, variations of arrangement, and even levels of style.[42] Paul's letters, with their undeniable characteristics of persuasive speech, were designed for a different type of context in which communities of faith needed encouragement, instruction, and correction both in understanding and in living out the new meaning of life engendered by the good news of God through Jesus Christ. While many of the goals and strategies of persuasive discourse represented in all three of these speech genres may be relevant to Paul's various purposes of persuasion, no one genre among them can tidily or adequately be used to categorize any one of his letters. Recent studies have shown that even the ancient Greeks and Romans did not conceptualize letters as orations. In fact, when they compared letters with orations, it was to assert that the style of language in letters should not be modelled on the close-knit and carefully crafted language of orations. Furthermore, if rhetoric is to be used as a tool of analysis, it appears more appropriate to use it from the perspective of a universal rhetoric that is basic to all human persuasive discourse.[43] The evidence simply does not seem to support the notion that Paul specifically assimilated Greco-Roman rhetoric *as a system* into his letters.[44]

In view of the diversity and complexity of his letters, it becomes necessary to carry out various types of close readings of each individual letter itself before applying any rhetorical or epistolary criteria of organization or structure that is genre specific. Such types of analysis help to focus on the many linguistic features that the text itself offers to make its own unique structure explicit. Modern text-linguistics is particularly relevant for this task.[45] It helps us to identify indicators of communicative function and changes in function, indicators of theme and changes in theme, indicators of predominant text-types such as narrative, argumentation, exposition, etc., shifts in verb moods such as the indicative and the imperative, and densities of recurring words, grammatical structures, etc. These all help us recognize natural units of the text. In other words, this approach is much more holistic and inclusive of various linguistic criteria that are relevant to establishing the structure of a document. Actually, people have always used these criteria, but intuitively rather than systematically. What this methodology does is to make such features explicit and so help a systematic application. Such an approach has led to the following structure of Galatians:[46]

1:1-5　　　　The letter opening
1:6-6:17　　The letter body
　　1:6-10　　Introduction: ironical surprise over Galatian attraction to a different gospel
　　1:11-2:14　Autobiographical argumentation for the origin/authority of Paul's gospel: divine, not human
　　2:15-4:11　Theological argumentation for the truth of the gospel: justification by faith, not works of the law
　　4:12-5:12　Personal and theological appeal to adhere to Paul's gospel: freedom with us, not bondage with them
　　5:13-6:10　Exhortation to the paradoxical freedom of loving servantship: to live by the spirit, not by the flesh
　　6:11-17　Summarizing subscript: neither circumcision nor uncircumcision counts, but a new creation
1:18　　　　Letter closing

This structure of Galatians does not pretend to be *the* definitive one. Texts are incredibly complex and a number of analyses by different scholars using the same methodology will no doubt come up with variations. These will bring new insights and enrich our knowledge as the journey of study goes on, hopefully toward greater accuracy and some sort of general consensus. The important thing is to find methodologies that are the most adequate to the text and appropriate to the goal one wishes to achieve with the text. Furthermore, text-linguistics and a universally conceived rhetoric are not mutually exclusive. In fact, they are well on their way to becoming theoretically combined in over-arching theories of communication.[47]

THE PAULINE LETTER GENRE AND SUBSEQUENT CHRISTIAN LETTERS

From the foregoing observations it becomes apparent that when Paul ministered the gospel to early Christian communities by means of letters, he was forging something new out of several rich literary and oral traditions. Not only was he selective in his use, but he also reshaped whatever conventions he used to suit the special contents of the Christian message and his particular role as apostle and Christian missionary. The structure, style and length of his letters lies closer to the familiar and diplomatic letters of antiquity than to official orders and decrees or the more formal, lengthy letter-essays of that time.[48] The contents, however, are even more diverse and complex than those of the letter-essays which tended to focus specifically on some philosophical issue or the biography of a particular person. In this way, his letters combined both personal warmth and theological complexity. They are indeed *real* letters to real people. And yet, they are written in a way that does not give subsequent readers that somewhat uneasy sense of being an uninvited eavesdropper on other peoples' private business.[49] There is much to be said for the view that Paul himself regarded the relevance and value of his letters to extend beyond their original recipients. This is even made explicit in Col 4:16 where he urges the exchange of his letters to the Colossians and the Laodiceans.

If we look around in the Jewish-Hellenistic world for the closest parallel to the Pauline letter, the exhortatory letter in 2 Macc 1:10-2:18 appears to provide some interesting comparisons. It is presented as being sent by Judas together with those in Jerusalem and Judea and the senate (2 Macc 1:10a). Compare this to Gal 1:1-2 where Paul includes "all the members of God's family who are with me" with himself as sender. It is sent to Aristobulus, priest and teacher in King Ptolemy's court, and the Jews in Egypt. Compare Phlm 1a-2 where the recipient is specifically Philemon, but with whom Apphia, Arichippus and "the church in your house" are included.

After the prescript there is a report of thanksgiving (2 Macc 1:11-17) for deliverance from the oppression of a king, apparently the Seleucid king, Antiochus IV. This is concluded with a "blessing" formula. Compare Paul's opening "blessing" paragraph in 2 Cor 1:3-7 and in Eph 1:3-22 where both blessing (1:3) and thanksgiving report (1:15) are combined. The report of the death of Antiochus in this thanksgiving/blessing introduction has the rhetorical function of appealing to goodwill from the recipients by way of evoking shared relief over the removal of a common threat.

Then comes the Jerusalem community's exhortation for their Jewish brothers in Alexandria to observe the festival of Hanukkah inaugurated to commemorate the purification of the temple after its desecration by Antiochus IV. This exhortation occurs at the beginning (2 Macc 1:18) and at the end (2:16) so as to frame a major message part of the letter (1:18-2:18). The exhortations to keep the feast are supported by sacred legends about Nehemiah and Jeremiah and by reference to Solomon's dedication of his temple (1:19-2:12). This is followed up by a reference to Nehemiah's work in preserving sacred writings (2:13), to which Judas' own work of preservation is compared (2:14-15), thereby enhancing his authority and integrity. Even though these materials are possibly added later to an original letter consisting of 2 Macc 1:11-18, for our purposes the form of this letter seems to have appeared acceptable to the redactor and as such provides a valid 'literary' example. The same holds true, even if this letter is pseudepigraphal, as it probably is. Apart from the formal parallels noticed above, the following parallels may be observed: As in Paul's letters the prescript assumes a certain authoritative status for Judas the sender, but the inclusion of others among the senders and recipients also expresses a strong sense of community of faith. Also, although the exhortation is to ritual rather than moral observance, the use of sacred tradition to support this can be taken as a very general parallel to Paul's pattern of theological exposition in relation to his admonitions. Compare Phil 2:1-18 where the sacred tradition of Christ's incarnation, death and exaltation (2:6-11) illustrates and validates the exhorted behavior framing it in 2:1-5 and 2:12-18.

While the above-mentioned parallels indicate some very general precedents, Paul himself obviously created a distinctive letter genre that became the model for subsequent Christian letters both within the New Testament and to some extent in the early church. First Peter gives the most obvious evidence of the influence of the Pauline letter. This is particularly apparent in the prescript (1:1-2) with its theological elaborations, the designation "an apostle of Jesus Christ," and the greeting of "grace and peace." Paul's influence is also to be seen in the opening "blessing" paragraph (1:3-12) modelled on Eph 1:3-14 and 2 Cor 1:3-7, in the general two-part sequence of theological exposition (1:3-2:10) followed by moral exhortation (2:11-5:11), and in the closing call to greet one another with a holy kiss (cf. 2 Cor 13:12) and the final benediction of peace (5:14). It also includes a section of household admonitions to slaves, wives and husbands (2:18-3:7) much like Eph 5:21-6:9 and Col 3:18-4:1. In the subscription (5:12-13) the secretary Silvanus may be the same close associate of Paul as in 1 Thess 1:1. This could explain the particularly close correspondences. In the Pastoral letters, the letter-openings and closings are close to Paul's typical formulations with the exception that in 1 Tim 1:2 and 2 Tim 1:2 the greeting is extended to form the tripartite "Grace, *mercy*, and peace." Second Timothy has the equivalent of an introductory thanksgiving and prayer report in 1:3-7, but uses "I am grateful to God" instead of the usual "I thank God." Neither 1 Timothy nor Titus have this typical introduction but immediately commence with exhortation and instruction. As mentioned above, all three of these letters differ so strikingly in both language, style and theological expression from the rest of Paul's letters that his direct authorship has been seriously questioned. Second Peter, which is clearly acquainted with Paul's letters (3:15-16), shows his influence only in the prescript (1:1-2). The same is true of Jude, vss 1-2.

The versatility of the letter form in early Christianity is particularly striking in the case of the Revelation of John. Here we find a complete apocalypse set within a very Pauline epistolary prescript (1:4-5) and closing benediction of grace (22:21). As for Hebrews, there is no epistolary opening at all, but in 13:18-19, 22-25 we find material typical of the Pauline letter-closing. Even the wish-prayer in 13:20-21 is modelled on, e.g., 1 Thess 3:11-13 and 5:23-24. There is also a recurrence of sections of theological exposition followed by sections of exhortation throughout it. Regarding 1, 2, and 3 John, it is sufficient to note that 1 John actually does not qualify as a letter at all. Second and 3 John, together with the letters reported by Luke in Acts 15:23-29 and 23:26-30, are the letters which stand the closest to the common letter tradition of the Greek papyri, both in form and length. Also, apart from the greeting in 2 John 3, they show no influence by the Pauline letter. Finally, James probably stands the closest of the New Testament letters to the Hellenistic letter-essay. The prescript is simple and very general. Instead of "grace and peace" the author simply uses the usual "greeting" (*chairein*). There are no other features in the letter that reflect the formulas and phraseology of the documentary Hellenistic letters (see the chapters on each of the above-mentioned works).

As we move down to the late first century and early second century C.E., we find Paul's literary influence most clearly in *1 Clement* and the *Letters of Ignatius*. In *1 Clement* we see it particularly in the prescript with the "grace and peace" greeting and at the conclusion with the closing wish-prayer and benediction of grace. In the opening and closing conventions used in Ignatius' letters Paul's influence appears in the use of theological elaborations attached to the sender, receivers, and the greetings. The greetings, however, are consistently the neutral "greeting" (*chairein*) and not "grace and peace." Also, he uses the closing "goodbye" (*erōsthe*) rather than Paul's typical benediction of grace or peace. Paul's influence is to be found more in the level of style used by Ignatius that combines personal warmth with theological reflection, practical warnings, and the conscious projection of authority and integrity by his willingness to suffer for Christ.

Beginning with the general epistles in the New Testament and moving down through the Apostolic Fathers and later Christian writers, we find in general that the letter form and style becomes more formal, lengthy and distant. Letter form becomes establishment form.[50] The contents are preoccupied less with grace and more with practical piety. Reflected in such changes is the whole process of a messianic movement becoming an established religion. If the form and phraseology of Paul's letters served to shape later New Testament letters and some of the letters in the post-apostolic period, such influence seems to have dropped off after that, except for a few isolated attempts at pseudepigraphy. This is probably due to Paul's letters being a part of the "apostolic" witness to the gospel. When apostles passed from the scene of history, apostolic authority found its place in their letters. The need to honor and preserve this authority would quite naturally discourage its precise emulation by later Christian writers. Perhaps this is a valid key to using "apostolic letter" as the most adequate description of the particular genre of letter created by Paul within the Hellenistic world of letter genres.[51]

FURTHER READING

Dahl, Nils A.
1976   "Letter," *Interpreter's Dictionary of the Bible.* Supplementary Vol., 538-541.
Davis, William H.
1933   *Greek Papyri of the First Century.* Chicago: Ares.
Doty, William G.
1973   *Letters in Primitive Christianity.* (Guides to Biblical Scholarship). Philadelphia: Fortress.
Elsom, H.
1987   "The New Testament and Greco-Roman Writing," *The Literary Guide to the Bible.* (Ed. by R. Alter and F. Kermode.) Cambridge, MA: Belknap Press of Harvard University Press.
Harris, William V.
1989   *Ancient Literacy.* Cambridge, MA: Harvard University Press.
Hartman, L.
1986   "On Reading Others' Letters," in *Christians Among Jews and Gentiles* (Essays in Honor of Krister Stendahl on His Sixty-fifth Birthday; Eds. G.W.E. Nickelsburg and G.W. MacRae.) Philadelphia: Fortress, 137-146.
Mack, Burton L.
1990   *Rhetoric and the New Testament.* (Guides to Biblical Scholarship). Minneapolis: Fortress, 25-48, 56-78.
Malherbe, Abraham J.
1988   *Ancient Epistolary Theorists.* (Society of Biblical Literature Sources for Biblical Study, Vol. 19). Atlanta: Scholars.
1977   *The Cynic Epistles.* (Society of Biblical Literature Sources for Biblical Study, Vol. 12). Missoula, MT: Scholars.

Milligan, G., Ed.
> 1980   *Selections from the Greek Papyri*. (With Translations and Notes;
> Reprint of Cambridge 1910 ed.) Chicago: Ares.

Porter, Stanley E.
> 1993   "The Theoretical Justification for Application of Rhetorical
> Categories to Pauline Epistolary Literature," in *Rhetoric and the New
> Testament*. (Essays from the 1992 Heidelberg Conference; Eds. S.E.
> Porter and T.H. Olbricht.) Sheffield: Journal for the Study of the
> Old Testament, 100-122.

Stowers, Stanley K.
> 1986   *Letter Writing in Greco-Roman Antiquity*. (Library of Early
> Christianity, Vol. 5). Philadelphia: Westminster.

White, John L.
> 1986   *Light from Ancient Letters*. (Foundations and Facets). Philadelphia:
> Fortress.
> 1983   "St. Paul and the Apostolic Letter Tradition," *Catholic Biblical
> Quarterly* 45, 433-444.

ENDNOTES

1. W.V. Harris, *Ancient Literacy* (Cambridge, MA: Harvard University Press, 1989) 88-89.

2. Harris, *Ancient Literacy*, 160-161.

3. Harris, *Ancient Literacy*, 127-128.

4. See S.K. Stowers, *Letter Writing in Greco-Roman Antiquity* (Library of Early Christianity, Vol. 5; Philadelphia: Westminster, 1986) 32-33.

5. See the summary of this situation in M.L. Stirewalt, "Paul's Evaluation of Letter-Writing," in *Search the Scriptures* (New Testament Studies in Honor of Raymond T. Stamm, Ed. by J.M. Myers, O. Reimherr, and H.N. Bream; Leiden: E.J. Brill, 1969) 179-186.

6. See the handy summary in A.J. Malherbe, *Ancient Epistolary Theorists* (Society of Biblical Literature Sources for Biblical Study, Vol. 19; Atlanta: Scholars, 1988) 2-14.

7. So, J.L. White, *Light from Ancient Letters* (Foundations and Facets, Philadelphia: Fortress, 1986) 193-197.

8. See W.G. Doty, *Letters in Primitive Christianity* (Guides to Biblical Scholarship, New Testament Series; Philadelphia: Fortress, 1973) 4-8; and especially Stowers, *Letter Writing*, 58-173.

9. So, H. Elsom, "The New Testament and Greco-Roman Writing," *The Literary Guide to the Bible* (Ed. by R. Alter and F. Kermode, Cambridge, MA: Belknap Press of Harvard University Press, 1987) 570-571.

10. See the handy collection of epistles by A.J. Malherbe, *The Cynic Epistles* (Society of Biblical Literature Sources for Biblical Study, Vol. 12; Missoula, MT: Scholars, 1977. For examples of even longer treatises in letter form, see the letters of Epicurus presented by Diogenes Laertius, 10.34-83, 84-116, 122-135 in *Diogenes Laertius II* (Trans. by R.D.

Hicks, Loeb Classical Library 185; Cambridge, MA: Harvard University Press, 1925).
11. Stowers, *Letter Writing*, 33.
12. For a good overview of pseudepigraphy, see K. Koch, "Pseudonymous Writing," *Interpreters' Dictionary of the Bible* (1976, Supp. Vol.) 712-714.
13. See Doty, *Letters*, 6-7.
14. See *The Apostolic Fathers* (Vol. 1, trans. by K. Lake, Loeb Classical Library; Cambridge, MA: Harvard University Press, 1912).
15. See *The Nag Hammadi Library* (Ed. by J.M. Robinson, third rev. ed.; San Francisco: Harper & Row, 1988) 434-437.
16. See E. Hennecke, *New Testament Apocrypha* (Vol. 2, Ed. by W. Schneemelcher, trans. by E. Best, D. Hill, G. Ogg, G.C. Stead and R.McL. Wilson from the German *Neutestamentliche Apokryphen*, Vol. II, 1964; London: SCM, 1965) 128-166.
17. H. Koskenniemi, *Studien zur Idee und Phraseologie des griechischen Briefes bis 400 n. Chr.* (Annales Academiae Scientiarum Fennicae, Ser. B., Vol. 102, 2; Helsinki: Suomalaisen Kirjallisuuden Kerjapaino, 1956)
18. See. J.L. White, *Light from Ancient Letters*, 198-202.
19. This outline follows the arrangement that includes the health-wish and other expressions of good will or expressions of aggravation *at the beginning of the body* of the letter. This view is predominant in Europe. See, e.g., Koskenniemi, *Studien zur Idee,* 155; O. Roller, *Das Formular der paulinischen Briefe* (Beiträge zur Wissenschaft vom Alten und Neuen Testament, Ser. 4, Vol. 6; Stuttgart: W. Kohlhammer, 1933) 54-55; Ph. Vielhauer, *Geschichte der urchristlichen Literatur* (Berlin and New York: de Gruyter, 1975) 65; and in North America see F.X.J. Exler, *The Form of the Ancient Greek Letter*. (Diss., Catholic University of America; Washington, D.C., 1923) 101 ff. On the other hand, most North American scholars include these features in the letter opening. For example, see P. Schubert, *Form and Function of the Pauline Thanksgivings* (Beihefte zur Zeitschrift für die neutestamentliche Wissenschaft, Vol. 20, Berlin: Alfred Töpelmann,1939) 5, 7, 24; J.T. Sanders, "The Transition from Opening Epistolary Thanksgiving to Body in the Letters of the Pauline Corpus." *Journal of Biblical Literature* 81 (1962) 348-62; R.W. Funk, *Language, Hermeneutic, and Word of God.* (New York: Harper & Row, 1966) 263 ff.; Doty, *Letters,* 27-47; and White, *Light from Ancient Letters*, 198-213. For a more detailed discussion see B.C. Johanson, *To All the Brethren: A Text-Linguistic and Rhetorical Approach to 1 Thessalonians* (Cultura Bíblica, New Testament Series, Vol. 16; Stockholm: Almqvist & Wiksell, 1987) 61-65.
20. See T.Y. Mullins, "Formulas in New Testament Epistles," *Journal of Biblical Literature* 91 (1972) 380-90. Also, White, *Light from Ancient Letters*, 203-213.
21. White, *Light from Ancient Letters*, 198-202.
22. G.J. Bahr, "The Subscriptions in the Pauline Letters," *Society of Biblical Literature* 87 (1968) 27-33.
23. The author's translation of a letter of introduction found in *Selections from the Greek Papyri* (Edited with Translations and Notes by G. Milligan; Reprint of Cambridge 1910 ed.; Chicago: Ares, 1980) 24-25.
24. The author's translation of the ship-master Irenaeus' personal letter to his brother found in *Selections*, 100-102.
25. The author's translation of the boy's letter found in *Selections*, 102-103.

26. The author's translation of the consolatory letter found in *Selections*, 96. Stowers, *Letter Writing*, 144, gives three fundamental elements in a letter of consolation, none of which involve typical conventional formulas: 1) a wide range of positive relationships between writer and recipient, 2) an experience of misfortune by the recipient that usually produces grief, and 3) the writer's expression of grief and reasons for the recipient to bear up under grief.

27. W.H. Davis, *Greek Papyri of the First Century* (Chicago: Ares, 1933) 57-58.

28. The following outline and account of phraseology are taken from J.A. Fitzmyer, "Aramaic Epistolography," *Semeia* 22 (1981) 30-39.

29. See Bahr, "The Subscriptions ...," 33-41. Bahr attempts to establish larger sections than just these references at the ends of the letters as being written in Paul's own hand, but in the absence of any autographs his evidence for this is highly conjectural and unconvincing.

30. See M.L. Stirewalt, "Paul's Evaluation," 186-196.

31. See Elsom, "The New Testament and Greco-Roman Writing," 571.

32. On this see T.Y. Mullins, "Visit Talk in New Testament Letters," *Catholic Biblical Quarterly* 35 (1973) 350-358.

33. Mullins, "Visit Talk," 355.

34. See B.C. Johanson, *To All the Brethren* (Cultura Bíblica, New Testament Series, Vol. 16; Stockholm: Almqvist & Wiksell, 1987) 176-181. My observations build a great deal on the work of K. Baltzer, *The Covenant Formulary in Old Testament, Jewish, and Early Christian Writings* (second German ed. *Das Bundesformular*, Wissenschaftliche Monographien zum Alten und Neuen Testament, Vol. 4; Trans. by D.E. Green; Oxford, 1971).

35. For a background in Hellenistic letter conventions, see P. Schubert, *Form and Function of the Pauline Thanksgiving* (Beihefte zur Zeitschrift für die neutestamentliche Wissenschaft, Vol. 20; Berlin: Alfred Töpelmann, 1939), and for a background in Old Testament, Jewish, and Christian prayers, see J.P. Audet, "Literary forms and contents of a Normal εὐχαριστία in the First Century," *Studia Evangelica* 1 (1959) 643-662; J.M. Robinson, "The Historicality of Biblical Language," in *The Old Testament and Christian Faith* (Ed. by B.W. Anderson; London, 1963) 124-158.

36. See L. Wills, "The Form of the Sermon in Hellenistic Judaism and Early Christianity," *Harvard Theological Review* 77 (1984) 277-299, and C.C. Black II, "The Rhetorical Form of the Hellenistic Jewish and Early Christian Sermon: A Response to Lawrence Wills," *Harvard Theological Review* 81 (1988) 1-18. A lot more comparative work with Old Testament and Jewish intertestamental speeches needs to be done before one can so easily assert a close connection with Greco-Roman rhetoric as Black does.

37. See J.C. Brunt, "The New Testament Haustafeln Passages," (unpublished study). For a good overview of the literature and an analysis that calls into question an all-too-easy connection with the so-called Stoic and Jewish-Hellenistic house-hold code form, see L. Hartman, 'Some Unorthodox thoughts on the "Household-code Form,"' in *The Social World of Formative Christianity and Judaism* (Essays in Tribute to Howard Clark Kee, Eds. J. Neusner, E.S. Frerichs, P. Borgen, and R. Horsley; Philadelphia: Fortress, 1988) 219-232.

38. See Doty, *Letters*, 55-63, and more recently J.M. Bailey and L.D. Vander Broek, *Literary Forms in the New Testament* (Louisville, KY: Westminster/John Knox, 1992) 23-87, for these types of materials and relevant literature on them.

39. Longenecker, *Galatians*, ((Word). Vol. 41, Dallas: Word, 1990) cix.

40. H.D. Betz, *Galatians*: A Commentary on Paul's Letter to the Churches in Galatia. (Hermeneia; Philadelphia: Fortress, 1979) 14-25.

41. B.L. Mack, *Rhetoric and the New Testament* (Guides to Biblical Scholarship; Minneapolis: Fortress, 1990) 66-73.

42. See G. Kennedy, *The Art of Persuasion in Greece* (Princeton, NJ: Princeton University Press, 1963) 10-12.

43. See S.E. Porter, "The Theoretical Justification for Application of Rhetorical Categories to Pauline Epistolary Literature," in *Rhetoric and the New Testament.* Essays from the 1992 Heidelberg Conference (Eds. S.E. Porter and T.H. Olbricht, Sheffield: Journal for the Study of the Old Testament, 1993) 100-122.

44. See, J.T. Reed, "Using Ancient Rhetorical Categories to Interpret Paul's Letters: A Question of Genre," also in *Rhetoric and the New Testament*, 292-324.

45. Unfortunately there is no book that provides a non-technical, popular description of text-linguistics for New Testament analysis as yet. For a somewhat technical model, see B.C. Johanson, *To All the Brethren*: A Text-Linguistic and Rhetorical Approach to 1 Thessalonians (Coniectanea Biblica, New Testament Series 16; Stockholm: Almquist and Wiksell, 1987) 3-34.

46. The following outline is based on an unpublished text-linguistic analysis of the structure of Galatians by the author.

47. See Johanson, *To All the Brethren*, 3-45, and the literature cited there.

48. N. Dahl, "Letter," in *Interpreters' Dictionary of the Bible* (Supplementary Volume, 1976) 540.

49. See L. Hartman, "On Reading Others' Letters," in *Christians Among Jews and Gentiles* (Essays in Honor of Krister Stendahl on His Sixty-fifth Birthday; Eds. G.W.E. Nickelsburg and G.W. MacRae; Philadelphia: Fortress, 1986) 137-146.

50. See Doty, *Letters*, 70.

51. Cf. J.L. White, "St. Paul and the Apostolic Letter Tradition," *Catholic Biblical Quarterly* 45 (1983) 433-444.

Chapter 5

Paul, Apostle to the Gentiles

John C. Brunt

In the history of the church Paul has been lauded as the true founder of Christianity and the only one to understand the message of God's grace. He has also been vilified as the chief perverter of the simple message of Jesus who complicated and distorted the true message of Christianity. Even though he is controversial, however, no student of the New Testament or early Christianity can ignore him. Not only does he play a central role in the book of Acts, but thirteen of the twenty-seven books of the New Testament bear his name. That these letters he wrote are not always easy to understand is affirmed even in the New Testament, for 2 Pet 3:15-16 says that Paul wrote difficult things that the unstable twist to their own destruction. *a controversial figure*

What are we to make of this controversial figure? We should probably begin with what Paul said about himself: he was a minister of Christ Jesus to the Gentiles (Rom 15:16) or an apostle to the Gentiles (Rom 11:13). Paul believed that God had called him to be an apostle, even though the call came at a different time than to the other apostles. He was as one "untimely born," but the Risen Jesus had appeared to him nevertheless (see 1 Cor 9:1; 15:8-11). His mission was different from that of the other apostles, particularly Peter, for Peter was commissioned to minister to the Jews, and Paul to the Gentiles (Gal 2:7-10). Paul was not, of course, the only one who carried the gospel to the Gentiles. The church at the empire's capital, Rome, was already a major church before Paul ever went there. We don't know who carried the gospel to Rome. Throughout Asia Minor and Europe, however, no one seems to have played a larger role in the spread of Christianity to the Gentiles than Paul.

Paul was not only an evangelist and pastor to the Gentiles, he was also the figure in the early church more than any other who thought about the meaning of the inclusion of Jews and Gentiles into a single unity in Christ Jesus. He not only fought for the reality of this idea, he provided the theological foundation that allowed the idea to become reality as well. Theologian, pastor, evangelist, letter-writer, and interesting human being. Paul was all of these.

We have no biography of Paul in the modern sense of the word, although Luke gives an overview of much of Paul's ministry as he tells the story of the spread of the gospel in the book of Acts. Yet it is obvious that telling the story of Paul wasn't Luke's major priority, or he would hardly have left Paul awaiting trial at the end of his book. But that gets us ahead of the story. Let us notice briefly what Acts tells us about Paul.

what Acts tells us

Paul first appears in Acts 7:58 giving his approval to the stoning of Stephen. He is initially called Saul, and although it is popular to refer to his change in name to Paul as part of his conversion, the name change occurs later in Luke, without explanation, possibly because Paul moves into a more Gentile context and therefore uses his Greco-Roman rather than his Jewish name.

Acts 9

In ch 9 Luke recounts the Damascus Road story, which Paul will re-tell two more times in Acts (22:30-23:11; 25:23-26:32). Paul was going to Damascus to persecute Christians, but the Risen Christ appeared to him on the way. Paul was

Saul on the Damascus Road

blinded for three days and sent to a disciple named Ananias. There he received his commission to take the gospel to the Gentiles. Although this radical change gave him a new perspective on Jesus as the Messiah or Christ, it was certainly *not a conversion from Judaism* not a conversion away from Judaism.

After many days (Acts 9:23) a plot to kill Paul led believers to help him escape from Damascus by being lowered down the wall in a basket (9:25). Paul then went to Jerusalem, where even the apostles were reluctant to have anything to do with him until Barnabas took it upon himself to speak for Paul and introduced him to the others. Soon controversy surrounded Paul again and he fled to his home city of Tarsus in Asia Minor, where he stayed for some time until Barna-

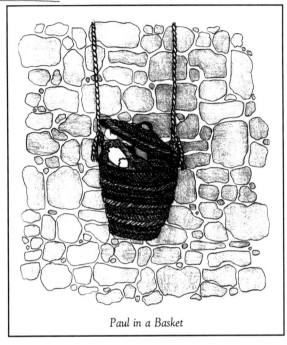

Paul in a Basket

bas, then ministering in Antioch, made a special trip to Tarsus to find Paul and bring him to Antioch to minister with him (Acts 11:25). In the course of their ministry, Paul and Barnabas made a trip to Jerusalem together with famine aid from Antioch (11:30).

Paul and Barnabas then set out on a trip to take the gospel around Asia Minor. We call it Paul's first missionary journey, although Paul would hardly have recognized the term. It is recorded in Acts 13-14. The two missionaries visited Cyprus, Perga, Pisidian Antioch, Iconium, Lystra, and Derbe. They began in the synagogues and often attracted the God-fearers, Gentiles who were attracted to Judaism but had not become full converts, and then with this core reached beyond to other Gentiles. At the end of this journey they stayed a long time with the disciples in Antioch (14:28).

In ch 15 Luke tells how Paul and Barnabas went to Jerusalem to discuss the *acts 15* matter of the gospel going to uncircumcised Gentiles. Their mission to the Gentiles was affirmed by the conference. Afterwards, however, Paul and Barnabas had a sharp dispute over whether to take John Mark, who had turned back part way through their first missionary journey, with them on their next travel itinerary (15:36-41). The result was that Paul and Barnabas split up, with

Barnabas taking John Mark and Paul going with Silas on what we call the second missionary journey, described in Acts 16:1-18:22. After retracing his steps through Derbe and Lystra Paul went through Phrygia and Galatia and on to Troas, where he had the famous vision calling him to come over to Macedonia (16:9). Paul then answered the call and traveled to the Macedonian cities of Philippi, Thessalonica, and Berea, then on to Athens and Corinth in Greece.

Paul stayed in Corinth for a year and half (18:11). This stay provides a peg for dating Paul's ministry there, for he appeared before the proconsul Galio (18:12) while he was there, and an inscription has been discovered that dates Galio's proconsulship from about 50-51 C.E. Paul then went on to Ephesus and returned to Antioch where he spent some time (18:22-23). Then on what we call Paul's third missionary journey he went to Galatia and Phrygia, then on to Ephesus, where he spent three years (Acts 19). While there he decided that he would go to Macedonia, Greece, Jerusalem, and then on to Rome (19:21-23).

Paul didn't complete this plan, however. When he arrived in Jerusalem he was arrested after he was falsely charged with taking a Gentile into the inner court of the temple, where Gentiles were prohibited on threat of death. As he was being arrested Paul told his Damascus Road story to the crowd from the steps that went from the temple area to the Roman fortress Antonia (22:1-29). He appeared before the Sanhedrin (22:30-23:11), Felix (24), Festus (25:1-22), and Agrippa (25:23-26:32), to whom he retold the Damascus story and finally appealed to Rome. Paul then was sent to Rome as a prisoner (27:1-28:10). The last verses of Acts (28:11-31) picture Paul under house arrest, free to preach, and awaiting trial for two years. Then the book abruptly ends.

Some have suggested that the book ends here because that is when Luke wrote, but this is quite unlikely. Acts seems to have been written much later. Luke probably ends here because he was telling the story of the spread of the gospel, and Paul preaching freely in Rome completes the story. This is supported by the fact that Luke is equally abrupt in dropping Peter in Acts 12:17. Obviously Luke is not writing a biography of either Peter or Paul, and what he tells us about them is both incomplete and selective.

There is material in Paul's letters, however, that confirms much of this basic outline of at least a portion of Paul's ministry. Paul confirms that before his conversion he persecuted the church (e.g. 1 Cor 9:9; Gal 1:13; Phil 3:6). Paul mentions his experience in Damascus (Gal 1:13) and his escape in a basket (2 Cor 11:30-33). He mentions his first visit to Jerusalem (Gal 1:19) and the Jerusalem Council (Gal 2:1-10), which is probably the same visit as recorded in Acts 15, although some scholars deny this (for details see the article on Paul's letter to the Galatians). Paul's letters also testify to his ministry in Macedonia and Greece (1 Thess 3) on his second journey, and his decision to leave Ephesus and travel to Macedonia, Greece, and then Jerusalem (2 Cor 1:16) and then go on to Rome (Rom 15:26-29), although Acts doesn't mention that Paul's ultimate goal was Spain.

There are differences between Acts and letters, even where they cover the same material, however. For example, Acts 15 and Gal 2 agree on the major decision of the Jerusalem conference—that Gentiles could become Christians without being circumcised. But Acts mentions the prohibition of food offered to idols and blood which Galatians doesn't, and Galatians mentions the provision that Paul should remember the poor in Judea, which Acts ignores. Another example is Paul's ministry in Thessalonica, which Acts implies only lasted three Sabbaths (17:2). Yet in Philippians Paul claims that the Philippians sent him aid again and again while he was in Thessalonica (Phil 4:16), which would seem to necessitate a longer stay.

More interesting than the outline of his ministry, however, is the information that the letters give us about Paul as a person. The following summary surveys some of the most important roles and characteristics of Paul that emerge from the letters.

Paul the Apostle to the Gentiles. In all the letters that carry his name except 1 and 2 Thessalonians, Philippians, and Philemon, Paul begins by reminding his readers that he is an apostle. His right to this title came in his experience of seeing the Lord (1 Cor 9:1). Paul certainly believed that God had sent (the term "apostle" means one who is sent) him on his mission to the Gentiles.

Paul the Jew. Even though he was an apostle to the Gentiles, Paul never put aside his Jewish identity. He tells us twice that he was from the tribe of Benjamin (Rom 11:1; Phil 3:5), and adds in the latter passage that he had been a Hebrew of Hebrews and a Pharisee. In Rom 11:1 Paul continues to call himself an Israelite who is part of the remnant of faithful in Israel. Nowhere does Paul more poignantly speak of his Jewishness than when he wishes that he could be accursed and cut off from Christ if it could mean the salvation of his people (Rom 9:3).

Paul the Evangelist. Paul loved taking the Gospel where it had never been before. He told the Romans that he wanted to go to Spain to preach the gospel because he didn't like building on someone else's foundation by preaching where the gospel had already been preached (Rom 15:20). He liked to be on the cutting edge of new frontiers.

Paul the Pastor. Even as Paul pressed to the new frontiers, he could never forget the new believers, his children, that he left behind. That is why he wrote letters. Read a letter like Philippians and see how warm Paul's feelings are for his people. Or read Paul's personal appeal to the Galatians. Paul was so angry with them that he didn't even include the usual thanksgiving for the congregation at the beginning of the letter, yet he could plead with pathos in Gal 4:12-20. We usually think of Paul primarily as theologian, but his theologizing was always in the specific service of ministry. He believed that what a person believes makes a difference in how a person lives, and so he ministered by laying a foundation of theology, but never was theology an end in itself. Even that most theological of letters, Romans, written to a congregation he had never visited, was a practical, pastoral letter (see the chapter on Romans in this volume).

Paul the Letter-Writer. We know that Paul wrote more letters than we have, for in 1 Corinthians he already refers to an earlier letter he had written to them (5:9). Paul wrote as a substitute for his personal presence. He certainly didn't know he was writing something that would eventually be considered Scripture, but he did write with a sense of apostolic authority. Apparently he dictated his letters. In Rom 16:22 the scribe who took the dictation greets the readers, and in 1 Cor 1:14-17 the content seems to reveal the process of oral dictation, with some changing of the mind going on even as Paul dictates.

At least one congregation seemed to think that Paul's presence through his letters was even more powerful than his personal presence, for in 1 Cor 10:10 Paul speaks of those who said of him: "His letters are weighty and strong, but his bodily presence is weak, and his speech contemptible."

Paul the Fundraiser. At the Jerusalem council, according to Gal 2, Paul agreed to raise money for the poor in Jerusalem. This task became an important part of Paul's ministry. Not only was it an obligation, Paul saw it as a theological opportunity to bind Jews and Gentiles together in unity. In Rom 15:25-28 he tells the Romans that even though his desire is to come to them and then go on to Spain, this collection of money he had raised from saints in Macedonia and Greece was so important that he would first go in the opposite direction to Jerusalem to deliver the money he had raised. He said that since the Jews had shared their spiritual blessings with the Gentiles, the Gentiles could now show their appreciation and confirm their unity by sharing their material blessings. Paul devotes two chapters (8 and 9) of 2 Corinthians to this collection. Yet he was afraid that the believers in Jerusalem would not accept it (Rom 15:31). Since Acts is totally silent on the collection, even though it records Paul's visit to Jerusalem, we don't know whether this important part of Paul's ministry was accepted or not.

Paul the Bold Ego. In Phil 3 Paul claims that if anyone has reason to be confident in the flesh, he had even more. He then goes on to list his pedigree: circumcised on the eighth day, of the people of Israel, from the tribe of Benjamin, a Hebrew of Hebrews, a Pharisee, a persecutor of the church, and blameless with regard to legalistic righteousness (3:4-6). Even though he goes on to proclaim this whole pedigree as rubbish or garbage (3:8) for the sake of Christ, one gets the idea that the speaker is a person of considerable ego strength.

Of course, a person with less ego strength probably wouldn't have survived the imprisonments, floggings, lashings, beatings, stonings, and shipwrecks Paul recounts in 2 Cor 11:23-29. Nor would a more timid person have been able to confront Peter to his face and call him a hypocrite for refusing to eat with Gentiles (Gal 2:11-15) even after Peter had come to see that God accepts all people, whether Jew or Gentile. A more shy person might have been intimidated by the other apostles, but Paul, even when he acknowledged that he was the least of the apostles, since he persecuted the church, could add that he worked harder than any of the rest (1 Cor 15:10).

Paul the Sufferer. Paul's mission inevitably led to suffering. None of us would want to endure his list of misfortunes. Yet Paul incorporated his suffering into his understanding of his mission. His scars were not merely reminders of injuries, they were the marks of Jesus (Gal 6:17), symbols of his faithfulness to the cross of Christ. Paul claimed to have learned the secret of being content in any and every situation, whether in plenty or want, because in Christ he could face anything (Phil 4:11-14). This is why he could rejoice even if he was in prison and faced the possibility of death (Phil 2:17-18).

According to Gal 4:13-15, Paul suffered some kind of physical infirmity or illness when he was at Galatia, although he doesn't say what it was. Suggestions have ranged from epilepsy to bad eyesight (based on the fact that Paul says the Galatians would have given him their own eyes if they could), but all suggestions are speculation. We don't know whether this infirmity at Galatia was with the same problem Paul talked about in 2 Cor 12:7-10, which he described as a thorn in his flesh. Paul says that he received this thorn to keep him from being too elated after his visionary experience with Christ. He prayed three times to be spared this thorn, but his answer from God was, My grace is sufficient for you (12:9). It was that promise that enabled Paul to endure suffering.

Paul the Servant of Christ. All that Paul was had been dedicated to Christ, and that intense, single purpose enabled God to use Paul as he did. In many ways Paul's background and personality ideally suited him for the special task of being an apostle to the Gentiles. He was a Jew, and yet he grew up (we do not know for how long) in the Diaspora, so the Greco-Roman city was a part of him as well. Most of Paul's ministry took place in the cities of the Roman empire. Whereas Jesus moved in rural Palestine and told stories about farmers, fishermen, seeds and plants, Paul moved in the cities and used illustrations about track meets and boxing matches (1 Cor 9:24-27).

From childhood he had had his feet planted in two different worlds. Who better to lead out in bringing those two worlds, Jew and Gentile, into a single unity in Christ.

Christ became so central to Paul that both his worlds could be radically criticized in the light of Christ. Something as vital as the Jewish necessity for circumcision could go in the light of his new reality in Christ. Yet Paul never turned his back on either world, for according to Paul's gospel, the new reality of God's grace revealed in Christ Jesus was the power of God for the salvation of all who believed, whether Jew or Gentile (Rom 1:16).

According to tradition Paul was executed outside the city of Rome in the early to mid sixties of the first century by being beheaded. This would have been the method of execution consistent with his Roman citizenship.

FURTHER READING

Knox, John
    1950   *Chapters in a Life of Paul.* Nashville: Abingdon.
Weiss, Harold
    1986   *Paul of Tarsus: His Gospel and Life.* Berrien Springs, MI: Andrews
            University Press.

Chapter 6

1 Thessalonians

Bruce C. Johanson

> *"But we do not want you to be uninformed, brothers and sisters, about those who have died, so that you may not grieve as others do who have no hope."*

BRIEF OVERVIEW OF THE BOOK

First Thessalonians is most likely the earliest letter of Paul that we have. He is writing to recent converts whom he had to leave prematurely due to an upsurge of opposition and persecution. Timothy had been sent back to visit them, and the letter reflects Paul's concerns for the Thessalonian Christians based on both his previous knowledge of them and Timothy's recent report. While there is much for which they are praised and commended, Paul's pastoral concern anticipates their perplexity and potential estrangement from the gospel due to the fact that some of them had unexpectedly died before the coming of Jesus Christ. Other factors that no doubt contributed to their anxiety and this potential danger were Paul's continued absence as well as the meaning of their past and present sufferings.

BACKGROUND CONCERNS

As the seat of government for the Roman province of Macedonia, Thessalonica was a city of importance. Paul, together with Silvanus (called Silas in Acts) and Timothy, made it his next focus of work after leaving Philippi (Acts 16:11-17:15; 1 Thess 2:1-2). According to Acts 17:1-9 he preached there for three weeks in the Jewish Synagogue with a favorable response predominantly from devout Greeks (cf. 1 Thess 1:10; 2:14), although there were also a few Jews. Acts also mentions that there were some "leading women" among the believers. In 2 Cor 8:2 we get a glimpse of the economic status of this early Christian community. Here Paul generally characterizes the Thessalonian community of believers along with other Macedonian believers in terms of "extreme poverty." *a place of extreme poverty*

71

The Jews who rejected the gospel instigated mob action which resulted in Paul and Silas being sent away by concerned brethren to Beroea at night. First Thess 2:17 appears to refer to this departure. After a good response to the gospel in Beroea, trouble was instigated there again by Jews from Thessalonica. Consequently Paul moved on to Athens.

According to 1 Thess 3:1-8 Paul, Silvanus and Timothy became anxious in Athens over the situation in Thessalonica. So they sent Timothy to encourage the believers there and to bring back news about them. Luke makes no mention of this visit in Acts, but simply reports that Paul went to Athens alone, leaving Silas and Timothy to continue working in Beroea. He also reports that, although Paul waited for them in Athens, they did not join him until later in Corinth (Acts 17:16; 18:1, 5).

If Paul wrote 1 Thessalonians from Corinth, it is most likely to be dated somewhere between 50-51 C.E. It was written no doubt in response to Timothy's report (3:1-8). From 2:14 and 3:3-4 we can gather that the believers there continued to undergo some persecution and sufferings at the hands of their own countrymen. Apparently the opposition initiated by the Jews was continued by the non-Jewish population. Thesssalonica prided itself on its good relations with Rome. So when Paul writes in 5:3, "When they say, 'There is peace and security,' then sudden destruction will come ...," he could be reflecting on the persecutors' loyal confidence in the Pax Romana and their consequent derision of the believers' trust in an imminent "Day of the Lord." Such derisive arguments would have been particularly trying in view of what appears to have been the recent converts' major problem: It seems that they were not prepared for some of their number to die before the parousia of Jesus Christ. When this actually happened they became perplexed and mourned the dead in a way that did not reflect Christian hope (4:13).

In view of his own fervent expectation of being alive at the imminent parousia (4:15), Paul may have bypassed or only lightly touched on the question of what happened to those believers who would die before that event. Also, it appears that he may have been in Thessalonica a relatively short time, if the three weeks of preaching in the synagogue (Acts 17:2) covers the entire period of stay. It could, however, refer to only the initial part of his ministry. In Phil 4:16, Paul mentions that the Philippian believers had repeatedly sent him financial support during his stay in Thessalonica. The distance and the time implied by such exchanges of correspondence would indicate that a somewhat longer period than three weeks was involved. On the other hand, the Hellenistic background of this predominantly Gentile community may have hindered their understanding of resurrection (see Greco-Roman Backgrounds).

However this may be, in spite of the addressees' continued good will (3:6), there was a very real potential danger of their questioning the actual nature of

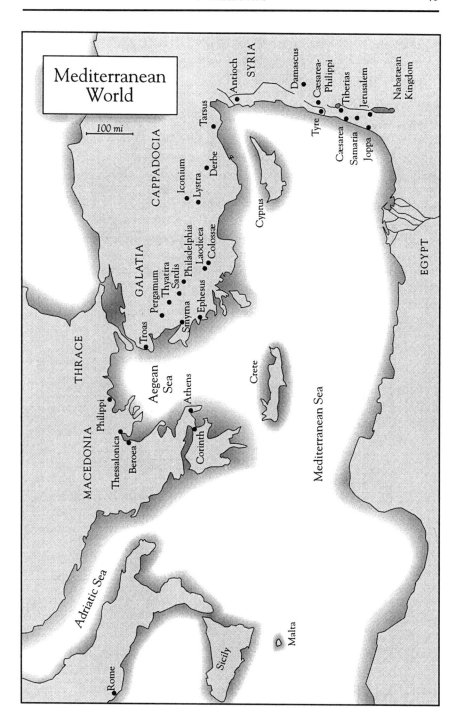

Mediterranean World

100 mi

THRACE

MACEDONIA
Philippi
Thessalonica
Beroea
Athens
Corinth

Aegean Sea

Crete

Adriatic Sea

Rome

Sicily

Malta

Mediterranean Sea

CAPPADOCIA

GALATIA
Troas
Pergamum
Thyatira
Sardis
Smyrna
Philadelphia
Ephesus
Laodicea
Colossæ
Iconium
Lystra
Derbe

Tarsus

Cyprus

SYRIA
Antioch
Damascus
Cæsarea-Philippi
Tiberias
Jerusalem
Tyre
Cæsarea
Samaria
Joppa

Nabataean Kingdom

EGYPT

their sufferings, the sincerity and reliability of Paul and company, and ultimately even the validity of the gospel itself.[1] In response, the tone of the letter is tender, pastoral, and delicately corrective.

LITERARY CONSIDERATIONS

With regard to literary aspects, 1 Thessalonians is puzzling in two major respects. First of all, there is the unusually long thanksgiving which stretches over chs 1-3. Secondly, why does Paul use the past tense in 2:16, "But God's wrath has overtaken them at last," when he pronounces what appears to be a future judgment on the Jews? Any satisfactory answers to these questions will involve a look at the very distinctive structure of the letter.

Framed by the letter opening in 1:1 and the letter closing in 5:25-28, two major sections of the letter may be distinguished: 1) The unusually long thanksgiving section in chs 1-3 which closes with a wish-prayer in 3:11-13, and 2) the exhortatory-instructional material in chs 4-5, also concluded by a wish-prayer in 5:23-24. Within these larger sections the material is quite clearly organized.

THE MESSAGE
Outline

If we look more carefully at the two-part structure of 1:2-3:13 and 4:1-5:24 we can observe that there is a three-part structure in both 1:2-2:16 and 2:17-3:13 similar to that found in 4:1-5:24.

A   1:2-10   Thanksgiving and praise for the believers' reception.

B   2:1-12   *Arguments* defending the character of Paul's ministry. *Paul's ministry*

A′   2:13-16   Thanksgiving and praise for the believers' reception and judgment against opponents.

C   2:17-20   Reminder of past efforts and longing to make a visit to believers.

D   3:1-8   Timothy's visit and return with good news framing an *argument* on the nature of Christian suffering. *nature of X an suffering*

C′   3:9-13   Thanksgiving with prayer for a future visit to believers and for their spiritual well-being.

E   4:1-12   Reminder of former moral exhortation and encouragement to excel more and more.

F   4:13-5:11   Eschatological instruction: *arguments* that the dead in Christ will *what about dead in X* not lose out at the second coming and encouragement for the living that God has indeed chosen them for salvation.

E′   5:12-24   More general exhortations on church and moral themes.

In each of these the material falls into an X Y X′ type of pattern to be seen both in the repetition of key words and phrases, of similar contents and of similar dominant persuasive functions.[2] In each case it is the central panel that *argument* contains a predominance of argumentative material, whereas the framing panels *surrounded* contain predominantly emotional appeals or appeals that enhance Paul's *by appeal* credibility. The points at issue are the genuine character of Paul's ministry (2:1-12), the question of Christian suffering (3:3-4), and especially the problem of those who had died and those who could still do so prior to the coming of Christ (4:13-5:11).

What is interesting from a rhetorical perspective is that in the extended thanksgiving section (1:2-3:13) the predominance of persuasive appeals are aimed at continuing and enhancing the good relations between the audience and Paul. This identifies it as having an extended introductory function in which the writer or speaker appeals to good will and thus prepares the audience for the main topic or problem he is going to treat. The more sensitive the topic or problem, the longer and more careful the preparation tends to be. This helps to explain the unusual length of the thanksgiving.

As for the problem in 2:16, some scholars have proposed that the past tense in "God's wrath *has overtaken* them at last" must refer to the destruction of the temple in Jerusalem in 70 C.E. Consequently they take this sentence together with 2:15-16 or all of 2:13-16 to be a later addition made by some scribe engaged in the work of copying the letter. As evidence against part of this view, the consistent three-part pattern of structure noted above would be destroyed if

2:13-16 were not original. Notice that the only references to "wrath" in the whole letter occur at the end of the panel sections 1:2-10 and 2:13-16. Furthermore, the past tense "has come" can be taken to have a dramatic function in Greek so as to indicate the certainty of judgment. Also "at last" can be translated as "utterly." This dramatic feature cannot be captured adequately in English by using a past tense, so the future tense is best used: "God's wrath will come on them utterly." In this way the wrath would refer to the "day of the Lord" (5:2) and not the destruction of the temple in 70 C.E., or any other lesser event that could be construed as a judgment.

Survey of contents

Paul repeatedly reminds the Thessalonian believers of their exemplary progress in the faith (1:2-10; 2:13-14, 19-20; 3:6-7; 4:1, 9-10). He defends the pure motives and honor of his ministry (2:1-12), hurls judgment indirectly at their oppressors by his judgment on Jews who hinder the gospel (2:14-16), expresses longing to visit them (2:17-3:13), explains the nature of their sufferings (3:3-4), and reminds them of his previous admonitions and instruction on sexual propriety and brotherly love which they continue to live up to (4:1-12). Only after this long preparation does he approach the issue that was troubling them and give comforting instruction on both the status of the dead in Christ (4:13-18) and also on the status of the elect who remain (5:1-11). It is most likely such a "deficiency" that Paul had in mind when he wrote about supplying "whatever is lacking in your faith" (3:10).

Some commentators have seen the admonitions in 4:1-12 and 5:12-22 as also reflecting actual deficiencies in the church, but this does not seem likely. In 4:1-12, they are *reminders* of previous instruction in which the addresses were obviously not at fault: "as you learned from us how you ought to live and to please God, *as, in fact, you are doing*, you should do so more and more" (4:1). Such reminders of previous, sound instruction may be seen as an indirect persuasive appeal for Paul's credibility prior to launching into corrective instruction on the touchy topic of 4:13ff. In 5:12-22 the admonitions are short, staccato and wind down for the close of the letter. Hardly a place or manner for taking up any pressing problems.

The primary messages, then, are that the dead in Christ will indeed be raised at the last trumpet call and together with the living will meet and remain with the Lord. Furthermore, after bypassing speculation as to when the Lord will come (5:1), Paul emphasizes the sudden, unexpected character of the "Day of the Lord" which will trap the wicked (5:2-3). By contrast, he emphasizes that his addressees are "children of the day" and not destined "for wrath, but for obtaining salvation through our Lord Jesus Christ" (5:4-10). Both the basis of hope for the resurrection of the dead in Christ and of the assurance of salvation for those who remain are grounded in the death and resurrection of Jesus Christ (4:14; 5:10). His message of hope is Christocentric to the core.

From 1 Thess 4:17 Paul appears to expect that he will be alive at the coming of Christ, although later in Phil 3:10-11 he anticipates taking part in the resurrection. It is appropriate to take a look at the practical advice he gives to those who await the parousia of Jesus: keeping sexual purity (particularly appropriate to his predominantly Gentile audience—4:3-8); love for fellow believers (4:9-10); quietness, productivity, and self-sufficiency in living (4:11-12); respect for God's workers, encouragement for the weak, and good will to all, even one's persecutors (5:12-15); joy, prayer and thanksgiving (5:16-18); openness to the Spirit and to prophecy, although the latter must be tested (5:19-20). Paul's concern for the whole person particularly comes to expression in the closing wish-prayer: "... may your spirit and soul and body be kept sound and blameless at the coming of our Lord Jesus Christ." The last words of the letter-body focus on the faithfulness of God: "The one who calls you is faithful, and he will do this."

RELEVANCE FOR TODAY

Paul spells out the very center of hope for all Christians who must face death. That center lies in the death and resurrection of Jesus Christ. For those who are still waiting for the parousia, his advice is still basic and sober: keep pure, love one another and keep occupied at honorable means of earning a living. There is no room here for getting carried away emotionally or for inordinate speculation on the time of the event, but rather a call to steady, quiet confidence in a faithful Savior.

ISSUES FOR DISCUSSION AND REFLECTION

1. How can Christians experience joy in the midst of affliction (1:6)? What do you think Paul means when he speaks of afflictions as something Christians were destined to undergo in 3:3-4?
2. Read several translations and commentaries on 4:4-6. What do you think Paul is referring to in these verses?
3. Analyze Paul's arguments in 4:13-18 and 5:1-11. Where does the focus of his message lie, on the how and when of the parousia and related events or on the certainty and assurance of resurrection, reunion and salvation?
4. In 2 Thess 2:3-12 Paul argues that certain events have to take place before the coming of Jesus Christ. How does this fit with 1 Thess 5:1-3 where he passes by "times and seasons" and emphasizes the suddenness and unexpectedness of the "Day of the Lord"?

FURTHER READING
Best, Ernest
> 1977   *A Commentary on the First and Second Epistles to the Thessalonians.* (Black's). London: Adam & Charles Black.

Collins, Raymond F.
> 1981   "Paul as Seen through His Own Eyes: A Reflection on the First Letter to the Thessalonians," *LS* 348-381. (also in Collins, 1984, 175-208).
> 1984   *Studies on the First Letter to the Thessalonians.* Bibliotheca Ephemeridum Theologicarum Lovaniensium, 66. Leuven: Leuven University Press.

Jewett, Robert
> 1986   *The Thessalonian Correspondence: Pauline Rhetoric and Millenarian Piety.* Hermeneia Foundations and Facets. Philadelphia: Fortress.

Johanson, Bruce C.
> 1987   *To All the Brethren: A Text-Linguistic and Rhetorical Approach to 1 Thessalonians.* Coniectanea Biblica, New Testament Series 16. Stockholm: Almquist and Wiksell.

Malherbe, Abraham J.
> 1987   *Paul and the Thessalonians: The Philosophic Tradition of Pastoral Care.* Philadelphia: Fortress.

Marshall, I. Howard
> 1983   *1 and 2 Thessalonians.* (New Century). Grand Rapids, MI: Eerdmans.

ENDNOTES
1. See A.J. Malherbe, *Paul and the Thessalonians* (1987) who represents the view that 1 Thessalonians is basically a general pastoral letter rather than one in which the matters reflected in 4:13-5:11 should be seen as the main exigence for which all else in the letter is a delicate preparation.

2. The categories for persuasive appeals are taken from Aristotle, *Rhet* 1.2.3 ff. *Pathos* indicates appeals to the emotions, *ethos* refers to appeals for the speaker's credibility, and *logos* refers to appeals to reason in a broad sense. For a discussion of these types of appeals and their application to 1 Thessalonians see Johanson, *To All the Brethren. A Text-Linguistic and Rhetorical Approach to 1 Thessalonians,* (1987) 36 ff, 81-141. For patterned repetitions of vocabulary that support this structure see pp 149-151.

Chapter 7

2 Thessalonians

Bruce C. Johanson

Day of the Lord: part of KOG idea

> *"And then the lawless one will be revealed, whom the Lord Jesus will destroy with the breath of his mouth, annihilating him by the manifestation of his coming."*

BRIEF OVERVIEW OF THE BOOK

Second Thessalonians primarily addresses two different but possibly related problems in the church at Thessalonica. First, someone was trying to secure support in the church for the view that "the day of the Lord is already here" (2:1-12). Apparently this was presented by the authority of ecstatic utterance ("spirit"), or authoritative pronouncement ("word"), or a letter ascribed to Paul himself (2:2; 3:17). Second, some of the believers were disorderly and living at the others' expense (3:6-13). These "busybodies" may have been the ones asserting the view that the day of the Lord had come. A claim for charismatic authority on their part could also involve a claim to be supported by the congregation.

BACKGROUND CONCERNS

Background concerns dealing with the city of Thessalonica and the social and economic composition of the church there have been covered in the previous chapter. Here we need to look at the relationship between 1 and 2 Thessalonians, the question of Paul's authorship of 2 Thessalonians, and some possible backgrounds for the issues in 2 Thess 2:1-12 and 3:6-13.[1]

First of all, the titles with their references to order, "First" and "Second" Thessalonians, are not original but were attached later when the letters were gathered together in some early collection. Consequently, this order reflects the opinion of a later editor and cannot be taken for granted as being correct. In fact, the actual historical order of the two letters could be reversed. Here are some of the observations presented by those who think that 2 Thessalonians may have actually preceded 1 Thessalonians:

1) When collecting letters of common destination there seems to have been a tendency to place the longer letter before the shorter one.

2) If 2 Thessalonians is the prior letter, Paul's reference to his personal signature in 3:17 would make more sense.

3) If the addressees had previously read 2 Thess 2:3-12, the remark in 1 Thess 5:1 that they have no need to be instructed about times and seasons would make more sense.

4) The topics introduced by "now concerning" in 1 Thess 4:9, 13 and 5:1 are interpreted by some as answers to questions occasioned by what Paul wrote in 2 Thessalonians.

*which covers
letter first?*

Those who are persuaded that the traditional ordering of the two letters is correct give the following typical responses to the objections above:

1) The first of these arguments cannot carry much weight by itself and the others are not in any way overwhelming.

2) The presupposition of a spurious letter in 2 Thess 2:2 is sufficient to explain Paul's reference to his personal signature in 3:17.

3) As for the remark of not needing to be instructed on times and seasons in 1 Thess 5:1, this can just as easily presuppose Paul's previous oral instructions.

4) Regarding the topics introduced by "now concerning" in 1 Thessalonians, none of them need to have had a previous letter to explain their occasion. In fact, the Greek represented by "now concerning" was commonly used simply to mark a topical transition and need not reflect an answer to some question.

To these observations we may add that the author's admonition in 2 Thess 2:15 explicitly refers not only to previous oral instruction but also to previous correspondence of which 1 Thessalonians may have been a part. According to these considerations there would be no overwhelming reason to question the canonical order of the two letters.

The next consideration has to do with whether or not it was Paul himself who wrote 2 Thessalonians. The whole question of someone writing in the authoritative name of an early apostle is not to be lightly dismissed as the product of faddish, liberal, modern scholarship. There are many letters in antiquity written in the name of Paul, Peter, and Barnabas, among others. Among these, the *Epistle of Barnabas* was even included in some of the earliest New Testament collections of authoritative works. It was a work which did not make it into the final form of the New Testament canon. It is also highly unlikely that Barnabas was its author. With this in mind, we should be willing to give a hearing to some of the main reasons why a number of scholars question Paul's authorship here:[2]

1) Many see an irreconcilable difference between 1 and 2 Thessalonians regarding eschatology. In 1 Thess 5:1-3 Paul's eschatology is characterized by the suddenness and unpredictability of the end, whereas in 2 Thess 2:1-12 the eschatology is characterized by predictability in that the end can be known not to have taken place yet since certain known eschatological events must first take place.

2) In conjunction with this first position it is observed that the view combatted in 2 Thess 2:2, namely that "the day of the Lord is already here," reflects a post-Pauline development. It represents an eschatology that is realized somehow in the present order and comes about as a reaction to the delayed parousia of Jesus Christ.

3) The presence of exact verbal parallels (e.g., see "work of faith" in 1 Thess 1:3 and 2 Thess 1:11, also compare 1 Thess 2:9 with 2 Thess 3:8) together with the use of un-Pauline expressions (e.g., the use of *epiphaneia* for the coming of Jesus Christ in 2:8; the shift to "Lord" in 2 Thess 2:13 and 3:16 from "God" in 1 Thess 1:4 and 5:23; the expression "we must always give thanks" in 2 Thess 1:3; 2:13 which Paul does not use elsewhere) are seen as supporting the non-Pauline literary dependence of 2 Thessalonians on 1 Thessalonians.

[handwritten margin note: was Paul author of 2 thess. ?]

These objections have been countered with the following arguments by those who are persuaded that Paul wrote 2 Thessalonians.

1) It is not strange to find a tension between the expression of the suddenness and unpredictability of the end in conjunction with anticipatory signs that must take place first. Both conceptions occur together in both Jewish and early Christian apocalyptic. Furthermore, given the nature of the problem faced by the church (2 Thess 2:3), it would be natural for Paul to dampen their runaway enthusiasm by reminders of primary events believed to precede the "day of the Lord" which he associates distinctly with the glorious coming of Christ (2 Thess 2:8; cf. 1:7-8).

2) Regarding the extreme realized eschatology of those troubling the church (2 Thess 2:3), interpreted as fitting most naturally during the late first century or the early second century, this is countered by pointing out that 2 Thess 2:4 was apparently written while the temple was still standing, namely prior to 70 C.E. Furthermore, the brevity of the text does not allow us to know for sure whether the claim "the day of the Lord is already here" reflects extreme realized eschatology. If it did, one would expect Paul to correct this mistaken view of the parousia rather than to argue for the prior occurrence of certain events.[3]

3) As for the parallels between 1 and 2 Thessalonians, it is argued that they are what one would expect between two documents written in close proximity. Also, no author is bound to use exactly the same terminology throughout his

or her writings. The Greeks were very aware that good writing even demands variation.

Besides these counter arguments, those who defend Paul's authorship point out that Paul's letters were occasioned for the most part by the needs of those he wrote to. Different needs would bring out different emphases in his teaching and theology. Apart from the altered state of affairs reflected in 2 Thess 2:1-12, he is seen as strengthening various aspects of his message already presented in 1 Thessalonians. For example, there is the unavoidable eschatological suffering and affliction (1 Thess 3:3-4; 2 Thess 1:4-5), the judgment that comes on their persecutors (1 Thess 2:14-16; 2 Thess 1:6-10); the instruction against idleness (1 Thess 4:11-12; 2 Thess 3:6-13), etc. In view of these considerations the defenders of Paul's authorship would place 2 Thessalonians fairly soon after 1 Thessalonians sometime around 50-51 C.E.

Finally, a word on the false view that "the day of the Lord is already here" (2 Thess 2:2). Some have seen this as due to some sort of intensely spirit-filled experience usually referred to as "enthusiasm." Such an experience often gives rise to some form of realized eschatology or secret rapture theology. There are different proposals regarding what the basis of this spiritual ecstasy or enthusiasm actually was.

One proposal is that the cause was a misunderstanding of Paul's previously given message. The false teaching was presented under the guise of coming from Paul himself (2:2; 3:17). Yet it is not clear whether this was by way of a forged letter or simply by someone's fixation with one particular expression of Paul's message to the exclusion of other balancing statements. In the latter case, one possibility would be to make a literal reading of 1 Thess 2:16c ("The wrath has come upon them at last" [RSV]) while ignoring 1 Thess 5:2 ("For you yourselves know very well that the day of the Lord will come like a thief in the night"). Another explanation is one which sees the enthusiasm as having a Gnostic origin. This, however, is highly questionable since some of the most characteristic features of Gnosticism are totally lacking in both 1 and 2 Thessalonians.[4]

A more recent explanation is proposed by R. Jewett. He notes that movements which are fixated with the millennium are often characterized by a strong resistance to such everyday life things as the work ethic, the sexual ethic and established authority. He finds Paul addressing such problems in 1 Thess 4:3-8, 11-12; 5:12-13. This resistance arises because they believe that the millennium has come. A future coming of Christ was unacceptable for them because they believed that they were experiencing and embodying it already in their ecstatic activities. This view, however, also has its problems. The arrival of persecution (1 Thess 3:3-4; 2 Thess 1:4 ff.) and the deaths of some believers (1 Thess 4:13 ff) would normally be expected to jeopardize such a claim of already participating in paradisiac conditions. What puts Jewett's view under doubt is that he cannot explain why, according to his hypothesis, this radicalism blossomed rather than wilted as it should have when all such evidence was against it.[5]

While it is important to make the effort to access better understanding by trying to reconstruct a probable or possible background to the view combatted in 2 Thess 2:1-12, one must concede with E. Best that the brevity of our text and our distance from it in time make it virtually impossible to know for sure what sort of belief lay behind it.[6]

THE MESSAGE
Outline

A careful reading of 2 Thessalonians reveals many similar structural features also found in 1 Thessalonians.[7] Apart from the letter opening in 1:1-2 and the letter closing in 3:17-18, we find two major sections of material that comprise the body of the letter as follows:

I. Letter opening 1:1-2
II. Letter body 1:3-3:16
    A. Instruction regarding the day of the Lord framed by passages expressing thanksgiving and prayer for the addressees . 1:3-2:16
    B. Specific commands regarding those who are idle in the community framed by topics regarding compliance and non-compliance with what Paul commands and by wish-prayers 3:1-16
III. Letter closing 3:17-18

Within the letter body the two major sections are made up of three subsections each. These subsections follow an X Y X' type of pattern:

A 1:3-12   A report of being bound to thank God regarding the addressees because of their faith, love and steadfastness under persecution (1:3-4). The mention of persecution issues into a lengthy digression on the retribution coming to those who afflict them (1:5-10). The passage ends with a report of prayer for the addressees' good resolve and work of faith in order that both they and the Lord may be glorified (1:11-12).

B 2:1-12   A warning not to be excited or persuaded by the view that "the day of the Lord is already here" (2:1-2). This is followed by *arguments* showing that it has not taken place yet, since the "rebellion," the revealing of the "lawless one," and the removal of who/what is restraining the revealing of the lawless one have not yet taken place (2:3-12).

note common X Y X' pattern

A' 2:13-17   A renewed report of being bound to thank God regarding the addressees because of their election for salvation (2:13-15). The passage closes with a wish-prayer for comfort and stability (2:16-17).

C   3:1-5   A request for the addressees' prayers (3:1-3a) followed by an expression of confidence regarding their compliance with Paul's commands (3:3b-4). The section closes with a wish-prayer (3:5).

D   3:6-12   Paul exhorts them to keep away from those who are idle and backs up the necessity of working (3:6) by *arguing* from the example given by himself and his co-workers (3:7-9). After reminding them of his previous instruction, "Anyone unwilling to word should not eat," he commands the idle to work and earn their own living (3:10-12).

C' 3:13-16   The final section opens with the general exhortation not to be weary in well-doing (3:13) and continues with commands on how to deal with those who manifest non-compliance with what Paul says in "this letter" as a whole (3:14-15). The section closes with a wish-prayer (3:16).

This patterning was observed in the previous chapter in the case of 1 Thessalonians. It is established by paying attention to parallels in the contents and types of contents as well as to the dominant types of persuasive appeals. In the framing panels an affective, emotional type of appeal tends to be dominant. Here the author reports and expresses his prayers for the addressees, encourages and comforts them in their persecutions and afflictions and express his sentiments and wishes regarding compliance with his commands. In the central sections the author tends to argue more on the basis of previous instruction and example. The X Y X' patterns place the focus on the materials in the central sections between the panels. Thus, it is in 2:1-12 and 3:6-13 that we find the primary concerns of the author where he warns against the false teaching that "the day of the Lord is already here" and instructs them on how to deal with the disorderly or lazy people among them.

Survey of contents

The message of 2 Thessalonians is basically a call to continue standing firm in the traditions taught by Paul to the community of believers in Thessalonica. In 2 Thess 2:1-12 the refutation of the claim that "the day of the Lord is already here" is based on two proofs: 1) there are events that must take place before the Day of the Lord (2:3b-5, 9-11); 2) there is a reason for the present delay of the Day (2:6-8). The passage is particularly difficult to interpret with regard to the nature of the "rebellion" (2:3), the identity of "the lawless one" (2:3), and who or what restrains this lawless one (2:6), all of which must take place before the parousia of Jesus Christ. The author had given previous instruction about all these things to his addressees (2:6—"you know") in a conversation that unfortunately is not available to us.

The bewildering array of interpretive suggestions in commentaries warn the modern interpreter of the danger of reading into the text what it may never have been intended to say. All we can surmise about the rebellion is that it must be against God in some way, given the context. The "lawless one" aspires to divine status by taking his seat in the temple and claiming to be God. The appearing of this lawless one is restrained for a time. The restrainer is first referred to in the Greek in the neuter gender ("what") and then in the masculine gender ("who"). Finally, the lawless one will come "in the working of Satan" with manifestations of power and deception for those who refuse to love the truth. He is then destroyed at the coming of Jesus.

Second, some of the community were living in idleness and at the other believers' expense (3:6-13). Is there any connection between this "idleness" and the false teaching in 2:1-2? Some think that the idleness was possibly due to the general Hellenistic scorn for manual labor and thus without any necessary connection with 2:1-2. Others see the idleness as a direct consequence of thinking that the day of the Lord had already arrived. Another view is that the word for "idle" here should be translated as "disorderly." Further on these persons are also described as "busybodies" (3:11). This view goes on to hold that they were the ones claiming that the Day of the Lord had come and that they regarded themselves as charismatic leaders worthy of financial support by the congregation.

Paul's reminder of his example of self-support is aimed against this behavior. Just as their teaching was not in line with the traditions taught by Paul (2:1-12, 15), so also their behavior was "not according to the tradition" received from Paul (3:6).

RELEVANCE FOR TODAY

On the general theological plane 2 Thessalonians depicts a God who is concerned for justice, who provides salvation for the righteous (2:13) and sends judgment to those who afflict the righteous (1:6 ff) and who take pleasure in unrighteousness (2:12). Justice is always relevant. More specifically, when read as a whole and in context, this letter provides a serious warning against escapist apocalyptic ecstasy in which a preoccupation with the day of the Lord can detract from "the eternal comfort and good hope through grace" that gives stability and growth in the present and "peace at all times in all ways" (3:16, 17 [RSV]).

In the practical sphere, the author can exhort people to earn their own living and not be an unnecessary burden to others in the church. But this does not mean that we are entitled to use this text to throw doubt unfairly on others and escape our Christian responsibility to help those who cannot or who have great difficulty in helping themselves.

ISSUES FOR DISCUSSION AND REFLECTION

1. What is the connection between vss 4 and 5 in ch 1? Does the word "evidence" in 1:5 refer back to a) persecutions and afflictions? b) steadfastness and faith? c) or to the author's boast regarding the addressees? Which of these makes the most sense?

2. In 1:5 is the "righteous judgment" something that is ongoing or future? In what way does the author see God's judgment as being righteous?

3. "Eternal" can mean "characteristic of the age" or it can mean "eternal" in a couple of differing senses, namely, eternal in the sense of "having a different quality" or in the sense of "final" where the idea of duration is lacking. Which of these makes the most sense of the expression "eternal destruction" in 1:9?

4. In 1:2-4, 11 the author refers several times to the "faith" of those he addresses. What significant characteristics regarding their faith can you observe from the context?

5. Read through 2:1-12 with the help of more than one commentary. How important do you think it is to be able to identify the "rebellion," the "lawless one" and what or who "restrains" him from being revealed? What is the primary purpose of this passage?

6. In 2:11 God is referred to as sending "a strong delusion" on those who reject the Gospel so that they would believe the lawless one. Does God really try to get people to believe what is false?

7. What is the meaning of the statement in 2:13 that "God chose you from the beginning to be saved"? How does God "choose"? What does "from the beginning" refer to?

8. Give an interpretation of the phrase "eternal comfort and good hope through grace" in 2:16.

9. Read through 3:6-15 with the help of a commentary. What are the arguments the author gives against idleness in favor of working and earning one's own living? Does he give any explicitly theological reasons? Would you argue the same way regarding idleness today? What do you think of the instruction on how the church should treat idlers and those who disregard the teaching in this letter? Would such a procedure work in your culture today?

- love increasing for one another
- steadfastness in persecution
-

FURTHER READING

Best, Ernest
1977 A Commentary on the First and Second Epistles to the Thessalonians. (Black's). London: Adam & Charles Black.

Bruce, Frederick F.
1982 *1 & 2 Thessalonians.* (Word). Waco, TX: Word.

Holland, G.S.
1988 *The Tradition that You Received from Us: 2 Thessalonians in the Pauline Tradition.* Tübingen: JLB Mohr.

Jewett, Robert
1986 *The Thessalonian Correspondence. Pauline Rhetoric and Millenarian Piety.* (Foundations & Facets). Philadelphia: Fortress.

Marshall, I. Howard
1983 *1 and 2 Thessalonians.* (New Century). Grand Rapids, MI: Eerdmans.

Nichols, Francis D., Ed.
1957 *Seventh-day Adventist Bible Commentary.* Vol. 7. Washington, D.C., 261-282.

ENDNOTES

1. Some scholars believe that more than one letter has been edited to make up what is presently 2 Thessalonians. For a critique of such views that question the unity of 2 Thessalonians see Best (1977, 45-50).

2. For a more detailed and complete treatment favoring Pauline authorship see Best (1977, 50-58) and for one of the most recent monographs rejecting Pauline authorship see G.S. Holland (1988).

3. See Best (1977, 276).

4. For a more detailed critique of the enthusiastic and Gnostic models see Jewett (1986, 142-149).

5. See Jewett (1986, 176-177).

6. See Best (1977, 278).

7. See the previous chapter on 1 Thessalonians.

Chapter 8

1 Corinthians
Sakae Kubo

"And now faith, hope, and love abide, these three; and the greatest of these is love."

BRIEF OVERVIEW OF THE BOOK

First Corinthians was one of the early letters of Paul. He wrote it from Ephesus in response to a letter which the Corinthians had written to him (7:1) and reports which he received from Chloe's people (1:11), and perhaps from Stephanas, Fortunatus, and Achaicus, as well (16:17). The letter deals with a series of problems existing in the church. He does not deal with doctrines as such but with the practical problems that a missionary church faces in an alien culture.

BACKGROUND CONCERNS

Paul came to Corinth for the first time on his second missionary journey. There he first met Aquila and Priscilla who had been forced out of Rome by the Emperor Claudius. According to his usual practice, he first preached in the synagogue. The ruler of the synagogue, Crispus, became a believer along with Titius Justus, "a worshiper of God." A "worshiper of God" was a Gentile who had not fully accepted the teachings of the Jews (a proselyte) but was sympathetic to the teaching of the Jews and attended the synagogue.

Gallio was proconsul in Corinth at the time Paul was there. This is important because it helps us to date Paul's time in Corinth. Gallio was proconsul beginning in July 51 C.E. Since Paul was a year and six months in Corinth, we can date the approximate time of his stay there.

Corinth was located at a strategic place in the four and a half mile isthmus that connected the Peloponnese and the mainland. This narrow spot on the isthmus served as a point for goods to be transported overland from the Gulf of Corinth to the Saronic Gulf. Today there is a canal that connects the two gulfs. This was completed in 1893, although Nero had already sought to dig it. The strategic location was enhanced by a hill, 1857 feet high, which added military advantages to the economic ones.

Old Corinth was destroyed in 146 B.C.E. by the Romans and remained desolate until 44 B.C.E. when Julius Caesar refound it as a Roman colony. The old city was so notorious for its immorality that the verb *korinthiazo* came to mean "to commit sexual immorality." The new city where Paul came was a typical Hellenistic port city with its usual vices. A Hebrew synagogue was located here. We know this because archaeologists have found a piece of the lintel which has enough letters (Greek) to tell us that it served for a synagogue of the Jews.

First Corinthians along with 2 Corinthians, Romans and Galatians has never been questioned as coming from the hands of Paul. Some have questioned, though, whether the letter as we have it today was the form in which Paul originally wrote it. We discuss this question in the next section.

LITERARY CONSIDERATIONS

In 1 Cor 5:9-11 Paul refers to a letter to the Corinthian church which he had written previous to 1 Corinthians. There he hints as to the nature of the letter. He had commanded them not to associate or even eat with any member of the church who was "guilty of immorality or greed, or is an idolater, reviler, drunkard, or robber" (5:11). Because of apparent differences in attitude in sections of 1 Corinthians, some scholars have sought to see in the harsher sections the contents of this previous letter. They seem to think that there is a contradiction between the rigorist attitude in 10:1-22 as compared to 8:1-13 and 10:23-11:1. Again some see a rather abrupt renewal in dealing with his apostleship (9) when the matter seemed to have been dealt with already in vs 4. The content of 2 Cor 6:14-7:1 also fits the tone of the previous letter. Since these seem to contradict portions of 1 Corinthians, and deal with a severe attitude, and since the previous letter seemed to reflect this attitude, these parts of 1 Corinthians must have come from the previous letter. This would make our 1 Corinthians a composite work edited from separate letters.

First of all it seems that the differences can be explained. For example, the rigorist attitude in 10:1-22 can be explained by the fact that this passage is dealing with a related but different issue than 8:1-13 or 10:23-11:1. This section deals with eating food offered to idols in pagan temples rather than buying such at a market or eating it in a private home. If these sections are as contradictory as they are made out to be, one would find it difficult to explain why they were joined together at all—not to say anything about the particular placement we find today. An editor must have had some reason to put these sections together. How would one explain this? Such considerations have led the vast majority of the vast majority of scholars to consider the previous letter to have been lost, and our 1 Corinthians to be a unity.

MESSAGE
Outline
First Corinthians can be outlined in the following manner:

Survey of contents

We see from the outline above that Paul deals with a good number of issues in this epistle: divisions in the church, immorality within the church, lawsuits with members of the church, liaisons with prostitutes, the Christian's relation to marriage, food offered to idols, conduct in worship (including women's dispensing of the veil in prophesying and the abuse of the Lord's supper), spiritual gifts and the place of glossolalia, and the resurrection of the dead.

There are several basic themes that run through these disparate issues. The first of these is Christian wisdom. The divisions in the church were due to the fact that they had lost sight of Jesus Christ and him crucified. Instead they were exalting human skills, accomplishments, and wisdom. They chose for their leaders those who had abilities they themselves desired and could vicariously enjoy. They reverted to the wisdom of the world rather than the wisdom of God.

The Jews demanded signs (miracles of power) that Christ was the Messiah and the Greeks sought wisdom, but in Christ and him crucified Paul was offering them both genuine power and true wisdom. He did not come with "lofty words" or "eloquent wisdom," but "in the demonstration of the Spirit and power." The Corinthians had gone back to the spirit of the world and had lost the Spirit which is from God and became "men of the flesh," "ordinary men." They forgot that God's workers are all on the same plane, all equal, whether one plants or waters over against God who makes things grow. They forgot because they did not understand the meaning of Christ and him crucified. They failed to understand that the cross signified that reliance on human efforts and strivings were futile in establishing one's standing before God. They failed to understand that God overturns human values and understandings. God chooses the weak not the strong, the low and despised not the elite, the humble not the proud to accomplish his purposes. In God's eyes the wisdom of man is nothing but foolishness. The human being has nothing to boast in except in God who does all things for him. "Let him who boasts, boast in the Lord."

Another important theme in this epistle is Christian freedom. Paul was an apostle of Christian freedom but he was not always understood rightly. People who heard him tended to go too far with their freedom. This is seen in the section on food offered to idols. Those who had knowledge that an idol was nothing felt free to eat food offered to idols. But some of these felt that their freedom should not be limited in any way. They would eat and exercise their freedom whenever and wherever they felt like it. If a weak brother should stumble, that was his problem. Paul says the Christian must exercise his freedom with love. Knowledge alone only puffs up; love builds up. Love must dictate to us how our freedom should be used. We cannot become a slave to our freedom.

This matter of Christian freedom is also discussed in connection with liaisons with prostitutes (6:12-20). The exercise of freedom, Paul says, must be determined by its outcome (whether it is profitable or not) and whether we become enslaved. In this case freedom should not be exercised because the outcome is not profitable. It leads to a break with the Lord. What we need to remember here is that our bodies are temples of the Holy Spirit and really belong to God. We cannot take what belongs to God and join it to a prostitute.

The problems regarding worship come under this heading as well. The women who were prophesying with their heads unveiled were influenced, no doubt, by Paul's message of Christian freedom. Yet the exercise of freedom here, while legitimate, went against the grain of the custom of the times. It is difficult for us to follow Paul's arguments, yet he was concerned that on this type of an issue the practice of the church should not become a scandal to the people in the church and the rest of society.

Christian freedom also does not mean that we are free to separate ourselves from members in the church who are not in our same class or ethnic group. The rich should not exercise their freedom

Paul the Missionary Preacher

to eat alone and leave the poor the crumbs of our rich repast. The Lord's supper is meant to unify. We eat from the one loaf and drink from the same cup, signifying our oneness with Christ and with one another.

A third theme that we find in this epistle is that of the church and the world. In the fifth chapter Paul calls for the church to expel the immoral person from the church "that his spirit may be saved in the day of the Lord Jesus" (5:5). Here we find Paul's concept of the already and not yet. In vs 7 he says, "Cleanse out the old leaven that you may be fresh dough, as you really are unleavened." This statement seems contradictory. If they are unleavened, how can they still have the old leaven in them? Christ's coming has made them unleavened (already) but their continuing life in this world makes it necessary for them to continue to cleanse out the old leaven (not yet). At any rate the old sinful ways of life practiced in such blatant form as in this chapter cannot be allowed to remain in the church.

This same theme is seen also in ch 6. Defrauding of a brother leading to lawsuits before unbelievers is a defeat and a disgrace that ought not continue. These kinds of things were part of the past life without God. Those who practice these things cannot inherit the kingdom of God. "But you were washed, you were sanctified, you were justified in the name of the Lord Jesus Christ and in the Spirit of our God" (6:11). Here again the idea of already and not yet is present.

Paul deals with marriage in the seventh chapter. He deals with this matter in the light of "an impending distress." He deals with sexual relations within marriage, the question of divorce in Christian and mixed marriages, whether virgins should marry or not, and the question of remarriage after the death of one's spouse. The underlying principle throughout in the light of the situation (and he brought in other matters besides marriage) is that one should remain in the state in which he was called, thus a single person should remain single and a married person should remain married.

The theme of spiritual gifts is discussed focusing particularly on the gift of speaking in tongues. Paul emphasizes first of all that though there are a variety of gifts, all gifts come from the same Giver, the Holy Spirit. He then says that like the members of a body, each individual Christian performs a function that is for the well being of the total body. We are interdependent. Then he lays down an important principle, i.e., that love must control each gift. Without love no gift, however great it may be, counts for anything. The second principle he lays down is that the gifts are given primarily for the edification of the church, and if they do not serve this function they should be exercised in private. The gift of tongues for this reason has been too highly valued in the church and should be placed in proper perspective.

The resurrection of the dead is a final important theme. There were those *5) resurr. of dead* in the church who denied this (15:12). Paul deals with the relationship between Christ's resurrection and ours, Christ's relationship to the first Adam, the nature of the resurrection body, and the final victory over death.

VALUE/RELEVANCE FOR TODAY

In the light of the practical nature of 1 Corinthians its relevance is more obvious than some other books of the Bible. The matter of divisions in the church, lawsuits among members, sexual immorality, the gift of tongues, the function and status of women in the church have particular relevance for us today. The issue of relationships among members is always relevant. Even the sections dealing with food offered to idols, women wearing veils while prophesying, and the treatment of the poor by the rich in connection with the Lord's supper provide principles which can be used today.

What are some of these principles? One is that Christian responsibility goes *X can* beyond the rightness of wrongness of a given act and must include the *responsible - ity* consequences of the action and its effect on other people. Even actions perfectly *includes* acceptable in one situation might be wrong in another context where they would *effect of* hurt a person. We also see that love and unity must be considered in every *act on* context. But Paul also shows that some actions, such as idolatry and sexual *others* immorality are always out of harmony with God's will (1 Cor 10).

ISSUES FOR DISCUSSION AND REFLECTION

1. Is Paul's treatment of division in the churches useful in dealing with the same problem today?
2. Should we ever disfellowship someone? What reasons would there be for it? Does disfellowship from the church today mean that such a person has been delivered to Satan?
3. Is our situation different today from Paul's regarding going to court? Are there some situations where it is out of our hands whether we go to court or not with fellow believers? Is there ever justification for the believer or the church to go to court with Christians of the same denomination? Of a different denomination?
4. Is Paul's counsel regarding remaining single valid for his situation? For ours? Ever? Are there some principles that are true regardless of circumstances?
5. How would you apply the principle regarding food offered to idols today? To what extent should one's freedom be curtailed by another person's scruples?
6. Should women be allowed to preach? Become ministers and be ordained?

7. What is the gift of tongues? Does it continue on today? What is the relationship of the Corinthian gift to the gift Pentecostals claim today? Is this something all churches should allow in the church today?
8. What meaning does the resurrection of the dead have for you? Is it something far fetched or something very meaningful to you in your daily life? How would you explain baptism for the dead in 1 Cor 15:29?

FURTHER READING

Barrett, Charles K.
>   1968   *A Commentary on the First Epistle to the Corinthians.* New York: Harper and Row.

Conzelmann, Hans
>   1975   *1 Corinthians: A Commentary.* Trans. by James W. Leitch. Ed. by George W. MacRae. (Hermeneia). Philadelphia: Fortress.

Fee, Gordon D.
>   1987   *The First Epistle to the Corinthians.* (New International). Grand Rapids, MI: Eerdmans.

Hering, Jean
>   1962   *The First Epistle of St. Paul to the Corinthians.* Trans. by A.W. Heathcote and P.J. Allcock. London: Epworth.

Hurd, John C.
>   1965   *The Origin of 1 Corinthians.* New York: Seabury.

Moffatt, James
>   1938   *The First Epistle of Paul to the Corinthians.* London: Hodder and Stoughton.

Morris, Leon
>   1988   *First Corinthians.* Rev. ed. (Tyndale). Grand Rapids, MI: Eerdmans.

Orr, William and James Arthur Walther
>   1976   *1 Corinthians.* (Anchor). Garden City, NY: Doubleday.

Chapter 9

2 Corinthians
Sakae Kubo

> *"So we are ambassadors for Christ, since God is making his appeal through us; we entreat you on behalf of Christ, be reconciled to God."*

BRIEF OVERVIEW OF THE BOOK

Second Corinthians, though written later than 1 Corinthians, is included among the early letters of Paul. It is the most personal and emotional of all Paul's letters. One writer describes 2 Corinthians as a "pathless forest" compared to the "carefully laid-out park" of 1 Corinthians. There are digressions here and there, emotional outbursts, irony, self-defense and vindication, attack and counterattack as Paul deals with problems in the church and with opponents who attacked him and his work. The first seven chapters deal with his recent relations with the Corinthians, the second part (8-9) deals with the collection, and the last four chapters deal specifically with the opponents who had come into the church from the outside.

BACKGROUND CONCERNS

Paul indicated at the end of 1 Corinthians (16:5-9) that his intention was to visit the Corinthians soon (4:19). Leaving Ephesus after Pentecost, his plan was to visit them after passing through Macedonia. Something happened that caused *a* him to change his plans. He made a "painful visit" (2 Cor 2:1) before the *painful* planned visit. Therefore, his next visit would be his third (2 Cor 12:14). He *visit* would like to visit them again on his way to Macedonia this time and visit them again on his return from Macedonia before going home to Judea (2 Cor 1:16). *sent* But he had second thoughts about returning again so soon (2 Cor 2:1). Instead *Titus* Paul sent Titus on to Corinth, and he went to Troas to meet Titus on his return *again to* (2:12), while he himself took advantage of the opportunity that opened up to *Corinth* preach the gospel in Troas. But for some reason Titus did not meet Paul in Troas. Paul's anxiety concerning the kind of response the Corinthians had made

97

drove him on to Macedonia so that he could find out sooner. There in Macedonia he did find Titus (7:5-6). He was relieved to know that they had responded positively to him. Second Corinthians is Paul's response to the news brought to him by Titus.

2 Cor Paul's response to Titus' news

LITERARY CONSIDERATIONS

The only canonical letters of Paul to the Corinthians in our possession today are 1 and 2 Corinthians. A 3 Corinthians is in existence, but it is clearly an apocryphal letter dating from a much later period than Paul. However, there is evidence that Paul wrote more than two letters to the Corinthian church. As indicated previously, there is a precanonical letter mentioned in 1 Cor 5:9. Paul also refers to a stern letter (2 Cor 2:3-4; 7:8, 12) which he wrote after 1 Corinthians. If we accept these data at face value, we have to assume that the precanonical letter and the stern letter are lost. In that case Paul wrote four letters to the church in Corinth.

an apocryphal 3 Cor

stern letter

precanonical letter

Some identify 1 Corinthians as the stern letter, reducing the total that Paul wrote to three. The description of the stern letter which Paul gives, however, has to be stretched to fit the contents of 1 Corinthians. On the other hand, some see 2 Cor 10-13 as a separate letter written after 2 Cor 1-9. This would increase the total to five letters.

Those who think that there are four letters feel that these are preserved in 1 and 2 Corinthians. The precanonical letter is found in parts of 1 and 2 Corinthians. The stern letter is 1 Cor 10-13 or 1 Corinthians. Some may even divide the letters to include six letters.

The traditional view is that 2 Corinthians is a single letter written by Paul in response to the good news brought to him by Titus. However, as we indicated earlier, some think that portions of 2 Corinthians, notably 6:14-18, belong to the "previous letter" (1 Cor 5:9). There are several reasons given for this. First, this passage does not fit smoothly where it is. If it were left out, the previous verse and the following verse connect very well. The content of the letter seems to fit well with what is described as part of the letter. However, abrupt transitions are present elsewhere (2:13-14; 7:4-5; 7:16-8:1). In such an emotionally charged letter these sort of abrupt transitions are not unexpected. The content of the "previous letter" did not deal with unbelievers, as this section does, but with believers.

Some feel that neither chs 8 nor 9 are part of the letter, and that because they are repetitious they could not have been originally written in the same document. These point to 9:1 as unnecessary duplication, since Paul had already been dealing with this matter in ch 8. It appears that Paul is taking up a new subject. But a close examination of the contents of vss 1-2 shows that what he is dealing with here is their readiness to contribute to the collection. He is not taking up a new subject; he is trying to show that he had boasted about their readiness and their zeal, and he does not want them to let him down. He is saying that because of their readiness he doesn't need to write to them about the collection.

Some see chs 10-13 as a separate letter. They suppose that its introduction has been lost and only later was it added to chs 1-9 to make our present 2 Corinthians. They feel that the change of tone is so great from the preceding section that it is psychologically improbable that it could have been written at the same time. However, the first section of the epistle is dealing with the church in general, while the last section is dealing specifically with his adversaries. The first section is Paul's response to the good news brought to him by Titus of the Corinthians' reconciliation to him. The last section deals with Paul's severe reaction to a new crisis brought on by outsiders, "the false apostles."

[handwritten margin notes: 1st part: church problems; 2nd part: Paul's opponents]

As indicated above, some feel that 2 Cor 10-13 was written after 1-9, and others before it, equating it with the stern letter. The latter suggestion is not generally accepted, because it does not refer to a single offender, and his punishment, to which Paul alludes, was included in this letter. Also, 12:17-18 refers back to 1-9. Supporters of this view also point to the fact that in 1:23-2:4 Paul is not ready to visit them, while in 13:1 he is ready.

THE MESSAGE
Outline

Survey of contents

There are basically three parts to this letter. The first part is a defense of Paul's actions; the second, an appeal for generosity toward the Jerusalem saints, and the third is an attack upon his adversaries in the church. His intent in this letter is, if possible, to win back the Corinthians to their original affection toward him and his message. The letter is charged with emotion and is characterized by digressions and, therefore, is not a systematic, logical presentation of themes. However, several important topics are discussed as he digresses and moves on toward his conclusion.

God is a God of comfort. He allows afflictions to come upon us, but he is always there to bring comfort. "We are afflicted in every way, but not crushed; perplexed, but not driven to despair; persecuted, but not forsaken; struck down, but not destroyed ..." (4:8-9). Also, affliction is slight and momentary compared to the "eternal weight of glory beyond all comparison" (4:17).

If such a one as Paul was misunderstood in spite of his sincerity and earnestness, it is possible for any of us to have the same experience. Nevertheless, Paul wished to be open and transparent in his ministry. He wished to be a fragrance of the knowledge of Jesus Christ, his aroma of life. He wished to be a treasure in an earthen vessel for the Lord. He wanted to be a minister of reconciliation, an ambassador of Christ, for Christ became sin for us that we might become the righteousness of God. He referred to the law as a dispensation of death and condemnation, and the new covenant ministry as the dispensation of the Spirit and of righteousness. The law in itself can only bring death and condemnation, but through Christ we can be freed from its condemnation and receive righteousness.

Paul also dealt with giving. Christians are sensitive about this area, and yet it is an important test of our Christianity. Christ spoke quite often about money, because it is a tangible evidence of our loyalty and dedication. In encouraging the Corinthians to give, Paul wrote the beautiful verse, "For you know the grace of our Lord Jesus Christ, that though he was rich, yet for your sake he became poor, so that by his poverty you might become rich" (8:9). He also pointed to the principle of reciprocity in sharing one's blessings (8:14). He encouraged also cheerful and generous giving (9:6-7), always reminding them of what God gave us in his "inexpressible gift!" (9:15).

Paul was loathe to boast, but the situation was such that he was forced to as he compared himself to these "superlative apostles." He wanted to show throughout that he had only their best interests in mind and not any selfish advantage.

RELEVANCE FOR TODAY

One cannot expect that such a personal letter would have as much relevance to us as did 1 Corinthians, a more practical letter. And yet there are values for us in this letter.

It points out clearly the importance of a ministry that is open and transparent, sincere and earnest, a ministry that does not need the help of underhanded or cunning ways. It also shows the danger of congregations being easily swayed by those who have ulterior motives rather than true Christian concern.

It shows the continuing importance, privilege, and responsibility of those who serve as ministers of reconciliation and ambassadors of God. These are the fragrance and aroma of God which can lead to death or life. These bear treasures in earthen vessels and must constantly recognize that they are but earthen vessels.

It points up the reality of afflictions in a Christian's life, but with the reality of God's presence and comfort. It puts afflictions in perspective as something slight and momentary over against the eternal weight of glory.

It also reveals the principles and motivations for giving and sharing of our blessings with others. What Christ did must serve as motivation, and there should be mutuality and reciprocity in helping one another.

ISSUES FOR DISCUSSION AND REFLECTION

1. Is there anything that we can do to remove all misunderstandings between people? Is some misunderstanding inevitable?
2. How does God bring comfort to us in our affliction? How can we keep from going under, being crushed, driven to despair, feeling forsaken?
3. What is the difference between the dispensation of death and the dispensation of righteousness? Is this to be equated to Old Testament times versus New Testament times? How would you explain this division?
4. Are appeals for giving out of place in a church or for Christians? Are all appeals good? How would you determine how to do this and what would be appropriate?
5. How do you reconcile Paul's call for love (1 Cor 13) with his remarks towards his adversaries in chs 10-13?

FURTHER READING
Barrett, Charles K.
  1974   *The Second Epistle to the Corinthians.* (Harper). San Francisco:
          Harper & Row.
Best, Ernest
  1987   *Second Corinthians.* (Interpretation). Philadelphia: Westminster.
Furnish, Victor
  1984   *Corinthians II.* (Anchor). New York: Doubleday.
Tasker, Randolph V.G.
  1958   *The Second Epistle of Paul to the Corinthians.* (Tyndale). Grand
          Rapids, MI: Eerdmans.

Chapter 10

Galatians

Bruce C. Johanson

> "There is no longer Jew or Greek, there is no longer slave or free, there is
> no longer male and female; for all of you are one in Christ Jesus."

BRIEF OVERVIEW OF THE BOOK

Galatians addresses a situation in which some persons had unsettled churches previously established by Paul in Galatia. They appear to have insisted that the gospel included the necessity of practicing Jewish rituals of the law. A concern for Gentile Christians to be circumcised appears to have been the primary issue. In opposition to this Paul vehemently contends that salvation is by grace through faith alone in Jesus Christ and not by any legal observances which he calls "works of the law." Grace brings freedom, but Christians must not allow this freedom to turn into a license for sin. They are called instead to the servantship of love, behavior that manifests the fruits of the Spirit in reciprocal love and care.

BACKGROUND CONCERNS

Before we can discuss who the possible addressees of the letter were, we need to take a brief look at the historical background of Galatia. During the first Millennium B.C.E., the Celts migrated out of the Danube River area of central Europe into northern Italy, Gaul and Britain. Around 281 B.C.E. they also moved down through Thrace, Macedonia, Thessaly and on into Asia Minor. They finally settled around Ancyra (modern Ankara). In 232 B.C.E. several battles kept them from overrunning the rest of Asia Minor and contained them in what became known as Galatia in north-central Asia Minor. All this helps explain why *Celts*, *Gauls* and *Galatians* were different terms used interchangeably in their Greek and Latin equivalents to designate the same ethnic group of people.

In 189 B.C.E. Galatia succumbed to Roman authority and subsequently became allies of Rome. In 166 B.C.E. they were granted independence as a kingdom. To reward their loyalty and support, various parts of neighboring areas were added to their kingdom. Finally in 25 B.C.E. after the death of the Galatian king Amyntas the kingdom was reorganized as the Roman *Provincia Galatia.* It reached from Pontus in the north to Pamphylia in the south and over a period of time came to include parts of Isauria, Lycaonia, Pamphylia, Paphlagonia, Phrygia, Pisidia and Pontus.

According to Acts, Paul established churches on his first missionary journey in the south-central part of Asia Minor which included Pisidia and Lycaonia, both in the Roman Province of Galatia (Acts 13:14-14:23). As for his second and third missionary journeys, it is probable that the references to "Phrygia and Galatia" in Acts 16:6 and 18:23 are ethnic names rather than provincial ones for areas in which he ministered. Thus, in Acts "Galatia" would more naturally refer to north Galatia where the ethnic Galatians were located.

The question has been raised as to whether Paul was writing to the ethnic Galatians in the north or to the people in the south who were not ethnic Galatians but who could be addressed as Galatians, since they belonged to Galatia as a Roman province. Suggested answers to this question have usually been closely tied to views of when and where the letter was written.

It has been traditionally suggested that Galatians was written just prior to the writing of Romans at the end of the third missionary journey. Two reasons are offered:

1. There are many topics, arguments and verbal expressions in Galatians that have close parallels and a more detailed development in Romans.
2. The combative tone and the kind of opponents found in Galatians are also reflected in 2 Corinthians, which was probably written just prior to Romans.

These connections would suggest an approximate date for Galatians between 54 and 58 C.E. somewhere in Greece or western Asia Minor at the end of the third missionary journey. This view typically takes "Galatians" (Gal 1:2; 3:1) to refer to the ethnic Galatians in north-central Asia Minor, since that was the part where Paul had been most recently.

On the other hand, towards the end of the nineteenth century W.M. Ramsay argued that when Paul uses "Galatians" it refers to the citizens of the Roman Province of Galatia which included more than ethnic Galatia.[1] The following are some of his more important arguments:

1. The status of a non-Roman citizen was that of a "provincial" whose relation to the Roman Empire was designated by province rather than by ethnic or national origin. Since slaves, enemies and foreigners were all lumped together in Roman eyes, a sensitive orator would address an audience in

southern Galatia either as *Galatae* or as *Coloni* rather than as Phrygians or Lycaonians, especially if any Roman citizens were in the audience.[2]

2. He also argued that Paul, as a Roman citizen, never uses wide geographical designations except for those of Roman provinces, whereas Luke, as an educated Greek, would tend to refer to ethnic groups within a province (e.g. Acts 14:6) or to use loose designations like "the Phrygian and Galatian region" (e.g. Acts 16:6; see NEB).[3]

If this is so, it allows for the possibility of Galatians being the earliest of Paul's letters that we have. It could have been written shortly after his first missionary journey, possibly from Antioch, sometime between 47-49 C.E. before the Jerusalem Council of Acts 15. Such a view usually correlates the Jerusalem visit in Gal 2:1-10 with the one in Acts 11:27-30 rather than Acts 15.

For the most part some form of the North Galatian theory has been the generally preferred view, although there is some recent support for the South Galatian theory.[4] Part of the puzzle has to do with the question of whether the Jerusalem visit referred to in Gal 2:1-10 corresponds to the visit in Acts 11 or to the one in Acts 15. The North Galatian theory places the letter long after the Jerusalem council of Acts 15. An objection frequently raised against it is Paul's silence in Galatians about the decisions of that council which freed Gentile Christians from practicing circumcision, a major issue in this letter. The South Galatian theory solves this by placing the letter prior to the Acts 15 visit.

By way of critique, even if Paul prefers to use Roman provincial designations, this certainly does not exclude North Galatia and prove South Galatia to be the destination of the letter. Furthermore, presupposing that Acts 15 represents the same Jerusalem Council as Gal 2:1-10, a reasonable explanation for his silence about the Council's decision on Gentile freedom from circumcision can be made.

1. It is fairly clear from Galatians that Paul was at pains to claim validity for his own apostolic status and authority apart from apostolic authority in Jerusalem (see Gal 1:1, 11-12, 15-17; 2:6-10). An appeal to the Council's decision would have weakened such a claim.

2. Also, what happened in Antioch after the Council according to Gal 2:11-14 must have made the intentions and the integrity of the Council's decision highly suspect. Paul reports that the faction insisting on circumcision came "from James" to Antioch and caused a serious breakdown in table fellowship between Jewish and Gentile Christians there. Thus, it is understandable if he should not appeal to the Jerusalem Council of Acts 15.

On the face of it, the noticeable similarities to 2 Corinthians and Romans make the later date for Galatians more attractive. Furthermore, if one subscribes to this, there really is nothing to *prove* that Paul could not have sent this letter to churches he had established in both northern and southern Galatia.

Finally, the letter's rhetorical complexity raises a question about the social composition of Paul's addressees. Since he typically established churches in cities, one can expect that whatever the predominant percentage of more-or-less educated recipients, there would have been enough acquaintance with Greco-Roman oratory by all to allow for an adequate comprehension of the letter's rhetoric when it was read to a particular church. After all, marketplace oratory was a fairly common phenomenon in that part of the world. Also, there were probably at least some persons sufficiently acquainted with the Greek Old Testament (the Septuagint) to be able to appreciate the scriptural arguments and to explain them to others who did not understand.

note Greco-Roman oratory + appeal to LXX for argument

HISTORICAL CONSIDERATIONS

Galatians 1-2 is our next most important source after Acts for reconstructing the history of the earliest church. For the period covered in Gal 1-2 it is actually the most important source, since Paul himself gives the information, whereas Luke presents it second hand. Galatians mentions two visits to Jerusalem, the first one three years after Paul's conversion (Gal 1:18-24) and the second one fourteen years later (Gal 2:1-10). Paul does not make it clear, but it is possible that the fourteen years is also reckoned from his conversion and so includes the three years already mentioned. As for Acts, five visits to Jerusalem are fairly clearly recorded: 9:26-30 (after Paul's conversion); 11:27-30 (with famine relief from Antioch); 15:1-29 (the Jerusalem council on the circumcision controversy); 18:22 (a hasty visit between the second and third missionary journeys); 21:15-17 (with the offering from the Gentile churches).

Gal. 2 Jerusalem visits

Acts: 5 visits to Jerusalem

A quick comparison indicates that there are enough similarities to make a connection between Gal 1:18-24 and Acts 9:26-30 as both recording the first Jerusalem visit by Paul after his conversion. Also, Gal 2:1-10 and Acts 15:1-29 both appear to record the Jerusalem council about the problem of Gentile circumcision.

A closer look reveals the following similarities and differences. As for the first visit, both record it as taking place after Paul's conversion. Both mention that he met apostles. Both mention that he journeyed from there to Cilicia ("Tarsus," mentioned in Acts 9:30, is in Cilicia). So much for the similarities. As for the differences, Luke states that Paul "went in and out among them in Jerusalem, speaking boldly in the name of the Lord" (Acts 9:28). He goes on to say that Paul's disputes with the Hellenists endangered his life, which was the reason he was shipped off to Tarsus. By contrast, in Gal 1:18-20 Paul insists on not having seen any of the apostles except for Peter and James during a short fifteen day visit. He also states that he was unknown by sight to the churches of Judea (1:22).

Gal. 1:18-24 + Acts 9:26-30

Gal 2.1-10
+
Acts 15,1-29

As for the next visit, Gal 2:1-10 and Acts 15:1-29 appear to refer to the same event. Both record that the question of circumcision for Gentile Christians was a major issue at stake. Both mention common participants, namely Paul and Barnabas, Peter and James. Both mention that Gentiles were not required to be circumcised. However, there are some problematic differences. The most significant difference is that the Acts 15 account records a very public meeting, whereas Gal 2:2 states that it was a private meeting between Paul, Barnabas and Titus and the "acknowledged leaders" (2:6) who turn out to be Peter, James and John (2:9). Also, Galatians does not mention the letter of reduced Jewish regulations required of Gentile Christians, and Acts does not mention the subsequent confrontation in Antioch when the "circumcision faction" from James scare Peter and even Barnabas into breaking table fellowship with Gentile Christians (Gal 2:11-14).

Such differences have led some to regard the Gal 2:1-10 event as having taken place during the famine visit recorded in Acts 11:27-30. A connection is seen between Agabus' prediction of a famine, which motivated Paul and Barnabas' visit with aid (Acts 11:28),[5] and Paul's mention of his visit as being "in response to a revelation" (Gal 2:2). This is possible, but a caution is in order. *Acts a* Many try to solve such problems in a way that seems to presume that we have *later* *all* the relevant facts in Acts. Whatever view one comes to prefer, it must be *account* remembered that Acts is not a comprehensive account of the history of the early church, but a selective one. Also, it is important to remember that Paul's letter was to and for insiders, while Acts was most likely written for outsiders. That usually has an impact on what an author chooses to include or leave out. *Paul* However one compares the accounts in Acts and Galatians, Paul provides a *shows* picture of a much sharper conflict than Acts does over how Jewish Christians *sharp* wanted to apply Torah to Gentile Christians. *conflict*

LITERARY CONSIDERATIONS

Recent debates over the literary structure of Galatians have not achieved much consensus. Older commentaries tended to divide Galatians into three parts: chs 1-2 as mostly narrative, covering personal matters; chs 3-4 as mostly argumentative, covering doctrinal matters; and chs 5-6 as mostly hortatory or admonishing, covering practical matters.[6] This is a fair assessment as far as it goes, but it rests on too high a level of generality to be useful in showing how these sections work together to achieve Paul's communicative purposes. Also, while it is true that chs 5-6 are mostly hortatory, the use of "mostly" hides the fact that exhortation is already strongly signalled at 4:12 and "practical matters" really only start at 5:13. Because of this commentators differ widely as to where they see the exhortation section starting.

THE MESSAGE
Outline
The following outline indicates that what starts in 4:12 is an appeal to adhere to Paul's version of the gospel which he has argued in what precedes. The specifically ethical exhortation starts at 5:13 (see the section on Galatians in the ch 4).

Survey of contents
In the opening prescript (1:1-5) Paul significantly expands what was typically a brief identification of the sender and recipient followed by a greeting. Paul already defends his apostleship as having not human but divine origin. Also, the greeting is expanded theologically by a brief statement of Christ's atonement for sins and deliverance from the "present evil age." Here already Paul signals what he is going to address, namely his authority and the gospel he preached.

When we compare the opening of letter body with Paul's other letters, the most striking difference is that there is neither thanksgiving-prayer report nor blessing section (see, e.g., 1 Cor 1:4-9 and 2 Cor 1:3-7). Instead we have a rebuke formula introducing a section of ironical censure (1:6-10). It signals the highly argumentative and anguished tone of the whole letter. Here he expresses surprise that they were turning to a different gospel and places all under a curse who preach a gospel different from the one he preached to the Galatian churches.

At the end of Galatians Paul adds a subscript (6:11-17), or postscript as some call it. In 2 Thess 3:17 a similar subscript serves merely to authenticate Paul as the sender. In Gal 6:11-17 it does this plus summarizes the main issue of the letter, namely the question of circumcision for Gentile believers. The shift to "large letters" noted in 6:11 probably indicates a change from a secretary's handwriting to Paul's larger style. (Does "large letters" indicate that he had poor eyesight?!) It is also notable that Paul sends no greetings at the end as he commonly does in his other letters. Perhaps the combative tone of the letter also explains this difference.

When we look at the rest of the letter, we find that in 1:11-2:14 the text type is predominantly narrative. However, the narration of Paul's conversion onwards to his confrontation with Peter in Antioch is not given primarily to inform his readers of such events. It has instead the argumentative purpose of establishing his personal integrity and apostolic authority apart from the Jerusalem apostles. This theme and purpose is explicitly expressed in 1:11-12. He starts by showing that even as a Jew before conversion he possessed superior integrity and zeal (1:13-14). After God's call it was three years before he met any of the apostles, and then it was only Peter and James that he visited for the short period of fifteen days (1:15-19). When he meets them again in Jerusalem it is by revelation, i.e. not human command (2:2). They discussed Gentile freedom from circumcision (2:1-10) and the Jerusalem apostles "contributed nothing" to him (2:6) but rather supported his mission to the Gentiles. Then again in Antioch, when threatened by the circumcision faction that came from James, it was Peter, one of the pillars (2:9) who buckled under the pressure to break from table fellowship with Gentile Christians. All of this is aimed at persuading the addressees' minds about Paul's integrity and apostolic authority.

Paul's public rebuke to Peter in 2:14 sets the stage for the next section which shifts to what is primarily theological argumentation in 2:15-4:11. Some see 2:15-21 as the speech addressed to Peter and, as such, the conclusion to the first section. However, the emphatically repeated statements in 2:15-16 that justification is "by faith" and not "by the works of the law" actually provides the theme and the thesis of the argumentation that continues to 4:11. In the rest of 2:15-21 Paul counters a view that regards Christ as an agent of sin when those seeking justification by faith are still found to be sinners (2:17). But, we should ask, "sinners" in what sense? For Paul, the real transgressor is the one who reverts back to law as a basis of justification (2:18). The law brings death, but Christ brings life through his death when we share in that death (2:19-20). The conclusion is that justification by law empties Christ's death of its purpose (2:21).

This theological argument is followed in 3:1-5 by an appeal to the Galatians' experience, namely that they received the Spirit by faith, not by any legal observance. In 3:6-9 he uses Scripture to prove that Abraham's real descendants who share his blessing are those who have faith like he did. In 3:10-14 he again uses Scripture to prove that the law places all under a curse which only Christ can remove by his death, so that Abraham's blessing and the promised Spirit are received by faith. Curse and blessing are characteristic features of the Old

Testament covenant concept. This makes the transition to the topic of covenant in 3:15-18 a natural one. Paul plays with the term *diatheke* which can mean both a human "will" as well as "covenant." On the analogy of a human "will" being irrevocable once it has been ratified, he argues that the promise made in God's covenant with Abraham is not revoked by the law of the Sinai covenant that came four hundred and thirty years later.

If the promise to Abraham takes precedence over the Mosaic law, then why the law? Paul answers this in 3:19-24 by indicating that the law had a custodial function until Christ should come. With Christ's coming faith in him dissolves distinctions of status, race and sex so that all become children of God, Abraham's seed and heirs by promise (3:25-29).

In 4:1-7 he goes on to develop the concept of sonship in terms of adoption through the redemption of Jesus Christ from bondage under the "rudiments of the world" (margin). This is a hard phrase to interpret, since one has to decide what kind of "rudiments" Paul has in mind. In the context it seems to refer to the law. Then in 4:8-11 he turns to the Gentile Galatians and describes their former bondage to "beings that by nature are not gods." He refers to their turning back in such a way that an analogy is implied between the "elementals" (their former gods, 4:8-9) and the "elementals" in 4:3 which appear to refer to the law. Paul is probably trying to shock them into the realization that going back to "works of the law" is virtually the same as returning to their former paganism.

So far, Paul has tried to persuade the Galatians' minds about his personal credibility (1:11-2:14) and the credibility of his gospel (2:15-4:11). Now in 4:12-5:12 he appeals to their will, to a decision to adhere to his gospel and the community of faith it fosters: "Friends, I beg you, become as I am" (4:12). This change of purpose is partly signalled by the letter's only explicit expressions of the author's will ("I beseech you," 4:12; "I wish," 4:20; 5:12) and the first appearance of imperative verbs (4:12, 21; 5:1). In 4:12-20 Paul appeals to them on the basis of their shared experience when he first brought the gospel to them. Notice the repeated references to "I" and "you." Then in 4:21-5:1 he interprets the two sons of Abraham, Isaac and Ishmael and their respective mothers, in an allegorical manner. The result is that Hagar and Ishmael belong to slavery and Sinai, whereas Sarah and Isaac belong to freedom by promise and to the Jerusalem above. The Galatians are then exhorted to adhere to the free children of promise. Then in 5:2 Paul spells out that the practice of circumcision actually would cut them off from Christ. He severely attacks whoever is troubling them and ends with the somewhat earthy, if not macabre, wish that those who were so eager about circumcision would get carried away and emasculate themselves!

In 5:13-6:10 imperative verbs continue to occur, only now they are used in moral exhortation. The concentration of moral contents is also highlighted by the reciprocal expression "one another" which occurs five times and only in this passage (5:13, 15, 26). Paul has previously urged the Galatians to stand fast in the freedom that Christ provides (5:1). Now he needs to spell out that this freedom is not license to serve the flesh. Paradoxically it is the freedom of loving servantship to "one another" (5:13-15). It is freedom which lives out of the Spirit that wars against the flesh. The "flesh" here designates the power of sin in a person and not just sexual lust, as the list of the works of the flesh illustrates. Those led by the Spirit are not under the law (5:18), for the Spirit bears all kinds of good fruit (5:22-23). Belonging to Christ puts the flesh to death (5:24-26). Finally, after a series of short admonitions (6:1-6), Paul warns that one reaps what one sows, corruption from the flesh, but eternal life from the Spirit, and concludes with an encouragement not to lose heart but do good to all, especially to fellow believers.

We have already mentioned the subscript (6:11-17). Paul's concluding summary in his own writing indicates that circumcision was the primary issue. He seems to think that the motivation for insisting on it was escape from persecution. It must have been hard for Jewish Christians caught between Gentile freedom and Jewish demands for purity. They most likely still felt a part of their Jewish brethren with whom many of them continued to worship in synagogues. However, their insistence on Gentile circumcision involved a legalism that jeopardized the message of grace, the heart of the gospel. Paul ends on an ironical note. If outward physical marks were important, he had the really important ones! He bore "the marks of Christ," a possible reference to the scars of numerous beatings endured for the sake of his gospel mission, one last proof of his personal integrity.

RELEVANCE FOR TODAY

Galatians powerfully maintains the unequivocal primacy and sufficiency of God's grace in Jesus Christ in the gospel of salvation. All "works of the law" used to claim a unique status in establishing a right relationship with God are excluded by grace. While this is applied in the context of Jewish and Gentile relations by Paul, in principle it applies to all who presume to claim an exclusive and unique relation to God based on anything they have accomplished themselves. Since grace is the universal basis of salvation, those who accept it by faith have all become one in Jesus Christ. They can no longer live in support of social, economic, ethnic and sexist prejudices and bigotry. In Paul's day such discrimination focused on Jew and Greek, slave and free, male and female. Today some of the names and circumstances may be different, but the categories remain much the same. Grace brings freedom, but it is the paradoxical freedom of love that calls us to serve one another. Such behavior cannot be motivated by commandments and rules, but grows as fruits of the Spirit. Indeed, the Spirit is the dynamic of the new life of true freedom in Christ. This powerful defense of Christian freedom has made Galatians a special source of inspiration whenever the church has subsequently become aware of and has had to deal with various forms of legalism and discrimination both within the community of faith as well as in the world at large.

ISSUES FOR DISCUSSION AND REFLECTION

1. Is it overly brash of Paul to suggest that even an angel who preached a gospel different than his gospel should be cursed? What do you think makes him so sure?
2. Compare the Jerusalem visits in Gal 1 and 2 with the visits in Acts 9, 11 and 15. Would you connect Gal 2:1-10 with Acts 11:27-30 or with Acts 15:1-29? Explain why.
3. How would you explain the significant differences in the accounts of Paul's first Jerusalem visit in Gal 1 and Acts 9? What do such differences say about how we should view the way revelation and inspiration work in Scripture?
4. Why do you think Paul refused to circumcise Titus (Gal 2:3) when, according to Acts 16:1-5, he circumcised Timothy?
5. Evaluate the dispute between Paul and Peter in Gal 2:11-14. Can anything be said in Peter's favor? What implications does this incident have for contemporary problems of segregation within the church or for diversity in mission outreach?
6. Are there issues in the church today that you would consider comparable to the issue of circumcision in Paul's day?
7. What sort of reasoning does Paul use to make Abraham's "seed" ("offspring" [RSV]) refer specifically to Jesus Christ in 3:16? Would you be able to use this type of interpretation to convince a modern person today? What made it possible for Paul to reason like that back then?
8. Look at several modern translations and commentaries to see how they translate "elementals of the universe" in 4:3. What are the most viable options in view of the context and how Paul uses the same expression in 4:9?
9. Compare and contrast the Spirit-led life and the life of the flesh as described in 5:16-26. What does Paul mean by the term "flesh"?

FURTHER READING

Betz, Hans D.
1979   *Galatians: A Commentary on Paul's Letter to the Churches in Galatia.* (Hermeneia). Philadelphia: Fortress.

Lightfoot, Joseph B.
1880   *St Paul's Epistle to the Galatians*. London: Macmillan.
Longenecker, Richard N.
1990   *Galatians*. (Word). Dallas: Word.
Lührmann, Dieter
1992   *Galatians: A Continental Commentary*. Trans. by O.C. Dean, Jr. Minneapolis: Fortress.
Ramsay, William M.
1899   *A Historical Commentary on St. Paul's Epistle to the Galatians*. London: Hodder & Stoughton.

ENDNOTES

1. W.M. Ramsay, *A Historical Commentary on St. Paul's Epistle to the Galatians*. London: Hodder & Stoughton, 1899, 84.

2. Ramsay, *Galatians*, 119-120.

3. Ramsay, *Galatians*, 314-16.

4. For an extensive discussion with good summaries see R.N. Longenecker, *Galatians*. (Word) Vol. 41. Dallas: Word, lxii-lxxii.

5. Josephus (*Ant.* iii. 15. 3; xx. 2. 5) refers to a famine in Judea which we can date to around 44-48 C.E. during the procuratorships of Cuspius Fadus and Tiberius Alexander. He writes that Queen Helena of Adiabene purchased corn and figs for distribution in Jerusalem during this famine. It may be the same famine recorded here in Acts.

6. See, e.g., J.B. Lightfoot, *St Paul's Epistle to the Galatians*. London: Macmillan, 1880, 65-67.

Chapter 11

Romans

John C. Brunt

> *"For I am not ashamed of the gospel; it is the power of God for salvation*
> *to everyone who has faith, to the Jew first and also to the Greek."*

a love theol. argument, not personal expression of concern

BRIEF OVERVIEW OF THE BOOK

Romans is not only Paul's longest letter, it is also different from most of the rest. Paul usually writes to churches that he has founded or known well and addresses specific problems. Paul had never been to Rome, however, and this letter contains the longest theological argument to be found in his writings. In it he sets forth the great themes of God's grace for all people, both Jew and Gentile, and of salvation through faith in Christ. And yet even this most theological of Paul's letters also puts us in touch with Paul the pastor, and at the end of the letter Paul speaks to specific problems concerning how Christians with different views and practices relate to each other. This letter is Paul's theological masterpiece, but it is nevertheless personal and pastoral as well.

BACKGROUND CONCERNS

No one doubts that Paul is the author of Romans. If Paul wrote anything, he wrote Romans. There is also general agreement on the time and place of writing. When, according to Acts, Paul was on what we call his third missionary journey, he decided that he would leave Ephesus, go to Macedonia, then on to Achaia (Greece), then to Jerusalem, and finally to Rome (Acts 19:21). He then went to Macedonia and spent three months in Greece (Acts 20:1-3).

This scenario fits well with what we find in Rom 15:25-26. There Paul tells us that he has just been to Macedonia and Achaia, where believers in both places have made contributions for the poor in Jerusalem. Now he plans to go on to Jerusalem, then to Rome, and finally to Spain (Rom 15:23-24). All this leads to the logical conclusion that Paul writes from Greece on his third missionary

[handwritten margin note: just before departure to Jerusalem from Corinth]

journey, just before his departure to Jerusalem. The date would be sometime in the late fifties of the common era.

The presence of several names in Rom 16 that are associated with Corinth or its suburb Cenchrea (but see the literary considerations section below) suggests Paul probably wrote from Corinth.

We do not know how Christianity initially entered Rome, although there is evidence that it was already there several years before Paul wrote this letter. The Roman historian Suetonius (ca. 100 C.E.) tells us that around the year 49 C.E. the emperor Claudius expelled Jews from Rome because of continuous disturbances at the instigation of one named Chrestus (*The Twelve Caesars*, "Claudius," 25). Chrestus is the Roman spelling for Christ, and this statement may well mean that the disturbances were between Christian Jews and opposing non-Christian Jews. This would place the arrival of Christianity in Rome at least by the late forties, and perhaps before.

LITERARY CONSIDERATIONS

The major literary question concerning Romans is the issue of the unity of the letter. Many scholars have suggested that the last chapter, Rom 16, is not part of the original letter as it was written to the Romans, but was either a separate letter of greetings sent to another congregation or was attached to a copy of Romans Paul sent to another congregation.

There are various theories, but the most popular is that Paul sent a copy of his letter to Rome to the Ephesian church as well, and this list of greetings was attached to that copy. Those who argue for this position point to the number of names, twenty-six in all, and question whether Paul could have known so many people in a church he had never visited. They also point out that many of the names were commonly used for slaves or former slaves, and they doubt that these people would have been sufficiently mobile for Paul to have known them in the east and then for them to have moved to Rome. They look specifically at names like Priscilla and Aquila, who, according to Acts 18, Paul had last met in Corinth, and Epenetus, who was the first convert in Asia (perhaps Ephesus), and conclude that these people would probably not have been in Rome.

Another line of evidence has to do with the various early manuscripts of the New Testament. Although most of the early manuscripts look like our versions, with Rom 16:25-27 as the conclusion to the letter, there are some manuscripts that place this final benediction at the end of Rom 14 as well, and the very oldest we have places it at the end of Rom 15, suggesting that perhaps the letter ended there, although it does go on to include ch 16 as well.

These are not compelling reasons, however, for assuming that Paul did not write these greetings as the conclusion of his letter to the Roman church and that the sixteen chapters as we have them do not form a unified composition. First, if Paul was writing to a church that he had never visited, it would have served his purpose to make every possible personal connection with the church there to establish rapport. And since all roads really did lead to Rome in the first century, it is not hard to believe that Paul would have known a number of the believers there. Paul himself is evidence of the mobility of the first century Greco-Roman population. And since Priscilla and Aquila, according to Acts 18:2, were among those forced to leave Rome by Claudius, it is not surprising that they would have returned to Rome after Nero lifted the ban. Second, the textual evidence is varied and does not give clear evidence for a break between chs 15 and 16. This leaves the assumption against unity with little support other than speculation.

Another literary issue concerns the relationship of the various sections of Romans to each other. The letter is easily divided into three sections: chs 1-8, 9-11, and 12-16. The first addresses the theological message of grace, the second the relationship between Jew and Gentile and God's continuing purpose for the Jews, and the third ethical and practical issues. How are these three related? Some see the first section as the central meat of Romans, with the last two added as almost appendices, somewhat detached from the first part. Others view the middle section as Paul's driving motive in writing the letter, and still others argue that the whole letter leads up to the final section.

When we look at links between different parts of the letter we find good evidence that all three sections are tied together in a coherent way. For example, in Rom 14 and 15 Paul addresses a problem between the weak and the strong Christians. The weak are more strict in observing certain days and eating only vegetables, whereas the strong have less strict practices on these matters (14:2-5). But already in ch 4 Paul begins using the language of weak and strong with reference to Abraham, who was not "weak in faith" (4:19).

Another example is seen in Paul's emphasis on not judging other Christians whose practices differ (14:10-13). Paul had already introduced the subject of judging in ch 2 (2:1-3). These and many other links suggest that the various parts of the letter form a coherent whole. The basic argument does not end in ch 8 but flows throughout the letter.

We can understand this best by working backward through the letter. In Rom 14 and 15 Paul speaks to the lack of unity in the Roman church and tries to bring the believers together into unity in Christ in preparation for his visit to them and his hoped-for participation with them in ministry to new worlds such as Spain.

Probably at least part of this disunity involved suspicions and debates between Jew and Gentile. Therefore it was important for Paul to discuss God's purpose for both within His plan of salvation. Romans 9-11 does just that. Here Paul shows that God's ultimate purpose is to save both Jew and Gentile. He also advises each as to how they should treat each other. This helps prepare the way for Paul's final advice about unity.

Paul knew, however, that the only real basis for unity in Christ is the realization that we are all sinners and that we all share the same basis for the hope of salvation—the grace revealed in Jesus Christ. Therefore he spent the first eight chapters laying the vital foundation of salvation in Christ.

This view holds that the whole letter of Romans forms a coherent argument. The letter is not a theological treatise with some attached appendices of generalized advice, as some hold. Nor is it three separate sections, virtually independent of each other, as others suggest. Rather it is a truly pastoral letter written to speak to the actual circumstances of the church at Rome.

At the same time, the letter certainly is theological. Paul was the kind of pastor who believed that good theology is relevant for how we live. The theological and the practical went together for him. Romans is therefore a theologically profound pastoral letter that bases Christian unity in God's grace for all people and applies this message to specific issues that threatened to divide Christians in Rome.

THE MESSAGE
Outline
Romans may be outlined as follows:

Survey of contents

Here we can review only a few of the major themes that emerge from a reading of Romans.

Unity in Christ and salvation for all. One of the most important theological terms in Romans is the simple term "all." With this term Paul obliterates the distinctions that build barriers between human beings and keep them from enjoying unity in Christ. With this term Paul puts all Christians in the same boat. All have sinned (3:23). All will stand before the judgment of Christ (14:10). All human beings stand under the wrath of sin with no claim they can make on salvation and nothing they could ever do to save themselves. Paul makes this universal condition of sin absolutely clear in the first three chapters of the letter.

But he does this only to pave the way for what follows. The universal need of humans leads to God's universal solution. Through Jesus Christ, God provides for the salvation of **all**. The good news of the gospel is the power for salvation to **all** who believe (1:16). God gave Jesus up for us **all** (8:32). Abraham is the father of **all** (4:11). God's goal is to have mercy on **all** (11:32). It doesn't matter whether a person is Jew or Gentile, God's saving action is for **all**. This theme accounts for Paul's emphasis on Jew and Gentile throughout the letter.

Yet for Paul the pastor this message is hardly an abstract, theoretical matter. It has all kinds of implications for life. If we are all in the same boat, sinners saved by God's grace, then we ought to be able to live in unity. So Paul advises that Christians, who have heard this universal message, should live at peace with **all** (12:18). They should be able to welcome each other (15:1).

This theme provides the basis for much practical advice in Romans, such as the counsel that Gentile Christians should not get big headed and think themselves superior to Jewish Christians (11:17-34), that the strict should not judge those who are more free, and vice versa, that those who are more free should not scorn the strict (14:1-5).

Thus we see that with this theme, as with so many others that he emphasizes, theological conviction and pastoral concern go hand in hand for Paul. The universality of God's provision for salvation calls us to recognize and act on our unity with all other Christians.

The free gift of grace. This theme is closely connected with the former. The universal provision for salvation comes to humans through God's initiative of grace. Paul uses this term "grace" twenty-two times in this letter. It refers to God's free acceptance of human beings apart from any human achievement.

Paul proclaims that God's grace is a gift (3:24) which brings believers justification or righteousness (5:16) and eternal life (5:21). Although it rules out all works or achievements as the basis for human salvation (11:6), it is not a license for irresponsible action (6:1, 15). It becomes the atmosphere in which Christians now stand (5:2) that allows them to live in peace with God and to have hope. No other term does a better job of capturing Paul's core conviction that Christians' only hope and ground for salvation is God's loving initiative to save them apart from any achievement of their own.

The obedience of faith. For Paul, the appropriate human response to God's initiative of grace is faith. Although the verbal form of this term Paul uses is often translated "believe," the term is much richer than that. Faith is a trusting commitment to God, a willingness to take him at his word and trust him for salvation.

Paul brackets the entire message of Romans with the interesting phrase, "the obedience of faith." Right at the beginning in 1:5 Paul says that through Jesus Christ he has received grace and apostleship to bring about the "obedience of faith" among all the Gentiles (or nations). He uses the phrase again at the end of the letter in the final benediction at 16:26. There he speaks of a mystery that was hidden but now has been made known, i.e. that all the nations or Gentiles should be brought to the obedience of faith.

By juxtaposing these two terms Paul is identifying them. The obedience that God wants is precisely faith. This obedience is not merely adherence to a set of rules. It is the total, personal commitment to God. The obedience God is looking for is faith. Paul feels so strongly about this that he dares to assert that whatever does not spring from faith, this total, trusting commitment to God, is sin (14:23). It is the only appropriate human attitude, and it is this attitude of faith that motivates responsible human action. This faith excludes all human boasting and pride (3:27). It leads Christians to lives of appreciative, appropriate service to God (12:3).

Righteousness in Christ. When Paul sets forth the thesis of his letter in 1:16, 17 he quotes from Hab 2:4, which introduces one of the most important analogies for salvation in Romans. When he says that the **righteous** will live by faith Paul is using language of the lawcourt. The terms translated "just," "justification," "justify," "righteous," and "righteousness" all come from the same root in Greek and have the scene of a judge in the background. Yet this background can be misleading, since the judge played a very different role in Paul's day than today. We think of judges as detached, objective deliberators who pass judgment. But in the first century the judge was one who became actively involved in working for the vindication of the oppressed. So to be righteous before God is not merely to be acquitted or declared not guilty, it is to be vindicated and set free.

According to Paul, we are vindicated by our trust in God's grace and therefore we enter into a new relationship with God. This new relationship changes our status, our outlook, and our direction. This is the experience of "righteousness." It is by faith from beginning to end (1:17).

In association with this theme Paul addresses the issue of law in Romans. This emphasis comes to a head in Romans seven where Paul shows that the law is holy, just, and good, even though it is powerless to save (7:11-12). It cannot provide righteousness, but that doesn't mean it is dispensable.

Paul's use of Scripture. This is not so much a theme as it is a part of Paul's method in writing this letter, but it is a method with great theological significance. Unless the reader makes continual reference to marginal notes (or has virtually memorized the Old Testament) it is easy to read and miss the fact that Paul is constantly quoting from the Old Testament. (The Old Testament, of course, was his Scripture. As Paul wrote Romans the gospels and most of the other New Testament works had not yet been written.)

Paul's use of the Old Testament is neither an accident nor a rhetorical device. He firmly believed that Christ was the fulfillment of the law and the prophets. The Scripture played an important part in an understanding of the gospel (see Rom 1:2; 3:21 and 10:4, for example).

Paul especially goes to the Old Testament when he presents a point of view that might seem controversial to his Jewish readers. Over and over again he shows that the Old Testament, if correctly understood, supports his message. It might seem strange that the Old Testament would permeate this letter so strongly when the majority of Paul's original readers were probably Gentile Christians. But Paul apparently believed that it was important for them too to have a firm grounding in Scripture as a foundation for the gospel.

RELEVANCE FOR TODAY

Romans speaks to the most basic issues of existence. It addresses universal questions of human need, God's activity in relationship to the world, and human relationships with God and other people. Even though the specific players and conflicts among them are different today, the basic issues of life are surprisingly the same.

Salvation is still found in God's grace alone, apart from any human status or achievement. And even those Christians who put their trust in God find themselves disagreeing with each other and needing to hear Paul's advice about how to live together in peace in spite of their disagreements.

Finally, in a century that has endured the holocaust, Paul's message of God's enduring love and purpose for the Jews is especially important to show that any prejudice against any of God's children, but especially against the Jews, is absolutely antithetical to the gospel. God's grace, when properly understood and embraced, leads to trust in God and love for others. This is still the essential message that women and men need to hear.

ISSUES FOR DISCUSSION AND REFLECTION

1. Why did Paul write this letter? Do you find any main purpose or driving force behind the letter?
2. What part of this letter best sums up Paul's overall purpose?
3. What major themes and terms do you find in the letter?
4. What do you learn about the Roman church and Paul's relationship to it from this letter?
5. After reading the letter, how would you define some of the key words in it such as grace, faith, and righteousness?

FURTHER STUDY

Achtemeier, Paul
    1985   *Romans*. (Interpretation). Atlanta: John Knox.
Barrett, Charles K.
    1957   *The Epistle of Paul to the Romans*. (Harpers). New York: Harper and Row.
Dodd, Charles H.
    1989   *The Epistle of Paul to the Romans*. New Haven: Yale University Press.
Donfried, Karl P., Ed.
    1991   *The Romans Debate*. Rev. and expanded ed. Peabody, MA: Hendrickson.

Dunn, James D.G.
  1989   *Romans 9-16.* (Word). Waco, TX: Word.
  1988   *Romans 1-8.* (Word). Waco, TX: Word.
Edwards, James R.
  1992   *Romans.* (New International). Peabody, MA: Hendrickson.
Kasemann, Ernst
  1980   *Commentary on Romans.* Trans. and Ed. by Geoffrey Bromiley. Grand Rapids, MI: Eerdmans.
Stuhlmacher, Peter
  1994   *Paul's Letter to the Romans: A Commentary.* Trans. by Scott J. Hafemann. Louisville: Westminster/John Knox.

Chapter 12

Philippians

John C. Brunt

"Rejoice in the Lord always; again I will say, Rejoice."

BRIEF OVERVIEW OF THE BOOK

Philippians is one of four letters (along with Colossians, Ephesians, and Philemon) known as the "prison letters." In it Paul writes from prison to one of his favorite and most supportive congregations to thank them for the support they have sent to him, let them know of his present circumstances and future plans, encourage them, and give admonitions and warnings. Clearly the dominant tone is one of warmth and gratitude as Paul thinks of and speaks to this congregation.

BACKGROUND CONCERNS

Paul's first visit to the Roman colony and major Macedonian city of Philippi was on his second missionary journey (see Acts 16). After his vision at Troas, where he heard the words "come over to Macedonia and help us" (vs 9), he traveled across the Aegean Sea to Neapolis and then on to Philippi, where he stayed "several days" (vs 12). Here he saw the conversion of both Lydia and a possessed slave girl. The latter incident sent Paul and Silas to jail, but an earthquake provided opportunity for them also to convert the jailer and his household before being escorted out of town by the officials. According to Paul (Phil 4:15-16) the Philippians had supported him after he left by sending gifts to Thessalonica (his next Macedonian stop) and other cities he visited.

Although no one questions that Paul wrote the letter to the Philippians, there are background matters about which scholars do differ. These include the place from which Paul wrote and the time of writing.

Since early times in the church's history, tradition has assumed that Paul wrote this letter during the imprisonment in Rome, about which Acts tells us in ch 28. The fact that Paul was in prison and that he speaks of the palace guard and Caesar's household supported this view. If true, the letter would have been written about 62 C.E.

Paul in Prison

Many recent scholars have questioned this tradition. They point out that terms like palace guard and Caesar's household were used loosely and could have been used in any Roman city that housed a Roman governing official. They also suggest that the trips Epaphroditus has made and the one Paul expects Epaphroditus and Timothy to make suggest a shorter distance than the 800 plus miles between Philippi and Rome. Some have proposed that Paul may have been in prison in Ephesus during his third journey and that this provides a more likely setting for Philippians. (Paul doesn't say he was imprisoned in Ephesus, but he does say in 1 Cor 15:32 that he fought wild beasts there.) If this is true, the letter would have been written around 56 C.E. There is no way to decide these issues with certainty. All we know for sure is that Paul was in prison when he wrote this letter and that it had been some time since his first visit to Philippi in 50-51 C.E.

Although the tone throughout most of this letter is warm and friendly, Paul does warn the Philippians about certain problems and people in ch 3. Who are these dangerous people? All we have to go on is what Paul says, therefore trying to find out who they are is something like trying to find out who your friend is talking to on the phone by listening to one side of the conversation. It isn't surprising that scholars have come to various conclusions. In the first part of the chapter Paul warns against circumcision and legalism, but in vss 12-16 he seems to be speaking against perfection. Then in vss 18-19 he warns against enemies of the cross whose god is their stomach and who glory in shame. Are these warnings all addressed to the same people, or does Paul have different groups in view?

The major argument is between those who see Paul speaking about one group and those who see two. But even those who see one group aren't agreed on who they are. Both Judaizers and Christians with gnostic leanings have been suggested. Some have even proposed three groups, while still others have suggested that Paul doesn't have any specific group in mind, but is just giving general warnings. Again, there is no way to tell for sure, but the vigor of Paul's response suggests that he is talking about real people. The way he argues also suggests that at least those addressed in the first part of the chapter had a Jewish background, although in the first century world where so many religious elements and ideas could be mixed together there may have been other influences on them as well.

LITERARY CONSIDERATIONS

The major literary problem of Philippians is its unity. Even though virtually all scholars believe the whole letter was written by Paul, many wonder if he wrote it all at one time or if it is a collection of two or three letter fragments put together by a later editor.

The most important evidence against the letter's unity is the break between 3:1 and 3:2. It sounds as if Paul is bringing the letter to a close by giving his future plans (compare Rom 15 and 1 Cor 16), then he abruptly changes both the subject and the tone in 3:2. It also seems strange that Paul waits until the end of the letter to thank the Philippians for their gift to him. (Sending support while he was in prison was no small matter. The empire didn't issue food and bedding to prisoners; they were dependent on such support.)

On the other hand there are common terms and themes that occur in both halves of the letter. For example, Paul uses language suggesting citizenship in 1:27 and 3:20, but nowhere else in his other letters. The term "gain" occurs only three times in the New Testament, and two of these occurrences are in Philippians, in sections that are often considered different letters. The theme of suffering appears in 1:29-30, 2:17, and 3:10. However, the theme of rejoicing, which occurs in 1:18, 2:17-18, 2:28, 3:1 as well as 4:4 and 4:10, is absent from 3:2-4:1, which some consider to be a separate letter.

The term "finally" in 3:1 seems to indicate that a letter is coming to an end. Yet although Paul uses this term to conclude letters (see 2 Cor 13:11), he can use it at other times as well (see 1 Cor 7:29, 1 Thess 4:1, and 2 Thess 3:1). All of this makes it impossible to know for sure whether the letter as we have it is in its original form or not.

Unfortunately, when we read this letter in English translation we lose some of the interesting literary devices Paul uses as he conveys his message. For example, he uses plays on words. In the first part of ch 3 he warns against those who demand circumcision, but he doesn't use the word at first. Instead he calls what they do "mutilation." The words mutilation and circumcision in the original language have the same root. The former literally means to cut down and the latter to cut around. Paul is playing with the two words to show his displeasure with their demand for circumcision.

Paul also uses plays that repeat the same words with different meanings. In 3:12 he repeats a word three times. The sense of the verse is that Paul has not already "taken hold," but he presses on to "take hold" of that for which Christ "took hold" of him. In 3:12 Paul affirms that he is not already "perfect," but then in 3:15 adds the ironic statement that "all of us who are perfect" will hold the same view. Trying to translate all Paul's playful usages of words into another language gives any translator fits.

The famous passage about Christ's willingness to suffer for us in 2:5-11 differs from the rest of the letter. It is written in poetic form. This leads most scholars to conclude that Paul is quoting from a hymn that was used in the early church. Of course, it could be that Paul himself was the author of the hymn, but probably he is using something familiar to the worship experience of the congregation to make a point, much as preachers often do in their sermons today.

THE MESSAGE
Outline
The content of Philippians may be outlined as follows:

Survey of contents

Paul begins this letter with a typical introduction and thanksgiving for the congregation. He then speaks of his own situation of imprisonment, stressing his contentment and assuring the Philippians of God's activity. In the second chapter he emphasizes their need to relate to each other with the humility of Christ and calls on them to live a blameless life. In ch 3 he warns them against those who put confidence in the flesh by demanding circumcision by contrasting his confidence in Christ alone. In the last chapter he gives final admonitions and expresses his gratitude for their generosity and support, before closing with final greetings.

Several important themes emerge from this letter. One is confirmed both by Paul's admonitions and his example. Even though Paul faces death, he rejoices in the Lord and he advises Christians to do the same. He declares that even if he is poured out as an offering or a sacrifice he is glad and rejoices (2:17). He has learned to be content in every situation, whether in want or plenty, for he knows that he can face anything through Christ (4:12-13). It is this total commitment of trust in Christ that makes a "peace that passes understanding" (4:7) possible for Paul. Because Christ is the central factor in his identity, he can already begin living life as a citizen of heaven that allows him to rejoice whatever his earthly situation. Paul is fond of financial metaphors in this letter, emphasizing that the only real value and worth in his life comes from Christ.

Another central theme is the Christian's responsibility to other Christians. Paul grounds this need to look out for other people's interests as well as one's own (2:4) in deep theological soil. In fact, this is the purpose for Paul's use of the beautiful hymn about Christ in 2:5-11. Unfortunately interpreters and theologians have often tried to use this hymn to figure out all the intricacies of the incarnation and the nature of Christ. But this is not at all Paul's purpose.

Paul uses the moving example of Christ's willingness to become human, suffer, and die, even death on a cross (the first century equivalent of the electric chair or gas chamber) not to satisfy theological curiosity or speak to abstract, ivory tower issues. He uses it to show us that if we commit ourselves to Christ there will be a shape to our lives. Following Jesus has ethical implications. It makes a difference in the way we live.

To commit our lives to Christ means adopting Christ's way of thinking about people. How sadly ironic that many have used these very verses that so profoundly call us to love each other as a means of fighting with each other about the nature of Christ.

This letter also has implications for the way we understand how we are saved. Paul makes it clear that no list of credentials that we can line up behind our names can ever contribute anything to our salvation (3:4-11). (In fact, when Paul says that he forgets what is behind he isn't talking about forgetting his past mistakes and sins but rather his achievements and accomplishments so that he can rely only on Christ.) He also warns us against thinking that we have already become perfect in this life before Christ's return (3:12-16).

All of these themes make a positive response to the central advice of the book possible. They all give reason for Christians to rejoice.

VALUE/RELEVANCE FOR TODAY

A recent (unscientific) poll of college students where I teach showed that the greatest barrier to faith was not the problem of science and religion, but the problem of suffering. Although this letter gives no propositional answer to the problem of suffering in the world, it does model a kind of faith that can take suffering seriously and still not only believe, but rejoice in that faith. By identifying with Christ's suffering, Paul finds meaning for his present existence and, because Christ's suffering culminates in resurrection, hope for the future as well. This perspective offers fruitful food for thought for those who struggle with the meaning of a world of suffering.

Paul's emphasis on finding all his worth and value in Christ also speaks to a culture that is as competitive and achievement oriented as ours. If Paul is right, when we allow ourselves to depend less on our accomplishments for our own self esteem, identity and sense of purpose and instead trust in Christ, we will experience a new freedom and peace in our own lives and a new ability to live for others as well. It is this joyful liberation that comes from putting aside every reason for confidence in ourselves and making Christ our only asset that is the chief contribution of Paul's letter to the Philippians.

ISSUES FOR DISCUSSION AND REFLECTION

1. Is the preaching of Christ from false motives effective in bringing people to faith? Does the motive of the preacher make a difference in effectiveness to the hearers or only in the preacher's relationship to God? (1:18)
2. Did Paul really wish to die or consider it just as good as living? (1:23-24) Or was this just his way of coming to terms with his possible conviction and execution?
3. Is it possible to live in our competitive society and maintain enough ambition to get up and go and do what needs to be done while living the kind of humble life Paul espouses in 2:1-11?
4. Why is Paul so down on circumcision? (3:2ff)
5. Is it emotionally healthy to consider everything in the world and in one's own history as "rubbish" for the sake of Christ? (3:8)
6. Where do you find the balance between being aware, realistic and not burying your head in the sand on one hand and thinking only on things that are pure and lovely on the other? (4:8)
7. What evidences do you see supporting either the unity of this letter or compilation theories about it?

FURTHER READING

Beare, Francis W.
> 1959 *A Commentary on the Epistle to the Philippians.* (Black's). London: Adam and Charles Black.

de Dietrich, Suzanne
> 1966 *Toward Fullness of Life: Studies in the Letter of Paul to the Philippians.* Philadelphia: Westminster.

Craddock, Fred B.
> 1985 *Philippians.* (Interpretation). Atlanta: John Knox.

Hawthorne, Gerald F.
> 1983 *Philippians.* (Word). Waco, TX: Word.
> 1987 *Word Biblical Themes: Philippians.* Waco, TX: Word.

Martin, Ralph P.
> 1976 *Philippians.* (New Century). Grand Rapids, MI: Eerdmans.

Plummer, Alfred
> 1919 *A Commentary on St. Paul's Epistle to the Philippians.* London: Robert Scott.

Chapter 13

Colossians
John C. Brunt

> *"For in him [Christ] the whole fullness of deity dwells bodily, and you have come to fullness in him, who is the head of every ruler and authority."*

BRIEF OVERVIEW OF THE BOOK

Colossians is another of the four letters known as the prison letters. In contrast to Philippians this letter was written to a congregation that was more distant from Paul and which he did not found. In it Paul sets forth the supremacy of Jesus Christ as well as the implications of Christ's supremacy for the Christian moral life. He also warns the Colossians about a Christian group that would intimidate them with certain rules and regulations.

BACKGROUND CONCERNS

A number of contemporary scholars have questioned whether it was actually Paul who wrote this letter. For many of these scholars this question has nothing to do with the value, inspiration, authority, or place in the canon of this letter, nor do they intend to suggest that there is any deception or lack of moral integrity of the author. Rather they hold that in the Greco-Roman world, one of the ways that students and subsequent followers of a great teacher would honor that teacher was to write in his or her name so that the teacher might speak to a new generation or situation.

Why is it that some scholars wonder whether Paul wrote this letter? There are several reasons. The first has to do with the language and style of the letter. There are some unquestionable differences in the style. The sentences are longer than Paul's sentences usually are, and some of Paul's common connecting words are absent. In addition, there are 34 words in this little letter that are found nowhere else in the New Testament.

Those who support Pauline authorship point out that most of these words are found in the section where Paul is combating false teachings. They suggest that

Paul was probably using the language of the false teachers to combat them. They also point out that differences in style might be accounted for by Paul's use of different scribes.

was Paul? the author

Some scholars also see evidence against Pauline authorship in this letter's relationship to other letters, namely Ephesians and Philemon. There is a very close relationship between Colossians and Ephesians, but we will save that discussion for the introductory section on Ephesians. When it comes to Philemon, this letter gives greetings from the same individuals (Epaphras, Aristarchus, Mark, Luke, and Demas). In addition, both letters speak to Archippus and both refer to Onesimus. Some suggest that the author is attempting to make this letter appear Pauline by using the names from Philemon. Others, however, point out that if Philemon and Colossians were written at the same time, these similarities would appear quite natural. It is also hard to believe that an author would take only these incidentals from a genuine letter when writing in Paul's name.

Because there are good explanations for the apparent differences between Colossians and the majority of Paul's other letters, it seems that the evidence is on the side of Pauline authorship, and in the remainder of this discussion that is what we will assume.

did Paul even visit Colossi

While Philippians was written to a congregation very close to Paul, Colossians is quite different. We have no specific evidence that Paul ever visited the city of Colossi, a relatively minor city in Asia Minor. Paul specifically says that Epaphras had introduced the Colossians to Christianity (1:7), and Paul implies that he was not known personally to the Colossians (2:1). It may well be that Paul wrote this letter primarily because of his attempts to get Philemon, a well-to-do Christian, to accept a run-away slave, Onesimus, back into his household (see the discussion on Philemon below). In this letter Paul specifically mentions Onesimus as one who carries the letter to them. He also includes a fairly lengthy section (3:22-41) on slavery. Perhaps when Paul sent Onesimus back to Philemon with the specific letter of request concerning Onesimus himself, he also wrote this more general letter to the broader Christian community there. It may be that Paul had also heard from Epaphras about certain false teachers and felt that he should write to the congregation.

Paul says nothing in the letter about his specific circumstances at the time, except that he is in prison. This leaves the question of the time that Paul wrote and the place from which he wrote in almost exactly the same state as with Philippians (see "background considerations" under that letter). The same arguments for and against Rome, Ephesus, and Caesarea as a place of writing apply.

One interesting feature in Colossians is Paul's mention of another letter within it. In Col 4:17 he tells the Colossians to read the letter that he is writing to Laodicia and suggests that they let the Laodicians read their's. We, of course, have no letter from Paul to Laodicia in the New Testament. Apparently this letter was lost, although some have speculated (with little direct evidence) that either Philemon or Ephesians might actually be the lost Laodician letter.

Another area of concern about Colossians is the nature and background of the false teaching that Paul addresses in ch 2. Some scholars have pointed out that a concern for eating and Sabbath suggest that the false teachers were Jews, and the combination of reverence for angels with calendar concerns might point to sectarian Jews such as those who produced the DSS. Others have emphasized that these false teachers talk about terms like "powers," "mystery," and "fullness," all of which are important in the later gnostic heresies. Thus they hold that these false teachers were probably forerunners of gnosticism. Still others argue that there is no group of false teachers against which Paul speaks. Instead Paul is merely giving general advice drawn from problems he has met in other places throughout the years. But the specificity of terms not usually used by Paul speaks against this.

[handwritten margin note: the false teachers in ch. 2: Jews, gnostics?]

Paul probably is addressing a specific heresy, but with our limited evidence it is impossible to say exactly who these false teachers were. They probably had concocted a mixture of Jewish, Christian, and perhaps pagan elements as well. It was certainly possible for such mixtures to arise spontaneously in the Greco-Roman world, and thus the Colossian heresy may not be specifically related to any other known group.

LITERARY CONSIDERATIONS

Paul's expression of the supremacy of Jesus Christ that begins in 1:15, takes on at least a partially poetic form, and may well be Paul's expansion of a hymn or poem concerning Christ. A number of scholars have attempted to sort out Paul's original source and his own comments, but the very diversity of results in this attempt shows the difficulty and speculative nature of the task.

An interesting literary feature of Paul's writing is his repeated yet richly varied use of certain words. In Colossians Paul repeatedly uses the term "body" with different meanings, and yet there is a unity and association that binds the whole together. Look at the following uses of body in Colossians.

1:18	Christ is the head of the body, the church
1:22	The Colossians are reconciled by the body of Christ's flesh
1:24	Paul in his flesh fills up what is still lacking in the sufferings of Christ for the sake of the body
2:11	Through a circumcision not done with hands, the Christian finds the removal of the body of flesh
2:17	The body belongs to Christ
2:19	The whole body is supported by Christ, the head

2:23   Paul speaks against the false teachers and their harsh treatment of the body

3:15   As members of one body, believers are called to peace

It is easy to see that there is an interplay going on between these various usages of the term "body." It is what happens in Christ's own body that makes possible the body of believers who are now directed by Christ the head. Paul's own suffering, which carries on the work of Christ (1:24, an unquestionably problematic passage), seems to be contrasted to the self-inflicted, harsh treatment of the body by the false teachers.

It is admittedly hard to put one's finger on Paul's precise meaning in some of these passages, but the above chart should be sufficient to show that there is a definite connection between Paul's literary style and the message he communicates. Understanding the way Paul plays with language is a definite aid to understanding what Paul is trying to say.

THE MESSAGE
Outline
Colossians may be outlined as follows:

Survey of contents

After his initial greeting Paul gives thanks for the Colossians' faith, which they have learned from Epaphras. He then goes on to uplift Jesus Christ and show his supremacy over all things. Far from being a mere abstract theological truth, Christ's supremacy has meant reconciliation with God and inclusion in the body of Christ for the Colossians. In the last part of the first chapter and the beginning of the second Paul explains the meaning of his own ministry.

In the remainder of the second chapter Paul deals with false teachings that threaten to intimidate the Colossians into certain regulations. In the last two chapters Paul portrays the shape of the moral life that will characterize Christians and gives final greetings. *themes:*

There are a number of important themes in Colossians, but we will limit our *supremacy* discussion to four of these. First in importance for Paul is the supremacy of *of J.C.* Jesus Christ over all things. This theme prepares the way for all that follows in Colossians. The Christology of Colossians is a very high Christology. All things were created through Christ (1:16). Whatever authorities and powers there might be in the world they all not only stand under Christ but owe their existence to him. The fullness of deity resides in Jesus Christ (1:19; 2:9).

Christ's supremacy, however, involves more than his power and authority over all things. It includes his specific action for human beings. In Colossians this especially includes the forgiveness that comes through Christ that is emphasized in 2:13-15. These verses have their difficulties in interpretation. For a long time scholars have debated the identification of the "written code," with its regulations, that was nailed to the cross. Some argued that this code was the ceremonial law of the Old Testament, while others made it the Ten Commandments. However, within its context the passage refers to neither. What is nailed to the cross is the guilt of the sinner. It is the IOU that stood against the sinner which is now totally canceled because of Christ's forgiving activity. The other themes that we shall study would not be possible without the truth of Jesus Christ and the good news about who he is and what he has done. *concern about*

A second major theme emerges from Paul's concern about the false teachers *about* in ch 2. Apparently these teachers have attempted to intimidate the Colossians *false* into obeying certain rules that involve festivals, rules about how to keep the *teachers* Sabbath, what they may touch, and what they may eat. From several indications within the chapter it appears that these rules, which attempt to deny the body, are tied up with a regard for supernatural powers such as angels and demons. The false teachers may have taught that by doing certain things and not doing other things the Colossians could stir up the wrath of demons, and in order to placate these demons they had to be very careful about their behavior.

Paul believes that these false teachings threaten the Colossians' experience of freedom in Christ. He urges the Colossians not to be intimidated by the false teachers but to realize that every religious practice, even those that are the most valid, are but shadows that receive their meaning from the true body, Jesus Christ. If they trust in Christ for forgiveness and salvation they need not be intimidated by these teachers and their regulations. And if Christ is truly supreme over every power and authority, they also need not be intimidated by the threat of demons and powers. At the cross Christ triumphed over every power, so if they are right with Christ they don't need to worry about any other power in the universe. Thus the Colossians are to live lives of confidence in Christ free from the intimidation of false teachers, regulations, and demonic powers.

Another major theme in Colossians is the Christian moral life. Although Christians are not to be intimidated by rules and regulations, they are to live a lifestyle that is worthy of the Lord who has saved them and a life that will please him by furthering his work in their lives and in the world (Col 1:10). (Notice similar statements in Eph 4:1; Phil 1:27; and 1 Thess 2:12.) A life of freedom in Christ is not a life of irresponsibility, nor is it a blank check for sin. The only appropriate response to Christ's love for us is a life that pleases him and promotes his cause. In this letter Paul gives the Colossians an idea of the shape that such a life will take.

This new life must begin with the mind. The Christian sets his or her mind on things above, focusing attention on Jesus Christ and the story of what he has done for us. This new mindset shapes both values and actions (Col 3:1-4).

Paul then gets quite specific and shows that sexual immorality, greed, anger, malice, and prejudice are all inconsistent with a life worthy of the Lord. He uses the metaphor of putting off clothes and putting on clothes, which is probably a baptismal metaphor. The old life with its actions are to be put off, and a new set of clothes is to be put on. This new life includes compassion, kindness, humility, gentleness, and patience (Col 3:12). It is a life of peace and fellowship with others as well as a life of worship where praise and hymns are directed toward God (Col 3:15-17). Finally it is a life where husbands and wives, children and parents, slaves and masters live in unity with each other (3:18-4:1).

Throughout Paul's discussion, the shape that the moral life takes is seen only in fellowship with others. Paul knows nothing of individual Christianity apart from a body of believers. In fact, the shape of this life is only possible through the fellowship of believers who become part of a body directed by Jesus Christ, the head. The moral life is not an individual life, but a life lived in community with others under the Lordship of Jesus Christ.

The final theme we mention comes in the latter part of ch 1 and the first part of ch 2. Here Paul discusses his own relationship to Christ and ministry for Christ. Part of what he says here is difficult to understand. He says that he not only suffers in his ministry for Christ but he makes up what is still lacking in

Christ's affliction. What can Paul possibly mean by this? Although it appears incredibly arrogant, that is not what Paul has in mind. He is trying to show that his ministry is an extension of Christ's work, but this is only possible because he allows Christ to be head and submits himself to Christ's Lordship, working under his direction.

VALUE/RELEVANCE FOR TODAY

We live in the world of a new polytheism where many lives are no longer centered in commitment to and worship of a single God but are rather scattered in many directions and governed by the values (and often whims) of a secular culture. When Paul uplifts Jesus Christ as the supreme Lord above all he is not merely writing theology. Properly understood, his words are a challenge that demand a response. We all must face the question of who will rule our lives. Will we adopt the philosophy of the autonomous man or woman who does his or her own thing? Will we be ruled by the values of our cultures or the gurus of the day? According to Paul, if we decide for any of these our decision is ultimately destructive. There is only one God who created us, knows us, has our best interest at heart, and we meet that God in Jesus Christ. True meaning is found only when he is the head and we are part of his body.

We also live in a modern, scientific age that has supposedly thrown off superstition, and yet our culture is full of superstition. The checkout counter tabloids proclaim that psychics and soothsayers can show us the way to the future. Paul proclaims that we need not be intimidated by any powers, for a life of commitment and trust to Jesus Christ truly frees us from fear and superstition.

The message of Colossians also frees us from intimidation from those who would impose their standards and rules on us, for although true Christian faith will always make a difference in life, there are many specifics of that life that must be a matter of our own decision based on our experience with Christ.

Finally, in our age of communication and mass media it appears that the point where Paul begins his description of the shape of the Christian moral life is especially crucial. Taking off the old life and putting on the new comes as we set our hearts and minds on what is above. This doesn't mean becoming hermits who are unaware of the world around us, but it does mean that Jesus Christ can only shape our minds as we focus our attention on him, what he has done for us, and the values that he holds dear. That certainly means saying, "No" to much of the media entertainment that upholds different values that are more in keeping with what Paul calls the old clothes that need to be taken off.

ISSUES FOR DISCUSSION AND REFLECTION

1. How do we experience the reality of the supremacy of Christ and actually make him the head in our lives and in the church when he is not here? How can an absent Christ be the head?
2. Is Paul's statement that he makes up what is lacking in Christ's suffering (1:24) something unique to him or could this be said of others as well? Would you feel it a lack of Christian humility to say it of yourself?
3. Is there a conflict between Paul's admonition about freedom from intimidation over rules and regulations in ch 2 and his own rule making in ch 3? Why should the Colossians ignore the false teachers rules and yet accept Paul's rules?
4. Is Paul's strong emphasis on the significance of the body, which he specifically identifies as the church, in conflict with his emphasis on individual freedom?
5. In what ways might Paul's emphasis on Christ's triumph over all powers an authorities influence your response if a friend came to you concerned that he or she might be possessed by demons?

FURTHER READING

Crouch, James E.
>   1972   *The Origin and Intention of the Colossian Haustafel.* Gottingen: Vandenhoeck and Ruprecht.

Lohse, Eduard
>   1971   *Colossians and Philemon: A Commentary.* Trans. by William R. Poehlmann and Robert J. Karris. Ed. by Helmut Koester. (Hermeneia). Philadelphia: Fortress.

Martin, Ralph P.
>   1973   *Colossians and Philemon.* (New Century). Grand Rapids, MI: Eerdmans.

Schweizer, Eduard
>   1982   *The Letter to the Colossians.* Trans. by Andrew Chester. Minneapolis: Augsburg.

Wright, Nicholas T.
>   1986   *The Epistles of Paul to the Colossians and to Philemon: An Introduction and Commentary.* (Tyndale). Grand Rapids, MI: Eerdmans.

Chapter 14

Ephesians
John C. Brunt

*"With all wisdom and insight he has made known to us the mystery of his will,
according to his good pleasure that he set forth in Christ, as a plan for the fullness
of time, to gather up all things in him, things in heaven and things on earth."*

BRIEF OVERVIEW OF THE BOOK

Ephesians is yet another of the prison letters in which Paul specifically
mentions that he writes from prison (3:1). In this letter Paul sets forth God's
secret plan which is now revealed. The plan is that all things in the universe
will come into unity under the headship of Jesus Christ. Most of the Ephesian
letter is spent working out the implications of this plan.

BACKGROUND CONCERNS

With the single exception of the pastoral letters, scholars have more doubts
about the Pauline authorship of Ephesians than any other of the letters that bear
his name. There are several reasons for this. The style and vocabulary of
Ephesians is similar to Colossians, but is even more different from the other *very*
Pauline letters than is Colossians. Ephesians contains long, torturous sentences *different*
that are not typical in Paul's other letters. Many scholars argue that the *vocab*
doctrinal content of Ephesians is also quite different from Paul's other letters. *from other*
More emphasis is placed on the church, so that its unity and position become *Paulines –*
more central to faith than we find in the other letters. The letter also lists church *more*
officials that many think that were not in place when Paul wrote. *emphasis*
on church
Most scholars also see the close relationship between Colossians and
Ephesians as evidence against Pauline authorship of Ephesians. The relationship
between the two letters is unmistakable. About one third of all the words found
in Colossians are also in Ephesians. And almost half of the verses in Ephesians *close //*
have verbal parallels with Colossians. There are even similarities of overall *to*
structure and order of topics presented. Many see this as evidence that the *Colossians*

141

author of Ephesians has copied Colossians. They question whether Paul would have written two letters with these kinds of parallels.

On the other hand, a minority of scholars point out that language and style differences could again be caused by a difference in scribes and a recognition that Paul gave his secretaries and/or co-authors a good bit of freedom of expression. They also point out that there are church officials in Philippians, which is generally accepted as Pauline, and that the similarities between Colossians and Ephesians could be explained if Paul wrote the two letters at the same time. If the letter is Pauline it probably was written at the same time as Colossians, since Eph 6:21 says that it was carried by Tychicus, who also carries Colossians, along with Onesimus (Col 4:7-9).

Earlier in this century the renowned New Testament scholar Edgar Goodspeed had an ingenious, elaborate, and highly speculative theory about the authorship of Ephesians. He held that the letter was written by Onesimus, the runaway slave whom Paul returned to Philemon (see the following chapter on Philemon). According to Goodspeed, Onesimus kept the letters to Philemon and Colossi, and then later decided to collect all of Paul's letters and publish them. He then wrote Ephesians as an introduction to the collection. Although this theory is ingenious, its speculative basis leaves it highly questionable.

If the letter is Pauline, the question of its date and the place from which it was written would be the same as Philippians and Colossians. See the discussion above (Background Concerns under Philippians). Even if the letter is considered Pauline there are serious questions about Ephesus as its destination. The oldest and best manuscripts of the New Testament omit the words "in Ephesus" in Eph 1:1 and thus give no place of destination within the letter itself. In addition, the content of the letter would hardly be what Paul would write to the believers at Ephesus. Paul had spent three years at Ephesus on his third missionary journey according to Acts. Acts 20 suggests that there was a deep personal relationship between Paul and the leaders of the church at Ephesus. And yet this letter has the most impersonal tone of all the letters that bear Paul's name. Paul neither greets specific friends nor shows the kind of personal warmth that we see in Philippians. This makes it very doubtful that the letter was written to Ephesus.

Some have suggested that this might be the lost letter to the Laodicians. Others suggest that it might have been a circular letter, not intended for any particular congregation. Perhaps Paul wrote this letter when he sent Colossians and Philemon and intended it for more general circulation in Asia Minor. The evidence is simply insufficient to form a conclusion.

LITERARY CONSIDERATIONS

One of the main question concerning Ephesians is its genre as a letter. As already mentioned, the letter has a much more impersonal tone than most of

Paul's letters and really borders on being an open letter or letter essay. It does not treat any specific problems within the church or false teachings that threaten the church as do both Philippians and Colossians. And as we shall see, Philemon is even more personal than Philippians or Colossians. Almost all of Paul's letters are clearly occasional literature (in other words, letters addressed to a very specific situation and to specific people). This letter is addressed simply to the saints, the faithful in Christ Jesus. At the end there are no greetings, simply the mention that Tychicus will carry the letter. If this were omitted, there would be no indication that the letter is actually occasional literature. Therefore, even if this letter is considered Pauline, it does bear a distinctive literary genre in relationship to the other letters.

THE MESSAGE
Outline
The following is an outline of the content of Ephesians:

Survey of contents

This letter begins with a statement of God's secret plan which has now been revealed. The secret plan is to unite all things under the head of Jesus Christ. Paul then works out the implications of this plan. It means that Christ has been exalted above all things and that those in Christ are exalted with him. It means that barriers between Jew and Gentile, between God and humans, and between various factions in the church have all been obliterated in Christ. It also means living a new life that is worthy of the God whose grace has made this life possible. This new life includes worship and the mutual submission of believers to each other, especially in the most significant relationships that exist within the Christian household.

The one important theme that weaves its way throughout this entire letter is that of unity. Ephesians 1:9 declares that God has a plan that has been a mystery. For the Greeks, however, a mystery is not something that cannot be known; rather it is a secret that is unknown except to those who are "in on it." This letter lets us all in on God's secret. God's secret is to unite all things in the entire universe, the human world, the heavenly world as well as the subhuman world, into harmonious unity. This is accomplished as all things are summed up under one head. That head is Jesus Christ who is now Lord of all.

The latter part of ch 1 shows how through the cross and resurrection, Jesus Christ has been exalted to the very throne of God where all things are placed under his feet. But Paul does not limit this exaltation to Jesus Christ alone. He goes on in the first part of ch 2 to proclaim that the Christian believer too has been exalted to the very realm of God to live a new life. Lest this startling, symbolic portrayal bring arrogance, Paul points out that it is possible purely by God's grace (2:8-9). He also makes it clear that this present exaltation with Christ does not rule out the future coming of Christ when Christ's victory and the resulting unity will actually become visible to the universe (2:7).

The revelation of this gracious plan results in reconciliation. Barriers between God and sinful humans are obliterated. And every Christian who recognizes his or her reconciliation with God also recognizes that now the barriers between humans are also obliterated, for all stand on the same footing when they become one with Jesus Christ. Paul's own ministry gives testimony to the revelation of this mystery as Gentiles come to God and are united in one body with Jewish believers.

Again, as in Colossians, there is a clear tie between the revelation of God's gracious plan and the life that Christians live. Again the call is to live a life that is worthy of the calling believers have received in Christ. And again Paul goes on to spell out the shape of this worthy life. It will result in unity within the church and the putting away of those things that God reveals are inconsistent with His purpose for human beings, in other words, those things that destroy fellowship with him and unity with others. Paul sees this new life as a life filled with God's spirit, which he specifically contrasts with being drunk with wine. While being drunk with wine leads to debauchery, being filled with the spirit of God leads to worship and moral responsibility. The worship involves singing *specifically* and praising God (5:18-20). The moral responsibility means submitting to each *re* other out of reverence for Christ (5:21). Paul goes on to show that this *3 pairs* submission is a mutual submission. He speaks to three pairs of relationships: wife-husband, child-parent, slave-master. In each case he begins by addressing the person who would usually be considered the underdog in the relationship. Then he goes on to turn the tables and place the responsibility for love and submission on the person of privilege as well. Thus he gives dignity and value to each person by addressing them specifically. (Much of the literature of the day addressed only the patriarch and told him to keep wives, children, and slaves in submission.)

Thus we see that God's plan to reconcile the world and bring everyone together in unity has very practical, everyday implications for life. It affects the way parents relate to their children, the way husbands and wives relate to each other, and the way we all live our lives from day to day. All of this is part of God's plan for unity which will eventually fill all in all and become visible in the entire universe. But the Christian has the privilege of already anticipating that future day by living according to the values of this plan for unity under the Lordship of Jesus Christ.

VALUE/RELEVANCE FOR TODAY

There are two basic ways that the revelation of God's plan to unite all things under the Lordship of Jesus Christ affects us today. First, we receive confidence, joy, and hope in the good news of this gracious plan, for if we take this letter seriously, it is not only Jesus Christ who was resurrected and is exalted to the right hand of God. We too have been made alive with Christ. If we are in Him, our destiny is sure. We have ultimate security. Whatever else may happen in this world, our destiny is in the heavenly realm, a destiny which no power or circumstance can take away from us. We have absolutely nothing to boast about (2:9), but we have everything to rejoice about, for God has raised us up with Christ and seated us with Him in the heavenly realms.

But second, this message presents us with a challenge. This great privilege brings responsibility as well. One who is grasped by this message of oneness with Christ can only live a life that is a worthy response by showing in everyday life that the barriers, indeed, have been broken down, and we are one. This means that every form of prejudice and discrimination is an affront to God's plan wherever it may be found. Isn't it obvious that this is especially true when it is found in the church? As long as there are congregations where people are excluded on the basis of race, as long as some churches limit full participation in the ministry on the basis of gender discrimination, and as long as we tolerate any form of domination of one group over another, we stand condemned by this letter. In fact, according to this letter, spirituality is not a matter of piety or external manifestations of power. It is rather a matter of joyful expression of praise to God and mutual submission to each other.

ISSUES FOR DISCUSSION AND REFLECTION

1. Does this letter present a danger of placing too much emphasis on the church? Is there a conflict between individual religious expression and this strong emphasis that being in Christ means being part of His body united to other believers?
2. Is there any place in today's world for racial, ethnic, and/or cultural separation for worship? How should the church witness to this message of unity? How does the church show that all barriers have been broken down?
3. What does Paul's instruction about Christian households (5:22-6:9) suggest for today? What specific shape, for instance, should mutual submission between husbands and wives take in today's world?
4. Is there a danger in Paul's emphasis on our exaltation to the right hand of God and our resurrection with Christ (2:1-10)? In both Rom 6 and Colossians Paul seems to be more restrained about the present reality of our resurrection with Christ. But here he speaks of the believers' present resurrection and exaltation in a way that is startling, even if symbolic. Could this lead to arrogance and/or unbridled enthusiasm?

FURTHER READING

Barth, Markus
      1974   *Ephesians.* 2 vols. (Anchor). Garden City, NY: Doubleday.
Mitton, C. Leslie
      1973   *Ephesians.* (New Century). Grand Rapids, MI: Eerdmans.
Stott, John R.W.
      1979   *God's New Society: The Message of Ephesians.* Downers Grove, IL: InterVarsity.

Chapter 15
Philemon
John C. Brunt

> *"I am appealing to you for my child, Onesimus, whose father I*
> *have become during my imprisonment."*

BRIEF OVERVIEW OF THE BOOK
Philemon is the most unusual of the letters in the New Testament. It is, in fact, unique to the entire Bible. It is a very short, personal appeal from Paul to a Christian householder and slave owner on behalf of a runaway slave. It is also one of the letters written from prison (vs 9).

BACKGROUND CONCERNS
All scholars agree that this letter was written by Paul. There are differences about the time of writing and the place from which it was written. These issues are virtually identical with those discussed in the previous prison letters. This letter certainly seems to have been written at the same time as Colossians, since Paul sends greetings from the same fellow-workers, and Onesimus is one who carries Colossians (for more details see the previous discussion on Colossians). Philemon probably lived at Colossai.

A story obviously stands behind this letter. Unfortunately we don't know all the details of the story, but we can piece together the basic picture from the letter itself. Paul addresses Philemon on behalf of his runaway slave, Onesimus. Verse 18 may suggest that Onesimus stole money from Philemon when he ran away. We have no idea how Onesimus came in contact with Paul, but through this contact Onesimus was converted and became Paul's close friend. Paul, however, felt that Onesimus needed to return to his master, and Paul sent this letter with Onesimus as he returned.

Since Paul's letter is the only source of information we have about the story, we don't know how the story ended. Did Philemon accept Onesimus back and forgive him? The very fact that the letter has survived probably indicates that he did (at least Philemon didn't tear it up and throw it into the fire). There is an interesting possibility that has absolutely no proof to back it up. About 50 years after Paul wrote this letter one of the early church fathers, Ignatius, wrote a letter to the church at Ephesus. He mentioned the name of the bishop there. His name was Onesimus. Ignatius even makes the same play on the meaning of Onesimus' name that Paul does (see literary considerations below). Could this elderly bishop 50 years later be the same Onesimus? Nobody knows, but it is an intriguing possibility.

Some scholars have suggested that it was not Philemon but Archippus who was the slave owner to whom Paul returned Onesimus (notice that Archippus is mentioned in vs 2). They speculate that Paul's instruction to Archippus in Col 4:17 ("See to it that you complete the work you have received in the Lord") also concerns Onesimus. But this is highly speculative and doubtful.

Paul's letter obviously assumes the practice of slavery. Slavery was wide spread in the Roman empire. As many as half of the population were slaves. The condition of slaves varied greatly. Some were cruelly exploited and oppressed. Others held very respected positions in wealthy households and were highly honored. People became slaves in many ways. Some were forced into slavery because of debt. Others had been captured in Rome's military exploits. Still others were born into families that had been slaves for generations. Many slaves were also set free in the first century Roman world. Some were allowed to earn money and buy their freedom while others were set free at the death of their master in his will. Potential punishment for runaway slaves was severe and could even include death. Often the slave was branded with a visible, permanent scar to avoid future escape attempts.

LITERARY CONSIDERATIONS

One of this letter's literary puzzles is its genre or type of literature. Is it merely a personal letter, or is it more like Paul's other letters, written with apostolic and pastoral authority as God's word for a community of believers? In many respects it is very personal. And yet we should notice that Paul addresses it not only to Philemon and to Apphia and Archippus (possibly members of Philemon's household), but also to the church that meets in Philemon's home. Thus even though the letter is very personal, it is more than a personal letter. Paul binds Philemon's decision regarding Onesimus with the church as a whole. It is not merely an individual, independent decision.

In this letter again Paul uses word plays and repetitive language as literary devices to enhance his message. This runaway slave's name, Onesimus, meant "useful." In vs 11 Paul tells Philemon that although "Mr. Useful" had been pretty useless to him in the past, now he was going to live up to his name and become useful to both Philemon and Paul.

One of the interesting words that Paul repeats is found in vss 7, 12, and 20. The word is a strange word. The King James Version of the Bible translates it quite literally. It means "bowels" or "viscera." But it was used figuratively in Greek to refer to the center of a person's being, a center that included both one's deepest emotions and strongest convictions. (Before we are too hard on the ancients for using the term "bowels" in this way, we should remind ourselves that when it comes to anatomy, our use of the term heart for the center of emotions isn't any better.) In vs 7 Paul concludes his thanksgiving for Philemon by rejoicing that Philemon has refreshed the bowels of the saints. In vs 12 he tells Philemon that in sending Onesimus back, he is sending back his very own bowels. Finally, in vs 20 Paul wraps up his argument by asking Philemon now to refresh Paul's bowels. This three-fold use of the term is hardly coincidental. With it Paul identifies his deepest feelings with the issue for which he pleads and makes a strong appeal to Philemon.

Another interesting literary feature is Paul's method of argumentation. There is no doubt that Paul pulls out all the stops. There is nothing subtle in his argument, even though Paul does his best to make it appear that way. For example, Paul claims that he could order Philemon to accept Onesimus, but that he will not do that, rather he will appeal on the basis of love (vs 8). He offers to pay Philemon back if he has been wronged, but then can't help adding that Philemon might be said to owe Paul his very life (vs 19). Even Paul's hints are not very subtle. Paul not only hopes that Philemon will accept Onesimus back, he would really like to see Philemon do more and release Onesimus altogether. Paul points out that if Philemon did that, Onesimus could come and be with him and help him as Philemon would if he could (vs 13). And he ends his appeal by expressing his confidence that Philemon will do even more than he asks (vs 21).

Does this type of argumentation really leave Philemon free, or is it manipulative? Even if it sounds manipulative to our ears we must remember what was at stake. Paul was writing on behalf of a dear friend and fellow Christian whose guilt could justify extremely cruel treatment or even death. If Paul is manipulative, it is certainly for a good cause.

THE MESSAGE
Outline
The outline of Philemon is brief:

Survey of contents

As we have already seen, this letter is Paul's personal appeal to Philemon on behalf of Onesimus. Paul begins by offering thanks for Philemon and then goes on to show that the admirable qualities which he appreciates in Philemon should logically lead Philemon to forgive Onesimus, accept him back, and perhaps going beyond that to release him altogether. Paul even offers Philemon an IOU written in his own handwriting and expresses his desire to come and visit Philemon.

There is an elegance to the specificity of this letter. There are no general theological teachings nor are there general ethical admonitions. Everything in the letter is directed to one specific goal, the forgiveness and acceptance of Onesimus.

VALUE/RELEVANCE FOR TODAY

There is a special value in the humanness and specificity of this letter. If inspiration of Scripture is a blending of the human and the divine, this is a letter that lets us in on the human side more than most. But it also lets us see Paul's gospel in concrete form. This real, live "exhibit A" speaks in a way that is disproportionate to its size. We see here the personal care and concern that Paul has for an erring and vulnerable individual. In others letters we have seen Paul argue theoretically that our faith in Jesus Christ should make a difference in the way we treat people. Here, as Paul personally pleads for forgiveness, we see a concrete example of Paul's teaching. But there are no theoretical arguments here. Everything is real, personal and concrete. It is, therefore, an especially powerful example of the compassion that the gospel produces.

If we do just a little reading between the lines in this story, we see a glimpse of how Paul thought the church should work. Paul doesn't address this letter, as we have seen, to Philemon alone. He addresses it to the church that meets in his house. (In the first century all Christian worship was held in the homes of believers. No buildings for worship were constructed by Christians.) Paul saw these house churches that met together as a close-knit bond of both fellowship and accountability (see 1 Cor 5 and 12 for example). Perhaps we would find it easier to live as we should, resist temptation, and make the right spiritual and moral decisions in our lives if our community were closer and we were willing to be more accountable for each other.

ISSUES FOR DISCUSSION AND REFLECTION

1. Was Paul manipulative? Are you comfortable with his method of argumentation? If you're not comfortable, does Paul's goal justify his method?

(handwritten margin note: Paul's personal concern)

2. Why didn't Paul just come out and condemn all slavery? Why did he argue only on behalf of one particular runaway slave rather than address the issue in general?
3. If you had been a part of early church councils deciding what would and what would not become a part of the church's canon of sacred writings, would you have included this small, personal letter? Why or why not?

FURTHER READING

Knox, John
    1959   *Philemon Among the Letters of Paul.* Rev. ed. Nashville: Abingdon.
Lohse, Eduard
    1971   *Colossians and Philemon: A Commentary.* Trans. by William R. Poehlmann and Robert J. Karris. Ed. by Helmut Koester. Hermeneia Series. Philadelphia: Fortress.
Martin, Ralph P.
    1973   *Colossians and Philemon.* (New Century). Grand Rapids, MI: Eerdmans.
Wright, Nicholas T.
    1986   *The Epistles of Paul to the Colossians and to Philemon: An Introduction and Commentary.* (Tyndale). Grand Rapids, MI: Eerdmans.

Chapter 16

The Pastoral Letters

John C. Brunt

> *"Let no one despise your youth, but set the believers an example*
> *in speech and conduct, in love, in faith, in purity."*

BRIEF OVERVIEW OF THE BOOK

The three letters known as the Pastoral letters, 1 and 2 Timothy and Titus, are linked together by common style, vocabulary, theological emphasis, and situation. All three are addressed from Paul to a younger co-worker, either Timothy in Ephesus or Titus in Crete, to admonish them about their ministry, including church order, the danger of false teachings and teachers, and how to live a godly life. Second Timothy differs from the other two in that it does not include specific qualifications for church officials and is written while the writer is in prison. It is also much more personal than the other two. All three letters primarily contain warnings and admonitions addressed to Timothy or Titus.

BACKGROUND CONCERNS

The chief area of controversy surrounding the pastoral letters is the question of authorship. All three letters carry Paul's name, yet even the beginning Greek student notices a jarring difference when she or he moves from the other Pauline letters to the Pastorals. The style and vocabulary are simply different. A total of over eight hundred words occur in these three letters, and over a third of them never occur in Paul's other letters.

Simple word statistics prove little, however. Much more difficult is the nature of the differences in vocabulary. They represent significant variations in the central concepts and concerns of the pastorals when compared with the other letters of Paul. For example, a central concept in the pastorals is godliness or piety (Greek, *eusebeia*). If we add together the noun, verb, and adverb forms of this root they are found thirteen times in the pastorals (1 Tim 2:2; 3:16; 4:7, 8; 5:4; 6:3, 5, 6, 11; 2 Tim 3:5, 12; Titus 1:1; 2:12) and not at all in the other ten

154

Introducing the New Testament

letters that carry Paul's name. The other letters certainly are concerned with moral responsibility, but never use this term, popular in the world of Greco-Roman morality, to express Christian responsibility.

The term "sound" to describe teaching (1 Tim 1:10; 2 Tim 4:3; Titus 1:9; 2:1), words (doctrine) (1 Tim 6:3; 2 Tim 1:13) or faith (Titus 1:13; 2:1) is central to the pastorals. One of the chief responsibilities with which Timothy and Titus are charged is the preservation of sound doctrine and teaching, yet the term never occurs in the other ten Pauline letters.

Another difficulty is the way that the same words can be used with different emphases. For example, the term "faith" in the other letters refers to a radical commitment to God's grace, which puts aside all claims of human achievement. In the pastorals, on the other hand, faith often refers to the teaching of the church, as when Christians today speak of being in the faith.

What are we to make of these differences? As you might expect, they have led to many speculative hypotheses, far too numerous to mention here. Four basic approaches have been suggested, however. First, some scholars seek to explain the differences on the basis of the different subject matter and situation in these letters. Few have held this position because the evidence seems to be too complex for a change in topic, time, and situation to explain it. Second, some have explained the differences on the basis of Paul's use of a scribe or secretary. Perhaps Paul directed an associate to write for him and gave that associate a good bit of freedom, so that the style and vocabulary, as well as some of the conceptual concerns and emphases, represent the work of the secretary rather than Paul. Others suggest that a later editor worked with genuine fragments from Paul but edited them into their current form after Paul's death. Fourth, the most popular position today is that the pastorals were written in Paul's name at a time after his death. Those who hold this position often point out that in antiquity writing in another person's name was not an attempt to deceive but to honor the memory of the departed teacher.

Although all proposals are speculative, and it is probably impossible to be absolutely certain about any of these suggestions, no one can deny that the pastorals are significantly different from the other letters that carry Paul's name, and that the connection between these letters and Paul, whatever it is, is not the same as the connection in the other letters. According to Rom 16:22, Paul wrote at least some of his letters by dictating them to a scribe. It is hard to imagine the same person who dictated Romans simply dictating the pastorals to a scribe. Whatever the Pastorals relationship to Paul might be, they are more distant than the other letters that bear his name.

Obviously the questions of date and setting depend on one's conclusions about authorship. If they are considered Pauline, they must be placed in a different portion of Paul's life than is covered by the book of Acts, for the

[handwritten margin note: do not fit in act. chron doesn]

situation represented would not fit with the chronological situation of Paul's life in Acts. In 1 Timothy Paul is free and has left Timothy in Ephesus to minister. In Titus he has left Titus to minister on the island of Crete. In 2 Timothy Paul is in prison and Timothy continues in Ephesus. Almost all who hold to Pauline authorship assume that Paul was released from the imprisonment described in Acts, and place these letters after that time: 1 Timothy and Titus during a period of freedom and 2 Timothy during a second Roman imprisonment that led to Paul's execution.

Those who hold to pseudonymous authorship date these letters after Paul's *[handwritten: Paul probably died in 60s]* death, which probably occurred sometime in the 60's C.E., and admit that little can be known about the situation. Since Polycarp seems to quote from the pastorals (although this is disputed by some), they would need to have been written by his time in the early part of the second century.

Another matter in question concerning the pastorals is the nature of the opponents against whom Timothy and Titus are warned. We know that they *[handwritten: who are the false teachers]* teach a different doctrine which includes myth, genealogies, and speculation (1 Tim 1:4; Titus 3:9). They also desire to be teachers of the law (1 Tim 1:7) and *[handwritten: ?]* appear to be ascetic, forbidding marriage and demanding abstinence from certain foods (1 Tim 4:3). Some problem people are actually mentioned by name, including Hymenaeus and Alexander, who were turned over to Satan (1 Tim 1:20), but there is no way of knowing if they were the same people promoting the other false teachings. It seems likely, however, since Hymenaeus appears again, this time coupled with someone named Philetus. Both of them are said to have swerved from the truth by claiming that the resurrection had already occurred (2 Tim 2:17-18).

From these clues there is no way to be definite about the identity or nature of these false teachers, but the combination of law, speculation, and some kind of denial of the future resurrection suggest that it had a Jewish element, but also included the kind of thinking that would eventuate in the full blown gnostic heresy of the second and third centuries.

Finally, who are the two figures to whom these letters are addressed? What do we know about Timothy and Titus? We look first at Timothy. *[handwritten: Timothy important to Paul]*

Timothy is listed as the co-sender of 2 Corinthians, Philippians, Colossians, 1 and 2 Thessalonians, Philemon, and as the recipient of 1 and 2 Timothy. Thus eight of the thirteen letters of Paul also include Timothy in one way or another. In both Acts and Paul's letters we see what an important role Timothy played in Paul's ministry.

According to Acts 16, Paul first encountered Timothy when he came to Lystra on what we have come to call his second missionary journey. Timothy was a "disciple" whose mother was a Jew and father was a Greek. Believers spoke well of Timothy, and Paul decided to include him on the mission team.

Paul circumcised him to avoid unnecessary prejudice against their ministry and took him along when Paul and Silas responded to the vision and crossed over to Macedonia.

In Acts 17:14-15 we discover that when Paul was escorted out of Berea, Silas and Timothy stayed behind, planning to join Paul soon. Acts 18:5 records that Silas and Timothy later met Paul in Corinth, still on the second missionary journey. According to 1 Thess 3:2-6, however, it appears that Timothy had met Paul in Athens before he reached Corinth, and had then been sent back to Thessalonica to strengthen the new believers there in the faith. Timothy carried out this mission and met Paul in Corinth (this corresponds with Acts 18:5) with good news about the continuing faith of the Thessalonians. Thus very early in Timothy's association with Paul he was sent by Paul on a significant mission.

This became the pattern in Paul's ministry. Timothy was also with Paul on his third missionary journey in Ephesus, where Paul stayed three years (Acts 19:22), and as Paul revisited Macedonia (Acts 20:4). But when there was trouble or a sensitive mission, Timothy often got the call. From Ephesus Paul sent Timothy to Corinth and called him "My son, whom I love, who is faithful in the Lord" (1 Cor 4:17). According to Heb 13:23, at some point in time Timothy, like Paul, became a prisoner and was released.

It is a puzzle that Titus, obviously an important co-worker of Paul's, is never mentioned in the book of Acts. This is especially curious given that according to Gal 2, Titus was a central figure at the Jerusalem council, which Acts 15 describes. Outside the pastorals, Titus appears in only two New Testament works, Galatians (2:1, 3) and 2 Corinthians (2:13; 7:6, 13, 14; 8:6, 16, 23; 12:18). From Galatians we learn that Paul took Titus to Jerusalem as exhibit A that it was possible to be an uncircumcised Christian Gentile. Second Corinthians shows us that Titus played a role in the collection at Corinth, and Paul was so personally fond of him that it was a personal crisis for Paul when he didn't meet Titus at Troas as well as a source of great joy when they finally did make contact in Macedonia. Paul calls him a partner and a co-worker (2 Cor 8:23).

LITERARY CONSIDERATIONS

Although 1 Timothy and Titus begin with a traditional letter opening, they do not bear most of the marks of a letter. They do not appear to be occasional, or addressed to a specific situation, in the way that most letters are. Rather they share the literary character of a manual of church discipline, perhaps a cross between a modern church manual and minister's manual. There are other examples of such writings in early Christianity, such as the *Didache*, probably written in the early part of the second century. This genre of literature often includes rules for church order and discipline along with qualifications for church officials, instructions with regard to worship, and behavioral and dogmatic standards for members.

Second Timothy, on the other hand, includes fewer of these elements *2 Tim* normally found in manuals of church discipline and more features of an *more an* occasional letter. In addition, it includes characteristics of another genre, the *occasional* farewell discourse found in works such as the pseudonymous *Testaments of the* *letter;* *Twelve Patriarchs*. This genre usually includes a recounting of the writer's *a* suffering and imminent death, the assurance that he or she has remained faithful *farewell* (see 2 Tim 4:6-8), and advice to the one who will carry the torch to endure with *discourse* faithfulness.

THE MESSAGE
Outline
These three letters may be outlined as follows:

1 Timothy

Survey of contents

Several concerns dominate the pastorals. One of the most important is the need for sound doctrine and godly or pious behavior. Some of the terminology relating to these concerns has already been discussed in the section above on background considerations. The pastorals are driven by the concern that the church was being threatened by false teachers who led believers astray. We have already noted that the pastorals give few details of this false teaching, but clearly the threat was not merely seen at the abstract level of theory; it was supposed to threaten behavior as well. In such a situation of threat the emphasis falls on keeping the tradition and protecting what has been entrusted to its leaders (1 Tim 6:20). Major Christian doctrines, such as salvation through Christ and the second coming are assumed and repeated rather than argued.

When the church feels the threat of false teachings and practice it is natural to emphasize church order and discipline as well. The pastorals are concerned that church leaders, such as elders and deacons, be qualified to lead the church well. (The *presbyteroi* of 1 Timothy and the *episkopoi* of Titus probably refer to the same group of elders.) The pastorals seem to represent a situation before the church developed a monarchical episcopate, where one leader, thought to have been succeeded from the apostles, led the church. Although Timothy and Titus are addressed, they are still assumed to be itinerant. Titus is to meet Paul at Nicopolis, and Timothy is to come to Rome. The permanent leadership of the church is group of elders and deacons.

It is not only church leaders, however, who are to be ordered in the proper way within the church. Older members (Titus 2:1-5), young men (Titus 2:6-8), slaves (Titus 2:9-10; 1 Tim 6:1-2), widows (1 Tim 5:3-16), and women in general (1 Tim 2:8-15) receive specific advice about their roles and behavior within the church. The community can only meet the threat that the false teachers present if everyone is not only faithful, but knows the limits, boundaries, and responsibilities of his or her role in the community. Emphasis is on behavior that is prudent, serious, temperate, self-controlled, godly, and hospitable. This appears to be a more conventional and less radical obedience than appears in other parts of the New Testament.

Another theme emphasized in all three of the pastorals is the danger of riches, or at least the greed that often accompanies riches. Elders (Titus 1:7) and deacons (1 Tim 3:8) are not to be greedy. Christians are to be content with food and clothing (1 Tim 6:8) and are warned about the temptations of the rich (1 Tim 6:9) and the teachers in the last days who will be lovers of money (2 Tim 3:2). Money is said to be a root of all kinds of evil (1 Tim 6:10).

RELEVANCE FOR TODAY

Many scholars tend to depreciate the message of the pastorals as inferior to the rest of the New Testament because of their emphasis on conventional morality and traditional teaching. But in our age of intense individualism, when we all tend to do it our way, we need to be reminded that there are limits and boundaries to both teaching and behavior which, when transgressed, present spiritual dangers. Already in 1 Cor 8-10 Paul had reminded the Corinthians that not all things are helpful nor do all things build up the church. The pastorals intensify this warning. Christian responsibility goes beyond conventional, cultural morality, but the pastorals remind us that it is never less than conventional morality. And in our age of the new and novel, it doesn't hurt to consider the value of what our foremothers and forefathers have entrusted to us.

We also need to be reminded that the church needs organization and order if it is to carry out its mission. The church's purpose goes beyond satisfying the individual needs of its members. Only when leaders and all members take responsibility can the church succeed.

[handwritten margin note: church goes beyond individual members]

ISSUES FOR DISCUSSION AND REFLECTION

1. If you were on a church nominating committee how would you want to condense, supplement, or modify the qualifications for church leaders today? Is it important to have a list of qualifications? If so, why?
2. How do you interpret some of the advice relating to women, such as 1 Tim 2:8-11? Should this instruction be followed in the church today? Why or why not?
3. What do you think are the most dangerous false teachings and practices that threaten the church today? How should the church respond to them?
4. In what practical ways might a Christian take the warnings in the pastorals about the dangers of money seriously in our capitalistic and often materialistic culture?

FURTHER READING

Dibelius, Martin
    1972   *The Pastoral Epistles.* (Hermeneia). Trans. by Philip Buttolph and Adela Yarbro, Ed. by Helmut Koester. Philadelphia: Fortress.
Guthrie, Donald
    1984   *The Pastoral Epistles.* (Tyndale). Grand Rapids, MI: Eerdmans.
Hanson, Anthony T.
    1982   *The Pastoral Epistles.* (New Century). Grand Rapids, MI: Eerdmans.
Quinn, Jerome D.
    1990   *The Letter to Titus.* (Anchor). New York: Doubleday.

Chapter 17

Narrative and Gospel Genre

Ronald L. Jolliffe

INTRODUCTION

Reading and understanding the gospels involves more than just knowing the meaning of words or even sentences. The gospels are the products of several generations of transmission, reflection, and development in thinking by the early church. This process began orally, with the telling and retelling of teachings of Jesus. Even at the written stage, the gospels have complex literary histories. This chapter will attempt a simplified introduction to two aspects of that history, narrative and genre.

Narrative has to do with all aspects of stories: content, composition, and the act of telling. When it comes to the gospels, narrative serves first as a reminder that the gospels began as stories—not stories carried around in books and read silently by a person before bed, but stories that were listened to and retold. Oral stories exist inside of people, and consist primarily of conceptual frameworks, patterns, or even pictures. No matter which of these metaphors one prefers, it is clear that oral stories are living, dynamic realities. On the other hand, written stories are located outside of people, in texts which build their conceptual framework a word at a time. Written stories are fixed and static in ways that oral stories are not.

The other topic treated in this chapter is genre (the *kind* of story). Genre and narrative are related to each other, but one is not a discrete category of the other. Genre is simply the word for *kind, style, or category.* In narrative, as in literature, genre has to do with different kinds of stories, much like one would find in a video store: drama, comedy, horror, action, adventure, classics, children's, etc. Some consider "gospel" to be a distinct genre of biblical literature. Whether or not this is the case, one can understand little of a text's actual meaning without knowing something of the text's genre. For example, if one reads a parable supposing it to be an apocalyptic text, a serious misunderstanding of the intended meaning of the text will be the result.

Narrative

Within biblical studies recently, there has been an increased interest in narrative. This interest can be comprehended in part as reaction against both conservative and liberal approaches to the Bible. Both the stark historicism of fundamentalism, given to mining the text for information, and the sterile historical-critical method given to analyzing the life out of texts in its complex observations, seem to have increased an interest in hearing the stories of the Bible as narrative. Narrative serves also as a reminder that story-telling involves community. In antiquity, stories were not enjoyed privately, as when one reads a book in silence. Stories were shared experiences between at least two, usually more, people.

It is difficult in the contemporary world, where everything important seems to have to be written down before it becomes important, to value orality. One of the few communication processes where orality still functions as a significant medium of transmission is jokes. While there are joke books, most people come in contact with jokes through hearing them told. Jokes can serve to provide a glimpse into the differences between the oral and the written transmission of information.

Jokes are relatively short by comparison with magazine articles, short stories, or newspaper articles. Jokes are rarely memorized word for word. They are remembered as the relationship between a set-up and a punch-line. Most jokes can then be adapted to a variety of particular circumstances, yet remain the same, even though the identities of people, places, and circumstances have been radically altered. With no intention to trivialize the stories of Jesus, the analogy of how the stories were initially transmitted is somewhat analogous to the transmission of jokes in contemporary western society.

Probably most stories in the gospels were told and retold long before they were written. It is important as modern readers of the gospels to read and think of (to hear) each pericope (story) as an individual unit, complete in itself, with introduction, plot development and conclusion, long before asking the ethical, moral, or theological meaning of a story. Furthermore, since most of the oral stories were originally circulated as individual units, the sequence of stories found in a written text is usually that of the author, not the original context of the story. The context of a story in any gospel provides information about what the editor of that gospel intended, but not necessarily about the story's context in its oral stage. These observations should caution against attempting to extract too much information from a pericope.

A distinction is frequently made between two basic uses of language. "First-order" language is the concrete language of story-telling (narrative). For example, it is the story of the Rich Man and Lazarus in Luke 16:19-31. "Second-order" language is the more abstract language of analysis. For example, when one asks what "Hades" is like from the story of the Rich Man and Lazarus, one is asking a second-order question that may not have been of particular interest to the story-teller. The gospels normally tell stories about Jesus without pausing to iterate what they want the hearer to know in second-order language, such as "Here we see that Jesus has power over nature." Second-order investigation is not inappropriate, but it often expresses the concern of the contemporary reader, and not necessarily the intention of the story-teller.

It seems that throughout much of the history of the church, as well as the history of scholarship, more energy has been invested in concerns about how to derive beliefs and teachings from the gospels than in hearing the stories as they are told. The first serious scholarly work with the issue of orality came with form-criticism, which investigates standard communication forms, both written and oral, in order to better understand how formal conventions shape human communication.

Genre

The word *genre* frequently worries persons new to literary study. Basically, genre refers to different categories of things. In the Bible, there are a variety of genre clearly apparent. There are letters, both personal, such as Philemon, and general, such as Galatians. There is apocalyptic, as in Revelation or Matt 24. In addition to these categories that treat whole documents, one can also distinguish the genre of certain smaller units that constitute parts of larger works. For example, there is allegory, such as the treatment of Hagar and Ishmael that appears in Gal 4:21-27. There are parables, which are distinguishable from proverbs, etc.

The importance of knowing something about the genre of a work is clear when one simply notes that one does not read a parable in the same way as a prayer. So also one reads myth, fable, legend, history, and allegory differently, for they utilize different devices for truth-telling. Readers intuitively know more about how to read different genres than they think they do. For example, a modern newspaper provides an assortment of different kinds of literary texts which readers have learned to read according to the appropriate literary genre without difficulty. While reading the front page one expects to learn accurate details and even-handed reporting about the news of the day. On the front page the views of the writers are not to skew the way the news is reported. But one turns to read the editorial page with quite different expectations. There one expects to find out whether the editor believes some news item is good or bad and why the editor holds that opinion. In other words, a reader seeks out the editorial page for a quite different reason than the front page.

When modern readers come to the reading of the New Testament gospels assuming they are going to read something like the front page of a newspaper, even though perhaps aware that it was written a long time ago, they are in danger of misapprehending the very thing the gospels were written to communicate. The gospel writers were not controlled by the urge merely to record their stories with objective chronological accuracy, nor to provide unbiased comprehensive coverage of the significant events in Jesus' life, nor in any other way to provide the neutral accounting that any reputable newspaper would require of its front-page writers. They were not dispassionate reporters, but evangelists. The gospel writers want the hearers of their works to commit their lives to Jesus, hardly a neutral stance for a reporter to assume!

Cool, objective reporting was not desirable to the writers of Matthew, Mark, Luke and John. The gospels were driven by a greater purpose, the proclamation of faith founded upon Jesus. This purpose controlled which stories were selected, which omitted; the arrangement of the narratives; how they were worded and the kinds of explanations attached to the words. The most direct statement of this kind of intention, which clearly reflects these observations is found in John 20:30, 31: "Although Jesus performed many more miracles for his disciples to see than could be written down in this book, these are written down so you will come to believe that Jesus is the Anointed, God's son—and by believing this have life in his name."

The concern of the gospels to *tell* the story of Jesus, rather than to *explain* who Jesus was or to *develop* a theology of who Jesus is, places the gospels in the genre of "narrative." Although it should now be clear why the gospels are not like front-page news stories, in that they lack the even-handed objective reporting expected in news reporting, it is also necessary to observe that the gospels are not much like the editorial page of a newspaper either. The editorial page overtly states the opinion of the editor, and normally provides the reasons for the editor's opinion. The editorial page, after describing the event or the pending legislation, then opines, "This editor finds the matter under discussion to be reprehensible (or admirable) because ...." The gospel writers do not often identify their personal views directly.

Gospel — *euangelion* — good news

The English word *gospel* is used as the translation of the New Testament Greek word *euangelion*, which also appears in English in the transliterated form evangelical. The root meaning is "good news."

The word gospel is used in several different ways. (a) It refers to the Christian faith. In this use, Christians confess, "I believe in the gospel of Jesus

Christ." (b) It is used to distinguish one way of being a Christian from another. In this use, one Christian might say of another, "She is so worried that she can't be good enough, it's too bad she doesn't understand the gospel." (c) In the use which is of interest to this chapter, gospel refers to a genre (kind, or category) of literature.

The gospels belong to an ancient world whose literary conventions governed how the gospels were written. Although people spoke of "good news" before the early Christians, *gospel* was not a name for a type of literature in existence. The early Christians applied the term *gospel* to their adaptation of ancient biography. Although scholarship continues to disagree over whether gospel is a unique genre distinct from ancient biography, it seems clear that gospel and biography share many things in common. Biography is not far off the mark as the *genre* to which gospel belongs, especially if one keeps in mind that people have always told stories about what other people said and did. Ancient biography did this formally, and so did the gospels. Furthermore, ancient biographers (like modern ones) always had personal reasons for writing about someone. The reasons changed from one biographer to another, but usually involved a desire for personal advancement in addition to the desire to influence the way the audience thought about the person whose story was being told. Whether personal advancement played a role with the gospel writers or not, the interest in influencing audiences is clear in the gospels. They intentionally assembled their stories to influence how hearers responded to what Jesus said and did. The gospels of the New Testament are not nearly so interested in merely recording the facts of Jesus' life, as in winning converts to the community of followers of Jesus.

Conclusion

So what difference does knowing about genre make? Understanding the differences between modern news reporting and ancient gospel writing prevents the assumption that the gospels were written only for the purpose of providing facts and information about Jesus' life and times. The gospels were not composed to record what the world was like in Jesus' day. They were written to proclaim the good news in such a way as to lead the hearers of the gospels to become disciples of Jesus. This is especially important to remember for readers who live in a world which gives primary importance to accurate data. The gospels do not want to serve as an encyclopedia of correct historical facts; they want to lead *you* to become a disciple of Jesus.

FURTHER READING
Bultmann, Rudolph
  1994   *History of the Synoptic Tradition*, Revised Edition. Peabody, MA:
         Hendrickson.
Funk, Robert W.
  1988   *The Poetics of Biblical Narrative.* Sonoma, CA: Polebridge.
Kelber, Werner H.
  1983   *The Oral and the Written Gospel: The Hermeneutics of Speaking and
         Writing in the Synoptic Tradition, Mark, Paul, and Q.* Philadelphia:
         Fortress.

Chapter 18

Gospel Relationships

Ronald L. Jolliffe

THE RELATIONSHIPS AMONG THE GOSPELS

Introduction

The New Testament contains four gospels, divided, on the basis of style and content into two groups, the Gospel of John and the three which, because they share a similar perspective, are called the "synoptic" gospels (Matthew, Mark, and Luke). This chapter will examine the relationships among the synoptic gospels, which will, of necessity, include a brief introduction to two other early Christian gospels, the *Sayings Gospel* (more commonly known as "*Q*") and the *Gospel of Thomas*.

This chapter will highlight the differences of viewpoint among the synoptic gospels, consider the sources used by the authors of the synoptics, and introduce a few works the student could read for more detail. As with the Gospel of John, each of the synoptic gospels represents a distinctive viewpoint on the meaning and significance of the life and death of the founder of the Christian religion, Jesus, called the Christ. For many centuries the differences among the gospels *representa-* have been illustrated by use of four creatures whose faces appear in the vision *tions of* of Ezek 1:10: Mark is represented by a lion, Luke by an ox, Matthew by a man, *4* and John by an eagle. Frequently artists using these symbols add wings to each *gospels* of the creatures.

The Gospel of John frequently tells its readers directly what they are to *John tells* believe about Jesus. The authors of the synoptic gospels also had clear goals *readers* about what they wanted their readers to understand, but for the most part, they *what to* chose to inform their readers about what Jesus' sayings and deeds meant through *believe* indirect methods. They normally do not make the overt statements common in the Gospel of John, but convey their purposes implicitly through a variety of means. They place the pericopae in particular sequences. They edit pericopae through omission and addition of information. They insert stories told in no

Sondergut: Stories told nowhere else [handwritten margin note]

other gospel (*Sondergut*). Occasionally they append explanations to some of Jesus' own stories, etc. These all combine to produce a certain "spin" on how the readers of each gospel are expected to respond to Jesus and his teaching.

The individual viewpoints of the Synoptic Gospels

Mark: a passion narrative — I am extended intro [handwritten margin note]

The Gospel of Mark. Mark, the first of the New Testament's gospels to be written, has been described as a Passion Narrative with an extended introduction. Peter's confession that Jesus is the Christ (Mark 8:27-30) forms an important division in the book. As soon as Peter's confession has been made, Jesus begins to teach his disciples that the Son of man must die (Mark 8:31), and the story moves inexorably forward, with Jesus' death in view, toward the cross.

Jesus has authority [handwritten margin note]

Mark's primary concern is Jesus' authority. In this gospel Jesus has authority that defeats his antagonists and conquers the natural world, disease and death. Jesus teaches as one who "has authority" (Mark 1:22). Jesus has authority to forgive sins (Mark 2:5-12); wins disputes concerning association with sinners (Mark 2:15-17), fasting (Mark 2:18-22), proper Sabbath observance (Mark 2:23-27, 3:1-6), being in alliance with Beelzebub (Mark 3:20-27), and over purification rituals (Mark 7:1-23). Jesus definitively answers his opponents concerning interpretation of the laws about divorce (Mark 10:2-9). He answers a challenge regarding payment of taxes (Mark 12:13-17), the resurrection (Mark 12:18-27); and the greatest commandment (Mark 12:28-34). Jesus even gives authority over diseases and demons to the twelve (Mark 6:7).

As to his authority over the natural world, Jesus exorcises demons (Mark 1:23-28, 5:1-13, 9:14-28); cures fever (Mark 1:29-31); heals leprosy, (Mark 1:40-45); restores mobility to a paralytic (Mark 2:15); restores a withered hand (Mark 3:1-5); holds power over the weather (Mark 4:35-41, 6:45-52); raises the dead (Mark 5:21-24, 35-42); heals chronic illness (Mark 5:25-34); feeds multitudes with small amounts of food (Mark 6:32-44, 8:1-9); heals a deaf-mute (Mark 7:31-37); heals the blind (Mark 8:22-26, 10:46-52).

no resurrection appearances [handwritten margin note]

Also of surprise, the Gospel of Mark does not record any resurrection appearances. The book simply ends with the women being afraid (Mark 16:8).

Matthew: five divisions [handwritten margin note]

The Gospel of Matthew. The structure of the Gospel of Matthew is surprisingly different from the Gospel of Mark. The book seems to be designed around five divisions. These divisions are framed by an introduction and a conclusion. The five divisions each consist of a section of deeds and teaching of Jesus and they each conclude with the phrase "when Jesus had finished ...." There are only five places in the book where this phrase appears. Each occurrence marks the conclusion of one of these sections of deeds and teaching (Matt 7:28; 11:1; 13:53; 19:1; 26:1).

|| Jesus - Moses [handwritten margin note]

Whereas Mark focused on Jesus' authority, Matthew seems to be interested in drawing parallels between Jesus and Moses. First there are the five "books" described in the last paragraph. Jewish tradition attributes five books to Moses, known as the Pentateuch, they are the first five books of the Jewish Bible, Genesis, Exodus, Leviticus, Numbers, and Deuteronomy.

Other interesting parallels can be made between Matthew's portrayal of Jesus and Moses. The ones which seem most significant appear only in the Gospel of Matthew. These include the decree to slaughter the infants (Matt 2:16, compare Exod 1:15-22); the flight into Egypt (Matt 2:19-21, compare Exod 1:1); the command to return because those seeking to kill are dead (Matt 2:20, compare Exod 4:19); the reference to the 40 days *and 40 nights* of fasting in the wilderness preceding the giving of the law (Matt 4:2, compare Exod 34:28); the law being given from a mountain (Matt 5:1, compare Exod 19:20-25). One should also compare Jesus' words, "You have heard it said, but I say to you ..." which appear early in the Sermon on the Mount and discuss commands from the books of Moses (Matt 5:21/Exod 20:13, 5:27/Exod 20:14, 5:31/Deut 24:1, 5:33/Lev 19:12, Num 30:2, Deut 23:23; 5:38/Lev 24:20; 5:43/Lev 19:18, Deut 23:6).

The Gospel of Matthew has often been considered the church's gospel since it seems most oriented toward the issues of how a congregation of people function together. In fact only the Gospel of Matthew mentions the church specifically, and both references have to do with church authority. The first is the famous "keys of the kingdom" speech of Jesus to Peter that he will build the church on "this rock" and give to Peter the keys of the kingdom of heaven. The second reference to the church comes in Matt 18:15-18 on how to restore fellowship after someone sins. These references to the church are anachronistic to Jesus' day, since there was no Christian church during Jesus' lifetime. Thus they represent Matthean interpretation of Jesus' words.

The Gospel of Luke   Luke holds yet a third emphasis, a focus on the matter of poverty. Luke's concerns for the poor can be noticed in the Lukan *Sondergut* materials. In the Lukan Christmas narratives there are no wealthy Magi bringing expensive gifts into the "house" (compare Matt 2:11), but only poor shepherds who find the baby in a manger because there is no room in the inn (Luke 2:8-20). The purification offering that Mary and Joseph take to the temple is the gift the poor are allowed to bring in place of a lamb, "a pair of turtledoves, or two young pigeons" (Luke 2:22-24, compare Lev 12:8). Luke's genealogy of Jesus does not trace Jesus' ancestors through the wealthy kings of Judah as in Matthew, but through obscure men (compare the kings in Matt 1:6-12 with Luke 3:27-32). The woes on the rich and comfortable in Luke 6:24-26 are Lukan *Sondergut* and correlate well with Luke's account of the beatitudes (Luke 6:20-21) which bless the poor and the hungry, in contrast to Matthew's blessing on "the poor *in spirit* and the ones who "hunger and thirst *after righteousness*" (Matt

5:3, 6). The following Lukan *Sondergut* also seem interested in the plight of the poor: the widow's son at Nain (Luke 7:11-17); the good Samaritan (Luke 10:29-37); the parable of the rich fool (Luke 12:16-21); the Pharisees being reproved for their love of money (Luke 16:14-16); the rich man and Lazarus (Luke 16:19-31); the parable of the persistent widow (Luke 18:1-8); and Zacchaeus (Luke 19:1-10).

The sources of the Synoptic Gospels

It is clear, when one compares the same story in each of the synoptic gospels, that a literary interdependence exists among the three. The easiest way to do this comparison is with a synopsis of the gospels (see the end of this chapter for bibliographic information on the most commonly used synopsis). Many stories and sayings are not only alike, but even share similar sentence structure and wording. This occurs not only in the sayings of Jesus, but also in descriptions of situations and in summary statements (compare Mark 3:1-2 with Matt 12:9-10 and Luke 6:6-7 for example).

The proposed solution to the literary interdependence of the gospels operates on a few basic observations. The first observation is that the Gospel of Mark was the first New Testament gospel to be written. A few basic observations confirm this. First, the Gospels of Matthew and Luke agree in the order of the stories they both tell only when there is also a parallel found in the Gospel of Mark. Secondly, Mark's stories are consistently longer and more awkward than the same story in Matthew or Luke. It is easier to explain why the gospels of Matthew and Luke would each choose to smooth out the difficulties in the Gospel of Mark, than to explain why Mark would have made Matthew's and/or Luke's stories more awkward and wordy.

The material in the gospels falls into one of two general categories; it is either 1) unique to only one gospel (*Sondergut*), or 2) it is shared with at least one other gospel. The way the material is shared between gospels is of two basic kinds; a) if it is found in all three synoptic gospels it is said to belong to the Triple Tradition; but if it is found only in Matthew and Luke (and not in Mark), it belongs to the Double Tradition.

Triple Tradition material is based on the Gospel of Mark. Mark was the first canonical gospel to be written, and was used extensively by Matthew and Luke as one of their sources for writing their own gospels. Nearly the entire Gospel of Mark is found in Matthew and Luke. But neither the Gospel of Matthew nor the Gospel of Luke report every account from the Gospel of Mark. Matthew includes about 90% of Mark, Luke about 55%. Only one saying and two healing stories in the Gospel of Mark are found neither in the Gospel of Matthew nor the Gospel of Luke, (namely, Mark 4:26-29, the Parable of the Seed Growing Secretly; Mark 7:32-37 healing a deaf-mute; and Mark 8:22-26 healing a blind man). In other words, material found in the Gospels of Matthew and Mark, or in Luke and Mark, is clearly based on Mark. Thus Triple Tradition material is really material that comes from the Gospel of Mark. So Mark is one of the primary sources for Matthew and Luke.

The other identifiable source is the Sayings Source. There are more than 200 verses that Matthew and Luke share in common that are not found in Mark. These verses have certain interesting characteristics. They consist almost entirely of sayings of Jesus. These Double Tradition verses appear to represent another gospel, in addition to Mark, that was used by the authors of the Gospels of Matthew and Luke when they were writing their gospels. This other gospel is called "*Q*" by scholars because it refers to a source used by Matthew and Luke (the German word for "source" begins with Q, *Quelle*). Because *Q* consists primarily of sayings of Jesus, it is also called the *Sayings Gospel* or the *Sayings Source*.

The history of scholarly work on *Q* has not been without problems. Even though compelling arguments substantiated the existence of *Q*, one difficulty seemed insurmountable—the fact that *Q* clearly lacked a Passion Narrative. It was thought impossible that any early Christian gospel could have been written that was interested in Jesus' teachings, but not in his death and resurrection. Consequently, *Q* was ignored by the majority of biblical scholars until a new archaeological discovery was made in the middle of the 20th century. An ancient gospel, which called itself the *Gospel of Thomas*, was found in 1945 near the village of Nag Hammadi in upper Egypt.

The *Gospel of Thomas* was an early Christian gospel which shared some characteristics similar to those described for *Q*. It was a gospel interested in the sayings of Jesus, rather than in Jesus' deeds. It contained 114 sayings of Jesus, but had no Passion Narrative. It was a gospel like *Q* in the sense that it was interested in Jesus as teacher rather than savior. The fact that such a document existed gave new impetus to the study of *Q*. Students interested in consulting the texts of *Q* and Thomas will find references to recent works where these documents are available in English translation at the end of this chapter.

In summary, there are three basic kinds of material found in the synoptics: a) *Sondergut*, b) material based on the Gospel of Mark, and c) material based on *Q*.

An example of source analysis

The preceding description in this chapter may be helpful for getting an overview of the relationships among the gospels, but there is no substitute for working with the materials themselves. The following simplified exploration of how the Gospel of Luke is structured demonstrates how Luke interfaced material from the Gospel of Mark, material from *Q*, and his own *Sondergut*.

Luke's gospel begins with the Lukan Christmas story 1:1-2:52 most of which is *Sondergut*. The first major section of the gospel (Luke 3-9:50) reports the Galilean ministry of Jesus. Luke uses the Gospel of Mark closely in Luke 4:31-44; 5:12-6:19; then uses *Q* in Luke 6:20-8:3. Because Luke has inserted *Q* material into this section which is following Mark so closely, scholars refer to it as Luke's "Lesser Interpolation." Luke finally returns to Mark for the last section of the Galilean ministry of Jesus in Luke 8:4-9:50. Luke uses nothing from Mark 6:45-8:26. This is called Luke's "Great Omission."

The next major section of the Gospel of Luke is Jesus' "Journey to Jerusalem" (Luke 9:51-19:28). No other gospel reports this journey. The majority of this section (Luke 9:51-18:14) is referred to as Luke's "Greater Interpolation" because this material is introduced into material taken from the Gospel of Mark. The Greater Interpolation is composed from *Q* and *Sondergut*.

Some features of this section of the Gospel of Luke are curious. The author reminds his readers frequently that Jesus is journeying to Jerusalem (9:51, 53; 13:22, 33; 17:11; 18:31; 19:11, 28). Within the nearly ten chapters of this journey to Jerusalem, not only is the Gospel of Mark almost never used, but major sections from *Q* appear, as well as approximately two-thirds of Luke's *Sondergut* pericopae (9:52-56; 10:29-37; 11:5-8, 27-28; 12:16-21; 13:10-17; 13:31-33; 14:1-6, 7-14; 15:8-10, 11-32; 16:10-12, 14-15, 19-31; 17:7-10, 11-19, 20-21; 18:1-8; 19:1-10, 41-44).

If you follow on a map the movements of Jesus in this "Journey to Jerusalem," you discover that there seems to be no specific direction to his travel throughout the section, until suddenly he arrives in Bethany, near Jerusalem in 19:29. It appears that the original materials the author used in developing this "Journey" indicated no sequence nor location, so the author devised it in order to have a place to incorporate these *Q* and *Sondergut* pericopae into the gospel.

The final section of Luke, the Passion Narrative begins with Luke 19:29 and the preparations for the last supper. The Passion Narrative of the Gospel of Luke uses material from Mark and *Sondergut* but there is no material from *Q*.

FURTHER READING

Aland, Kurt, Ed.
    1982   *Synopsis of the Four Gospels*. London: United Bible Societies.
Goehring, James E., Charles W. Hedrick, Jack T. Sanders, and Hans Dieter Betz, Eds.
    1990   *Gospel Origins and Christian Beginnings, in Honor of James M. Robinson*. Sonoma, CA: Polebridge.
Grant, Frederick C.
    1957   *The Gospels, their Origin and Growth*. New York: Harper & Row.

Jacobson, Arland D.
   1992   *The First Gospel: An Introduction to Q.* Sonoma, CA: Polebridge.
Miller, Robert J., Ed.
   1994   *The Complete Gospels, Annotated Scholars Version.* San Francisco: Harper Collins.
Stein, Robert H.
   1991   *Gospels and Tradition. Studies on Redaction Criticism of the Synoptic Gospels.* Grand Rapids, MI: Baker.

Chapter 19

Mark

Ernest J. Bursey

"[W]hoever wishes to become great among you must be your servant, and whoever wishes to be first among must be slave of all. For the Son of Man came not to be served but to serve, and to give his life a ransom for many."

BRIEF OVERVIEW OF THE BOOK

The book of Mark begins in the middle of the stream. After a few words of introduction from the Old Testament and John the Baptist, an adult Jesus is baptized in the river Jordan as God's voice claims him as "beloved Son."

The book divides into roughly two halves on either side of Peter's confession that Jesus is the Messiah (8:27-30). Both halves contain an extended discourse by Jesus (a series of parables in 4:1-34; an overview of events around the destruction of the temple and the coming of the Son of Man 13:1-37). The first half of the book defies obvious division as the wide variety of

The Baptism of Jesus

suggestions indicates. The second half contains three obvious divisions. Jesus immediately announces his coming death, a theme that dominates the journey to Jerusalem (8:31; See also 8:34-37; 9:9, 30-32; 10:32-34). His presence at the

175

temple is the setting for chs 11-13. *c)* Jesus' arrest, crucifixion and resurrection constitute chs 14-16.

BACKGROUND CONCERNS

Mark, the name affixed to the beginning of the book by as early as the end of the first century, was one of the most common names in the Roman world. For the name elsewhere in the New Testament see Acts 12:12 (John Mark), 12:25 (John Mark), 15:37, 39 (John Mark), Col 4:10 (Mark the cousin of Barnabas, 2 Tim 4:11 (Mark), Phlm 24 (Mark), 1 Pet 5:13 (Mark, "my son"). All these New Testament references to (John) Mark could point to the same person associated with both Peter and Paul.

External evidence exists for linking the book with the apostle Peter. Papias, a second century bishop from Hieropolis, claimed he had been told by "John the elder":

> Mark became Peter's interpreter and wrote accurately all that he remembered, not, indeed, in order, of the things said or done by the Lord. For he had not heard the Lord, nor had he followed him, but later on, as I said, followed Peter, who used to give teaching as necessity demanded but not making, as it were, an arrangement of the Lord's oracles, so that Mark did nothing wrong in thus writing down single points as he remembered them. For to one thing he gave attention, to leave out nothing of what he had heard and to make no false statements in them.[1]

At least some of the intended readers were Gentiles who were not familiar with Jewish practices, as the elementary explanation in 7:3-4 about ritual washing indicates. The phrase, "all the Jews," in 7:3 suggests a distinction between the Jews and the readers of Mark. Gentile readers would appreciate that Jesus commanded a demoniac in the Gentile territory of Decapolis to announce what Jesus had done for him even before sending his own Jewish disciples out into Galilee (5:19, 20).

Frequent allusions to the Old Testament show the author assumes the intended readers possess a familiarity with the Old Testament. Since the Old Testament was the Bible of the early Christians, even Gentile Christians would be acquainted with it. Concerns over ritual defilement lurk throughout much of Mark, suggesting this was more than an antiquarian interest for the author (1:40-45; 2:16; 2:27, 30-34). His disciples are singled out by the Pharisees for not observing the rituals of purification before eating (7:1-5), invoking a stinging and lengthy counterattack by Jesus (7:6-23) who declares that whatever goes into a man cannot defile him (7:18). Perhaps the intended readership was in a situation analogous to the Galatian Christians to whom Paul wrote his painful letter warning against Judaizers, who arrived after his departure and who sought to impose a brand of Jewish practice on the fledgling Christian churches in Galatia.

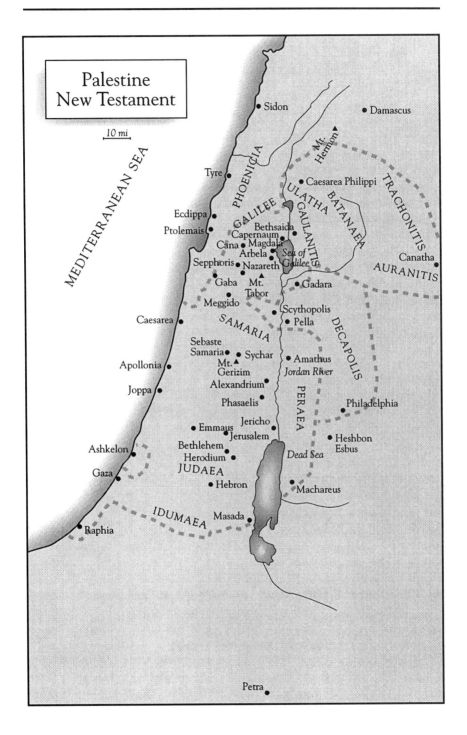

Palestine
New Testament

10 mi

MEDITERRANEAN SEA

Sidon

Damascus

PHOENICIA

Mt. Hermon ▲

Caesarea Philippi

Tyre

Ecdippa

Ptolemais

GALILEE

ULATHA

GAULANITIS

BATANAEA

TRACHONITIS

Bethsaida

Capernaum

Cana

Magdala

Arbela

Sea of Galilee

Canatha

AURANITIS

Sepphoris

Nazareth

Gaba

Mt. Tabor ▲

Gadara

Meggido

SAMARIA

Caesarea

Scythopolis

Pella

DECAPOLIS

Sebaste

Samaria

Sychar

Amathus

Jordan River

Apollonia

Mt. Gerizim ▲

Joppa

Alexandrium

PERAEA

Philadelphia

Phasaelis

Jericho

Emmaus

Jerusalem

Heshbon

Esbus

Ashkelon

Bethlehem

Herodium

Dead Sea

Gaza

JUDAEA

Hebron

Machaerus

IDUMAEA

Masada

Raphia

Petra

Rome? *all use of Latin terms*

Clement states that the book was written in Rome when Peter was there.[2] The extensive use of Latin words and construction drawn from the military, judicial and economic spheres, supports a Roman setting. See *modius* (4:21); *legio* (5:9, 15); *speculator* (6:27); *denarius* (6:37); *sextarius* (7:4); *census* (12:14); *quadrans* (12:42); *fragello* (15:15); *praetorium* (15:16); *centurio* (15:39, 44, 45). See especially the explanation of Greek words in 12:42 and 15:16 by the use of Latin equivalents. This evidence does not prove the intended readers were Romans since Rome's military conquests had encouraged the spread of Latin far beyond the city of Rome.

author, readers not knew Aramaic

The book's frequent use of Aramaic words and, on occasion, its explanation of Aramaic words with a Greek translation (3:17; 5:41; 7:11, 34; 10:46; 14:36; 15:22, 34), suggest that the author, unlike the intended readers, was familiar with Aramaic, the basic language spoken in Palestine. The quality of the Greek indicates it was a second language for the author. The way all three languages are used in the book would support authorship by a Palestinian Jew, like John Mark, who became a Christian and engaged in mission in the wider Greco-Roman world and, if Papias' and Clement's words are accepted, wrote the gospel for Roman Christians while in Rome with Peter.

If the book was written while Peter was alive as Papias and Clement claimed, it would have been completed before the outbreak of persecution by Nero against Christians in Rome in 64 C.E. Presumably the warning of Jesus in Mark 13:14 would not be couched in the mysterious language of Daniel if written after the actual destruction of the temple in 70 C.E.[3]

comparison. 1. compare view of J.B. to D.S.S. 2. death of John in Josephus

For a better understanding of this gospel in its first-century setting, Mark's use of Isa 40:3 in 1:2-5 to point to the work of John the Baptist should be compared to its use in 1QS VIII of the Dead Sea Scrolls to point to the study of the Law by the righteous community living in the wilderness. Mark's account of the work and death of John in 1:2-8 and 6:14-29 should be compared with Josephus' account in *Antiquities* 18:116-119 of why Herod executed John. Likewise readers of Mark ought to compare the description of Jesus' royal entrance into Jerusalem according to Mark 11:1-11, with Josephus' account in *War* 7.63-74, 123-162 of the triumphal entries of Vespasian and Titus into the city of Rome.

LITERARY AND RHETORICAL CONSIDERATIONS

gospel: Jesus' first, message

Mark's narrative about Jesus may have been the first of a new literary species, the gospel. Actually the term, "gospel," first referred to the contents of the message Jesus proclaimed (1:14).

several endings added

The book has been provided with several different endings. All existing endings that go beyond 16:8 did not originate from Mark's hand but are attempts to produce a more satisfactory conclusion to the book. The longest ending, 16:9-

20 in the King James Version, appears to have been composed independently as early as the first half of the second century prior to its association with the book of Mark and deserves respect for its antiquity. The central issue is whether the ending at 16:8 can be sustained or whether we must conclude the original ending to be lost. In 16:6-7 the divine messenger points the women to the empty tomb, declares Jesus is risen and then commands them to tell the disciples that Jesus would be waiting for them in Galilee. However, due to utter fear the women flee "and they said nothing to anyone, for they were afraid" *(kai oudeni ouden eipan ephobounto gar)*. The specific interpretative challenge is to make a case for the author intending to end with these words. Modern interpreters ready to end the book at 16:8 point to the pattern of fear, faithlessness and the failure to comprehend that characterizes Jesus' disciples throughout the book. By ending this way the author has invited us readers to break that pattern by responding to the good news Jesus offers and to follow him wherever he leads us.

[margin note: was original ending lost?]

[margin note: did the author intend to end here?]

How well-written is the book? No one denies the book's uncouth use of the Greek language. Modern translations remove the annoyance of Mark's sentences often hitched together like railroad cars with "and" (Greek: *kai*). In the first chapter alone "immediately" (Greek: *euthus*) is used eleven times. Yet the book conveys a vividness and level of dramatic interest that makes it the best story of the four in the New Testament.

[margin note: crude but vivid]

Almost diametrically opposite views have been expressed about the writer's skill. A century ago Mark was seen more as an editor with a sloppy scissors and tape technique. Low estimates of Mark's literary skill can still be found. John Meagher characterizes various sections of the book as "disordered detail," "irretrievably awkward," "very ordinary, homely, untrained prose," etc. and asserts, "I think Mark writes rather badly."[4] On the other hand, high estimates of the author abound. Robert Fowler speaks of Mark's "masterful rhetoric of indirection" and declares the book as a whole to be "a valley of paradox" in which "the incongruous and ambiguous greet us at every turn."[5] This gulf between the opinions of literary critics comes in part from the differing assessment of the frequent gaps in the flow of the Markan narrative—are they due to clumsy or skillful writing?

[margin note: what about the gaps]

Ancient authors knew that the way most of their readers experienced a work of literature was through listening to it being read aloud and so took into consideration the aural capabilities of their audience. When we try to understand the book of Mark there is additional reason to consider the author's use of oral rhetoric. The gospel was heir to the substance and forms from thirty or forty years of oral preaching and story-telling by early Christian preachers and teachers, themselves imitators of the manner of Jesus, the book's main character. We take the aurality of Mark's intended audience seriously when we ask of any

[margin note: ancient writers wrote for hearers]

proposed outline or interpretation whether persons listening to the book as a whole at one sitting would be likely to notice it amid the flow of words.

Mark provides the hearer with a variety of resources for holding his extended narrative together in their minds while it is being spoken to them one word at a time.

similar stories

(a) Similar stories are clumped together (e.g. the conflict stories of 2:1-3:6; the parables of 4:1-34; the miracles of 4:35-6:6; the serial confrontations with priests, Pharisees, Herodians, Sadducees and scribes in 11:27-12:34).

Jesus' miracles in couplets

(b) Several of Jesus' miracles occur in separated couplets: the two supernatural feedings (6:30-44; 8:1-10); two stilling of the storms (4:35-41; 6:30-44), two healings of blind men (8:22-26; 10:46-52). The fates of John the Baptist and Jesus before are paired (6:17-22, 29; 9:12f) and their baptisms and authority compared (1:8; 11:27-33). Rather than a needless repetition, the paired stories are never identical.

Series of 3

(c) Series of threes hold the hearers' attention. There are three opinions about John (6:14f); three opinions about Jesus (8:27f);

Jesus & the Cripple

three announcements of Jesus' arrest, death and resurrection (8:31; 9:31; 10:33f); the disciples' three failures to keep awake (14:32-42); Peter's three denials (14:66-72); three non-demonic declarations that Jesus is the Son of God (1:11; 9:7; 15:39). The three predictions of Jesus' impending death and the disciples' failure to comprehend serve as a ramp for the reader to grasp the enormity of their abandonment and denial of him when he was arrested.

Stories attached to teaching

(d) Stories are attached to teachings to which they apply. The episode with the Gentile "dog," 7:24-30, follows the dispute over defilement, 7:1-23. Jesus' three announcements of his coming death (8:31; 9:31; 10:32-34) are each followed by scenes exposing the crass efforts of his disciples to gain advantage over each other. Jesus' warning to his disciples, and Mark his readers, to keep watch for the return of the Master (13:32-37), is followed by the account of the disciples' failure to keep watch (14:32-42).

Jesus Heals the Paralytic

conflict stories in pairs

(e) The five brief conflict stories appear to be arranged in two pairs; the first pair around sin and sinners (2:1-17), the second pair around Sabbath (2:23-3:6). These pairs surround the incident about fasting (2:18-22). Yet structurally the first and last stories are quite similar, while the second and fourth match. Accounting for this degree of complexity remains a challenge to interpreters.

2d half – waiting for Jesus' prediction + be fulfilled

(f) Through the latter half of the book we wait for the fulfillment of Jesus' predictions and promises (e.g. 9:1, 10:39; 14:27-30, 14:62; 8:31; 9:31; 10:32ff).

use of bracketing NOTE:

(g) A favorite strategy is the use of bracketing or the insertion of interludes. After Jesus' family leaves their house to come after Jesus because he is out of his mind (3:20f) and before they stand outside Jesus' house (3:31-35), Mark inserts the scribes' decision that Jesus is possessed by Beelzebul (3:22-30). After Jesus starts towards Jairus' home to heal his daughter (5:21-24) and before he arrives and raises her up (5:35-43), a woman touches Jesus' garments and is healed (5:21-34). After Jesus sends the disciples out (6:7-13) and before they return (6:30), Mark relates the death of John the Baptist (6:14-29). After the fig tree is cursed

(11:12-14) and before the disciples see it withered (11:20-21), Jesus drives the merchants out of the temple (11:15-19). These interruptions provide a sense of the passage of time but at a price—in each of these sandwich like constructions the readers' attention is diverted. Why then would Mark write this way? Interpreters are prone to look for thematic connections between the interlude and the story encompassing it. For instance, the woman who touches Jesus' garment is commended publicly for her belief (5:34). Then Jairus, told his daughter has died, is told by Jesus, "Do not fear, only believe" (5:36).

The Christian practice of reading the miracle stories as invitations to spiritual salvation assumes an allegorical sense to the narrative which may have been intended by Mark. If the fig tree is intended as a symbol of the temple and/or the Jewish nation, then Jesus' curse on the tree matches his shutting down of the temple service and gives weight to the accusation that Jesus plans to destroy the temple (14:58). The danger from allegorical approaches to the narrative comes from seizing on plausible interpretations never suspected by the author. It is helpful to keep in mind the pastoral purpose of the book. Whatever deeper meanings might be intended or surmised ought to square with the obvious and plain reading of the book.

THE MESSAGE
Outline
Mark may be briefly outlined as follows:

I. Jesus' deeds of the kingdom 1:1-8:26
II. Movement toward the cross 8:27-16:8
    A. Jesus announces his death, calls disciples to serve . . 8:27-10:52
    B. Jesus in the temple 11:1-13:37
    C. Jesus' passion and resurrection 14:1-16:8

Survey of contents
Mark's choice to write a narrative warns us against assuming we can bypass the book once we have an analysis of it in hand. When a rich narrative is reduced to a handful of themes a lot is destroyed, including its persuasive power. However, to trace the underlying conceptual structure of the gospel demands dissecting it as if it were a corpse on the autopsy table. We ought to treat the body with respect and pray for its resurrection after we are finished with our carving.

Mark planted the opening words by which we gain access to the story and its truths: "The beginning of the good news of Jesus Christ, Son of God." From these few words we grasp that the story Mark tells is at least part of "the good news," that this good news is from Jesus and/or about him, and that Mark claims for Jesus as the central character a special relationship with God.

[handwritten margin: Jesus' first lines]

So we pay attention to the first lines spoken by Jesus: "The time is fulfilled, and the kingdom of God has come near; repent and believe in the good news" (1:15). The second line of Jesus' speech points back to the first line: "the good news" is the arrival of the kingdom of God. Understanding what Jesus means by "the *[handwritten: understand the KOG — major task of players]* kingdom of God" will be a major assignment for the other characters in the story and for us as well. Jesus calls for us to repent and entrust our lives to the kingdom of God. The fact that he asks for this kind of response suggests belief won't be automatic or easy.

From this starting point Mark has given us several interwoven lines to trace in our journey through the rest of the story: (1) the arrival of the awaited *[handwritten: keep to story]* kingdom of God; (2) the role of Jesus, who we already know to be more than simply a messenger; and (3) the human responses, appropriate and inappropriate, to both the news of the arrival of God's kingdom and to Jesus, God's son.

The kingdom of God

The phrase, "kingdom of God," or its shortened form, "the kingdom," appears *[handwritten: KOG]* 14 times in the book of Mark, almost exclusively on the lips of Jesus. No one in the narrative ever asks Jesus about the meaning of the phrase nor is it ever defined or explained by the author.

Presumably Mark's intended readers were familiar with the term, but how? The Old Testament book of Daniel tells a dream about a stone that smashed a metal statue and then grew into a great mountain. The stone represented a future indestructible kingdom set up by the God of heaven that will break into pieces all existing human kingdoms (2:44). Jews who heard Jesus' preaching about the arrival of the kingdom would have supplied their own mental picture of the large stone smashing the statue. Living under the rule of Rome they longed for a deliverer from God. Many expected the future kingdom to be headed by an anointed king like David. When Jesus entered Jerusalem riding on a colt the crowds cried, "Blessed is the coming kingdom of our ancestor David" (11:10).

Imagine the confusion when Jesus compared the kingdom of God to a tiny mustard seed that grew to a large bush (4:31-32)! No wonder Jesus spoke of the "secret of the kingdom of God" (4:11). Yet Jesus promised that some in the hearing of his voice would not die before the kingdom of God would come with power (9:1).

To further complicate matters, Jesus revealed to his disciples the unusual and *[handwritten: strange entrance requirements]* stringent entrance requirements into this kingdom. Those who enter will come as children (10:14, 15). Threading a camel through the eye of a needle would be easier than a rich man gaining entrance into the kingdom of God (10:23-25). If one's eye causes sin, better to pluck it out and enter the kingdom of God than to end up two-eyed in hell (9:43, 45, 47). A scribe declares that to love God with all one's heart and strength and to love one's neighbor as oneself is much more than all the sacrifices offered in the temple. Jesus pronounces the man as "not far from the kingdom of God" (12:34). Presumably the scribe needs to act on his own teaching.

Jesus

Jesus, the principal character in the gospel, stands out as a person of action and obvious authority. All other characters in the book are divided up on the basis of how they relate to him. Bestowing titles to indicate importance or status was an accepted practice in the ancient world (e.g. Isa 9:6). But knowing which titles belong to Jesus is not a simple task for the characters in the book. Jesus' disciples wonder, "Who is this, that even wind and sea obey him (4:41)?" Herod thinks Jesus is John the Baptizer returned from the dead (6:14). Others conclude him to be Elijah or some other ancient prophet (6:15; see also 8:28). His unconventional message and awesome behavior made it difficult to identify him readily with the usual categories (4:41).

Jesus' initial ministry marks him as an itinerant preacher who practices exorcism and healing (1:21-39). He came "from Nazareth of Galilee" (1:9) and so is identified as "Jesus of Nazareth" by a shrieking demon (1:24; see also 10:47 and 16:6). However, there is little honor to be gained from Nazareth. Even the unclean spirit went on to declare, "I know who you are, the Holy One of God" (1:24; see also 3:11 and 5:7). Earlier at Jesus' baptism the voice of God from heaven told Jesus, "You are my Son, the beloved" (1:11). Much later in the hearing of the disciple the Voice claims Jesus as "my Son, the beloved" (9:7). Apparently only Jesus heard the heavenly voice at his baptism, and the testimony of unholy demons is suspect. Jesus' religious opponents considered him possessed by Beelzebul and working with the aid of Satan (3:22). While the readers of the book know from the start who Jesus is, no humans within the narrative acknowledge Jesus as the Son of God until the very end when the centurion executing Jesus confirms, "Truly this was God's Son" (15:39).

When Jesus presses his disciples to identify him, Peter declares, "You are the Christ." "Christ" is the Greek equivalent of the Hebrew based "Messiah" or "Anointed One." Past Jewish kings had been appointed by being anointed with oil (Saul, 1 Sam 10:1; David, 16:1). It was understood that the Messiah would be a descendant of king David (12:35). To speak of Jesus as "the Christ/Messiah" implies kingship over the Jews, accompanied by special evidence of God's favor. So Pilate and the mocking Roman soldiers speak of him as "the King of the Jews" (15:9, 12, 18, 26). The priests join the titles when they demand, "Let the Christ, the King of Israel, come down."

Jesus refers to himself by the enigmatic title, "the Son of Man," especially when he speaks of his arrest and death (8:31; 9:9, 12, 31; 10:33, 45; 14:21, 41). As the Son of Man he has authority to forgive sins and authority over the Sabbath (2:10, 28). As the Son of Man he promises to come with great authority and glory on the clouds accompanied by the angels and at the right hand of God as he gathers his chosen ones from the earth (8:38; 13:26; 14:62). Scholars have labored mightily to explain Jesus' use of the term when speaking of both his humiliation and his divine authority. The title in the Old Testament can refer to humans in their weakness. So the Psalmist asks of God, "What is man that thou art mindful of him, and the son of man that thou dost care for him?" (Ps 8:4 RSV). But Daniel sees "one like a son of man" presented to the Ancient of Days in the heavenly court and receiving authority and kingship that will last forever (Dan 7:13, 14 RSV). Perhaps Mark preserved the self-designation, "Son of Man," in order to speak of both Jesus' crucifixion and his divine role. By exercising supernatural powers in feeding the masses and stilling the storm, Jesus went beyond what his disciples or anyone else were expecting of the Christ/Messiah. His execution by crucifixion fell far below their expectations of the Christ/Messiah.[6]

Jesus is more than God's messenger announcing God's kingdom. In the Old Testament the God of Israel, Yahweh, has power over the waves and sea (i.e. Job 9:8; Ps 65:7; 77:16-19; 89:9; 104:6, 7; 107:23-32; Isa 43:16; 51:9-10). According to Exod 16:35 God provided manna to feed the huge multitude of Israelites in the Sinai wilderness. Mark takes extensive space to show that he is God's Son with his Father's power to still storms and feed multitudes in the desert (4:35-41; 6:30-52; 8:1-10).

How does the attention on the person of Jesus square with his emphasis on the kingdom of God? Right after Jesus tells the crowds and his disciples that some of them will see the kingdom of God come with power (9:1), Jesus himself is transformed into a splendid being of light who terrifies three of his disciples (9:1-6). Later he promises to return as the heavenly Son of Man with great power after the bodies of heaven are shaken (13:26). So the arrival of the kingdom of God coincides with the arrival of Jesus, the Son of God. Its power is manifested by him, both in the present and the future.

What is the connection between Jesus' death, which occupies so much of the book's attention, and the kingdom of God? At his trial and execution he is declared "King of the Jews." At his death, accompanied by supernatural signs, he is recognized as "Son of God." Mark makes it clear that when Jesus travels to Jerusalem he is acting in accord with a divine plan. Before his ascent to the right hand of God the Son of Man must be arrested, abused, handed over to violent men to be killed. Jesus viewed his own death as an act of ransom for many (10:45; 14:24 speaks of Jesus' blood poured out for many). Those who are ransomed are then to be gathered as Jesus' chosen ones when he returns as the heavenly Son of Man (13:26, 27).

Human Response

Jesus strides across Galilee preaching, "The time is fulfilled and the kingdom of God has come near; repent, and believe in the good news" (1:15). The call for repentance in Jesus' preaching was carried through from John's preaching (1:4) and later picked up by the Twelve whom Jesus sent out preaching and healing (6:12). So much for the mention of repentance in the book. But collectively the words, "faith/belief" "to believe" and "unbelief" appear 17 times in the book. Mark shows considerable interest in Jesus' call for faith/belief in the good news of the arrival of the kingdom of God already evident in his healing and exorcisms. This suggests that the book was written with more than just believers in mind, though Jesus's most extensive comments on faith are given to his disciples (11:22-25). How is "believing in the good news" to be related to the faith required for healing? Presumably the healing comes from the presence of God's kingdom realized through the miracles Jesus performs. Taken as a whole, Jesus' scattered comments on faith are remarkably positive (see 5:34, 36; 9:23; 10:52; 11:22-24). The cry of the father, "I believe; help my unbelief!" (9:24) echoes the inner prayer of every struggling believer.

As soon as Mark speaks of Jesus' preaching (1:14, 15), we hear of Jesus calling four fishermen to follow him and become fishers of men (1:16-20). For the rest of the story Jesus is scarcely ever out of sight of his disciples. He selects twelve to be with him and to go out preaching and exorcising demons (3:14, 15; see 6:7-13), thus extending his ministry through these disciples under his authority.

In spite of the disciples' immediate favorable responses to Jesus' invitations (1:18, 20; 2:14; 3:13) and their subsequent success in preaching and healing (6:12, 13), Jesus later announces to the crowds and his disciples, "If any want to become my followers, let them deny themselves and take up their cross and follow me" (8:34). The condition of self-denial and cross-bearing are added by Jesus to the original arrangements for discipleship after he announces his own death (8:31). Nothing appears to be taken for granted about the disciples' prior commitments. The demand that a rich man give away all he owns as a condition for discipleship and eternal life (10:21) is a specific application of Jesus announcement.

Jesus invests considerable effort and time on his disciples. They receive private instruction (4:10-20; 34; 7:17-23; 9:30-31). Yet they have difficulty grasping even the basic lessons and Jesus appears disappointed in them (4:13; 7:18; and especially 8:17-21). Each time Jesus announces his coming death they respond in a highly inappropriate or insensitive manner (8:32, 33; 9:32-34; 10:35-37). The last we see of the disciples in Mark they are disappearing into the darkness at Jesus' arrest in spite of their vow to stand with him to death (14:31; 14:50). Under oath Peter denies any knowledge of Jesus (14:71).

Interpreters grapple with the question of how the author intended us to view these disciples. Some scholars understand the disciples in Mark to be like the uncomprehending and fickle crowds or even Jesus' fearful enemies. Why then tell the painful story of their failures? From this point of view, Mark may have intended to undermine their authority in the infant church. *[How understand disciples?]*

Robert Fowler points to the distance between Jesus and his disciples that grows throughout the narrative

> Unevenly but irreversibly, until at last at the level of story all of the disciples abandon Jesus, at which point the distance between Jesus and the Twelve has become total, which means that at the level of discourse the burden of discipleship now falls squarely upon the shoulders of the only remaining candidate for discipleship—the recipient of the narrator's discourse, the reader of the Gospel.[7]

It is unlikely, though, that the readers are to see themselves as replacements for unredeemable disciples. After all, they were handpicked by Jesus and left everything to follow him (10:28; see also 1:16-20). Only among the disciples is Jesus recognized as the Christ/Messiah (8:27-29). Jesus solemnly promised them that no one leaving family or property for his sake and the sake of the gospel will lose a rich reward in the present age and the age to come (10:29-30). And at no place in the narrative does he indicate that he is finished with them, even after they all abandon him. His final message was an invitation to meet him in Galilee (16:7). At one point the whole group of disciples exclaimed in astonishment, "Then who can be saved?" Jesus looked at them (Greek: *enblepsas autois*) and said, "For mortals it is impossible, but not for God; for God all things are possible." (10:26, 27; see also 9:23 for the call to faith). *[readers are not replacements for the disciples]*

The preaching of the coming kingdom of God presumes a community of faith springing up in response. The twelve selected to preach are joined by others who listen to Jesus with a level of interest that sets them apart from the general crowds (3:31-34; 4:10; also 3:13 and 4:36). Looking at those gathered around him Jesus declares, "Here are my mother and my brothers" (3:34). The task of preaching by the twelve and others is to continue beyond Jesus' death and resurrection (9:9; 13:9-11; 14:9). Jesus' use of "any" and "whoever" (3:35; 8:34-35) conveys an invitation to any reader or hearer to join the disciples in their arduous yet ultimately rewarding role (10:29, 30). *[KOG presumes a faith comm. in response]*

Jesus offers instruction for the fledgling community most systematically within chs 8-10 and especially in connection with the announcements of his coming death. Not only must his followers reckon with the possibility of their *[ch 8-10 instruction]* own deaths for the sake of the gospel and Jesus (8:35-37; 10:30, 38-39; 13:11-13), but would be leaders among his followers must be last in line and slave of all, showing particular regard to the least significant, and modeling their use of power after the Son of Man who came to give his life as a ransom for many (9:36-37, 42; 10:13-15; 10:42-45). Disciples are to maintain high standards of personal conduct including the absence of divorce (9:43-10:12) and the keeping of peace among themselves (9:43-10:12).

Much of the book's contents make particular sense in light of an atmosphere of hostility and persecution. The perplexity that naturally arises when persecution strikes is to be met by the story of Jesus' death and resurrection and return with power to gather his elect. Jesus' power to save, shown in the miracle stories, and his call to suffer, declared in his teaching and exemplified in the passion narrative, bound together in one book are an antidote to despair and loss of confidence. The parables of the kingdom remind the readers not to overlook the presence of the kingdom in its apparent smallness. The eschatological discourse points out the bad conditions that lead up to the consummation. "But the one who endures to the end will be saved" (13:13).

RELEVANCE FOR TODAY

The underlying message about Jesus and the description of discipleship is the same in each of the New Testament gospels. All the gospels are written to encourage persecuted and ostracized believers to bear the shame of Jesus' name. All the gospels offer deliverance from demonic powers. Jesus' radical inversion of power as service impresses the thoughtful reader of each of the gospels. Jesus' scandalous warnings against wealth and his call for prospective disciples to give up everything are part of each of the Synoptics. Yet it is appropriate to ask wherein lies Mark's distinctiveness.

Mark's position in the New Testament canon remained secure because of its connection with Peter, yet it has been largely ignored for nearly two millennia. For much of the Christian era Matthew was held to be the source of the book of Mark, a view still held by a minority of scholars. Ninety-five percent of Mark's contents are closely paralleled in Matthew and Luke.

Why read the book of Mark today if you are not a literary critic or historian? For starters Mark offers a vivid story not yet expanded by the sermonic asides and the parables found in Matthew and Luke. Attention in Mark remains on Jesus and his disciples. Even the book's two sermons are closely connected with the story line. The crowds' problems over understanding Jesus' parables (4:11, 12) turn out to be shared by Jesus' closest followers (8:17-21). Jesus' teachings on how to prepare for the coming of the Son of Man (13:3-37) find illustration in the stories connected with Jesus' arrest in the garden and his trial (14:32-42, 53-72).

What would a reflective reading of Mark bring to the spiritually sensitive reader? Taken seriously, the book demolishes all pictures of a domesticated Jesus. The way he terrified those who had given up everything to follow him threatens our prospects for a conventional association with him. Whether any spiritual benefit accrues from reading Mark depends on whether we can see and hear without fleeing to our tamed depictions of Jesus and whether we have the courage to draw a connecting line between the ambitious disciples and ourselves. The abrupt ending, whether original or not, leaves the reader off balance but with the possibility of writing a more satisfactory ending that includes a personal response. Jesus' final invitation for the disciples to meet him in Galilee (16:7), even after they had abandoned and denied him, speaks volumes about his commitment to them. The disciples may not be suitable role models, but, as defective as they are, they still stand inside the circle of those Jesus calls his brothers and sisters and mother (3:34, 35). This alone brings hope to those who find themselves stumbling after God.

ISSUES FOR DISCUSSION AND REFLECTION

1. Descriptions of Jesus as a warm and loving person who inspires spiritual intimacy fall short of the Markan Jesus, who more often left terror and amazement in his wake.
   What place is there today for a mysterious Jesus who inspires awe and even terrifies his closest companions?
2. Jesus declared to his disciples, "Do you not see that whatever goes into a man from outside cannot defile him" (7:18). From this statement the author of Mark extrapolates the position that Jesus had declared all foods clean (7:19b), thus apparently eliminating the Old Testament dietary restrictions against unclean foods.
   Is there a basis on which a Christian could legitimately observe any of the Old Testament ritual laws?
3. Jesus told the crowds, "Truly I say to you, there are some standing here who will not taste death before they see that the kingdom of God has come with power" (9:1). Later he told his disciples about the events that will precede the coming of the Son of Man and declares, "Truly I say to you, this generation will not pass away before all these things take place" (13:30). Nearly 2000 years have elapsed.
   How should these assertions by Jesus be understood?
   Was Jesus mistaken?
   Were there extenuating circumstances that have caused a delay?

4. Jesus told a friendly prospect who wanted the assurance of eternal life
   (10:17) to "sell out that you have, and give to the poor, ... and come, follow
   me" (10:21). Mark reports that "the man went away sorrowful; for he had
   great possessions. Jesus made no effort to block the retreat of such a
   promising follower whom he held in warm esteem. There was no
   negotiating over the terms.
   Why did Jesus impose such stringent conditions?
   Would Jesus demand the same terms today from those interested in securing
   eternal life?

FURTHER READING

Best, Ernest
   1981   *Following Jesus: Discipleship in the Gospel of Mark.* Journal for the
          Study of the New Testament, Supl. Series, 4. Sheffield: Journal for
          the Study of the Old Testament.
Blevins, James L.
   1981   *The Messianic Secret in Markan Research, 1901-1976.* Washington,
          DC: University.
Burdon, Christopher
   1990   *Stumbling on God. Faith and Vision through Mark's Gospel.* Grand
          Rapids, MI: Eerdmans.
Dewey, Joanna
   1980   *Markan Public Debate: Literary Technique, Concentric Structure,
          and Theology in Mark 2:1-3:6.* Society of Biblical Literature
          Dissertation Series 48. Chico, CA: Scholars.
Guelich, Robert A.
   1989   *Mark 1:1-8:26.* Vol. 34A. (Word). Waco, TX: Word.
Gundry, Robert
   1993   *Mark: A Commentary on His Apology for the Cross.* Grand Rapids,
          MI: Eerdmans.
Fowler, Robert M.
   1991   *Let the Reader Understand: Reader-Response Criticism and the
          Gospel of Mark.* Minneapolis: Augsburg Fortress.
Hengel, Martin
   1985   *Studies in the Gospel of Mark.* Philadelphia: Fortress.
Hooker, Morna D.
   1991   *The Gospel According to Saint Mark.* (Black's). Peabody, MA:
          Hendrickson.
Humphrey, Hugh M.
   1981   *A Bibliography for the Gospel of Mark, 1954-1980.* (Studies in the
          Bible and Early Christianity, Vol. 1). New York: Edwin Mellen.

Kermode, Frank

    1979   *The Genesis of Secrecy: On the Interpretation of Narrative.* Cambridge, MA: Harvard University Press.

Meagher, John C.

    1979   *Clumsy Construction in Mark's Gospel.*   Toronto Studies in Theology, Vol. 3. New York: Edwin Mellen.

Raisanen, Heikki

    1990   *The Messianic Secret in Mark.* Edinburgh: T & T Clark. See especially pp 1-37, "Methodogical Issues in the Study of Mark's Gospel."

Rhoads, David and Donald Michie

    1982   *Mark as Story: An Introduction to the Narrative of a Gospel.* Philadelphia: Fortress.

ENDNOTES

1. Quoted by Eusebius of Caesarea in *H.E.* 3.39.14-15 Loeb Classical Library.

2. Eusebius *H.E.* 2.15; 6.14.

3. According to Hengel 1985, pp 14-28. Compare with Luke 21:20, "Jerusalem surrounded by armies."

4. 1979, p 34; See also Raisanen, 1990.

5. 1991, pp 155, 193.

6. Right after Peter's confession that Jesus is the Christ/Messiah Jesus commands that his disciples tell no one about him (8:29, 30). The disciples are commanded to tell no one about Jesus' transfiguration (9:9). This secrecy has been interpreted by W. Wrede and others as a fiction created by the early church explaining why Jesus didn't publicly declare himself as the Messiah. On the other hand, the Messiahship of Jesus according to Mark was wide of the Messianic standard of his contemporaries' expectations. Any public announcement that Jesus was the Messiah would have created immense difficulties for him. When he does admit before the high priest that he is the Christ, along with being the Son of the Blessed and the heavenly Son of Man, the assembly determines to kill him for blasphemy (14:61-64).

7. 1991, pp 70, 71.

Chapter 20

Matthew

Ernest J. Bursey

"The kingdom of heaven has come near."

BRIEF OVERVIEW OF THE BOOK

The book of Matthew presents a narrative about Jesus and his first followers largely after the order found in the book of Mark. F.C. Burkitt noted long ago, "Matthew is a *fresh edition* of Mark, revised, rearranged, and enriched with new material."[1] Much of the book is taken up with a series of short, loosely connected episodes woven into a continuous quilt. However, several long and uninterrupted speeches of Jesus directed to his disciples appear spaced throughout the Matthean narrative. Like benches placed along a pathway inviting hikers to stop and view the scenery at hand, these speeches in Matthew invite the listener to attend more closely to an aspect of Jesus' teaching where it stands in close connection with the developing story of Jesus.[2]

Matthew replicates nearly all of the contents and thematic emphases of the book of Mark. But the two books are different. Matthew is much larger than Mark, due to considerable new material. Matthew's story begins with the newborn Jesus' adoption by Joseph (ch 1) and his narrow escape from being murdered in Bethlehem as an infant (ch 2), both additions to the story in Mark. Matthew also includes a description of the devil's temptations (4:1-11), Jesus' impressive inaugural sermon (chs 5-7), and a concentrated string of miracle stories (chs 8-9) found spread over the first six chapters of Mark. Jesus' brief mission instructions in Mark 6:7-13 are expanded to a comprehensive mission discourse (ch 10), followed by a speech against unrepentant Galilean cities (ch 11) and a long tirade against the Pharisees who accuse him a second time of demonic aid (ch 12). The Markan parables of the kingdom (4:1-34) are partially taken over and augmented by stories of judgement (ch 13). The rest of the book largely follows the Markan story line, while making room for a discourse to

Jesus' disciples on community discipline (ch 18), a lengthy series of woes against the scribes and Pharisees and Jerusalem itself (ch 23), and more than doubling of the eschatological discourse in Mark (chs 24-25). After dealing with a Jewish rumor about Jesus' body (28:11-15), the gospel closes with a final commissioning scene (28:16-20).

Resurrection of Jesus

BACKGROUND CONCERNS

a Jewish-Xian perspective

Most students of Matthew have concluded that the book was written from a Jewish-Christian perspective for the guidance of Christians with a Jewish heritage. A minority of New Testament scholars hold the contrary view, based partly on (a) the strong statements against Jewish leaders throughout the book; (b) alleged anti-Jewish statements in 21:43 and 27:25; and (c) an alleged lack of knowledge about inner Jewish teachings as evidenced in the phrase, "the teaching of the Pharisees and Sadducees" in 16:12, in view of the strong differences between these two groups.[3]

While all the gospels show an awareness of the Jewish world in which Jesus arose, certain elements favored in Matthew were characteristic of Jewish religious life. In the debate over what defiles, Matthew directs our attention on the matter of eating with unclean hands, while apparently upholding the Old

Testament laws regarding clean and unclean (15:1-20, especially vss 2, 20). By contrast, compare the version in Matt 15 with Mark 7:1-23, especially vss 3, 19b, where the whole notion of distinction between clean and unclean appears to be set aside.

Tithing of spice seeds is supported, though not as a replacement for justice *uses* and mercy (23:23). Matthew's preference for "kingdom of heaven" is consistent *KOH* with a Jewish practice of avoiding unnecessary use of the name of God. The phrase is missing from Mark and Luke where the more direct language of "the kingdom of God" appears.

When facing persecution the disciples are to pray that they will not have to flee on the Sabbath (24:20). In the other New Testament gospels there are no parallels to this statement. Stanton[4] argues on the basis of 12:1-8 that Matthew and his readers would not have felt bound to rigid Sabbath observance but would face additional hostility from fellow Jewish nationals if traveling on the Sabbath in Jewish territory. It is less likely that Matthew's readers obeyed the rabbinic strictures on Sabbath travel along the lines later described in the Jewish Mishnah (written 210 C.E.).

Other lines of evidence are less compelling but nonetheless supportive *extended* Opening the book with an extended genealogy for Joseph, "Son of David," *genealogy* starting with Abraham (1:1-18), is consistent with a Jewish interest in ancestry. *from* The absence of conflict over circumcision probably indicates a continued practice *Abraham* of this Jewish rite by Matthew and the original recipients of the book. In *↓* contrast to the letters of Paul, there is no mention of circumcision in Matthew, *Joseph* much less any debate over the practice.

The extensive use of quotations from the Old Testament is consistent with *extensive* a Jewish Christian setting. However, the mere use of the Old Testament is no *use of* evidence of a Jewish setting. The book of Mark, whose readers were more *OT* distant from Judaism according to Mark 7:1-4, nevertheless also regularly draws attention to the Old Testament through direct quotation and indirect allusion. Apparently non-Jewish converts to Christianity were immersed in the study of the Old Testament. But Matthew draws on less obvious citations from the Old Testament, as if providing new "tidbits" for those already familiar with the more obvious candidates.[5] The introductory phrase, "This took place to fulfill what had been spoken by the Lord through the prophet" occurs with variations a dozen times in the book, followed by a quotation from the Old Testament. The phrase was almost certainly was composed by the author. The Old Testament quotations that follow have drawn extensive attention for their distinctive wording that relies on Hebrew text traditions in addition the Greek Old Testament.

Scholars of Matthew have long divided themselves over the question of whether the original readers of Matthew still considered themselves Jews and whether they were so considered by others.[6]

Interpreters have long been perplexed over the positive tone of Jesus' command to his disciples to do and observe whatever the Pharisees and scribes sitting on the seat of Moses speak (23:2-4). Elsewhere in Matthew Jesus consistently counters their teaching. What Matthew has in view, according to Powell,[7] is the physical control of access to the Torah, due to the Pharisees' and scribes' social and educational privilege. Jesus' command implies a situation of continuing dependance on these Jewish leaders, and thereby association with them, by at least some of Matthew's readers.

Jews = a troubled relationship c̄ their own people

While the religious and cultural world of Matthew's first readers was Jewish, their relationship with that world appears to have been troubled. The followers of Jesus to whom Matthew is directed either are experiencing the promised persecution from their kinsmen or are on the verge of undergoing it (10:16-23; 23:34-36). Strong statements against the Pharisees and scribes take up a whole chapter (23; see also 3:7), pointing to a struggle between the followers of Jesus and the Pharisees and scribes for the mind and heart of the Jewish population. Three times in Matthew the charge arises against Jesus that a demon helps with his exorcisms (9:32-34; 10:25; 12:22-24). Twice the Pharisees publicly voice this charge. Jesus warns his followers to expect the same treatment (10:25; 5:11; see also 12:33-37, and "false witness and slander," 15:19). This points to efforts to discredit Jewish Christian missionaries with the charge of demonic assistance. Further evidence that the book envisions traveling missionaries performing exorcisms along healings without fee (10:1, 8) is supported by Jesus' warnings against false prophets and charismatic figures (7:15, 22, 23; see also 24:11, 24). Jesus does not dismiss the miracle workers for their miracles but because of their failure to conform their conduct to the will of God.

Those who identify the author as Matthew, one of Jesus' disciples and a former tax collector, find support in the title, "The Gospel According to Matthew," found in early manuscripts, and in the wording of Jesus' call to Matthew in 9:9 which corresponds closely to the call of Levi in Mark 2:14 and Luke 5:27. In all three of the Synoptic gospels this brief account is followed by an episode of Jesus at a feast with tax collectors. The lists of the Twelve in Mark 3:16-19 and Luke 6:13-16 include the name of Matthew but not Levi.

Early church tra- *church tradition: Matthew as author*
dition unanimously
claimed the apostle
Matthew, a former tax
collector, as the author
of the book (9:9; 10:3).
The title, "The Gospel
According to Matthew"
and the supporting tes-
timony of Papias may
date from as early as
the first decades of the
second century.   The
dating of the title is a
conjectural matter since
no first century copies
of Matthew exist today.

Matthew the Tax Collector

Papias' statement has
been preserved by Eusebius (260-340) in *H.E.* 3:39, "Now Matthew made an
ordered arrangement of the oracles [*ta logia*] in the Hebrew language ...."
Papias' claim that the book was written originally in the Hebrew (or Aramaic)
language has been largely dismissed by most modern scholars.[8]   Both bear
witness to an already existing tradition that connected the book with the apostle
Matthew. Most scholars recognize the author brought a strong Jewish heritage *difficulty ē Matthean authorship*
to the writing of the book, but find difficulty with direct authorship by Matthew
of the twelve apostles, due in part to the apparent use of Mark, itself not written
by an apostle, and in part to the later date assigned for the writing of Matthew.[9]

Decisions about when the book was written depend on a series of historical
and literary judgments. Grounds for these judgments are based in part on
whether the author and his Jewish Christian readers are viewed as still involved
in mission to or even dialogue with the Jews, and thereby affected by the
massive dislocations within Judaism during and after the War of 67-70 against *when? after Jewish War*
the Romans; and partly by a sifting through the gospel for hints that allow for
comparisons with other early Christian literature, some more datable than
Matthew, such as the letters of Paul. In particular, Matt 22:7 is seen as referring
to the destruction of Jerusalem, either by the way of prophecy on the part of
Jesus or by a subsequent historical allusion added by the author.[10] While most
scholars place the book's date in the last quarter of the first century, a vigorous
minority hold to a date well before the destruction of Jerusalem in 70 C.E.

Egypt, Syria, Transjordan, and Galilee have all been proposed as the locale
for the book and/or its intended readers; in fact, it could have been written for

readers in any of a number of cities on the eastern side of the Mediterranean Sea, except the city of Jerusalem.

LITERARY CONSIDERATIONS[11]

The writer of Matthew apparently drew upon the book of Mark as a major source. Ninety percent of the contents of Mark appear in Matthew and in the same order from ch 12 onward. Matthew and Luke may have used an earlier or different version of Mark than the one found in our present New Testament. The opposite possibility that Mark is a condensed version of Matthew and Luke, has drawn some support in recent years, though most scholars still view Mark as prior to Matthew. The modern revival of this view began in earnest with W.R. Farmer.[12] These two options do not exhaust the possibilities offered to account for the complex and even confusing relationships between the three Synoptic gospels. For a discussion of the relationships between the gospels see ch 18 of this volume. Along with Luke, Matthew appears to have used another source known as Q, particularly in chs 5-6, 10-11, and 23-25.

Matthew shows skill in his use of the Greek language, often improving on Mark's rough language. For instance, Matthew eliminates or replaces the numerous "and" (Greek. *kai*) and "immediately" (Greek: *euthus*) that pepper the book of Mark. But he writes with a Semitic flavor characteristic of a bilingual speaker immersed in the Greek Old Testament. Some changes Matthew makes in Mark's wording uphold the honor of Jesus and his followers. (Compare Mark 4:11, 12 and Matt 13:11-13; Mark 6:3, 5 and Matt 13:55, 58; Mark 8:15, 21 and Matt 16:6, 11-12.) Others reduce the possibility for an inexperienced reader to draw the wrong conclusion from Mark's more ambiguous account. (Compare Mark 3:34 and Matt 12:49; Mark 7:29 and Matt 15:28).

Among the three Synoptic gospels, Matthew typically takes the fewest words to relate an individual story, leaving space in a manuscript of fixed length for the large influx of Jesus' words. For instance, the story of the woman with a hemorrhage is rendered in Mark 5:25-34 with 154 words, in Luke 8:42-48 with 114 words, but with only 48 words in Matt 9:20-22.

By contrast, the five major discourses in Matt 5-7, 10, 13, 18, 23-25 are greatly expanded beyond their counterparts in the other Synoptic gospels. Each shows Matthew's skill in collating and arranging other sayings on the topic at hand. For instance, Matt 10:1-16 is paralleled in Mark 6 and Luke 9 and 10, but 10:17-42 is composed of material either unique to Matthew or found in quite different places in the other gospels. Matthew 24 is closely paralleled in both Mark 13 and Luke 21, though two of the three stories in Matt 25 are unique to Matthew.

Jesus Teaching From the Boat

As a story about Jesus and his disciples, the book of Matthew defies precise outline. This has not stopped scholars, encouraged by Matthew's obvious organization of some of the material at his disposal, from trying to discern an overall structure. In the most notable attempt, B.W. Bacon (1918) considered the five speeches of Matthew to be a deliberate counterpart to the five books of Moses.[13]

With the narrative of Mark as an outline the author of Matthew did not try to create a new structure from scratch. Matthew has followed Mark's story most closely from chs 14-28. Not surprisingly, it is particularly difficult to ferret a distinct outline from chs 14-28.

While no comprehensive structure can be discerned, Matthew has told the story of Jesus with the skill of a preacher or teacher intent on his hearers retaining as much of the authoritative teachings of Jesus as possible. After all, the final words of Jesus, "teaching them to obey everything that I have commanded you" (28:20), must refer to Jesus' instructions in the book, especially the discourses. To this end the author employs a wide range of aids, including extensive first person address from Jesus. Jesus, himself an effective oral communicator, can be seen as the inspiration behind Matthew's careful compiling

[handwritten margin notes: compared to 5 books of Moses]

[handwritten margin notes: Jesus an effective oral communicator]

and editing. Consider the impact on those hearing the Sermon on the Mount read aloud. For instance, Jesus' direct speech, "I say to you," repeated without interruption (5:21; 28, 32, 34, 39, 44), gives Jesus' words a living power over Matthew's listeners. See also Jesus' invitation in 11:28-30, "Come to me, all you that are weary and are carrying heavy burdens, and I will give you rest. Take my yoke upon you and learn from me ...."

memory aids

blessed

The Sermon on the Mount (5-7) illustrates Matthew's skill in organizing the material to aid memory.[14] The introduction in 5:1-2 convey a two-beat cadence that continues in the beatitudes for the next nine verses. The word "blessed" (*makarioi*) introduces each new sentence in 5:3-11. There is no known parallel in the ancient world to this long cascade of blessings. Most of the rest of the chapter is organized around the two phrases, "You have heard that it was said to those of ancient times ... but I say to you" (5:21, 27, 31, 33, 38, 43).

"you have heard, but"

alliteration

Alliteration abounds throughout the Sermon, easing the task of recall. For instance, after the words "blessed [are] the" (*makarioi hoi*) the first four beatitudes all begin with the Greek consonant "p."

inclusios

The use of framing verses or inclusios also allows the hearer to hold related materials together. The rewards offered in the first and eighth beatitudes are the same: "for theirs is the kingdom of heaven" (5:3, 10). In this way the other rewards in vss 4-9 are all gathered as part of the blessings that accompany "the kingdom of heaven." The phrase, "the law and the prophets," frames an even larger section of the Sermon between two key statements at 5:17 and 7:12. The Sermon (5-7) and the collection of miracle stories (8:1-9:34) are bound together by a summary found at 4:23 and repeated again at 9:35, "Jesus went throughout Galilee teaching in their synagogues and preaching the good news of the kingdom and curing every disease and every sickness among the people." In this way Matthew offers the Sermon and the diverse cluster of miracles as premier examples of Jesus' authority as teacher and healer.

non-Jews in genealogy

The beginning and end of the book have similar emphases. The surprising appearance of four non-Jews in the opening genealogy prepares us for Jesus' final explosive command to his Jewish disciples: "Go therefore and make disciples of all nations" (28:19). In the genealogy David's wife is described as "the wife of Uriah," rather than as Bathsheba (1:5). Uriah was a Hittite, and therefore also a non-Jew, as were Tamar, Rahab and Ruth, the other three women mentioned in the genealogy. Likewise, the last words of Jesus, "I am with you always, to the end of the age" (28:18-20) return the hearer full circle to the book's beginning where Jesus is given the name Emmanuel, "which means, 'God with us'" (1:23).

The discourses, differing from one another in topic, are arranged in a logical order. First Jesus lays out the conditions for discipleship (chs 5-7), then he gives the disciples specific mission instructions (ch 10). A series of stories or parables suitable for public hearing and private explanation offer content to the missionary teaching and explanation for the diverse reactions they will receive (ch 13). The fourth discourse lays the basis for dealing with problems within the body of disciples, the church (ch 18). The last discourse (chs 24-25) deals with the end of the world and the arrival of the Son of Man, the fulfillment of the prayer "Your kingdom come" expressed in the first discourse (6:10). The first and last of the discourses appear to balance each other, not only in size. The Sermon on the Mount opens with multiple blessings (5:3-12); Jesus' final discourse about the end of the age is prefaced with a series of "woes" throughout ch 23. In contrast, Luke's counterpart to the Sermon on the Mount places the blessings and woes side by side (Luke 6:20-26 within 6:20-49).

It would be a mistake to read any of the discourses in isolation from the rest of the book. Like an exemplary teacher, the Matthean Jesus often illustrates his instruction in the discourses or shows by his own actions how it is to be applied. For instance, Jesus warns his disciples when persecuted to flee to the next city (10:23). Soon the reader is informed that Jesus is aware of the Pharisees' plan to kill him and so withdraws (12:14, 15; compare Mark 3:6, 7). After John's disciples tell Jesus of John's death at the hands of Herod (14:12), Jesus hears and withdraws from there (14:13; compare Mark 6:29-32). For other instances of Jesus living within his own instructions, see 10:5, 6 and 15:24; 10:14-15 and 11:20-24. See also the connection Matthew intends the reader to make between Jesus' warning against uttering oaths (5:33-37), and the foolhardy oaths of Herod (14:7, 9; compare Mark 6:23, 26), and of Peter (26:72; compare Mark 14:70).

While vivid metaphors are scattered throughout the book (e.g. 3:10-12, 5:13-16, 10:16; 15:14), Matthew has included short stories or parables in several strategic locations to summarize and keep fresh what has already been learned by the listener, and to make unforgettably explicit what is already implicit in the discourses and narrative. The cluster of seven parables of the kingdom in ch 13 offer little that is not already explicit in the first twelve chapters.[15]

In his speech to the religious leaders in Jerusalem, Jesus told three parables that describe the coming rejection by God of those who have been rejecting his Son, Jesus, using the familiar settings of the vineyard and the wedding (21:28-22:14). But this rejection of Jesus has already been evident from the opening chapter of the book, and God's intention to invite outsiders to the banquet table instead of the expected guests has already been announced by Jesus in 8:11, 12.

Jesus' discourses typically end with a parable. For example, the parable about the fate of two houses in the flood at the end of the Sermon on the Mount (7:24-27) builds on Jesus' claim in 7:21 that only the one "who does the will of my Father" will enter the kingdom of heaven. The parable makes clear that

Jesus' own teaching constitute God's will and so directs the listener back to a careful listening of the whole sermon before it.

In the final cluster of parables in ch 25, two parables point the hearers back to earlier statements of Jesus (25:13 repeats 24:42; 25:29 repeats 13:12). The last story (25:31-46) passes beyond the world of metaphor and parable to bring the listener into the court of the coming judge, Jesus himself. His accusation against those on his left hand, "Truly I tell you, just as you did not do it to one of the least of these you did not do it to me" (25:45), match his equally terrifying words in 7:23, "I never knew you; go away from me, you evildoers." In the first instance, Jesus' would-be associates are stripped of their claims on him (7:21-23); in the final scene, all the nations of the world are assembled before him and judged on the basis of their response to the needs of the least of his family (25:31-46), presumably those preaching in his name.

THE MESSAGE
Outline

Survey of contents

Most of the major themes in Mark are retained in Matthew and are often further developed. The author demonstrates Jesus' identity as Son of God and Messiah within the framework of the Old Testament promises to those he considered to be the rightful heirs to these promises.

The author is intent on displaying Jesus' understanding of God's will. Jesus upholds the authority of the Old Testament, calling for absolute obedience to the least of the commandments (5:19). Yet, as the Messiah and Son of God, he brings his own authority to reveal the intent of God. Some commandments are intensified (5:21-30, 43-48; 19:16-22), still others apparently set aside on the basis of their misuse or provisional nature (5:31-42; 19:3-9).

Throughout the book Matthew displays an over-arching interest in the kingdom of heaven. The phrase, "kingdom of heaven," appears 33 times; "the kingdom of God," four times, and figures in the identical brief announcements of John the Baptist (3:2), Jesus (4:17) and the disciples (10:7). The term is never defined, but serves as a large conceptual canvass on which to portray the active rule of God. The term is secondary to, though integral with, Matthew's primary interest in Jesus. The infant messianic King is introduced in 2:1-6 before the first mention of the kingdom of heaven by John (3:2). Jesus' ministry, including his exorcisms, is the key evidence that God's rule has come (12:28). With the arrival of the kingdom, Jesus sets forth God's unequivocable will, setting aside both the traditions of men (15:1-9) and the temporary concessions to human hardness of heart (19:8).

Yet the kingdom of heaven is also still to come, as the disciples' prayer indicates, "Your kingdom come," (6:10). God's kingdom will arrive in its fullness when Jesus returns "on the clouds of heaven with power and great glory" (24:30). At its onset Jesus will divide humanity at a final judgment on the basis of whether Jesus teachings have been received and performed as the will of his Father (7:21; 25:31-46; see also 26:64). Those who give even a cup of cold water to one coming as a messenger of Jesus will be rewarded (10:40, 42), while disregard for those who bear Jesus' message is grounds for eternal punishment (25:31-46; 10:32-33, 40). The specter of the coming judgment is kept before the readers. Each of the five discourses ends on a note of certain judgment (7:24-27; 10:41-42; 13:47-50; 18:32-35; 25:45, 46), though the uncertain time of the heavenly Son of Man calls for constant readiness (24:36-51).

In the meantime, the community of Jesus' followers possesses the assurance of his presence (28:20). As their Lord (*kurios*), he acknowledges them as "little faith ones" (*oligopistoi*, 6:30, 8:26, 14:31, 16:8, lit. trans.) and calls for faith in the face of persecution and danger (8:25, 26; 14:27, 31; see also 6:25-33). His continued presence as their Master and sole teacher blocks any hierarchy or privileged status; instead they are to consider themselves all brothers and sisters (23:8-10).

His followers stand under a mandate to disciple all nations. The explicit statements of 5:13-16; 10:5-33, 40-41; 23:34-37; 24:14; 25:14-46; and especially the final commissioning scene of 28:18-20 convey the strong emphasis on mission. It would be only a slight exaggeration to characterize Matthew as a manual for church planting within a hostile environment. While the first hearers of the book may be largely Jewish and the author upholds a mission within Judaism (10:23), Matthew envisions a world wide discipling of non-Jews (24:14; 28:19, 10:23).

A challenge to the author of Matthew and other followers of Jesus was the unavoidable fact that Jesus was not acknowledged as the Messiah by most of his or the author's Jewish contemporaries; instead, he was crucified by a Roman at the request of Jewish leaders who accuse him of demonic aid (9:34, 10:25, 12:24). Matthew's explanation for this clear rejection is pointed and sustained: from start to finish the Pharisees, scribes and priests operate as a "brood of vipers" (3:7-8); as hypocrites intent on public praise and financial gain (6:1-18; 23:5-7, 25-26); as blind guides and fools (15:14, 23:16-24) who bar the entrance to the kingdom of heaven (23:13). Vigorously debated among modern interpreters of Matthew is whether the book teaches the rejection of the Jewish people as a result of the leaders' rejection of Jesus (21:42, 43). Closely related is the issue of whether the author viewed his community as still within the circle of Judaism.[16]

Part of the difficulty lay in the unexpected character of Jesus' messiahship. As a healer and exorcist who appeared reluctant to champion militaristic ventures Jesus didn't fit the Messianic mold (26:51-54). Even John the Baptist appears to waver over Jesus (11:2, 3). The disciples have considerable difficulty seeing Jesus as the Jewish Messiah. They all acknowledge him to be the Son of God (14:33) before even one of Jesus' disciples, Peter, acknowledges him as the Messiah (16:16). In this instance Jesus explains Peter's insight into his Messiahship as a revelation from "my Father in heaven" (16:17). When Jesus goes on to reveal his impending death, Peter rises in rebuke (16:21-23). For Jews to embrace a crucified Jesus as the Messiah called for a new understanding of the promised Messiah.

Early on, Matthew prepares the way for this new understanding. Joseph, a "son of David" (1:16, 20), bequeaths his lineage to Jesus who, as the royal "Son of David" performs miracles of healing (9:27, 12:23, 15:22, 20:30, 31). Scripture is marshalled to legitimate Jesus' ministry. Matthew presents the healing Jesus as the Messianic bearer of his people's diseases (8:17; Isa 53:4). Jesus assures John with a recital of his deeds cast in the language of the prophet Isaiah (11:3-5; see Isa 29:18; 35:5, 6; 42:18). At the beginning an angel of the Lord introduces Jesus as one who saves his people from their sins (1:21). Near the end Jesus speaks of his death as a ransom for many (20:28) and the pouring out of his blood for many for the forgiveness of sins (26:28).

RELEVANCE FOR TODAY

The Sermon on the Mount (Matt 5-7), as well as the rest of the book, was composed primarily for followers of Jesus, his church (*ekklesia*, 16:18, 18:17) who assembled themselves for instruction and prayer (7:7; 18:19, 20; 28:19).

The Sermon, with its concentration of Jesus' teachings, has held pride of place in influence among Christian pastors and teachers from the *Didache* of the early second century onward. The Beatitudes (5:3-11) and the Lord's Prayer (6:9-13), both part of the Sermon, have drawn extensive attention on their own, as well.[17] There is little evidence of any slowing down in interest if the outpouring of books and articles on the Sermon is any indication.

But Christian readers of the Sermon over the last two millennia have widely differed in their understanding of its purpose and application, especially in light of its challenging demands. The view that the highest standards of the Sermon were reserved for the spiritually elite first emerged during the late medieval period. Some Protestants, especially among Lutherans, have considered the Sermon's high standards impossible for any person to reach and so, like the law as described by Paul in Romans and Galatians, leading the reader to a profound sense of one's sinfulness and then to Christ through whom the believer is granted righteousness. On the surface the Sermon itself does not betray a sense of moral failure or lack of confidence in fulfilling the demands. Anabaptist Christians have embraced the Sermon's teachings as the calling of every follower of Jesus within a community of faith. Other Christians see the Sermon with its call to uphold the commandments as a throwback to the religious demands of the Old Testament. Still others envision the terms of the Sermon to be most fitting for a future time when the kingdom of heaven arrives in its fullness. Prominent world figures of recent generations, including Leo Tolstoy, Mahatma Gandhi, Dietrich Bonhoeffer, and Martin Luther King, Jr., have found a clear sense of direction from the mandates of the Sermon and its strategies for peaceful protest.

Throughout the Sermon is an unavoidable emphasis on Christian action. The truly great ones in the kingdom both do and teach the commandments (5:19); those Jesus allows to enter the kingdom have been doing the will of God (7:21); the wise man whose spiritual house withstands the flood has listened to the words of Jesus and then done them (7:24). Yet the inner life is of immense ethical significance. Jesus' declaration that whoever looks on another person with lust has already committed adultery in the heart (5:27, 28) moves the realm of action back into the inner world of imagination.

Matthew emphasizes that character can be judged by observable "fruits" (7:16-20), though prophetic charlatans may attempt to substitute other more dramatic actions for the instructions of Jesus (7:15, 22). The inner world of the heart flowers in the outer world of deeds and speech, discernable to those instructed in the principles of the kingdom (15:18, 19; see 23:2-36 as an exercise in unmasking the pretensions of self-blinded hypocrites). This inseparable solidarity Matthew poses among thought, word, and deed may seem naïve today when those who seek to influence us do not live among us but present themselves through professional media. On a more personal and enduring level, Matthew's grasp of the unity of the person proves immensely helpful. To embrace the way of holistic righteousness in chs 5-7 is to possess a security against moral deception from others and oneself.

High expectations of personal conduct are balanced in Matthew by a shared pastoral interest in the spiritual welfare of one another that seeks to avoid the spirit of condemnation and a blindness to one's own deficiencies (7:1-5). Sin is taken with utter seriousness threatening even those within the circle of discipleship (18:6-9). The four steps by which the church aids a brother struggling with a sin (18:15-20) follow the parable of the shepherd in pursuit of the straying sheep (18:12, 13) and Jesus' declaration that it is not the will of "My Father in heaven that one of these little ones should be lost" (18:14, margin).

In Matthew's day followers of Jesus assembled in the living quarters of the more affluent members, thus limiting the size of the church and allowing for personal knowledge of one another. For many today the church is a larger collection of persons who do not know one another at an intimate spiritual level. Furthermore, the notion of spiritual accountability runs against the grain of Western individualism. But the present growth of small groups within and without the organized churches confirms the prerequisite for spiritual security of a circle of like-minded persons who will notice and respond when one is absent.

Matthew 16:18, 19 has been a warrant for centuries of ecclesiastical control and hierarchical development, including the papal office. But most scholars today agree that Matthew envisions an egalitarian church in which church leaders couldn't even claim the title of "teacher." Matthew has taken from Mark the sayings on servanthood (Mark 10:35-45; Matt 20:20-28), then given it concrete application in the instruction to avoid titles of honor and positions of power (23:8-11), ending with the warning that the self-exalted will be humbled (23:12). Even privilege accruing from seniority in service is called into question. The parable of the workers who all got the same pay regardless of how long they worked (20:1-15) is framed by similar sayings that the first will be last and the last first (19:30; 20:16). There is little evidence that any ancient Christian community consistently followed the egalitarian vision of Matthew, even while the gospel was being widely read and copied. The *Didache*, an early second century Christian manual shows much affinity to the gospel of Matthew, yet speaks of church offices contrary to the clear statements of Matthew.[18] But Matthew's stubborn picture of true equality within the inner life of the believers under the lordship of Christ still challenges all hierarchical structures within the church.

The disciples of Jesus are called to make disciples of all nations, in spite of horrendous cost to themselves and their converts (4:18-22; 10:16-23, 34-38; 13:44-46; 24:9-14; 28:18-20). In the most telling way Matthew has harnessed together the high ethical demands characteristic of the Old Testament prophets with the call for world wide evangelism. Notice how the sayings on the salt of the earth and the light of the world, with the command to perform works that lead others to give honor to God (5:13-16), are followed by Jesus' demand for a greater righteousness (5:20) and then by the series of vivid examples of that greater righteousness that comprise the ethical heart of the Sermon (5:21-48). The kingdom of heaven requires mercy and justice particularly from those proclaiming it. On the other hand, the traditional acts of the religious life are to be done away from the scrutiny of others for their approval (6:1-18). In the increasingly secular world of North America such advice may be incomplete.

ISSUES FOR DISCUSSION AND REFLECTION

1. Jesus' last words to his followers were, according to Matthew, "And remember, I am with you always, to the end of the age" (28:20), and there the book ends with Jesus in the midst of his disciples. Earlier Jesus had told them, "Where two or three are gathered in my name, there I am there among them" (18:20).
   Why is there no ascension scene in the book?
   According to Matthew, how is Jesus to be understood as present today?
   Through his teachings or even simply through the book itself?
   From the point of view of the book of Matthew, has Jesus ever left?
2. In Matt 5:48 Jesus urges, "Be perfect, therefore, as your heavenly Father is perfect," while Paul in Rom 3:23 declares "all have sinned and fall short of the glory of God." In Matthew Jesus insists that whoever keeps and teaches the least of the commandments will be called great in the kingdom of heaven (5:19) and "the one who does the will of my Father" will enter the kingdom of heaven (7:21), while Paul insists that "no one will be justified by the works of the law" (Gal 2:16). In Matthew Jesus promises "until heaven and earth pass away, not one letter, not one stroke of a letter will pass from the law" (5:18), while Paul explains, "The law was our disciplinarian until Christ came .... But now that faith has come, we are no longer subject to a disciplinarian" (Gal 3:24, 25).
   Do Matthew and Paul share any common ground?
   Are these two in irreconcilable disagreement?
   Does the Matthean Jesus teach a salvation by human achievement?
3. A searching for the roots of the Holocaust has led some to look again at the New Testament. At the trial of Jesus, according to Matt 27:25, the Jewish crowd shouted, "His blood be on us and on our children!" These words and others in Matthew (i.e. 22:43; 23:37-38) have indeed been pressed into service to validate anti-Semitic attitudes and violence against Jewish people, of which the Holocaust is the most horrific example.
   How should the cry of the crowd in 27:25 be understood?
   Are there statements elsewhere in the book that would need to be considered before concluding that the book is anti-Semitic or that violence against Jews is justifiable?
4. Read through the Sermon on the Mount in Matt 5-7.
   What do you find to be memorable?
   Do you consider the overall message to be good or bad news? Are the teachings of Jesus easier to keep than the laws of Moses?

5. According to Matt 5:1, 2 and 7:28, Jesus directed the Sermon on the Mount to his disciples in the presence of crowds of people.

    Do these teachings describe how a person can be successful today in business or politics or advertising?

    Does the Sermon give "church rules" or universal principles? Of what value would the teachings of Jesus in the Sermon be for persons who are not followers of Jesus?

    Can one follow the teachings of Jesus without accepting Jesus?

6. The final scenario when all humanity like sheep and goats stands divided before Jesus (25:31-46) has been widely used on behalf of the poor and dispossessed of the world. However, recent interpreters are likely to hold that "the least of these who are members of [Jesus'] family" are those who engaged in mission for Jesus' sake. According to this interpretation this glimpse ahead to the final judgement scene serves as an encouragement to those undergoing hardships in proclaiming the gospel, rather than as a warning to those indifferent to social injustice. Let's assume this second interpretation is closer to the author's understanding.

    What reasons could you offer for affirming the first interpretation? Would these reasons make sense to the author of Matthew?

    Would it be inappropriate or dishonest to extend Matthew's or Jesus' intended meaning of the "least of these" to include the poor and disadvantaged?

7. The statements on divorce and remarriage in the Synoptics (Matt 5:31, 32, 19:3-9; Mark 10:2-12; Luke 16:18) agree that divorce and remarriage amounts to adultery, although Matthew includes an apparent exception for unchastity (*porneia*). Yet divorce and remarriage are widespread in today's world even among Christians.

    How ought these statements on divorce and remarriage be viewed by Christians today?

    Does the exception clause in Matthew open the door to additional grounds for divorce?

    What should be the role of the church when one of its families is undergoing divorce?

8. In Matt 23:8-11 Jesus eliminates the titles of "rabbi," "father" and "master" (*kathegetes*). His disciples are all brothers with only Jesus, the Christ, as master and teacher. Completely absent from Matthew are the offices of bishops, elders, deacons, although prophets, scribes, the wise ones, and the righteous are mentioned (10:41; 13:52; 23:34).

    Does the author of Matthew intend his readers to exclude the church offices not mentioned in the book?

Did the author Matthew intend to write off all church ecclesiastical hierarchies?

What should be made of the words to Peter in 16:18-19, "You are Peter [petros] and on this rock [petra] I will build my church"?

In general, how have the words of Jesus in Matt 23:8-11 fared in the history of the Christian church?

FURTHER READING

Balch, David L.

1991   *Social History of the Matthean Community: Cross-Disciplinary Approaches.* Minneapolis: Fortress.

Betz, Hans Dieter

1995   *The Sermon on the Mount: A Commentary on the Sermon on the Mount, Including the Sermon on the Plain (Matthew 5:3-7:27 and Luke 6:20-49).* Ed. by Adela Y. Collins. (Hermeneia). Minneapolis: Fortress.

Bonhoeffer, Dietrich

1948   *The Cost of Discipleship.* London: SCM.

Bornkamm, Guenther, Gerhard Barth, and Heinz Joachim Held

1963   *Tradition and Interpretation in Matthew.* Philadelphia: Westminster.

Carson, D.A.

1984   *Matthew.* (Expositor's, Vol. 8, pp 1-599). Grand Rapids, MI: Zondervan.

Carter, Warren

1994   *What Are They Saying about Matthew's Sermon on the Mount?* New York: Paulist Press.

Davies, W.D. and Dale C. Allison, Jr.

1988   *Matthew.* (International). Vol. I, Matthew I-VII. Edinburgh: T & T Clark.

1991   *Matthew.* (International). Vol. II, Matthew VIII-XVIII. Edinburgh: T & T Clark.

France, R.T.

1989   *Matthew: Evangelist and Teacher.* Grand Rapids, MI: Zondervan.

Guelich, Robert A.

1982   *The Sermon on the Mount. A Foundation for Understanding.* Waco, TX: Word.

Gundry, Robert

1982   *Matthew: A Commentary on His Literary and Theological Art.* Grand Rapids, MI: Eerdmans.

1994   *Matthew: A Commentary on His Handbook for a Mixed Church Under Persecution.* Grand Rapids, MI: Eerdmans.

Hagner, Donald A.
    1993   *Matthew 1-13*. (Word). Waco, TX: Word.
    1995   *Matthew 14-28*. (Word). Waco, TX: Word.
Johnsson, William G.
    1977   *Religion in Overalls*. Nashville, TN: Southern.
Kingsbury, Jack Dean
    1988   *Matthew as Story*. Second rev. ed. Philadelphia: Fortress.
Kissinger, Warren S.
    1975   *The Sermon on the Mount: A History of Interpretation and Bibliography*. ATLA Bibliography Series, No. 3. Metuchen, NJ: Scarecrow & American Theological Library Association.
Luz, Ulrich
    1993   *The Theology of the Gospel of Matthew*. New Testament Theology. Cambridge: Cambridge University.
    1994   *Matthew in History: Interpretation, Influence, and Effects*. Minneapolis: Fortress.
Overman, J. Andrew
    1990   *Matthew's Gospel and Formative Judaism: The Social World of the Matthean Community*. Minneapolis: Fortress.
Powell, Mark Allen
    1995   "Do and Keep What Moses Says," *Journal of Biblical Literature* 114/3:419-35.
Senior, Donald
    1996   *What Are They Saying about Matthew?* New York/Mahwah, NJ: Paulist, Revised and expanded edition.
Stanton, Graham N., Ed.
    1983   *The Interpretation of Matthew*. Issues in Religion and Theology 3. Philadelphia: Fortress.
    1992   *A Gospel for a New People: Studies in Matthew*. Edinburgh: T & T Clark.
Wainwright, Elaine Mary
    1994   "The Gospel of Matthew," in Elisabeth Schlüsser Fiorenza (Ed.), *Search the Scriptures: A Feminist Commentary*. Vol. 2. New York: Crossroad, 635-77.
White, Ellen G.
    1956   *Thoughts from the Mount of Blessing*. Mountain View, CA: Pacific.

ENDNOTES

1. *The Earliest Sources for the Life of Jesus* [London: 1922] 97 and cited in Stanton (1992) 52.
2. For a cogent display of the fit between the discourses and their immediate narrative settings see France 154-156.

3. For surveys and critiques of the evidence see France 102-108, Senior 15-16, Stanton (1992) 131-139.

4. Stanton (1992), 192-206.

5. See 2:18-19, 23; 4:15-17.

6. See Stanton (1984) 1911-21 for a helpful survey up to 1980. For specific proposals that place Matthew and its readers in tension with contemporary Judaism see Overman; Anthony Saldarini, "The Gospel of Matthew and Jewish-Christian Conflict," in Balch; and Stanton (1992) 113-283.

7. Powell (431-35).

8. See France 50-80 and Davies-Allison (1988) 1.7-18 on the title and the witness of Papias.

9. For a vigorous attempt to connect the author with the apostle Matthew, see France 50-80.

10. See also the reference to the destruction of the temple in Jerusalem in 23:38; 24:1-2, 15.

11. For fuller discussions of the literary structure and style of Matthew see Davies-Allison (1988) 58-96; France 123-165; and Goulder, M.D., *Midrash and Lection in Matthew* (London: 1974) 70-115.

12. See Farmer, *The Synoptic Problem* (New York: Macmillan, 1964).

13. See France 141-153 or Senior 25-37, for a survey and critique of the proposed structures from Bacon onwards.

14. For a attempt to show how the Sermon was organized for the benefit of listeners rather than readers see Bernard Brandon Scott and Margaret E. Dean, "A Sound Map of the Sermon on the Mount," *Society of Biblical Literature 1993 Seminar Papers*, Ed. Eugene H. Lovering, Jr. (Atlanta: Scholars, 1993):672-725.

15. Warren Carter, "Challenging by Confirming, Renewing by Repeating: The Parables of "the Reign of the Heavens" in Matt 13 as Embedded Narratives," *Society of Biblical Literature Seminar Papers* 34, 399-424.

16. See Stanton (1992) 113-281 and Senior 7-16 for a survey of the discussion.

17. See the bibliographies of Kissinger and Betz 643-663.

18. See Stanton (1992).

Chapter 21

The Gospel of Luke

Sakae Kubo

> *"The Spirit of the Lord is upon me,*
> *because he has anointed me to bring good news to the poor.*
> *He has sent me to proclaim release to the captives*
> *and recovery of sight to the blind,*
> *to let the oppressed go free,*
> *to proclaim the year of the Lord's favor."*

BRIEF OVERVIEW OF THE BOOK

Luke is one of the three Synoptic Gospels. While it treats the life of Jesus in a way similar to Matthew and Mark, there are some significant differences. *author* First of all the author is not a Jew and he is not writing to Jewish Christians. *not a Jew,* Second, his introduction is quite different from those of the other two. Third, *not writing to Jewish xeans* his Gospel is only the first part of a two part work which traces the spread of the gospel from Jerusalem to Rome. Fourth, he has some very distinctive emphases which ˉwe shall expand on later. *a 2 part work*

The outline of Luke's Gospel is similar to the other two. He has an infancy narrative, the ministry of Jesus in Galilee and Jerusalem, the passion narrative, and the resur-

Mary & Joseph

rection. However, he has added an extensive account of Jesus' journey from Galilee to Jerusalem after His ministry in Galilee.

BACKGROUND CONCERNS

The author is not identified in the Gospel. This, however, is a common feature of all four Gospels. The Muratorian Canon, dated about 170-180 C.E., named Luke the physician as the author. He is called "the beloved physician" in Col 4:14. The church father, Irenaeus, who lived about 185 C.E. said Luke, the companion of Paul, wrote the Gospel which Paul preached. Other later church fathers, Tertullian and Clement of Alexandria, support this. Many scholars today accept this tradition since there is nothing within the Gospel to contradict it. The contents of the Gospel support the idea that it was not written by a Jew. While there are parts of the Gospel that reflect the Greek Old Testament, the Gospel as a whole and the Acts evidence a high quality of Greek. Where other Gospel writers include Semitic words, he avoids them. He also leaves out some issues which would not be appreciated by those unacquainted with Jewish concerns. Also Paul, after mentioning Mark and Jesus Justus as "the only men of the circumcision among my fellow workers" (Col 4:11), goes on to mention Epaphras, Luke, and Demas, who then must obviously be Gentiles. It has been suggested that since Luke was relatively obscure, the fact that the Gospel is ascribed to him is strong reason for its acceptance. Who would have ascribed such a Gospel to him if he didn't in fact write it?

Some date the Gospel before the destruction of Jerusalem (70 C.E.). J.A.T. Robinson dates it as early as 57-60 C.E. Some, because the ending of Acts presents events which occur as late as 63 C.E., feel that both the Gospel and the Acts were completed in the 60's. However, because of the change in the description of the destruction of the temple in Luke 21 from that in Mark, others feel that the Gospel and Acts must have been written after the destruction of the temple. The signal to flee Jerusalem in Mark is "when you see the desolating sacrilege set up" (Mark 13:14), while in Luke it is "when you see Jerusalem surrounded by armies" (21:20). The assumption is that Mark, written before the destruction, was not as precise as Luke, who has the advantage of looking back to what had already happened.

If Luke used Mark, then he must have written after Mark. But if he wrote after the destruction of Jerusalem, then it must have been after 70 C.E. as well. Some have given it a wide range, 70-90; others 80-90, but the usual date selected is 80-85. I would prefer a date before 70. Luke's description of the destruction of Jerusalem may have been influenced by the Old Testament description of the fall of Jerusalem. What is puzzling, on the other hand, is the fact that Luke completes the Acts with Paul's two years in relative freedom in Rome without any further description of what happened to Paul. If he wrote after 70, he wrote after Paul had been executed. One would expect that he would have included an account of Paul's death in Acts if he wrote it later. One can counter by saying that Luke's intent had been accomplished, but even if that were the case, one would expect some type of concluding remark about Paul's preaching in Caesar's household.

LITERARY CONSIDERATIONS

As indicated earlier, there is a general consensus that Luke was dependent on Mark for some of his material. He mentions in his introduction that he was acquainted with others who had written about what had transpired. The other sources that scholars think Luke used are *Q*, a collection of the sayings of Jesus, and *L*, his own private source. The latter could be material he mentions in his introduction.

[handwritten margin notes: 3 sources: Mark, Q, L]

Another interesting literary feature concerns the style of the first two chapters of Luke's gospel. The Greek Luke employs in these two chapters has a more Jewish character than that of the rest of the gospel. Perhaps Luke does this intentionally to emphasize the Jewish origin of the gospel story. In addition, Luke records several hymns that come from those who witness to God's activity in the birth of Jesus.

THE MESSAGE
Outline

Survey of contents

While the Synoptic Gospels obviously have major similarities in content, there are certain characteristic themes and emphases in Luke that are peculiar to his Gospel. One of these is the universality of salvation. One would expect this when looked at from the vantage point of Acts and the spread of the gospel from Jerusalem to Judea to Samaria to the ends of the earth (Acts 1:8). But even within the confines of the Gospel, this idea is present. Whereas Matthew's genealogy goes back to Abraham, Luke's goes beyond the bounds of Judaism to the beginning of the human race—to Adam, the son of God. While Matthew's concern is a Jewish concern to demonstrate that Jesus was the Messiah to come, predicted in the Old Testament, Luke wants to show that Jesus is the Savior and

[margin annotations: universality of salvation; genealogy to Adam]

The Good Samaritan

Redeemer of the whole world. Luke has included the story of a *good* Samaritan traveler and a *grateful* Samaritan leper. He includes also Jesus' reference to the faith of the widow of Zarephath and Naaman the Syrian officer. The table in the kingdom of God will have people "from the east and west, and from north and south" (13:29), and "repentance and forgiveness of sins should be preached in his name to all nations" (24:47). Again, when we look at Acts, we find Luke intent on showing how the gospel has gone primarily through the missionary endeavors of Paul to the Gentiles in the Gentile world of Asia Minor and to eastern Europe and to Rome itself.

Luke's Gospel also shows concern for the social outcasts and the underprivileged. It has the story of the sinful woman (7:36-50), Jesus' defense of his association with tax collectors and sinners (15), his inviting himself and

[margin annotations: stories include Samaritans; concern for outcasts]

becoming "the guest of a man who is a sinner" (19:8), the chief tax collector of Jericho. In his inaugural sermon Jesus, quoting the words from Isaiah, set forth his mission "to preach good news to the poor, to proclaim release to the captives and recovering of sight to the blind, to set at liberty those who are oppressed" (4:18). In the Magnificat, Mary refers to her "low estate" and then goes on to say how God humbles the proud and mighty. While he fills the hungry with good things, he sends the rich away empty (1:48, 51-53).

The same type of reversal is seen in Luke's version of the Sermon on the *reversal in Sermon on Plain* Mount. Those who are poor, hungry, and who weep will be blessed while those who are rich, full, and who laugh have woes pronounced upon them. The poor man, Lazarus, ends up in the bosom of Abraham while the rich man finds himself in Hades.

Women play a sig- *Women* nificant part in Luke's Gospel. The main actors in the birth narratives are, of course, Mary and Elizabeth, but Anna the prophetess is also mentioned. Mary and Martha play their part. Mary Magdalene, Joanna, the wife of Chuza, and Susanna provided for Jesus and the disciples. The widow of Nain, the woman sinner, the woman who

Mary at the Tomb

had a spirit of infirmity for eighteen years were all recipients of Jesus' kindness and mercy. Jesus praised the woman who gave her mite.

A strong emphasis in Luke is the importance of prayer. Jesus not only *prayer* teaches much about prayer, he is seen often in prayer, especially at every important occasion (3:21; 5:16; 6:12; 9:18, 28-29; 10:21-22; 11:1; 22:41-45; 23:46). Luke has recorded seven instances which the other Gospels have not mentioned.

Anyone who has studied the Acts knows how important the Holy Spirit is *Holy Spirit* in Luke. From Pentecost on, the church and her leaders were guided by the Holy Spirit. But even in Luke, the Holy Spirit is present. The Holy Spirit is prominent in the birth narratives. John the Baptist, Elizabeth, Zechariah are all filled with the Spirit. It is through the Spirit that Jesus is conceived and it is the

Spirit who descends on him at baptism. It was with the Spirit that the disciples were to be "clothed with power from on high" (24:49).

Finally, a characteristic emphasis of Luke is joy. Words with the root of joy or rejoicing are found many more times in Luke than the other Gospels. People praise God throughout (2:20; 5:25-26; 7:16; 13:13; 17:15; 18:43). Heaven rejoices when sinners are reclaimed and people rejoice when lost things are found. The infancy narratives are suffused with joy from the time that Zechariah is told that Elizabeth would bear a son (1:14) to the time when the heavenly host praised God with their Gloria in Excelsis and the shepherds glorified and praised God for all they had heard and seen.

Shepherds Visit the Child

RELEVANCE FOR TODAY

As we look at the themes we find in Luke, we are impressed with their relevance. The gospel of universality needs emphasis today, though, of course, with a different perspective. In Luke's day the Jews owned the gospel and they needed a universal perspective so that the world of the Gentiles would be included. Today the gospel has been owned by the Western World but the universal perspective needs to include the Third World. We need above all a sense of true brotherhood and sisterhood that would cause racial, ethnic, and cultural barriers to cease to exist in a worldwide church and that each member of the church, no matter where he or she comes from, may feel that he or she truly belongs and is a part of God's rainbow family.

Universality needs to be viewed, not only geographically but also socially. Jesus' concern for social outcasts and the underprivileged needs attention by Christians today. Jesus' attitude toward and treatment of women especially needs to be noticed. In his day when women had no social standing, what he did and taught was revolutionary. Women should be treated as equally as men in every way.

Luke's emphasis on prayer and the Holy Spirit continues to be relevant for Christian spiritual life. Many in the world today struggle to find some kind of meaningful spirituality that transcends the mundane world of busy schedules and financial pressures. Luke points Christians to spiritual meaning in prayer and through the Spirit.

An aspect of Luke's teaching which has generated much discussion is his view of eschatology. The contention of some, notably Hans Conzelmann, is that Luke has shifted the emphasis of the early church from the imminent second coming to the earthly concerns of the Christian community. Others hold that Conzelmann's view is an extreme position. They believe that Luke has not eliminated the teaching of the imminent second coming and that his dealing with the history of the church is not antithetic to the belief in the soon coming of Christ. An understanding of the interplay between the Christian's relationship to the present earthly concerns of life and to the coming of Christ is relevant for those who try to live responsibly in this world as they hope for the coming of Christ as well.

what is Luke's view of eschatology?

ISSUES FOR DISCUSSION AND REFLECTION

1. Why do you think Luke emphasizes the universality of the gospel more than the other Gospel writers?
2. Is the emphasis on universality and the favorable view on social outcasts, including women, due to Luke's selection of events, or is it indeed the emphasis and view of Jesus Himself? In other words, do we like Luke because he agrees with us or because he is faithfully recording Jesus' life and teachings?
3. In light of the significant part Jesus gives to women in Luke, why do you think many churches continue to place women in a secondary role?
4. In reading Luke, do you find that he seems to have placed the second coming a little farther off than Mark or Matthew? In what way is his view different from the others if at all?
5. In what ways do you find Luke's Gospel different from the other Synoptic Gospels?

FURTHER READING

Conzelmann, Hans
>   1961   *The Theology of St. Luke.* Translated by Geoffrey Buswell. New York: Harper and Row.

Fitzmyer, Joseph A.
>   1985   *The Gospel According to Luke.* (Anchor). Vol. 28, 29. Garden City, NY: Doubleday.

Geldenhuys, Johannes N.
>   1951   *Commentary on The Gospel of Luke.* (New International). Grand Rapids, MI: Eerdmans.

Karris, Robert J.
>   1985   *Luke: Artist and Theologian: Luke's Passion Account as Literature.* New York: Paulist.

Marshall, I. Howard
>   1978   *The Gospel of Luke: A Commentary on the Greek Text.* (New International Greek Testament). Grand Rapids, MI: Eerdmans.

Morris, Leon
>   1988   *The Gospel According to St. Luke.* Rev. ed. (Tyndale's). Grand Rapids, MI: Eerdmans.

Chapter 22

Acts
Sakae Kubo

"But you will receive power when the Holy Spirit has come upon you; and you will be my witnesses in Jerusalem, in all Judea and Samaria, and to the ends of the earth."

BRIEF OVERVIEW OF THE BOOK

Acts is a sequel to Luke as is evident from the introduction to the Gospel and the Acts. The book begins after the resurrection and then goes on to show how the gospel went from Jerusalem, Judea and Samaria, and to Asia Minor, eastern Europe, and to Rome. In it Luke also shows how the early church, comprised of Jewish believers, struggled with the command of Christ to preach the gospel to the Gentile world. He also shows how Christianity was treated by the Roman government as it sought to proclaim the gospel.

BACKGROUND CONCERNS

What we have said regarding the authorship of the Gospel of Luke would hold true for Acts, since they were obviously written by the same person. We are assuming, therefore, that the author of Acts is also Luke. (See also the comments regarding the date of this book under Luke.)

One of the unique features of the book of Acts is the presence of two quite different textual traditions among the ancient manuscripts of the gospel. One is the so-called Western text. The text from which most translations are made is the Alexandrian text. The Western text, found primarily in Manuscript D, is characterized by longer readings, making it ten percent longer than the Alexandrian text. It has some very interesting details that appear plausible. Some of these readings are found in 13:27; 15:29; 18:27; 19:1; 28:21. Eldon Epp has found an anti-Jewish tendency in these readings.

221

LITERARY CONSIDERATIONS

Luke obviously was dependent on sources in the writing of his Gospel as he indicates in his introduction (1:1-4), and as a comparison with Mark and Matthew shows. There is no reason to think that he did otherwise in Acts.

One interesting aspect of the narrative of Acts is the presence of the "we sections" (16:10-17; 20:5-15; 21:1-18; 27:1-28). These are sections where the first person plural is used in place of the third person forms. A good number of scholars feel that these are sections where Luke was himself an eyewitness and was writing from first hand experience.

For the other parts of the Acts, some refer to a Jerusalem source and an Antiochene source. He also had access to individuals, especially Paul himself, who reported to him some of the things that took place.

Throughout the book Luke has added summaries: longer summaries (2:42-47; 4:32-35; 5:11-16), shorter summaries (1:14; 6:7; 9:31; 12:24; 16:5; 19:20; 28:30-31), and numerical summaries (2:41; 4:4; 5:14; 6:1, 7; 9:31; 11:21-22; 14:1; 19:20). Some have tried to divide the contents of the book on the basis of these summaries.

Another feature in Acts is the relatively large number of speeches. Some feel that these discourses are Luke's work and are made to fit his theological orientation because they are of Lukan style. Therefore, it is concluded that they are not reliable or an authentic reflection of what was actually said. Others contend that though they may be in Luke's style, and while they are not verbatim reports, they actually reflect the basic content of the speeches. Luke did not just make them up, but was dependent upon those who were present. These discourses are found in 2:14-39; 3:11-26; 4:8-12; 5:29-32; 7:2-53; 10:34-43; 13:16-41; 17:22-31; 20:18-35; 22:2-21; 24:10-21; 26:1-23; 28:17-20, 25-29.

THE MESSAGE

Outline

I. Introduction 1:1-26
   A. Preface 1:1-2
   B. Post resurrection experience 1:3-8
   C. Ascension 1:9-11
   D. The upper room and the appointment of Matthias 1:12-26
II. Witness in Jerusalem, Judea, and Samaria 2:1-9:43
   A. Witnesses in Jerusalem 2:1-8:3
      1. Pentecost and its aftermath 2:1-47
      2. Peter's healing miracle 3:1-26
      3. Persecution by the priestly faction 4:1-31
      4. Common possession and the story of Ananias and Sapphira 5:1-11

Survey of contents

The Book of Acts begins in the interim between the resurrection and the ascension. The disciples are given the promise of the Holy Spirit to empower them to witness "in Jerusalem and in all Judea and Samaria and to the end of the earth" (1:8). The fulfillment of this promise begins with Pentecost and the witness in Jerusalem and Judea. In spite of the fact that the disciples are persecuted from without, and threatened by deception and division from within, the gospel is proclaimed.

Soon the gospel is proclaimed in Samaria, and an Ethiopian eunuch is converted. Now the gospel must go beyond the familiar perimeters of Judea and Samaria out to the Gentile world. The conversion of the Ethiopian eunuch was perhaps the first minuscule step. The next event, however, is more significant; that is, the conversion of Cornelius the centurion, because of the remarkable occurrences that took place. The vision of Peter, the providential synchronization of the event, the pouring out of the Spirit upon Gentiles convinced not only Peter, but the other disciples as well, that God was leading them in this experience. But this was viewed as an exceptional individual experience.

The dispersal of the disciples into the Diaspora because of persecution in Jerusalem led to contact with Greeks (11:20), and many believed. Barnabas and Saul were leaders in this movement. Appropriately they were set aside specifically for a historic Gentile mission to Cyprus and Asia Minor. Their strategy was to go to the synagogues and proclaim that Jesus was the Christ to the Jews and to the Gentile proselytes and God-fearers. When they returned to Antioch, "they gathered the church together and declared all that God had done with them, and how he had opened a door of faith to the Gentiles" (14:27).

inclusion of Gentiles However, this new development among the Gentiles brought the issue of what must be expected of them, if they were to join the church, which until now had been made up of Jewish Christians. The issue was brought before the apostles in Jerusalem, and their decision was that circumcision would not be required, but that Gentiles should "abstain from the pollutions of idols and from unchastity and from what is strangled and from blood" (15:20).

Thus with this major issue settled, the work among the Gentiles went ahead with the second missionary journey to Asia Minor and Europe. In their mission to the Gentiles, the disciples had to reckon with the Jews, on the one hand, and the Roman government on the other. They had to establish their identity and *Roman officials portrayed as fair* their legitimacy in Roman society. In all their encounters with the Roman officials, the Christians were treated fairly, e.g., at Philippi, Corinth, and Ephesus.

The third missionary journey was primarily centered in Ephesus. After the close of this journey, Paul received many warnings against returning to Jerusalem, but he steadfastly set his course in that direction. When he returned to Jerusalem, the first thing he was asked to do was to participate in a purification ceremony to allay fears that he had abandoned all Jewish practices and had taught that all Jews should forsake Moses. But Jews from Asia Minor who recognized him, charged him with doing these things and also with bringing Greeks into the temple. This led to an attempt to kill him, but he was rescued by Roman soldiers.

He was then imprisoned in Jerusalem and later was sent to Caesarea because of a threat to kill him. While in Caesarea, he appeared before Felix, Festus, and Agrippa. He appealed to Caesar and thus was sent to Rome.

A complete reading of the book of Acts reveals that its message transcends the story of any single individual. It is not the story of Peter, although he is prominent in the early part of the book. Yet Luke seems to leave Peter's story dangling when he says simply that Peter went to another place (12:17). Nor is it the story of Paul, although he is the most prominent player in the last half of the book. It is the story of the spreading gospel, that begins in Judea and extends to the ends of the earth. The preaching of the gospel in Rome, the political, economic, and communications center of the empire, serves as a fitting symbol of the spread of the gospel to the world.

preaching *at Rome* *is* *symbolic*

RELEVANCE FOR TODAY

The book of Acts shows how God constantly pushes his people to break from their narrow boundaries. Too often people think God and Christ belong to them in an exclusive sense. The Jews felt that way. The Christian Gentiles felt that way. Western Christians felt that way. American Christians often feel that way. And yet today, as in the time of the disciples, God is going beyond the narrow boundaries, this time from a North American Christianity to Third World Christianity. It is ironic that the bases from which Christianity sent forth its missionaries are becoming secular while the former mission fields are becoming Christian. It is important to take a good look at Acts to see how God works and is still working today, and not to resist his guidance and leadership in this direction.

The Holy Spirit is not imprisoned in Scripture. He is working today, and we need to be sensitive to his leadership in our lives and in our church.

ISSUES FOR DISCUSSION AND REFLECTION

1. Can Pentecost be repeated today to empower us to finish the work?
2. At the Jerusalem Council comparatively few requirements were set for Gentile membership into the church. What should we expect, especially of non-Western peoples, as they join the church? What about polygamy? How long should we wait to baptize these peoples?
3. If most of a denomination's membership is in the third world, but most of its financial support comes from America, from where should its leadership be chosen? How would you feel about Third World missionaries to the Western world?
4. How should the church relate to governmental authorities, especially where the government is hostile to the church? Should they proclaim the gospel openly and face persecution, or should they fall in line with government policies and work quietly within the restrictions set forth?

FURTHER READING

Bruce, Frederick F.
    1953   *A Commentary on the Book of Acts*. Grand Rapids, MI: Eerdmans.
Hengel, Martin
    1980   *Acts and the History of Earliest Christianity*. Philadelphia: Fortress.

Marshall, I. Howard
    1980   *Acts of the Apostles*. (Tyndale's). Grand Rapids, MI: Eerdmans.

Packer, John W.
    1966   *Acts of the Apostles*. (Cambridge). Cambridge: Cambridge University Press.

Chapter 23

John and the Synoptics
Ronald L. Jolliffe

GENERAL INTRODUCTION: WHY FOUR GOSPELS?

One of the puzzles of the New Testament is why the New Testament has *why 4?*
four gospels all telling the story of the life of Jesus. It seems one gospel, telling
all the stories without duplication could reduce the length of this section of the
New Testament by half. So why have four which contain so many interesting
differences, especially since some of the differences even appear contradictory?

One early Christian scholar, Tatian, in the last half of the second century, *Tatian's solution*
saw the difficulties of four gospels and wrote a single gospel, the *Diatessaron*,
which attempted to include every saying and story of Jesus without duplication
or omission. But Christians seemed to prefer four gospels to one, and Tatian's
Diatessaron enjoyed only regional popularity. The differences in viewpoint,
culture, and emphasis seemed to add a vitality to the story of Jesus that perhaps
was absent in Tatian's work.

The four gospels tell the story of Jesus from four different viewpoints for *4 viewpoints,*
four different kinds of audiences. Mark, the first of the gospels to be written, *4 audiences*
was clearly written for people who knew almost nothing about Jewish beliefs and
practices (for example Mark 7 goes to great lengths to explain some very basic
Jewish practices to his readers). Matthew, however, is written to an audience
that knows much about Judaism and the Old Testament, and seems to continue
practicing some Jewish purity laws that Mark assumes have been abandoned
(compare Mark 7:14-23 with Matt 15:10-20). Luke shares with Mark a non-
Jewish audience, but Luke has a particular interest in the matter of poverty.
Contrast Luke 6:20, 21 with Matt 5:3, 6 and Luke 6:6-12 with Matt 2:7-11.
Also note Lukan *Sondergut* like Luke 7:11-17; 16:19-31. Still, the differences *synoptics*
between the synoptics (Matthew, Mark and Luke) are slight in contrast to their *very*
differences with the Gospel of John. They are so similar when compared to it *different*
that they are called the synoptics (meaning *through the same eyes*). *from John*

The accompanying table provides a quick overview of some of the differences that exist between the synoptics and the Gospel of John. The first column lists sequentially the pericope[1] in the Gospel of John. The next three columns compare the parallels found in the synoptics. A blank line in a column indicates no parallel in that gospel. The table shows that the layout of the Gospel of John does not align easily with the design of the synoptics. The fourth gospel agrees with the basic outline of Jesus' life as told in the synoptics only at a very elementary level. It begins at the start of Jesus' ministry with the preaching of the Baptist and Jesus' baptism and concludes with accounts of his crucifixion and resurrection. Beyond this rudimentary outline, there is little agreement in content or order of events between the synoptic gospels and the Gospel of John.

John	*Mark*	*Matthew*	*Luke*
1:1-18 Prologue: the word of God	—	—	—
1:19-34 Baptist and Jesus' baptism	1:1-16; 3:1-6	4:18-22; 16:17f	5:1-11; 6:14
1:35-51 First disciples	—	—	—
2:1-13 Cana marriage	—	—	—
2:14-25 Cleansing temple	11:15ff, 27-33	21:12f, 23-27	19:45f; 20:1-8
3:1-21 Nicodemus	—	—	—
3:22-36 Baptist's testimony	—	—	—
4:1-42 Samaritan woman	—	—	—
4:43-46a Ministry in Galilee	1:14b-15	4:13-17	4:14b-15
4:46b-54 Centurion	—	8:5-13	7:1-10
5:1-47 Bethzatha Pool	—	—	—
6:1-15 Feeding 5000	6:32-44	14:13-21	9:10b-17
6:16-25 Miracles	6:45-56	14:22-36	—
6:29-59 Bread of Life	—	—	—
6:60-66 Taking offense at Jesus	—	—	—
6:67-71 Peter's confession	8:27-30	16:13-20	9:18-21
7:1-52 Tabernacles	—	—	—
[7:53-8:11 Woman taken in adultery]	—	—	—
8:12-59 Discussion with the Jews	—	—	—
9:1-41 Blind man	—	—	—
10:1-21 Good Shepherd	—	—	—
10:22-42 Jerusalem and Jordan	—	—	—
11:1-44 Raising Lazarus	—	—	—
11:45-53 Taking counsel against Jesus	11:18; 14:1f	26:1-5	19:47f; 22:1f
11:54-57 Jesus retires to Ephraim	—	—	—
12:1-8 Anointing at Bethany	14:3-9	26:6-13	7:36-50
12:9-11 Plotting to kill Lazarus	—	—	—
12:12-19 Triumphal entry	11:1-10	21:1-9	18:28-40
12:30-36 Death discourse	—	—	—
12:37-50 Judgment by the Word	—	—	—
13:1-20 Washing disciples' feet	—	—	—
13:21-38 Betrayal and denial predicted	14:18-31	26:21-35	22:15-34

14:1-17:26 Farewell discourse	—	—	—
18:1-19:42 Arrest, trial, Crucifixion	14:32-15:47	26:36-27:66	22:39-23:56
20:1-23 Resurrection appearances	14:32-15:47	26:36-27:66	22:39-23:56
20:24-29 Appearance to Thomas	—	—	—
20:30-21:25 Ending and appendix	—	—	—

It is also readily apparent that the Gospel of John only occasionally reports the same stories as the synoptics. Only about ten percent of the Gospel of John has parallel passages in the synoptics. Notice that the synoptics do not even mention most of the stories told in the Gospel of John.

Location of Jesus' ministry

While Jesus' ministry is confined to Galilee in the synoptics, his ministry continually moves him back and forth between Galilee and Judea in the Gospel of John, where Jesus spends far more time in Judea than Galilee. In the synoptics Jesus only goes to Jerusalem once during his adult life, to die (Mark 11:11; Matt 21:1; Luke 19:41). In the Gospel of John, Jesus moves back and forth between Galilee and Jerusalem (1:28 in Bethany near Jerusalem; 1:43 → Galilee; 2:13 → Jerusalem; 4:43 → Galilee [via Samaria 4:3-42]; 5:1 → Jerusalem; 6:1 → Galilee; 7:10 → Jerusalem. From John 7:10 to the end of the book, Jesus never returns to Galilee, placing Jesus, according to the Gospel of John, in Galilee for only 113 of 842 verses (1:43-2:12; 4:43-54; and 6:1-7:9).

Length of Jesus' ministry

In the Gospel of John, Jesus' ministry extends over three different Passovers (2:13; 6:1; 11:55), whereas the synoptics agree that, as an adult, Jesus only goes to Jerusalem once, to his death at Passover time. The view that Jesus' ministry lasted three and a half years is based on the chronology of the three Passovers in the Gospel of John. The view of some that Jesus' ministry lasted only one year accepts the validity of the synoptic gospels' chronology.

Some have tried to harmonize the two chronologies by noting that each gospel reports one time that Jesus cleanses the temple. If one assumes, then, that Jesus cleanses the temple only once, just prior to the crucifixion, then the cleansing in John 2:14-21 is this same cleansing, meaning one should not count this Passover as an additional year. They also speculate that the reference to the second Passover, in John 6:4, was inserted by the author to make a connection for the reader between Jesus' statement at the Last Supper, "This is my body," with his multiplication of the loaves here. Thus they reduce the number of

The Fish & the Loaves

Passovers in John to one, as in the synoptics. (There is no reference to the Passover in any of the synoptic gospel accounts of feeding the multitudes, Mark 6:32-44; 8:1-10; Matt 14:13-21; 15:32-39, Luke 9:10-17). John's symbolic connection of the Passover, feeding of the multitude, and the Lord's Supper may help explain why there is no Last Supper in the Gospel of John, since it has been replaced by the chapters in the Gospel of John dealing with the bread (John 6) and the vine (John 15).

Jesus' actions

Several significant differences exist between Jesus' activities in the synoptics and in the Gospel of John. The first has to do with the activity of exorcism. In the synoptic gospels, the reader is frequently confronted by "unclean spirits" which possess persons and require powerful means to be expelled (for starters see Mark 1:23-27; 5:2-13; 6:7; 7:25; 9:17-25; and parallels). It is surprising to discover that there is not a single reference to this phenomenon in the entire Gospel of John.

We also notice with some surprise that Jesus does not associate with "losers" in the Gospel of John. Although we do find him speaking with the Samaritan woman in John 4, he is not the friend of publicans and sinners, nor does he suggest they will enter the kingdom before the religious leaders.

Jesus' teaching

Parables are short, pithy, enigmatic stories which normally contain no explanation. In the synoptics Jesus teaches in parables. In fact, Jesus does not teach without using parables (Mark 4:34; Matt 13:34), but in the Gospel of John, Jesus tells no parables. The Greek word for parable (*parabole*) does not even appear in the entire Greek text. In the Gospel of John, Jesus teaches with lengthy speeches built on single themes. As examples, consider the "born again" section of John 3; the "living water" of John 4; the bread of life of John 6; the good shepherd of John 10, the way, truth and life of John 14; the vine and branches of John 15; the comforter of John 16.

[handwritten margin notes: "no exorcisms in John", "Jesus not with 'losers'", "no parables"]

The Sower

By contrast consider the many quips, riddles, proverbs and parables that make up the Sermon on the Mount in Matt 5-7, which has many unconnected themes: the beatitudes of 5:3-12; the salt 5:13; light 5:14-16; law 5:17-22; reconciliation 5:23-26; adultery 5:27-28; offending body parts 5:29-30; divorce 5:31-32; oaths 5:33-37; retribution 5:38-42; loving one's enemies 5:43-48 all in just the first chapter of the Sermon on the Mount!

In summary, the Gospel of John seems less concerned with quoting the teachings of Jesus than with providing extended meditations (or sermons) on the meaning of Jesus' words.

not quoting Jesus — meditating on meaning of his words

Not only is the manner of Jesus' teaching different, the content is also different. The increased attention to the devotional and meditative life seems to have displaced the ethical concerns and appeals for justice of the synoptics. In the Gospel of John, Jesus commands his followers to love one another (13:35), but there is no command to love one's enemies!

"Belief" in Jesus

Frequently repeated words and phrases can be important clues to significant themes in a biblical book. Two different basic themes form an important contrast between the synoptics and the Gospel of John. The synoptic gospels make frequent references to the "reign" (or "kingdom") of God, which appears about 54 times in Matthew, 19 in Mark, 44 in Luke, but only four times in the Gospel of John. This primary theme in the synoptic gospels of the reign of God (in Matthew "of heaven"), characterizes Jesus' teaching and preaching. It means that people are called to account for themselves before God in the way they live upon this earth. The very first words Jesus speaks in Mark (1:14) are a call to allow God's reign to control how one behaves: "The time has come; the kingdom of God is upon you; repent, and believe the Gospel."

For the Gospel of John, the Greek verb *pisteuō,* "to believe, to trust, to have faith in," is important enough to appear more than 90 times, compared to about 10 times in each of the synoptic gospels. And the difference is not just quantitative. In the Gospel of John, repeatedly, one is asked to trust Jesus or his words, or even to trust in Jesus as one trusts in God (John 14:3). This contrasts with the synoptics, where the *only* reference to trusting in Jesus is what the children sitting on his lap are to do (Mark 9:42). In the synoptic gospels, the dominant theme is the reign of God, which calls for people to live upon this earth as though living before God. Additionally, in the Gospel of John, Jesus frequently builds entire sermons upon the simple phrase "I am ...." In the synoptic gospels there are only a few places where Jesus says, "I am ...," and none of these passages hints at the dominical the significance of John's usage.

Theology and history in the Gospel of John

An interesting experiment can be made which shows that the Gospel of John is more interested in what belief in Jesus means than in the mundane details of a chronology of the life of Jesus. The synoptics make it very clear that the last supper was instituted at a Passover Seder (Mark 14:12-19, Matt 26:17-20, Luke 22:7-13). The commonly understood chronology of Jesus' trial, crucifixion, burial and resurrection (based on the synoptics), then, is that Jesus' last supper with his disciples was on Thursday, the eve of Passover; his trial and crucifixion were on Friday, the Jewish Passover; he lay buried in the tomb on Saturday; and lives as the resurrected Lord since Easter Sunday.

Before surveying the Gospel of John's record of the events, it is helpful to make a few basic observations relating to Passover. Passover, like all Jewish days begins at sunset (not midnight). The day preceding the Sabbath and the day preceding a festival are called a "preparation" days. According to Exod 12 the Passover lamb is to be killed at the beginning of Passover, that is, on the eve of Passover.

The Gospel of John agrees with the synoptics as to the week days for Jesus' arrest, trial, crucifixion, burial, and resurrection. The difference is that in the Gospel of John, the Passover comes on Saturday, the Jewish Sabbath, and not on Friday, as in the synoptics. The following observations make this clear. John

18:28 inserts the note that the ones who brought Jesus to Caiaphas "did not enter the praetorium, so that they might not be defiled, but might eat the passover." The note is not found in any of the synoptics because according to their chronology, the Passover meal has already been eaten. John 19:14 clearly states that the day of the crucifixion is the day of preparation for the Passover. John 19:31 calls the day of crucifixion a day of preparation for "a high day," apparently a day when the weekly Sabbath and the Passover fell on the same day.

It may be that the Gospel of John places the day of the crucifixion on the day preceding the Passover in order to correlate Jesus' death with the time the Passover lambs are slaughtered. Of course this creates a problem for the author as to what Jesus and the disciples were doing at a feast on Thursday evening where the synoptics report Jesus and the disciples sharing their last supper at a Passover *Seder*. To avoid this difficulty, there is no Passover *per se* in John 13, where the Gospel of John takes up the report of the Thursday evening meal. Clearly it is the same meal that the synoptics make the Lord's Supper. In the Gospel of John there is also a supper with the disciples that includes bread and Judas taking his leave to betray Jesus, but it is not to be understood as a Passover.

So while some things are the same, everything is different. Notice that John 13:1 places the events of this chapter "*before* the Passover." During supper, Jesus gets up and washes the disciples' feet. There is no sharing the cup. There is no cup. There are no words instituting the Lord's Supper, no "This is my body, this is my blood." There is bread, and it is shared. But it is only given to Judas after Jesus dipped it in the dish. When Judas received it, Satan entered into him and he left.

That brings us full circle to our beginning observation. In John there is no "last" supper. Jesus never says, "I will not eat of this bread nor drink of this fruit of the vine until I eat and drink new with you in my Father's kingdom." In the Gospel of John words somewhat like those of the Lord's Supper appear in John 6:46-58. To believe in Jesus is to eat Jesus' body and drink Jesus' blood (John 6:29).

For the Christian, every meal is a breaking of bread, and a sharing in the life of Jesus. Every drink of water is to drink the living water. Every day connected to the wine-producing Vine is to remain connected with him (John 15). In the Gospel of John, the Lord's Supper is not something that happened "back then" in the days of Jesus and the apostles, but something that all who believe share—and especially those who have never seen him (John 20:29). Here we see how John masterfully connects the life of Jesus with the spiritual life of the believer.

Conclusion

It may have sounded surprising earlier in this chapter to state that the fourth gospel is not intended as merely a history of the life of Jesus, but as a collection of meditations, perhaps even evangelistic sermons, designed to lead to belief in Jesus. This is not speculation, but the way the book itself defines its purpose: "These things have been recorded so that you can all believe that Jesus is the Christ-son of God, and through believing come to have life in his name" (John 20:31). This statement of the purpose of the book serves as the conclusion to the gospel. It is immediately preceded by the last story of the gospel. Thomas, who doubted that Jesus was raised, saw the resurrected Jesus and confessed, "My Lord and my God!" The final words of Jesus to Thomas speak to all Christians who live without seeing Jesus, "You have come to believe because you have seen me. The ones who are truly happy are the ones who believe without seeing." The Fourth Gospel was written to establish belief in the resurrected Lord.

ENDNOTES

1. The word "pericope" (pronounced pə-'ri-kə-pN) comes from two Greek words *peri* meaning "around" and *koptein* "to cut." It refers to a complete individual unit of the gospel, such as a story (like the Wedding at Cana), a parable (there are no parables in the Gospel of John), a hymn (the hymn to the "Word" in John 1), etc.

[Handwritten marginal note: John not def / gospel / not / meditations / to cause / to belief]

Chapter 24

The Gospel of John

Ronald L. Jolliffe

"Now Jesus did many other signs in the presence of his disciples, which are not written in this book. But these are written so that you may come to believe that Jesus is the Messiah, the Son of God, and that through believing you may have life in his name."

BRIEF OVERVIEW OF THE BOOK

The Gospel of John ranks as the favorite and most frequently read gospel in the New Testament. Aside from the Lord's Prayer, the most frequently memorized text is probably John 3:16, "God so loved the world that he gave his only Son." This gospel, like no other, takes time for extensive and profound meditation on who Christ is and on the meaning of Jesus' words.

The Gospel of John was written to lead its hearers to believe in Jesus. This theme opens (1:7) and closes the book (20:30-31). The book was not written to chronicle all the events of Jesus' life, nor to provide a chronology of Jesus' ministry, nor for any other mundane purpose. It was written to lead people to believe in Jesus and to find life in his name.

The prominent ideas in this gospel take focus when one considers some frequently occurring words: "truth" and "love;" the contrasting terms "light" versus "darkness;" and the verb "to believe." Although the verb "to believe" appears about three times more frequently in this gospel than in all the synoptics combined, the noun form, "belief" or "faith," never appears because, for the Gospel of John, it is something one practices, not something one belongs to.

[handwritten margin note: belief is what one practices (an idea from Hebrew scripture)]

To avoid confusion this chapter will use "John" when referring to the apostle and "*GJ*" for the Gospel of John.

BACKGROUND CONCERNS

The question of authorship for the *GJ* is complex. Two sources provide relevant information about the authorship: the *GJ* itself and early church tradition. Like the synoptics, the *GJ* is anonymous. The title, referring to John, is a later addition. Aside from John the baptizer, the *GJ* never refers to any person named John, his brother James, nor to "sons of Thunder," (in the addendum one does find "sons of Zebedee"). The book indicates something of its literary complexity when it refers to the authors as "we" (1:14, 16; 3:11; mimicked in 21:24) and to the apostolic witness, as "he" (19:35).

[handwritten margin note: author- "the beloved" disciple]

The addendum, ch 21, seems to have as one of its purposes, the identification of the author of the book with the "beloved disciple." John 21:24 claims this disciple "has written these things." But this verse also clearly indicates the presence of other writers, the "we" who "know that his testimony is true." It is also clear that ch 21 was written after the death of the "beloved disciple" as indicated by the chapter's careful exegesis of the words of Jesus in 21:20-23.

[handwritten margin note: ch. 21 - added after this disciple's death]

As to the early church tradition, explicit claims of Johannine authorship do not exist before the last quarter of the second century. Perhaps the first is Irenaeus (ca. 130-202 C.E.) who wrote, "Then John, the Lord's disciple closest to his heart, himself put out his gospel, while living in Ephesus of Asia."[1]

Earlier, the situation is more complicated. Papias of Hierapolis about 130 C.E., wrote,

> But if someone coming through was a follower of any of the presbyters, I closely examined the words of the presbyters, about what Andrew or what Peter said, or what Philip, or what Thomas or James said, or what John or Matthew or any other of the Lord's disciples said, or what things Aristion and the presbyter John, the disciples of the Lord are saying. For I didn't think the things out of so many books helped me as much as the living and continuing voice.[2]

[handwritten margin note: H.E. 3.39.4]

Notice that two Johns are ranked among the "disciples," one named with Peter, the other called "the presbyter." You will notice later when you read the epistles of John (they are the books in the New Testament most similar in language and world view to the *GJ*) that 2 and 3 John name the author as "the elder."

In light of the lack of any mention who the author is within the book, there are dangers in a dogmatic assumption that the apostle John was the author, for it invites speculations unfounded on the text itself. For example, if a similar story appears in both the *GJ* and a gospel not written by an "eyewitness" (such as Luke), with important differences of detail, the assumption of apostolic authorship for the *GJ* has lead to accepting the *GJ* as correct and discounting the other as corrupted. But when this happens, the reader's assumptions have become more important than the text. Another problem is the temptation to form psychological explanations based on the assumed personality profile of the assumed author. For example, one might explain away a difficult saying of Jesus as somehow skewed by the temper of the "son of Thunder." The book is too important for us to jump blindly into its study believing we already know more *book does not tell us author*

than the book itself tells us. Remember the book never names its author. The best course seems to be to leave the identity of the author unresolved.

Date of composition

The gospel was the last of the four canonical gospels to be written. It is normally dated during the last decade of the first century because of its distance from "the Jews" (which will be discussed near the end of the section on background concerns) and its developed theological understandings. The discovery of a small manuscript fragment (P^{52}) of John 18 in Egypt, which dates from the first half of the second century provides the *terminus ad quem* (latest possible date) for the gospel's composition.

P^{52} from early 2d c.

Provenance

The *provenance* (place where something comes from) of the *GJ* has been identified traditionally with Ephesus on the basis of the quotation from Irenaeus, quoted above, who claims John the apostle sent out his gospel while in Ephesus of Asia. Papias also refers to Ephesus. But references to John's presence in Ephesus by people who lived or worked there are lacking. Other areas have also been suggested. More recently a developing consensus favors a provenance in Syria, due in part to the large number of early Christian texts coming from there, and to the gnostic concerns of the *GJ* and the strong gnostic movement in Syria.

Ephesus or Syria (because of gnostic flavor)

LITERARY CONSIDERATIONS

As ch 24 has already observed, the *GJ* is unique in many ways when compared to the synoptics. A quick survey of a synopsis of the gospels clearly shows that the *GJ* only occasionally reports the same stories as the synoptics. While Jesus' ministry is confined to Galilee in the synoptics, his ministry continually moves him back and forth between Judea and Galilee in the *GJ*. Jesus' ministry appears to extend over three Passovers, whereas the synoptics agree that, as an adult, Jesus only goes to Jerusalem once, to his death.

GJ unique

Galilee ↑ Jerusalem

Jesus' teaching style is different in the *GJ* than in the synoptics. Although in the synoptics Jesus "did not speak to them without a parable" (Mark 4:34), in the *GJ*, Jesus never uses a parable. In fact the word "parable" does not appear in the Greek text. The sermons in the *GJ* are extended meditations on single thematic units (bread, water, shepherd, vine, etc.) in contrast to the collections of independent aphorisms and proverbs which stand as sermons in the synoptics.

no parables

lengthy meditation

Even the content of Jesus' proclamation changes. In the synoptics Jesus continually proclaims the Reign of God and the need to trust in God. In the *GJ* the focus is changed. Jesus encourages his followers to believe in him in order to have life. After 2000 years of Christian theology, this perhaps sounds like an insignificant difference, but without that 2000 years of history it is absolutely shocking. Remember that the Judaism in which Jesus lived was a thorough-going monotheistic religion. Devout Israelites daily repeated the "Hear O Israel, the Lord our God is one Lord." The *GJ* is direct in its affirmations of Jesus' divinity. The frequent use of the first-person hypostatic verb "I am" is distinctive to this gospel with Jesus saying things like: "Before Abraham was, I am" or "I am ... the life," etc. The *GJ* has been extremely influential in guiding Christian theology's understanding of the relationship between God and Jesus.

The *GJ* gives clear evidence of layers of editorial work. Perhaps no sentence in the Bible looks more like the work of a committee than 4:1-3, "Now when the Lord knew that the Pharisees had heard that Jesus was making and baptizing more disciples than John (although Jesus himself did not baptize, but only his disciples), he left Judea and departed again to Galilee."

The book opens with an ancient hymn (1:1-18) probably originally addressed to Wisdom that has been adapted to apply to Jesus. The author, or an editor, has interrupted the poetic structure with commentary twice (1:6-8, 15). The hymn now stands as an overview of the theme of the entire *GJ* that Jesus is the Word of God.

An observation of modern scholarship that seems to have become generally accepted is the identifiable presence within the *GJ* of an earlier written work which was incorporated into the *GJ* that, in its original form, was composed of a collection of miracles (signs) which Jesus performed. This *Signs Gospel* appears to have been a collection of seven miracles of Jesus found in 2:1-11; 4:46-54; 5:1-9; 6:1-15, 16-21; 9:1-41 and 11:1-44. This hypothesis begins by observing the numbering of the signs in 2:11 and 4:54. It helps explain why in some places in the *GJ*, people believe, or are encouraged to believe, or are approved for believing because of the signs (1:50; 2:11, 18-23; 4:48-54; 5:20, 36; 6:2, 14, 26; 7:31; 9:16; 10:37-38; 11:45-48; 12:18; 12:37; 13:19; 14:11, 29), yet in other places they are cautioned against basing belief on miracles (3:2-5; 20:24-29) or clearly encouraged to believe on the basis of the words spoken where no signs have been given (4:39-42; 5:24, 46-47; 6:28-51; 8:28-31). The *Signs Gospel* held the miracles of Jesus up as a basis for faith. The *GJ* seems hesitant about this view, since at the time of writing, miracles seem to be a thing of the past, yet people must still come to faith in Jesus. Therefore there appears to be an ambivalent attitude toward miracles in the *GJ*.

The *Signs Gospel* is reconstructed by some scholars as composed of 1:6-7, 19-49; 2:1-12a, 14-19; 4:46b-54; 5:2-9; 6:1-25; 9:1-8; 11:1-45, 47-53; 12:1-8, 12-15, 37-40; 18:1-20:22, 30-31b; 21:1-4.

Chapter 21 is clearly a later addendum to chs 1-20. The most obvious evidence is that the conclusion to chs 1-20 found in 20:30-31 immediately follows the climactic confession of Thomas that Jesus is "My Lord and my God!" Furthermore, 21:2 refers to "the sons of Zebedee" as though the reader knows who they are, yet no reference to James and John, to the "sons of thunder" (see Mark 3:17), nor to "the sons of Zebedee" is to be found in chs 1-20. John 21:15-24 indicates that it was written not only after the death of Peter, but 21:23 indicates it was also written after the death of "the beloved disciple."

The story of "The Woman Taken in Adultery," provides another window on *location of woman taken in adultery* the editorial work of composing a gospel. This story (7:53-8:11) properly belongs to the gospel tradition, but probably not to the *GJ*. Notice that in your Bible, if it is a more recent translation, this pericope is treated in some special way. It is either printed with a notation, in italics, within double square brackets or at the bottom of the page in small type to indicate that the earlier and more reliable manuscripts do not have this story. Some manuscripts locate it in other places e.g., following Luke 21:38 or John 7:36; 7:52 or 21:24.

The way the story is written seems to indicate that it does not belong to the *GJ*. Consider the following observations: (1) 8:1 speaks of "the Mount of Olives." This is the only place in the entire *GJ* where the hill is referred to by name. On the other hand, reference to the Mount of Olives appears in each of the synoptics at least three times; (2) the synoptics continually refer to the "scribes" (Mark ca. 21 times, Matthew 22 times and Luke 14 times). The term "scribes" never appears in the *GJ*, except here in 8:3. These observations, combined with the absence of the pericope in most manuscripts, suggest that the pericope should not be considered an original part of the *GJ* though it has a place in early Christian tradition.

"The Jews"

There is one additional difficulty which should be addressed before we turn to the outline of the gospel. The *GJ* is the most self-consciously "Christian" of all the canonical gospels. As such, the *GJ* uses "the Jews" as a term for Jesus' enemies. But not only the enemies of Jesus were Jews, so were Jesus' friends and Jesus himself. This use is unlike the use in the synoptics, where Jesus' enemies are spoken of as particular groups of community members or leaders, such as the "scribes and Pharisees," or the "leaders of the Jews." In the *GJ*, the most common term used to refer to Jesus' opponents is "the Jews." The history of relationships between Christians and Jews has probably been far more difficult because of this often unfortunate misunderstood usage in the *GJ*. Many Christians in the past have specifically quoted this book to justify their anti-Jewish sentiments.

In terms of authorship, it is difficult to imagine a Christian who lived as a Jew into adulthood speaking of the enemies of Jesus as "the Jews" when he himself, as well as his Lord, were Jewish. This observation seems to indicate that the gospel, in the stage in which we have it, was not completed by an eyewitness. Second, as to dating, it indicates that this gospel could not have been written until Christians no longer thought of themselves as a Jewish denomination.

Third, and most difficult is the matter of what is meant by, as well as how to speak and write about "the Jews" in the *GJ*. Some suggestions have been blatantly anti-Jewish. More recently suggestions include reading "Judeans" (in contrast to "Galileans"), understanding "the Jews" to refer to a particular faction of Israel such as those affiliated with the temple cult in contrast to the rest of the Jews, or that the term was originally used at a time when Christians were a small, despised group with no political power against a much larger and more powerful antagonist. None of the suggestions is fully satisfactory, but all of them serve to remind us that the term "the Jews" does not refer to all Jews. When speaking or writing about the *GJ,* "the Jews" should be referred to as "some of 'the Jews'" or a similar phrase as a continual reminder that God's children are to be found among all people everywhere.

You may be concerned about all the difficulties this introduction to the *GJ* has raised and especially about the freedoms the *GJ* seems to have taken with the story of Jesus. All this theological reflection, adaptation of the events to meet the needs of parishioners, changes in the opponents, etc., makes it sound as if the author were manipulating the story to suit his own purposes. It may be helpful to observe how the author himself understands his role in this process. It is described quite nicely in John 16. The disciples who sat and listened to Jesus did not clearly understand Jesus' message. It was for their own good that Jesus would go away. Then the Spirit of truth would be able to come in order to lead them into all truth. The author recognizes the complexity of understanding who Jesus is and what his words mean and clearly teaches that it is only under the influence of the Spirit of truth (who works through teachers like the author of the *GJ*) that Jesus' message can become clear.

[handwritten margin note: author Spirit of truth works through him]

THE MESSAGE
Outline

The following outline attempts to hear the entire text in terms of the gospel's statement of purpose contained in the original conclusion to the book found in 20:30, 31. Only this gospel out of the four canonical gospels contains an explicit statement of purpose: "... these are written that you may believe that Jesus is the Christ, the Son of God, and that believing you may have life in his name."

Survey of contents

Many proposals have been made about what *the* message of the *GJ* is. This section accepts the view that the primary historical influence of the *GJ* upon Christianity has been its view of Jesus. In dramatic contrast to the synoptics, where Jesus is wise teacher, exorcist, miracle worker, healer and Messiah, the *GJ* portrays Jesus as equal to God. Nearly every chapter reaffirms the intimate relationship and near equality of Jesus with God.

In the following examples, one gets a flavor of this emphasis which is unique to the *GJ*. Jesus is God's very Word who is indeed truly God (1:1-5). John the Baptist gives his own personal testimony to Jesus as the one who is to be his successor and superior, "He is the Son of God" (1:19-34). At various places we are confronted with Jesus' omniscience (1:50; 6:64; 18:4; etc.). Statements like Jesus "comes from heaven and is above all," that he "utters the words of God," that whoever "does not obey the Son shall not see life, but the wrath of God rests upon him" appear throughout the book beginning with 3:22-36. In the account of the Samaritan woman, Jesus is identified not only as the Messiah, but also as the Savior of the world. Jesus is said to make "himself equal with God" (5:18). The Son knows and does what the Father does (5:19, 20) and is to be honored in the same way that the Father is honored (5:23). The has life in himself just as the Father has life in himself (5:26). The Son has authority to execute judgment (5:27). The Son is the source of life (5:40). Jesus comes from the one who sent him (7:29), and he will return to the one who sent him (7:33). It is "the Father" who sent Jesus (8:18), and Jesus is "not of this world" (8:23). In 8:32-36 the freedom that comes from the truth is revealed to come only from the Son. In 8:39-58 a discussion of Abraham ends with Jesus striking response, "Before Abraham was, I am." Jesus accepts the worship of the healed blind man (9:38). Jesus says, "I know the Father" (10:15) and "I and the Father are one" (10:30). These claims to deity are not missed by the people who object "... you, being a man, make yourself God" (10:33). Jesus is the resurrection and the life, and whoever believes in him will not die (11:25-26). In ch 14, Jesus is going to God to prepare places for those who believe in him. No one comes to the Father except through Jesus (14:6). In response to Philip's request that Jesus reveal the Father to them, Jesus responds,

The Resurrection of Lazarus

"He who has seen me has seen the Father" (14:9). This theme builds to its climax in the final speech of Thomas who falls down and exclaims to Jesus, "My Lord and my God" (20:28). This exaltation of Jesus has made this the preferred gospel for Christian devotional meditation as well as for showing the deity of Jesus.

The second chapter introduces the beginning of Jesus' signs, which appear throughout the second and third major divisions of the book's outline The signs are significant in establishing the *GJ*'s claims concerning Jesus, they lead to belief in Jesus, and they reveal Jesus' glory. The first of these signs (changing water to wine) forms the core of the story of the wedding at Cana which also introduces the language of "my hour," referring to the death and resurrection of Jesus (2:1-11). In the remainder of the chapter Jesus cleanses the temple, an act that the synoptics reserve for passion week. Many believe in his name because of the signs they see him do (2:23). The second "sign," which leads the "official" of Capernaum and all his household to believe in Jesus does not come until 4:43-54.

A common phenomenon in the *GJ* is illustrated in Jesus' night conversation with Nicodemus (3:1-21). The dialogue mixes two time levels, the time when Jesus lived on earth and the time of the author writing the story 60+ years later (this mixing of the time of the author and of Jesus is also interesting to follow in ch 9 where the healing of the blind man is mixed with the later expulsion of followers of Jesus from the synagogues). This results in an unusual conversation in which Jesus' sometimes refers to himself as "I" and other times as "we" even though no one else has joined the conversation. The same is seen with "you" which has two separate forms in Greek, one for singular and one for plural, though not in English. In other words, Jesus sometimes speaks as though Nicodemus is more than one person, even though this is not discernible in English. The following verses have the plural form of "you" in this story in Greek: 3:7b, 11b, 12a, b, c, d. It is probably easiest to think of this section as a sermon being preached around 90 C.E. built upon the story of Jesus and Nicodemus, rather than as a transcript of the dialogue between them.

Samaria separates Galilee from Judea. Animosities are strong between the Judeans and the Samaritans as rivals over who are the true heirs to Moses. The Samaritans accepted the first five books of the Jewish scriptures as their own. Rivalry was most prominent over the proper place of worship, which dated back to the time of Ezra and the construction of the second temple. These animosities were intensified when the Maccabees destroyed the Samaritan temple on Mt. Gerizim. These strong sentiments are clear in 4:1-42, (cf. 8:48). The chapter agrees (as does the entire *GJ*) with the synoptics in affirming Jesus' full inclusion of women, even though it clearly violates social convention. Consider the aghast response of his own disciples (4:27).

Chapter 5 opens the next section of the gospel where opposition to Jesus begins to build. In the pericope of the man by the pool (5:1-18) people began to seek to kill Jesus because he made "himself equal with God" (5:18). The words and actions of Jesus were an affront to the views of some regarding what constitutes appropriate Sabbath observance. But the story was not inserted at this point in the narrative to discuss proper Sabbath keeping. It stands here to continue the discussion between the author and his readers about who Jesus is and the relationship of Jesus with God. This is clear when we read the story and look at its various parts.

To begin with we notice that the story has three scenes followed by a summary. The summary includes events that happen later than the story itself. The first scene (at the pool 5:2-9), although a spectacular miracle, does not even pause to reflect on the wonder, for other points are being scored. In the second scene (among the crowds presumably near the pool or on the street, 5:9b-13), the man is carrying his pallet. In the third scene, (in the temple 5:14-15), Jesus meets the man and makes his identity known to the man.

The sequence of events narrated in the summary (5:16-18) reveals the author's agenda. First, because Jesus violated the Sabbath, they persecuted Jesus. Because they persecuted Jesus, Jesus said that he and his Father are both working. Because Jesus said this, they sought all the more to kill him, not only for Sabbath violation, but also because he "called God his Father, making himself equal with God." The entire summary relates events from a later time than what happened at the pool. Notice that it is the author, not Jesus, who introduces the "equal with God" comment.

The Crucifixion

In 10:22 Jesus is in Jerusalem for the Feast of Dedication. This is the holiday season called Hanukkah. It commemorates the cleansing of the Jewish temple in 165 C.E. after the Seleucid ruler Antiochus Epiphanes had taken control of the temple, dedicated the temple to Zeus and sacrificed a pig on the altar of burnt offering in 167 C.E. An account of these events is found in the Apocrypha's book of 1 Macc. Each winter, near Christmas, Jews continue to celebrate this rededication of the temple which Jesus celebrated.

Although there is no account of the Lord's supper in the GJ, which we would expect at ch 13 (consult the end of ch 24 of this volume for further details), ch 6 is woven together on the basis of stories about bread which seem to serve as a sort of meditation on the meaning of the Lord's supper. This becomes explicit in 6:52-59 where bread and blood appear together.

The triumphal entry follows the anointing of Jesus' feet at a feast. The discussion following the request of the Greeks to see Jesus makes clear that Jesus' glorification refers to his death (12:23-28). The cross, a symbol of shame and embarrassment to many of the early followers of Jesus, becomes, in the *GJ*, the elevation of the son of God to honor and worship.

Chapter 13 marks the beginning of the final section of the *GJ* known as the passion narrative. This section of the *GJ* is more like the synoptics than any other part of the *GJ*. Chapter 13 reflects the *GJ* version of the Lord's supper, which has a foot washing, but no last meal or institution of the communion service. The chapter in this text dealing with John and the synoptics ends with an explanation of why this is the case, which will not be repeated here.

The coming of the Counselor is introduced in 14:25 and remains an intermittent theme of the discourse into ch 16. The differences between the teaching of Jesus (for example, as reported in the synoptics) and the teaching of the *GJ* is perhaps best explained in 16:12-15—that the Spirit of Truth would teach things that the disciples were not yet ready to bear. In 16:25-33, Jesus is said to speak to them in figures, which they think they understand (16:29) but Jesus denies that they do yet (16:31).

RELEVANCE FOR TODAY

An important theme in the book is love. (*Agape*, the word for selfless love, *love a theme* occurs 31 times as a verb and another six times as a noun. In addition, *philos*, the love of friendship, occurs six times as a noun and an additional thirteen times in its verbal form.) It is love that binds Christians to one another (13:34; 15:12, 17) and to Christ (8:42; 13:34). It is love that led the Father to send his Son (3:16, 35). Love results in keeping Jesus' words (14:15, 23), and in rejoicing (14:28). When so many come from homes where divorce, abuse, neglect, and "busy-ness" have caused people to feel unloved, the *GJ* is a very important gospel. Perhaps no other lesson could be more important. What a wonderful world it would be if all who claim to belong to Christ actually loved all others!

ISSUES FOR DISCUSSION AND REFLECTION

1. In the *GJ* Jesus goes to Jerusalem for Passover (and the immediately following Feast of Tabernacles) in 2:13; 6:4 (7:2-10); and 11:55. This requires a ministry of at least two years in length (since he goes to three different Passovers). The synoptics each speak of Jesus only going to Jerusalem once in his adult life for the Passover connected with his death (Mark 10:32-14:17; Matt 20:17-26:20; Luke 9:51-22:7). What explanations are possible for the differences?

2. Select three people to perform 3:1-21 as a one-act play. The three parts are Jesus, Nicodemus and the writer of the gospel as the story teller. While the story is only about two people (Jesus and Nicodemus), there is clearly also the narrator. Consider carefully the assignment of vss 11-21. In the second half of vs 11 the pronouns change from "I" to "we" and from "you (singular)" to "you (plural)." Who is speaking in these verses? Jesus? The narrator? (Remember that modern editors have decided what words to print in red as the words of Jesus. The Greek does not have quotation marks, so the players must assign many of the dialogue parts to the various actors.)

3. In the discussion of "provenance" under "Background Concerns" the textbook says traditionally Ephesus in Asia Minor was considered the location of the writing of the *GJ*, but more recently a consensus for Syria has been developing. Locate both areas on the map of the "Mediterranean Area in the Time of Paul." Read about these two areas. What kinds of differences might it make to the author and his audience if they lived in Syria rather than Ephesus? Consider factors of climate, geography, access to trade, language, etc.

4. Now that you have read all four gospels, (Matthew, Mark and Luke, as part of the material for section III and the *GJ* for this chapter), which gospel did you like best? What elements made you prefer one over another?

5. The healing of the man who was blind from birth in ch 9 is introduced by the question whether the blindness is because of the sin of the parents or the man himself. How would you frame a response to this question based on the information in John 9?

6. The term "the Jews" appears in the *GJ* in the following verses. Read each use and compile a list of texts that speak a) positively, b) neutrally, and c) negatively of "the Jews." 1:19; 2:6, 13, 18, 20; 3:1, 25; 4:9, 22; 5:1, 10, 15, 16, 18; 6:4, 41, 52; 7:1, 2, 11, 13, 15, 35; 8:22, 31, 48, 52, 57; 9:18, 22 (2x); 10:19, 24, 31, 33; 11:8, 19, 31, 33; 11:36, 45, 54, 55; 12:9, 11; 13:33; 18:12, 14, 20, 31, 33, 35, 36, 38, 39; 19:3, 7, 12, 14, 19, 21, 31, 40, 42; 20:19.

FURTHER READING

Barrett, Charles K.
    1965   *The Gospel According to St. John: An Introduction with Commentary and Notes on the Greek Text.* London: SPCK.

Brown, Raymond E.
    1979   *The Community of the Beloved Disciple*, New York: Paulist.

Bultmann, Rudolf
    1964   *The Gospel of John, A Commentary.* Translated from the German by Basil Blackwell. Philadelphia: Westminster.

Marrow, Stanley B.
   1995   *The Gospel of John: A Reading.* New York: Paulist.
Martyn, J. Louis
   1979   *History and Theology in the Fourth Gospel,* revised and enlarged, Nashville: Abingdon.
Newman, Barclay M. and Eugene A. Nida
   1980   *A Handbook on the Gospel of John.* New York: United Bible Society.
Sloyan, Gerard S.
   1991   *What are they saying about John?* New York: Paulist.

ENDNOTES

1. *Adversus haereses*, III, 1, 1; translation by author.
2. Quoted in Eusebius, *H.E. III, XXXIX, 4;* translation by author.

Chapter 25

Johannine Letters

Bruce C. Johanson

> *"Beloved, let us love one another, because love is from God; everyone who loves is born of God and knows God."*

BRIEF OVERVIEW OF THE BOOKS

First John appears to be a homily addressed to a group of early Christians [1 Jn: homily to abandoned Xian community] who had been abandoned by a significant number of their community. Those who had departed apparently taught that Jesus Christ had not come *in the flesh.* Those who remained are encouraged to hold onto what they had heard from the beginning. The writer gives them several basic norms by which they can assure themselves of belonging to the truth. These have to do with confession that Jesus is the Christ, the Son of God come in the flesh, assurances of forgiveness for confessed sins through the atonement of Jesus Christ, and the need of genuine love for one another and for God. In particular, mutual love is what gives confidence as the judgement approaches. [2 John: from elder to elect lady] Second John is a short letter from the "elder" to the "elect lady" who is presumably a specific church. Although very much shorter than 1 John, it gives approximately the same message regarding christological confession and mutual love. Third John is a brief letter from the "elder" to "Gaius." He applauds Gaius for hospitality to [3 Jn: elder to Gaius] brethren he has sent. He goes on to complain about Diotrephes, who refuses such hospitality and does not recognize his authority. The message closes with a commendation of Demetrius.

BACKGROUND CONCERNS

It is a difficult task to reconstruct the background of the Johannine epistles. First John makes no explicit mention of who the author is, where it was written, or to whom it was addressed. Second and 3 John identify the sender simply as "the elder." Second John is addressed to "the elect lady," most likely a veiled reference to a church. Third John is addressed to someone by the name of Gaius.

John the disciple? [handwritten marginal note]

From a fairly early date the author of 1 John has been regarded as John the son of Zebedee, the disciple of Jesus referred to in, e.g., Mark 1:19. By contrast, 2 and 3 John received such recognition much later and not without some serious doubts along the way. Eusebius records a tradition that John the disciple was located in Ephesus and traveled about in the surrounding region (*H.E. 3.23.6*). If this is reliable, both the place of writing and of the addressees may possibly have been somewhere in or around Ephesus in western Asia Minor. For various reasons, however, many modern scholars have felt the need to question the authorship of even 1 John by John the disciple. The following are some of the more important observations on the competing sides of this question.

John, the Beloved, and Jesus

In support of the traditional view, the opening lines of 1 John have been taken to indicate that the author was among the eye-witnesses of Jesus:

1 Jn 1: an eyewitness report [handwritten marginal note]

> That which was from the beginning, which we have heard, which we have seen with our eyes, which we have looked upon and touched with our hands, concerning the word of life—the life was made manifest, and we saw it, and testify to it, and proclaim to you the eternal life which was with the Father and was made manifest to us (1 John 1:1-2, RSV).

Those who reject this view note that, although these words appear to indicate an eyewitness, the object of the witness does not seem to be Jesus' life on earth.

The repeated expression "that which" is neuter gender in the Greek and therefore impersonal. Consequently "word" in the expression "the word of life" should be understood as the "message" or the "revelation" of life. This focus on the truth of the "message" continues in the letter (1:5, 8, 21, 24, 26-27, etc.). By contrast, the Gospel of John uses "word" of Jesus himself (John 1:1). Even "life" in 1 John 1:1-2 may be understood as a reference to what the message brings to believers, since it is qualified as "eternal life." Furthermore, the expressions of "seeing" and "looking at" may be taken to mean enlightenment rather than physical sight. Finally, the expression "touched with our hands" does not need to be understood literally, if the "we" is a group of persons who have had direct contact with the apostles. In this way, they claim that their mediation of the message is authoritative and genuine.

In favor of the traditional interpretation, there is evidence that in 1 John 5:20 Jesus Christ himself is referred to not only as "true God" but also as "eternal life." Such usage shows that it is quite within the author's style to use words with rich, multiple meanings. Jesus may be referred to as both person, message, and benefit to the believer. The same phenomenon is found in the Gospel of John: "I am the way, and the truth, and the life" (John 14:6). Consequently, the author may be including himself among the original eyewitnesses of Jesus who could quite literally say, "which ... we have touched with our hands" (RSV). These contrasting observations simply underline the ambiguity of the primary passage in 1 John that could tie it to one of Jesus' disciples.

Another part of the puzzle comes from 2 and 3 John. Here the author identifies himself as the "elder" (2 John 1; 3 John 1). A quotation of Papias (ca. 150 C.E.) by Eusebius has fueled speculation that a certain John the elder, as distinct from the John of the original twelve disciples, may have been the author, not only of Revelation, but also of 1, 2, and 3 John:

> But if ever anyone came who had followed the elders, I inquired into the words of the elders, what Andrew or Peter or Philip or Thomas or James or John or Matthew, or any other of the Lord's disciples said, and what Aristion and the elder John, the Lord's disciples, are saying *(H.E. 3.39.4).*

What is significant here is that, whereas all are called elders and disciples, the former John is included among the disciples who were part of the original twelve. The latter John is called "the elder John" and mentioned with Aristion who was not among the twelve. The past tense "said" suggests that the former John was no longer alive, while the present tense "are saying" suggests that the elder John and Aristion were still alive when Papias wrote. Eusebius (ca. 325 C.E.) notes this and goes on to suggest that Revelation was most likely the work of the elder John. Many modern scholars have extended the same possibility to include the Johannine epistles.

All this is, of course, highly speculative. Besides, as 1 Pet 5:1 indicates, the title "elder" could quite naturally be applied to an apostle, even as it was done at a later time by Papias. Also, in favor of the traditional view, we find that the author's authority appears to have carried across different churches (2 John, 3 John). This must be seen as characteristic for an apostle rather than an elder who was not an apostle.

Another approach to the question of authorship is based on comparisons of language and style among the Johannine writings. A comparison of 1 John and the Gospel of John shows an impressive number of parallels in both language and style.[1] In general, however, the style of 1 John is simpler and more repetitive. Some of the more significant differences are as follows: 1) the use of "word" (*logos*) personally in John (1:1, 14), but impersonally in 1 John (1:1-2); 2) the use of "paraclete" (*parakletos*) for the Holy Spirit in John (chs 14-16), but for Jesus Christ in 1 John (2:1); 3) Jesus' death in the gospel is expressed in terms of his glorification (John 12:16, 23; 13:31), but in terms of atonement in 1 John (2:2; 4:10); 4) the eschatology in the gospel appears to emphasize eschatology as the present possession and experience of eternal life (John 3:36; 5:24), whereas the emphasis in 1 John is more on the future coming of Christ (2:28; 3:2; 4:17). In this last instance, it must be pointed out that 1 John also has texts that equally express the present possession and experience of eternal life (1 John 3:14-15; 5:11-13). As for 1 John compared to 2 and 3 John, the latter two have much in common with 1 John in terms of typical terms and phrases.[2] However, in style they are more sophisticated. It appears that in all such comparisons the similarities weigh heavily in favor of common authorship, while the differences are explainable as what one may reasonably expect when an author writes in and for different situations.

Finally there is the witness of tradition to the acceptance of 1 John as coming from the disciple John. While many allusions to 1 John are apparent in parallel expressions and phraseology in Christian literature between ca. 100-150 C.E., Papias gives the earliest explicit reference to it. Then around 180 C.E. Irenaeus (*Adv. Haer. 3.16.18*) and Clement of Alexandria (*Strom. 2.15.66*) also recognize it. After that, there are abundant references, none of which question its apostolic origin. As for 2 and 3 John, Eusebius' quotation from Origen (ca. 230 C.E.) provides our earliest record of their existence. Origen refers to both letters and remarks that not everyone regarded them to be genuine (*H.E. 6.25.10*). It is not until the fourth century that they come to be widely regarded as John the disciple's work and a part of the New Testament canon.

Among scholars who question John the disciple's authorship as a whole or in part, some have tried to establish an original source which was commented on by the author and further revised by a later editor.[3] The original source was seen as consisting of the many antithetical statements in 1 John and the hortatory parts as the subsequently added commentary. Others have proposed theories of a [handwritten: 2) a "school"] Johannine school. In other words, both the gospel and the epistles are seen as the products of John and his close associates and followers. This theory is based on efforts to discern stages of composition and editorial work that reflect struggles between progressive and conservative tendencies within the so-called school.[4] Both source and school theories, because of their complexity and largely speculative character, do not help us arrive at any assured results.

Before turning to deal with literary considerations, it is necessary to sketch what we can possibly reconstruct of the situations reflected in these writings. Explicit reference is made in 1 John 2:19 to a group of persons who had abandoned the community of believers. In the context of 1 John 2:18-27 it is quite obvious that the secession was over differences in belief. The first explicit reference to false teaching is found in 2:22: The one who "denies that Jesus is the Christ" is a "liar" and an "antichrist." It is possible to understand "Christ" (*Christos*) as the Greek equivalent for "the Anointed One," i.e. "Messiah." As such, it could reflect a Jewish denial that Jesus qualified as the Messiah. If that were the case, we would expect to see at least a few quotations from the Old Testament used in support of Jesus' messiahship. All that we find is a passing allusion to Cain as an example of one who's deeds were evil. There is not a single quotation from the Old Testament in all of 1, 2 and 3 John. We most [handwritten: no OT quote in 1-2-3 Jn.] likely have to search elsewhere for a probable background.

In 4:2-3 we find another explicit reference to false Christological teaching, again linked with the designation "antichrist:"

> By this you know the Spirit of God: every spirit that confesses that Jesus Christ
> has come in the flesh is from God, and every spirit that does not confess Jesus
> is not from God. This is the spirit of the antichrist, of which you have heard
> that it is coming, and now it is already in the world.

The phrase "has come in the flesh" seems to indicate that some did not believe he became a physical human being. We find virtually the same characterization of the false teaching warned against in 2 John 7: "Many deceivers have gone out into the world, those who do not confess that Jesus Christ has come in the flesh; any such person is the deceiver and the antichrist. In 2 John 9 those who hold this view of Christ are described as trying to "go ahead" (RSV) of the church. Perhaps they regarded themselves as the *avant garde* or spiritual elite among the believers. How may all this be interpreted?

There is evidence, beginning in the first century, of a dualistic world view [handwritten: a dualistic worldview: matter = evil] that was quite widely spread. Such a dualistic outlook regarded physical phenomena as evil in contrast to spirit which was seen as good. We know from later sources that such a dualism led many early Christians to make a distinction between Christ as spirit being and Jesus as human being. This way of thinking made it very hard for many to believe that the heavenly being Christ actually *became* the flesh-and-blood man, Jesus. They thought he only *appeared* to be a man. One version of this was expressed in the view that at baptism the spirit being Christ somehow took up existence in the man Jesus, but left him before he died on the cross. This type of christology came to be called "Docetism." It is possible that 1 John 5:6 is aimed against such a view. Here the author insists that Jesus Christ came with both the water (baptism?) and the blood (death on the cross?). With this in mind, the phrase "has come in the flesh" could be the author's way of affirming the reality of the incarnation. Furthermore, the second part in 1 John 4:3, "every spirit that does not confess Jesus is not from God," may be interpreted as attacking a denial of the human element in the incarnation represented by "Jesus." As such, it may be another version of "who denies that *Jesus* is the Christ" (2:22). By contrast, the true child of God "believes that *Jesus* is the Christ" (5:1).

Along with these observations there are several other indications that fit the pattern of religious phenomena which developed in the second century into what is known as Gnosticism. The words "light" and "darkness" were widely used in religious discourse to contrast good and evil. They were especially used by Gnostics and people with Gnostic-like tendencies to express the goodness of "spirit" and the evil nature of "matter," i.e. a *metaphysical* dualism. First John seems to make a point of giving these terms an *ethical* content where "light" is associated with loving behavior and "darkness" with hating (1:6-7; 2:9-11). Also, those who espoused a metaphysical dualism often regarded salvation in terms of enlightenment, i.e. an awakening to the liberating knowledge that the divine as "spirit" was present within one's physical being. It is possible that some such view of enlightenment lay behind the claims to "sinlessness" that John counters in 1:8-10. Finally, people with Gnostic-like tendencies, who claimed special knowledge, tended to be elitist. If such elitism was a part of the characteristics of those who abandoned the community, it would have augmented the insecurity of those left behind. Such a background may account for John's frequently given tests and assurances that his addressees *know* God and what is true (2:3-5, 12-14, 20-29; 3:18-24; 4:2-6, 7, 13-16; 5:2, 18-20). Taken together, these inferences suggest that 1 and 2 John were concerned to refute some early Christian form of budding Gnosticism. Eusebius (*H.E. 3.1.4*) tells us about a certain Cerinthus whom John repudiated as a false teacher. According to Irenaeus (*Ad. Haer. 1.26.1*), Cerinthus held a docetic view of Christ. There is, however, not enough evidence to prove that it was exactly his form of docetism that 1 John argued against.

There are some interpreters who dispute whether the phrase "has come in the flesh" (4:2) is at all the focus of a dispute on Christology. They think that it was simply part of the confessional tradition current in the area and that the focus is primarily a question of confessing or denying Jesus Christ.[5] They hold that 1 John in primarily a letter of pastoral exhortation and comfort. When the author writes about confession and denial of Jesus Christ, he is thought to be primarily concerned to keep those who remained after the schism committed to faith in Jesus Christ. Such an interpretation is definitely a possibility. However, it does not do justice to the significant clusters of closely connected references in both 1 and 2 John to false teaching, antichrist, and christological confessions or denials that involve the fleshly existence of Jesus Christ.

What are we to make of 3 John? In this letter the elder commends Gaius for supporting some traveling missionaries who have returned with good reports about him. He goes on to complain about a certain Diotrephes who does not recognize the elder's authority, refuses to welcome those sent presumably by the elder, and excludes from church fellowship anyone who welcomes them. It is possible that Gaius himself had been ostracized by Diotrephes. Is the positive reference to Demetrius in 3 John 12 intended to support his replacement of Diotrephes as the authoritative figure in that church? Was the struggle over authority connected with the false teaching combatted in 1 and 2 John? One can only speculate. There is nothing in the text of 3 John to make any such connection.

We cannot securely narrow down the probable date of any of the three Johannine epistles to a particular year. The late eighties or early nineties C.E. is a likely guess for 1 John. These limits are suggested by what appear to be allusions to 1 John in other early Christian writings, a few of which can be dated in the late nineties C.E. To try to tie the date of 1 John to that of the Gospel of John does not get one very far, since the date for the Gospel is itself difficult to establish. If John the disciple is the author of all three epistles, it would seem difficult to push a date for any of them beyond the early nineties C.E.

LITERARY CONSIDERATIONS

Of all the New Testament epistolary literature 2 John and especially 3 John stand the closest to Greco-Roman conventions of the common letter, in terms of both length and form.[6] As to form, 3 John has a brief prescript in which sender and receiver are identified (vs 1), reports of prayer for the addressees' well being and health and of joy over news received about him (vs 2-4), the message part of the letter (vs 5-12), the expression of a need to write more, but preferring to speak directly soon in a personal visit (vs 13-14), and the closing expression of greetings and request for greetings to be passed on (vs 15). The only departure from the common letter conventions is the absence of a "salutation" (Greek: *chairein*) in the prescript after the identification of sender and receiver. In 2 John the identification of sender and receiver is followed by a Christian salutation of "Grace, mercy, and peace," etc. (2 John 1-3). Instead of a report of prayer for the addressees' health and well-being, there is an expression of joy over the their spiritual condition (vs 4). Then comes the message section (vs 5-11). After that, there is the expression of a need to write more, but preferring to speak directly soon in a personal visit (vs 12), much as in 3 John. A simple greeting from the elder's church to the addressees closes the letter (vs 13).

It is not hard to see that, if 1 John had not been preserved together with 2 and 3 John, it would most likely not have been called an "epistle." It has neither opening nor closing epistolary features. The only significant characteristic that makes a connection with the letter genre is the frequent expression of "I am writing to you" (e.g., 2:1, 7-8, 12-13 [RSV]) and "I have written to you" (2:14, 21, 26; 5:13 [RSV]). The use of the past tense in the latter instances is typically epistolary in that a writer often referred to his or her letter from the later perspective of when it would be read by the addressee. On the other hand, the style of the writing is certainly not typical of letters. A brief introduction presents the topic, i.e. "the word of life," which the author says that he and his co-witnesses wish to share with the addressees. The rest of the writing goes on to unfold what this "word of life" means for the addressees' faith in general as well as for the particular situation in which they find themselves. The author alternates between series of short aphoristic announcements of essential truths and longer hortatory, pastoral sequences that admonish and comfort the addressees. He expresses a basic idea and then expresses it again with subtle differences so that one gets a sense of both progression and circularity. For example, in 1:8 the author writes, "If we say that we have no sin, we deceive ourselves, and the truth is not in us" (RSV), and again in 1:10 we find, "If we say that we have not sinned, we make him a liar, and his word is not in us" (RSV). This also occurs on a larger scale where the theme of loving/hating one's "brothers and sisters" recurs in 2:9-11, 3:10-17, and 4:20-21.

In view of such observations it is widely held that 1 John be regarded primarily as a theological tract or manifesto. However, a tract is usually formulated to address a more general audience in less personal terms than seems to be the case with this writing. The references to recent schism over differences of belief in the community (2:18-27) intimates a particular situation being specifically addressed. Right after 2:18-27 the author hurries to exhort his addressees to confidence (2:28), and then three more times in 3:19-21, 4:17 and 5:14. The secession over conflicting beliefs about Christ apparently left those who remained feeling insecure over their own status in face of the impending judgment. There is also the familiarity and warmth of the address "children," "little children" or "my little children" which recurs often (2:1, 12, 13, 18, 28; 3:7, 10, 18; 4:4; 5:2, 21). These features suggest that it is closer in genre to a homily written and sent to a particular church or even a group of closely associated churches which had all been more or less divided for the same reason.

THE MESSAGE

Because of the subtle, repetitive, circular style in 1 John, critics have not come to any consensus on its structure. In fact, some believe that it is a hopeless undertaking. If, however, we turn to the developing discipline of text-linguistics, we find criteria which make the task less hopeless. This discipline *recurring features are important* has shown that different kinds of recurring features in a text serve as a principal means of achieving a text's coherence and cohesion. In other words, coherence and cohesion have to do with the *unity* of a text and its subsections.[7] The repetition of thought coupled with the simple vocabulary of 1 John results in the frequent repetitions of specific words, word groups and phrases. As one reads through, one can observe the shifting *densities* of these recurring expressions. Such densities coupled with the flow of thought can help us to isolate fairly securely shorter sections of text. The larger twofold or threefold divisions found in most commentaries do not appear to be supported by any such clearly demonstrable criteria in the text itself.[8]

In *1:1-4* the author expresses his intent to communicate his experience of the *word of life* "word of life" with his addresses in order that they may have fellowship with one another and with God. The passage is obviously introductory. Supporting this division is a density of references to "life" and "fellowship" and of verbs of perception and communication.

In *1:5-2:11* the focus is on behavior characterized by light or darkness. The *light-darkness* recurring references to "light" and "darkness" and "being/walking in the light/darkness" occur at the beginning (1:5-7) and the end (2:8-11) of the section like a frame. In between the author spells out what light and darkness mean, first in relation to claims of sinlessness and Christ's atonement for sin (1:8-2:2) and then in relation to keeping God's commandments. The latter is expressed in terms of mutual love (2:3-11). Significant word and phrase recurrences in the subunits are "sin(s)," "if we should say/claim" and "commandment(s)," "he who says/claims."

This is followed by two shorter passages. In *2:12-14* we find the most *children- fathers- youngmen (repeated)* highly structured unit in the whole document. It has two strophes of three lines each. By repeatedly addressing first children, then fathers, then young men the author emphasizes his assurance to the readers that their sins are forgiven and that they know God, that they know "him who is from the beginning," and that they have overcome evil. Then in *2:15-17* admonitions warn against love of the world and its captivating desires. Note the repetitions of "world" and "desire." Then in *2:18-27* we again find a longer passage that warns against the views of those who had left their community of faith. Their apostasy is a sign that the end is near. Tests of belief in Jesus and the Father in terms of denial and confession are presented. Also, assurances are given that those remaining have genuine knowledge by the anointing of the Spirit. Significant word repetitions here are "antichrist(s)," "true/false," "anointing," and "deny."

behavior in view of parousia   In *2:28-3:9* the author moves on to the believers' behavior and status in view of the approaching coming (*parousia*) of Christ. This is expressed in terms of "doing/practicing righteousness" and "not doing/practicing sin" and in terms of a "Father/children" relationship to God. "Born of him/God" in 2:29 and 3:9 forms a frame for the unit. Other word recurrences are "appear" and "sin." Connecting closely with this passage, we find that in *3:10-24* "doing what is right" is spelled out in terms of reciprocal love in the community with concrete examples given. When there is love in action and belief in Jesus Christ, God's commandments are fulfilled and there is confidence before God. Repetition of "that we should love one another" provides a frame for the unit in 3:11 and 3:23. The most significant recurrences are the references to "love." Other recurring terms are "brother(s)," "heart" and "commandment(s)."

antichrist   In *4:1-5* we return again to the problem of false teaching, this time in terms of false spirits, i.e. "false prophets" and "antichrist." The test is whether or not they confess that Jesus Christ really came in the flesh. If so, they are of God. If not, they are of the world. Recurring expressions are "spirit(s)" and "world."

God is love   In *4:7-21* the focus is again on reciprocal love in the community. The fact that "God is love" (4:8, 16) and that this is expressed concretely through Christ's atonement for sin evokes the believers' love. When such love is complete in the believer, it displaces all fear and gives confidence for the day of judgment. Besides the recurring references to "love," there are four references to love being "perfected" in believers (4:12, 17, 18).

faith   In *5:1-12* the focus turns to faith, first in terms of belief "that Jesus is the Christ" (5:1) and "that Jesus is the Son of God" (5:5), and then in terms of faith "in the Son of God" and "in God" (5:10). Belief that Jesus is the Christ involves loving both God and Jesus as well as the children of God and keeping his commandments. This faith gives victory over the world. That Jesus is the Son of God is witnessed to by the Spirit, the water and the blood. The one who believes this has God's witness within. The person who has the Son has eternal life. The expression "who believes" is the main recurring feature that gives this passage coherence (5:1, 5, 10). Other important recurring words are "born" and "witness."

confidence   Finally, in *5:13-20* the focus is on confidence in the knowledge they have. They know that prayer requests to God are answered, particularly prayer requests for those who are committing sin that is not "mortal" (lit. "unto death"), whatever that may mean. They also know that the Evil One cannot touch the person who is born of God. To conclude, they know the One who is true, that they are in the One who is true, i.e. Jesus Christ his son, who is true God and eternal life. The most important recurring expressions are "you know" once and "we know" five times. Other significant recurrences are the petitioning words "ask," "requests," "pray," and references to "sin," "mortal sin." The sentiments in 5:20 make a fitting conclusion in keeping with themes and concerns expressed throughout the writing. In view of this the final exhortation in 5:21, admonishing them to guard themselves from idols, comes as a curious closing, since this is a topic never mentioned once throughout the writing.

These observations on 1 John and the previous remarks on the form of 2 and 3 John help us to arrive at the following outlines:

Outline
1 John

    I. Introduction: the author desires to proclaim his and his co-witnesses' experience of the "word of life" so that his readers may have fellowship and joy 1:1-4

   II. Body of the writing 1:5-5:20

      A. Instructions about light and darkness. Walking in the light means to acknowledge sin, to accept forgiveness through Jesus Christ, and to love one's brother. Walking in darkness means to deny sin and to hate one's brother 1:5-2:11

      B. Assurances that the addressees' sins are forgiven, that they know God and the one who is from the beginning, and that they have overcome the evil one 2:12-14

      C. Admonitions to guard against love of the world and its captivating desires 2:15-17

      D. Assurances that those now abandoned by antichrists may be confident in their knowledge about Jesus and God, because they have the anointing of the Spirit 2:18-27

      E. Encouragement for confidence before the parousia, because those born of God practice righteousness and cannot practice sin 2:28-3:9

      F. Instructions that to practice righteousness means active, mutual love and belief in Jesus Christ. This fulfills God's commandments and gives confidence before him 3:10-24

      G. Warnings against false prophets, spirits of antichrist and of deception, who deny that Jesus Christ has come in the flesh 4:1-6

H. Admonitions to mutual love because God is love and has demonstrated his love in his Son's atoning death. Love gets rid of fear and gives confidence in the day of judgment 4:7-21

I. Instructions about faith: both faith *that* Jesus is the Christ and the Son of God and faith *in* God and his Son give victory over the world and eternal life 5:1-12

J. Assurances that God answers their requests, that they are protected from the evil one, and that they truly know Jesus Christ, who is true God and eternal life 5:13-20

III. Closing: an admonition to guard against idols 5:21

2 John

I. Letter opening: the "elder" writes to the "elect lady" (most likely a church) and sends a salutation of grace, mercy and peace 1-3

II. Letter body 4-11

A. Opening report of joy over the spiritual condition of the addressees 4

B. Exhortation to mutual love and a warning to beware of those who do not acknowledge the coming of Jesus Christ in the flesh 5-11

III. Letter closing: the desire is expressed to visit the addressees rather than to communicate by letter and a greeting is sent from the "elect sister" to the addressees 12-13

3 John

I. Letter opening: the "elder" writes to the "beloved Gaius" whom he loves in truth 1

II. Letter body 2-12

A. Opening report of prayer for the health and well-being of Gaius and of joy over good news of his spiritual condition 2-4

B. Commendation of Gaius for his hospitality to travelling brothers apparently sent by the elder 5-8

C. Complaint about Diotrephes, who does not acknowledge the elder's authority and refuses to let the church welcome and support brothers sent by him 9-10

D. Exhortation to imitate good, not evil. This is followed by a commendation of Demetrius 11-12

III. Letter closing: the desire is expressed to visit the addressees rather than to communicate by letter. There is a wish of peace followed by greetings and a request to pass them on 13-15

Survey of contents

First John calls upon its addressees to find assurance and encouragement from the basic truths of the gospel they had heard from the beginning (1 John 1:1; 2:7, 24; 2 John 5-6). The message about God is that he is "light" (1 John 1:5) and "love" (4:8, 16). God's love is manifested in the sending of his Son to be an expiation for our sins (4:9-10). There are many more references to God than to either Christ or the Holy Spirit. In fact, it has the third highest ratio of references to God in the New Testament after Romans and 1 Peter.[9] This is not a proof, but simply a symptom of the fact that the message of 1 John is God-centered. It is primarily about the addressees' relationship to God. The message about Christ is that belief *in* him (3:23; 5:10) as well as belief *about* him (4:15; 5:1) are what secure that relationship: "No one who denies the Son has the Father; everyone who confesses the Son has the Father also" (2:23). He came in the flesh in order to become the savior of human kind by the expiation of sins (1:1; 2:1-2; 4:2, 10, 14). The message about the Spirit is that it anoints its recipients with knowledge of the truth (2:20, 27). Its presence is evidence that God dwells in the believer (3:24). In particular, it stands as witness to the reality of Christ's incarnation (4:2; 5:6-8). The Spirit is never referred to as the "Holy Spirit," but simply as "the Spirit" (3:24; 5:7) or "the Spirit of God" (4:2, 13) or the "Holy One" (2:20). Finally, the message to the addressees is that they are called to have fellowship with God, Christ and one another (1:3). Important elements pertaining to that fellowship are acceptance of the forgiveness of sins (1:9-2:2) and keeping God's commandments (2:3). His commandment is twofold: "believe in the name of his Son Jesus Christ and love one another" (3:23). Such love is to be tangible, mutual love in the community of faith (1:6, 9-11; 3:11-18). It removes fear and gives confidence on the day of judgment (3:19-22; 4:17-18). Believers may commit sins and be forgiven (2:1), but they cannot lead a life that is centrally controlled by sin (3:4-9). In fact, there is "sin unto death," i.e. sin that *tends* to death. This may be either hate for other believers (3:14b-15) or rejection of Christ (5:12).[10] However, when mutual love is at the center, then one has already "passed from death to life" (3:14a).

Second John simply reiterates the two central ideas of 1 John regarding mutual love (5-6) and belief in the incarnate Christ (7-9). It also warns against fellowship with those who do not hold to this teaching. Third John is about the positive relations of Gaius and the negative relations of Diotrephes to the author. The focus is on authority without spelling out the basis of that authority. If all three writings arise out of a common situation, the elder's authority may be seen as based on either direct or mediated apostolic witness.

RELEVANCE FOR TODAY

The simplicity of 1 John at a first reading is somewhat beguiling. On further reflection, one finds it to be a simplicity that arises from a profundity that is timeless. The author guides the readers from their anxiety to assurance, from fear to love. He does not amass intricate arguments with elaborate proofs. With an unfolding tapestry of simple, recurring topics and themes he leads them back to the basic essentials of the gospel. He shows that when either faith or action deviates from the revelation of God's love in the atonement of Jesus Christ, genuine Christianity is in jeopardy. Belief in the incarnation, namely that Jesus Christ *became* human rather than merely *appeared to be* human, makes a vital difference. By taking on flesh, living, dying and rising again, Jesus Christ provides the primary, tangible evidence of God's love. If he had only taken on a human appearance, the revelation he brought would have been exclusively a revelation of word without any supporting evidence in flesh and blood reality. When the concept of incarnation is understood as the revelation of God's love *both in word and in action*, it captures the essence of the Christian faith. In this way, there is a very real connection between belief that Jesus Christ came in the flesh (4:2) and love for one another both in word and in deed (3:18).

The enduring wisdom of 1 John manifests itself in the testing of new theological formulations by the basic essentials of the gospel. This abbreviation to such basics as faith in Jesus Christ and mutual love is a reminder that not all doctrinal truths are of equal standing. Also, the author's avoidance of legislating how mutual love is to be carried out, other than being tangible, is noteworthy. This allows for cultural and situational sensitivity and flexibility. Above all, the continuing relevance of 1 John manifests itself in the discernment of gospel truth as embracing the whole person in relation to community and God. Belief that has no connection with loving action has no connection with life. Loving action without belief has no direction in life. When Christian belief and action connect, there is both human and divine fellowship, "that our joy may be complete" (1 John 1:4).

ISSUES FOR DISCUSSION AND REFLECTION

1. Compare 1 John 1:8-2:2 with 3:6-9 and 5:18. Is it possible to reconcile what appear to be contradictory statements about the Christian and sin? Compare the NRSV and the NIV on these passages and read the study by Sakae Kubo noted in the bibliography below.

2. In the light of the messages of 1 John as a whole, attempt to explain what the author possibly meant when he refers to "mortal sin" in 5:16-17. A literal translation of the Greek is "sin unto death."

3. Use a concordance to find all the passages in 1 John that refer to "commandment(s)." Study the contexts and explain the different meanings the author gives to this word.

4. Analyze the passage 1 John 2:12-14. What patterns of repetition do you find? Is there any theological significance to the parallels? What was the author trying to communicate to his audience?

5. Use a concordance to find all the passages in 1 John that refer to "life." What does this author mean by "life" and when does the believer have "eternal life"?

6. Use a concordance to find all the passages in 1 John that refer to "confidence." According to 1 John, what do you find to be the ultimate basis of Christian confidence?

7. What concept of "antichrist" do we find in 1 John 2:18; 4:3 and 2 John 7?

8. Study 1 John 2:22-24; 4:2-3; 5:6-8 and 2 John 7. What sort of christological debate seems to have been going on? Check the commentaries and other literature for alternatives to the one proposed in this introduction.

FURTHER READING

Brooke, Alan E.
  1912 *A Critical and Exegetical Commentary on the Johannine Epistles.* (International). Edinburgh: T & T Clark.
Brown, Raymond E.
  1982 *The Epistles of John.* (Anchor). Vol. 30. Garden City, NY: Doubleday.
Bultmann, Rudolph
  1973 *The Johannine Epistles.* (Hermeneia). English translation from the second German ed., 1967. Philadelphia: Fortress.
Carson, D.A., Douglas J. Moo, and Leon Morris
  1992 *An Introduction to the New Testament.* Grand Rapids, MI: Zondervan, 445-458.
Funk, Robert W.
  1967 "The Form and Structure of II and III John," *Journal of Biblical Literature* 86, 424-30.
Grayston, Kenneth
  1984 *The Johannine Epistles.* (New Century). Grand Rapids, MI: Eerdmans.
Houlden, James L.
  1973 *A Commentary on the Johannine Epistles.* London: Adam & Charles Black.

Kubo, Sakae
 1969 "I John 3:9: Absolute or Habitual?" *Andrews University Seminary Studies* 7, 47-56.
Lieu, Judith
 1991 *The Theology of the Johannine Epistles.* Cambridge: Cambridge University Press.
Malatesta, Edward
 1973 *The Epistles of St. John: Greek Text and English Translation Schematically Arranged.* Rome: E. Vicariatu Urbis.
Westcott, Brooke F.
 1966 *The Epistles of John.* (New ed. with forward by F.F. Bruce, orig. ed. 1883.) Appleford Abingdon Berkshire: Marcham Manor.

ENDNOTES

1. See A.E. Brooke, *The Johannine Epistles*, (ICC; Edinburgh: T & T Clark, 1912) i-xix.
2. See A.E. Brooke, *Johannine Epistles*, lxxiii-lxxv.
3. E.g., see R. Bultmann, *The Johannine Epistles*, (Hermeneia; Philadelphia: Fortress, 1973; second German ed. 1967) 17ff. Bultmann's development of this view is scattered in several articles before and after his commentary. For a good overview see R.E. Brown, *The Epistles of John*, (The Anchor Bible, Vol. 30; Garden City, NY: Doubleday, 1982) 38-41.
4. For a couple of examples of this type of approach see Brown, *The Epistles of John*, 69-115, and K. Grayston, *The Johannine Epistles*, (NCBC; Grand Rapids, MI: Eerdmans, 1984) 9-14.
5. See, e.g., J. Lieu, *The Theology of the Johannine Epistles* (Cambridge: Cambridge University Press, 1991) 8-16, 75-77.
6. See R.W. Funk, "The Form and Structure of II and III John," *Journal of Biblical Literature* 86 (1967), 424-30.
7. See R.A. de Beaugrande and W.U. Dressler, *Introduction to Text Linguistics* (London and New York: Longman, 1981) 48-112.
8. The commentary that stands closest to this procedure with somewhat similar results is that of J.L. Houlden, *A Commentary on the Johannine Epistles* (London: Adam & Charles Black, 1973) 22-24. Another author that works with word recurrences, particularly in terms of concentric patterns, etc., is E. Malatesta, S.J., *The Epistles of St. John: Greek Text and English Translation Schematically Arranged* (Rome: E. Vicariatu Urbis, 1973). However, he still forces an overarching, three-part division on the material. The focus in 1:5-2:28 is supposed to be "God is Light," but the "light" motif is quite absent in 2:12-28. The focus in 2:29-4:6 is supposed to be "God is Just." However, apart from 2:29 where this is stated, the rest of the section does not develop this topic, but focuses on "being born of God," "doing righteousness," "loving one another" and discerning "false prophets." Also, the only other significant reference to God being just is in 1:9. Finally, the focus in 4:7-5:13 is supposed to be "God is Love," but that focus only fits 4:7-21.

9. See D.A. Carson, D.J. Moo, and L. Morris, *An Introduction to the New Testament* (Grand Rapids, MI: Zondervan, 1992) 428.

10. See B.F. Westcott, *The Epistles of John* (New ed. with forward by F.F. Bruce; Appleford Abingdon Berkshire: Marcham Manor, 1966; orig. ed. 1883), 209-214. Although old, this commentary is a classic and still useful.

Chapter 26

Revelation

Ernest J. Bursey

"Worthy is the Lamb that was slaughtered to receive power and wealth
and wisdom and might and honor and glory and blessing!"

BRIEF OVERVIEW OF THE BOOK   *title: apocalypse self-identification: prophecy*

Revelation is the only book in the New Testament to be identified as a "prophecy" (1:3). It is largely a description of visions seen by its author, John. The battle of Armageddon, the number 666, a great red dragon, the seven last plagues, and a new Jerusalem 1500 miles across are just a few of the parade of strange words and pictures we meet in this book that still fascinates its readers.

BACKGROUND CONCERNS

The author speaks of himself as John, the slave of Jesus Christ (1:1 RSV); *John calls himself* as a prophet (22:9); and as one who had been persecuted with his readers (1:9). Though this John never calls himself an apostle, early Christian tradition identified him as the apostle John and the author of the Gospel of John. He apparently writes from the island of Patmos in the Aegean Sea, 37 miles from the mainland of Turkey. While on Patmos John had received the visions that make up the bulk of the book of Revelation (1:9).

According to early Christian tradition,[1] John was banished to Patmos during the final years of the emperor Domitian (81-96 C.E.) as punishment for his witness. Most scholars agree that Revelation was written during Domitian's reign,[2] though some place the book earlier either during the reign of Nero (54-68 C.E.) or Vespasian (69-79 C.E.). According to the Roman historian Suetonius, Domitian insisted on being treated as a god while he was still alive.[3] According to Dio, another Roman historian, Domitian initiated persecution against Jews and possibly Christians who were members of the imperial family.[4]

The book of Revelation was written to churches located in seven major cities in what was in John's time the province of Asia Minor. A look at the map shows that these cities—Ephesus, Smyrna, Pergamos, Thyatira, Sardis, Philadelphia, and Laodicea—lay along a circular highway in the western half of the province. The letters in chs 2-3 that are addressed to the churches are arranged in the precise order a traveler on the road would pass through the seven cities, starting with Ephesus on the coast and ending with Laodicea in the Lycus valley. Presumably John arranged for the book of Revelation to be smuggled over to the mainland and then read to each of the churches.

7 churches on a highway

death of Antipas

Christ Among the Lampstands

By examining the letters to the seven churches, we discover John wrote to remind the readers of certain dangers to their faith. The death of Antipas, a Christian in Pergamus (2:13), was just the beginning. The readers could expect even more persecution for their faith in Christ (2:10). There were conflicts with Jewish neighbors (2:9; 3:9). Failure to take part in the rituals of the cult of the emperor, including the worship of the reigning emperor's statue, could result in death at the command of Roman authorities, according to the letters of the Roman governor, Pliny.

But the most serious dangers came from the inside. The church members in Laodicea foolishly relied on their share of the economic prosperity of their city (3:17) when they were spiritually poor. The letters to members in Ephesus and Sardis warn against serious backsliding.

Certain church leaders blurred the lines between Christian faith and the dominant culture. They were willing to accommodate to the demands to take part in the pagan rituals. For this compromise they are vilified in Revelation as "Balaam" and "Jezebel" to show how dangerous they were (2:14; 20). In earlier times Balaam and Jezebel had led the Jews into immorality and idolatry away

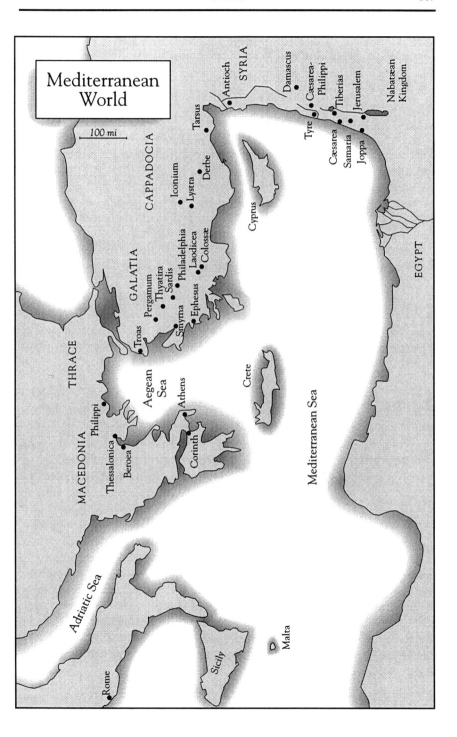

Mediterranean
World

100 mi

CAPPADOCIA

SYRIA

Antioch

Damascus

Tarsus

Caesarea-
Philippi

Tiberias

Jerusalem

Nabataean
Kingdom

Tyre

Caesarea

Samaria

Joppa

Iconium

Lystra

Derbe

Cyprus

GALATIA

Pergamum

Thyatira

Sardis

Philadelphia

Laodicea

Colossæ

Smyrna

Ephesus

Troas

THRACE

Aegean
Sea

Athens

Crete

EGYPT

MACEDONIA

Philippi

Thessalonica

Beroea

Corinth

Mediterranean Sea

Adriatic Sea

Malta

Sicily

Rome

from the worship of God with devastating results. John insists the only safe course lies in a strict obedience to the commandments of God and an unflinching allegiance to Jesus Christ as their "Lord" instead of the "Lord" emperor.

Part of the power of Revelation comes from the creative—even surprising— way John mines from the quarry of the Old Testament, the Bible of early Christians. In Revelation there are hundreds of direct parallels and obvious references to the Old Testament. But the Old Testament is never quoted in the book beyond a word or two! Instead the familiar Old Testament is paraphrased and woven into the fabric of a new prophecy.

Many of the symbols and much of the overarching structures of the book come from the Old Testament. The monsters of Rev 13 remind us of the four animals of Dan 7. A long list of parallels can be drawn between Revelation and the book of Ezekiel, including the eating of a book (Ezek 3; Rev 10:8-11) and the measuring of the temple (Ezek 40-43; Rev 11:1-3). But nearly always Revelation reshapes or blends and even transforms what is borrowed from the Old Testament.

From the way John describes the dragon and the lady in labor in ch 12, it is obvious he wants to remind us of several stories at once: Not only how Herod tried to kill baby Jesus but also the story the of serpent and Eve and the promise regarding her offspring in Gen 3. We must also keep in mind the story of God providing for Elijah in the wilderness away from Ahab and Jezebel.

The sea monster of Rev 13 is a collage of body parts from the four animals of Dan 7. And unlike Ezekiel, the prophet in Revelation finds the sweet book in his mouth bitter in his stomach. The temple turns up missing from the new Jerusalem—we are even reminded that it is gone (21:22).

While the author of Revelation speaks of his book as "prophecy," the book is similar to a number of widely circulated Jewish books, now classified as apocalyptic writings. Most of these apocalyptic books were written before the book of Revelation. The word, "apocalyptic," is taken from the Greek words in the opening phrase of the book. "The revelation (*apokalypsis*) of Jesus Christ" (1:1). With the exception of Daniel and Revelation, these apocalyptic books are not part of the Bible. But like the book of Revelation (4:1, 2), they typically portray the writer ascending to heaven or traveling to some vantage point in order to see the impending cosmic disasters.[5] The keen interest in symbolic numbers like 144,000 and 666 (7:4-8; 13:18) is characteristic of a number of other apocalyptic books.[6] The descriptions of many-headed monsters in 12:3; 13:1, etc., so strange to us, would have been less surprising to Christians who knew about the monstrosities in *1 Enoch*, *4 Esdras* and other Jewish books. All this indicates that Revelation draws upon a pool of symbols and conventions widely known to Jews and Jewish Christians of the time.

[margin note: Revelation differs from other apoc.]

Yet the book of Revelation clearly stands apart from these Jewish apocalyptic writings by its fresh use of the familiar. For instance, in *4 Ezra* 12:31-34 we are introduced to the Messiah as the Lion whom God holds in reserve until the end when he will be released to punish the wicked. But in Rev 5:5 John is told the Lion has already conquered. To compound surprises, when John looks he doesn't see a lion but a lamb! And even though this Lamb carries the marks of its slaughter, John sees it alive standing on its feet!

[margin note: salvation for all, not just Jews]

In both the Old Testament and the Jewish books written afterwards the emphasis lies on the restoration of Judaism and its fortunes. But in Revelation, the horizons of salvation reach to every nation and people. After hearing the roll call of the 144,000 from the twelve tribes, John looks and sees a great horde beyond all possibility of counting drawn from "every nation, from all tribes and peoples and languages" standing before the throne of God (7:4-9).

The fundamental cause for these and other differences is not John's creative imagination but the death and resurrection of Jesus Christ. Along with the rest of the New Testament, Revelation sees these past events as profoundly decisive in determining the outcome of all the rest of history. The future victory over evil has been secured by the past victory of Jesus' death.

LITERARY CONSIDERATIONS

[margin note: similar titles to John]

As part of the New Testament writings linked with the apostle John, Revelation stands with the gospel of John and the three letters, 1, 2 and 3 John. Similarities to the gospel of John include the titles given to Jesus as "the Lamb" (John 1:29; Rev 5:6) and the "Word of God" (John 1:1-14; Rev 19:13). Both books use water, light, life as symbols pointing to Jesus' offer of salvation. Both put their readers in open conflict with the Jews and both describe Jesus and His followers as bearing faithful witness to the truth.

[margin note: hard to classify]

As a unique mixture of literary genres, the book defies easy classification. The book is presented as a "revelation" (1:1) and as a "prophecy" (1:3). Yet the book incorporates the features of an early Christian letter, including the addresser and addressees (1:4), the invoking of grace and peace at the beginning (1:4-5) and the benediction at the end (22:21). Each of these letters directed to the angels of the seven churches follows the same stylized pattern that ends with a promise of reward to the overcomer and an appeal to hear "what the Spirit says to the churches."

[margin note: intended to be heard]

A blessing is bestowed on the one who reads aloud and those who listen to the book (Rev 1:3). Most of the book's intended readers were expected to experience the book through hearing someone else read it out loud. At the end of each of the seven letters we meet the same appeal, "He who has an ear, let him hear." The book was written as a dramatic whole to be heard at one sitting. The brief glimpses of the rewards promised the conquerors in chs 2 and 3 must still be in our memories when we meet their full description at the end of the book.

At the time of the writing of Revelation Christians were not permitted to build or dedicate places of worship in the Roman empire. So the members of the seven churches would have heard Revelation read to them in the private homes in which they regularly assembled to worship. A message from the exiled prophet would provide an out-of-the-ordinary worship service in these house churches.

full of worship language The book itself is filled with the language and experience of worship usually directed towards the Lord God Almighty and Jesus Christ. This is not surprising since a major issue in Revelation is over who ought to be worshiped.

hymns Hymns are spaced throughout the book, often at the beginning and end of visions (e.g. 4:8-11; 5:9-14; 7:9-12; 11:15-19; 15:3-4; etc). Modern readers are tempted to hurry past these hymns in order to delve into the fascinating and complicated symbols of the book. This is a mistake. The hymns lay bare for us the essential issues and truths which the symbols illustrate. They provide windows and doors for us to enter the book. While poetic, they are more than poems. They are the words believers used when they worshiped God and Christ.

why symbols? Why does Revelation rely so much on symbols? What is gained by communicating this way? What would be lost if we reduced Revelation to a series of statements or principles? It has been suggested that much of Revelation is coded to protect the author or readers if the book fell into the hands of authorities. The obscure details of some of the symbols have worked to the advan-

Angel on Land & Sea

tage of interpreters who try to show the prophecies were fulfilled centuries afterwards.

But the lasting impact of the vivid symbolism reminds us that Revelation is *creates* not merely to be interpreted. It creates in our mind's eye another world strong *another* enough to push back this world at the edge of our senses. The choice of *world* symbols helps us to feel deeply and to respond with more than nodding agreement to the vital issues. The nice mask of evil is ripped away. Instead we see a woman drinking the blood of those she has murdered (17:6) and hideous monsters grasping for adoration from craven humans (13:1-4, 12).

On the outer edges of the book are two key visions: First, John is *outer edge:* commissioned to write what he will see (1:10-20) by Christ who is holding the *vision* angels of the seven churches in his hand (1:10-20); and second, the description *of X +* of the luminous new Jerusalem in which God and the Lamb dwell with humans *new Jerusalem* forever (21-22).

Two visions serve as anchors within the body of the book. The throne room *anchor:* vision of chs 4-5 provides the basic theme and setting for the visions of chs 6- *vision* 11. Then in ch 12 we meet the Devil in the guise of a dragon bent on *throne* destroying the Manchild, his mother and the rest of her children. All the while *room (4-5)* the dragon is doomed himself to die. Chapters 13-20 plot out the emergence of *dragon (12)* the dragon's allies, their rough grasping for power and their downfall.

For first century readers certain numbers carried special meaning. *numbers* Revelation has plucked several out of sacred history: the completion of creation in seven days, the roots of Israel in the 12 sons of Jacob, and the three and a half years of drought when the evil king Ahab was in power while Elijah hid in the wilderness (Luke 4:25; Jas 5:17; see also Dan 7:19-25 for the horn that persecutes for three and a half years).

Throughout Revelation we meet these and other numbers.[7] There are the *7 :* seven churches, the seven seals, the seven trumpets, etc. that convey the sense *complete-* of completeness and universality. In the mention of the 12 tribes (ch 7) *ness* Revelation has preserved the Jewish traditions connected with the number 12. The two dead witnesses come to life after three and a half days (11:11). The woman is fed in the wilderness for three and a half times. (12:14).

Yet again, we see the fresh approach of Revelation even to numbers. Just before the series of seals and trumpets are completed, between the sixth and seventh items in each case, we are treated with a long unannounced interruption (7; 10-11:13). Numbers are multiplied and manipulated. The role call of the 12 tribes turns up exactly 12 times 1,000 from each tribes to make up a grand and precise total of 144,000. The symbolic weight of 12 is multiplied in the walls of the new Jerusalem, 144 cubits high, with the names of the New Testament apostles on its 12 foundations and the names of the Old Testament tribes of Israel on its 12 gates (21:12-21).

THE MESSAGE
Outline

The content of Revelation may be outlined as follows:

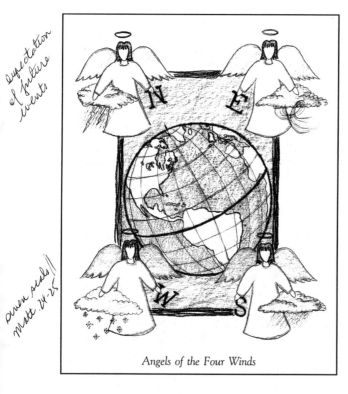

Angels of the Four Winds

Survey of contents

The book of Revelation presents itself as a report of "things which must shortly take place" (1:1; see also 1:19; 4:1). It may seem to be very different from the other books of the New Testament. But this is not true. Instead it builds on the expectations of future events we can find elsewhere in the New Testament.

The seven seals present the same outline of events as we find in Jesus' list of the signs of the end found in Matt 24-25 (parallels in Mark 13 and Luke 21). In a symbolic format Rev 6 shows the proclamation of the gospel, the effects of wars, famine, disease and death, the persecution of believers, the physical signs of the end in the heavens and on the earth, and the appearance of the Son of Man.

The descriptions of the rise and fall of the Satanic trinity are an expanded version of the teachings about the lawless one and the man of sin found in 2 Thess 2. The only place in the Bible that speaks of the 1000 years when Satan is bound is Rev 20. But even here the ties with the rest of the New Testament can be seen. Revelation 20:1-4 provides the setting for the future judgment of the world by the saints mentioned by Paul in 1 Cor 6:2-3. But Revelation is far more than a schedule of what is to happen or even an expansion of the teachings of the New Testament on the events of the last days. *heavenly*

By taking us back and forth between heaven and earth John shows us how *earthly* close is the connection between what happens in heaven and what happens on *events* earth, and especially between God and his people.[8] The prayers of the saints *are* bring results (6:9-11; 8:3-5). Soon God will act to bring justice against the *linked* arrogant powers.

The book repeatedly affirms that God is in charge, regardless of appearances *God in* and regardless of what the powers of this world may claim. The disasters of the *charge* seals, trumpets and plagues are unleashed on cue from God's throne room. The devil's entrance in the book is delayed until ch 12 where he appears as an angry dragon already defeated in heaven. As a prophecy from God, the book itself is evidence that he knows the future and is in charge of directing the outcome of this world's affairs.

Three Angels

Revelation lifts us up to a holy God who is to be praised because He will rid the world of evil (19:1-6) and create a new earth without defect, decay or devil. In the meantime we face the specter of a hodgepodge sea monster and a land monster acting as the devil's fronts in his desperate counter-attack at God and the Lamb (ch 13). In spite of the monstrous threats of the dragon and his cohorts, the outcome should never be in question. Much of the last half of the book details the future defeat on earth of this ludicrous threesome who clamor to be worshiped, along with the harlot Babylon.

A dominant issue in the book is over who is worthy to be worshiped. Clearly the devil and the beasts do not qualify. Does anyone else? Near the end of the book John is tempted two times to worship his angel guide. Each time he is warned to stop and instead to "worship God" (19:10; 22:8, 9). Exalted as they are, even angels dare not accept the worship of humans.

In Revelation the issues stand out in the starkest terms. The lines are sharply drawn between those who obey the commands of God and those who succumb to the beasts and the harlot Babylon. The book creates a vivid sense of the evil character of the institutions and powers that threaten to bully and seduce the unwary Christian. Warnings against cowards and those who do not tell the truth are emphasized (21:8; 21:27; 22:15). All this suggests that those first Christians for whom John wrote were losing their sense of the importance of Christian worship and lifestyle. They were questioning if openly witnessing for their faith was the wise approach. Against this backdrop of confusing grays John paints a picture in black and white.

Revelation goes beyond reminding us of God's ultimate victory. Revelation is a call to arms, not to swords and spears, but to open and irrepressible witness. It urges us to join God and the Lamb in the victory march. The book demands toughness and stamina in the present combat. Rewards are offered only to those who fight and overcome the dragon even to the point of death (2:7; 2:11; 2:17; etc.). And in this book, death at the hands of the dragon means his defeat (12:10-12)! Only one who knew that Jesus held the keys to the grave (1:18) could write this way.

Though Revelation places great emphasis on the deeds of the faithful, still salvation comes through Christ. They overcome the devil through the blood of the Lamb (12:11). The robes of the great multitude have been washed and made "white in the blood of the Lamb" (7:14).

The importance of Jesus in the book cannot be doubted. After all, it is "The revelation of Jesus Christ" (1:1). John must mean either that the book is from Jesus or that it is about Jesus. Possibly he has both in mind.

The scene in ch 5 where Jesus takes the sealed scroll probably means that Jesus has secured salvation and enabled his followers to receive their eternal inheritance, written as a will on the scroll.[9] As the Lamb Jesus will continue to shepherd the redeemed before the throne of God (7:17). Like a bodyguard, the 144,000 follow him wherever he goes (14:4)

Jesus also inspires terror as the One who carries out judgment. The kings *judge* of the earth cry out for the rocks to hide them from the "wrath of the Lamb" (6:16). Those who worship the beast are warned of their future torment in the presence of the angels and the Lamb (14:9-11). The armies of heaven are led by "Faithful and True" (19:11), "The Word of God" (19:13), who Himself treads the wine press of God's wrath (19:15; 14:19, 20).

Along with God, who sits on the throne, Christ is praised and even ^ *praised* worshiped in Revelation (5:12-14; 7:9-10). The basic difference between early + *worshiped* Christians and their neighbors, Jewish and pagan, lay over the respect Christians gave Jesus Christ. If he was merely a human being, then Christians were guilty of idolatry. And if Christ was to be praised, why not include the gods and goddesses of the Greeks and Romans? Why Jesus and only Jesus? Could Christians worship Christ without compromising their belief and worship of the one God? A careful reading of the book of Revelation helps us to see some ways these challenges could be met.

In Rev 4 God on his throne is worshiped by 24 crowned elders and four living creatures in heaven because he is the Creator of everything. In Rev 14:7 the angel urges the whole world to worship God for the same reason and because the hour of his judgment is come. But even in ch 4 we can sense the difference between the praise God deserves from his creation and the praise he has received. It is the Lamb that changes all that. The achievement of the Lamb is his death that redeems *"for God"* persons from every corner of the earth to be "a kingdom and priests *to our God"* (5:9, 10). The number of the saved is beyond counting (7:9). Through Jesus, humanity is saved and lifted to reign with God, and through Jesus God is given a kingdom of priests who offer their praise. The Lamb brings together God and his people (21:3). When this double achievement is announced all heaven breaks out in praise (5:8-13). Now the millions of angels praise the Lamb. And at last every living being from the heights of heaven to the depths below the seas unite in one vast issue of praise to both the One Sitting on the Throne and to the Lamb!!!

Like most of the rest of the New Testament, Revelation doesn't come right *Jesus –* out and say, "Jesus is God." Instead, some of the titles that are given only to *Lord* God at the beginning of the book are transferred to Jesus before the end. The treatment of the title, "Lord" (in Greek: *kurios*) is particularly revealing. This title was employed by the Roman emperor Domitian and others as an expression of divinity. In Rev 1:8 John speaks of the "Lord God." Throughout the book the title, "Lord" is reserved for God until Jesus comes riding a white horse and leading the armies of heaven. On His thigh the words are written: "King of Kings and Lord of Lords" (19:16). Only at the very end of the book in a dramatic finale (22:20) does John join together for the first time the words, "Lord" and "Jesus" in the terse prayer, "Come, Lord Jesus."

In Revelation Jesus is given special recognition, even worship, because of what he has accomplished. No other person in the universe can match his past and future accomplishments as the One who secures the worship of the redeemed and as the executor of God's judgment.

VALUE/RELEVANCE FOR TODAY

Several basic ways of interpreting Revelation have developed over the centuries of study of the book.

A *preterist* approach to Revelation views the book as directed largely to known events of the first century. The first readers of the book would have tried to understand it through their own world. For instance, Lady Babylon who sits on seven hills would have been recognized as the city of Rome, capital of the Roman empire, while the horns and heads of the beast would be identified with specific Roman emperors and leaders. Frequently the preterist view is tied up with the conclusion that John was largely mistaken about the second coming. The limits of the preterist view arise in part from deciding that John was attempting to describe events and figures of his own time and then from observing that the particulars of first century history do not match the particulars of the visions.[10]

The *futurist* approach treats the book as largely prophetic of what still hasn't happened. *Dispensationalists* (or pretribulationists), popular among conservative Christians, read Rev 4:1 as a reference to a secret rapture of Christians, while the seals, trumpets and the rest of the prophecies of the book are placed in the future. In general, futurists have failed to give the symbolic and apocalyptic nature of the book enough weight in favor of an excessive literalism. By putting the bulk of the book into the future, futurists run the dangers of trivializing history and losing interest in the activity of God over nearly 2000 years of history.

The *historicist* approach, widely favored among Protestant interpreters in an earlier time, sees the visions of chs 6-13 as prophecies of major events in history, particularly in the Middle East and Europe. Some have also viewed the letters to the seven churches as providing a sketch of the history of the Christian church from the first century to the last.[11] Frequently the time periods in the book are seen as "prophetic," with a prophetic day equal to a literal year. Most historicists have concluded that the various visions in chs 2-12 cover the course of history several times, but from different perspectives.[12] In this way the visions of the seven seals and seven trumpets overlap chronologically, each ending with the second coming and the final judgments. Given the human tendency to interpret events differently, it is not surprising that historicists have been publishing their disagreements with each other for centuries. A strong basis for an historicist interpretation of Revelation lies in the remarkable correspondence between the events and signs of Matt 24 (and parallels) and the seven seals of Rev 6-8:1.[13] Clearly some of the items in Matt 24 have occurred in history and some have not. The same would be true of the seven seals.

A fourth approach to Revelation, the *idealistic* or *mythological*, allows for multiple fulfillment and application. Rather than identifying the beasts of Rev 13 and 14 with a particular entity, what is important is the character of the beast. On this reading the beasts show up on a fairly regular basis! The gain from looking at principles and issues is obvious. But the losses from cutting completely the ties with historical particularity will be too high a price to pay for believers in the first and second comings of Jesus Christ. To treat the specific prophecies as capable of almost endless fulfillment reduces them to vagaries.

There are elements of truth in each of the approaches. The book of Revelation spoke directly to the needs of first century Christians. It is hard to imagine that Christians in Asia minor could read in ch 13 of the demand to worship the "image to the beast" without thinking of the pressures they were experiencing to show allegiance to the statue of the emperor.[14] Certainly the end of the world has not yet happened as John, along with Paul and Jesus, described it.

The book was offered to first century Christians to help them. Yet, as is true of Old Testament prophecy,[15] the initial application did not necessarily exhaust or complete the potential within the visions. If one is willing to allow that God is involved in the prophetic experience, then the notion of future fulfillment beyond the prophet's understanding is reasonable. Particularly helpful would be the inspired interpretations of future prophets.

Probably no other book in the Bible has been the locus of so much speculation and not all of it harmless, either. The dangers from misusing Revelation have a long history. Revelation has been used as a tool for damning one's theological, political and even racial opponents. As Christian history approaches the end of the second millennium we can expect to see a growing interest in Revelation, too often at the service of sensationalists. The belief that things will get worse before they get better, common to Revelation and the New Testament, shouldn't provide a blanket endorsement for any novel interpretation. The greatest care ought to be taken to ground our interpretations in this book on a thorough knowledge of the whole book and of the basic issues, convictions and theology that it shares with the rest of the New Testament and even the Old Testament.

The conviction that God is in ultimate control and the powers of this world are passing away has made the book of Revelation a haven for the oppressed of all ages.[16] Revelation's sharp distinctions between church and world ought to keep us wary of the notion of a "Christian nation." The kingdom of God remains in conflict with the kingdoms of this world. Their symbols of success, the Lamb and the Harlot, cannot be meshed.

The King at Harvest Time

The demand to bear witness by deed and testimony remains in force. The Evil One does not lie still. Christians must not sleep, either. Remembering that time is short and growing shorter helps us sort through the decisions of our own lives. An absolute loyalty toward God can free us from the shallow pretensions of our age. Revelation 18 reminds us that the price of prosperity for some is too often the degradation of others.

When humans have it in their power to annihilate themselves and destroy the planet, hope in a sovereign God finds reception. In the reading of the book the voice of Jesus is still heard, "Surely I am coming soon" (22:20).

Amen. Come Lord Jesus.

ISSUES FOR DISCUSSION AND REFLECTION
1. To gain a sense of the book of Revelation as a whole, read it out loud at a single sitting. What basic convictions shine through?
2. You can easily locate the hymns in the book of Revelation if you use a translation that indents the poetry. Examine the contents of the hymns for yourself to discover the basic issues of the book.
3. Compare the strong statements about governing powers in Rev 14 and 18 with the advice of Paul in Rom 13 and with 1 Pet 2.

4. Does Revelation teach that God is responsible for evil? What are the risks in linking God with the disasters that occur in our world?
5. Compare the "wrath of God" in Revelation with Rom 1. Are they the same?
6. The sense of the soonness of Christ's coming appears throughout the book of Revelation. Was it true to say that Christ is coming soon? Can this sense of the soonness of the second coming be maintained today?

FURTHER READING
Selected Primary Sources (In addition to the Old Testament)
Pliny

> *Letters, 10.96-97.* Of fundamental importance in illustrating the attitudes of Roman representatives in Asia minor towards Christianity.

Anonymous

> *4 Ezra 11-13.* Helpful illustration of the strong parallels between Revelation and Jewish apocalyptic writings.

Suetonius

> "Domitian" 12-13, *The Twelve Caesars.* Provides evidence for Domitian's insistence on his divinity.

Selected Resources on the Book of Revelation
Aune, David E.

> 1983 "The Influence of Roman Imperial Court Ceremonial on the Apocalypse of John," *Biblical Research 38* (1983) 5-26.

Barr, David L.

> 1986 "The Apocalypse of John as Oral Enactment," *Interpretation.* Vol. 40, No. 3, 243-256.

Bauckham, Richard

> 1993 *The Theology of the Book of Revelation.* Cambridge: Cambridge University Press.

Caird, George B.

> 1976 *A Commentary on the Revelation of St. John the Divine.* New York: Harper & Row.

Collins, Adela Y.

> 1984 *Crisis & Catharsis.* Philadelphia: Westminster.

Froom, LeRoy E.

> 1954 *The Prophetic Faith of Our Fathers*, 4 vols. Washington, DC: Review & Herald.

Hemer, Colin J.

> 1986 *The Letters to the Seven Churches of Asia in Their Local Setting.* Sheffield: Journal for the Study of the Old Testament.

Ladd, George E.
  1972   *A Commentary on the Revelation of John.* Grand Rapids, MI:
          Eerdmans.
LaRondelle, Hans K.
  1987   *Chariots of Salvation.* Washington, DC: Review and Herald.
Maxwell, C. Mervyn
  1985   *God Cares*, Vol. 2. Boise: Pacific.
Muse, Robert L.
  1996   *The Book of Revelation: An Annotated Bibliography.* New York:
          Garland. [Over 1400 entries published between 1940-1990.]
Nichols, Francis D., Ed.
  1957   *The Seventh-day Adventist Bible Commentary*, Vol. 7, pp 715-899.
          Washington, DC: Review and Herald.
Paulien, Jon
  1987   *Decoding Revelation's Trumpets: Literary Allusions and
          Interpretation of Revelation 8:7-12.* Berrien Springs, MI: Andrews
          University Press.
Peterson, Eugene H.
  1988   *Reversed Thunder: The Revelation of John and the Praying
          Imagination.* San Francisco: Harper and Row.
Strand, Kenneth
  1979   *Interpreting the Book of Revelation.* Worthington, OH: Ann Arbor.
Walvoord, John F.
  1966   *The Revelation of Jesus Christ.* Chicago: Moody.

ENDNOTES

1. Victorinus, *Commentary on the Apocalypse*, ANF, vol. 7, p 353. Victorinus died a martyr in 304 C.E.

2. In his work, *Against Heresies* 5.30.3, Irenaeus (ca. 130-ca.202 C.E.) stated Revelation was written in the time of Domitian.

3. Suetonius, "Domitian," 12-13, *The Twelve Caesars.*

4. Dio, *Roman History* 67.14.1-3.

5. For example *1 Enoch* 14 and *2 Enoch* 1.

6. For instance, *Jubilees* recounts Israel's history from jubilee to jubilee. The space between jubilees was 49 years (7 squared).

7. For a helpful summary of the use and meaning of symbolic numbers in Revelation, see Henry B. Swete, *The Apocalypse of St. John* (1908) pp cxxxv-cxxxviii.

8. For a similar conclusion see Ellen G. White, *Testimonies to Ministers and Gospel Workers* (Mountain View, CA: Pacific, 1923) p 114.

9. Kenneth Strand, *Interpreting the Book of Revelation* (Ann Arbor: Worthington, OH, 1976) p 55. In personal conversation Professor Strand has pointed to Jer 32:1-25 and suggested the scroll of Rev 5 can be seen as a title deed to the new earth.

10. For a discussion of the difficulties facing a preterist interpretations of Rev 17 and the solutions proposed, see J. Massyngberde Ford, *Revelation*, The Anchor Bible (New York: Doubleday, 1975) pp 289-291.

11. An historicist reading of the letters to the seven churches faces a serious challenge—each of the differing letters was written to the needs of a specific group of Christians in John's day. The apparent basis for the sequence of the letters is geographical not chronological.

12. For this reason, some interpreters prefer the term, "recapitulationist." The classic Adventist work, *Thoughts on Daniel and the Revelation*, by Uriah Smith (rev. ed. Nashville, Tenn: Southern, 1944), as well as *God Cares*, Vol. 2 by C. Mervyn Maxwell (listed in the bibliography) fit in this category.

13. Maxwell provides a convenient table in *God Cares*, Vol. 2, p 181.

14. Here Pliny's correspondence with the emperor Trajan over the trial of Christians (*Letters*, 10.96-97), ca. 110 C.E., is invaluable. Pliny insists that Christians worship the emperors statue along with images of the other gods.

15. First Pet 1:10-12 and Matt 13:17 speak of the limits of the Old Testament prophets in understanding what they have seen or written.

16. For a recent "colored" South African reading of Revelation, see Allan A. Boesak, *Comfort and Protest* (Philadelphia: Westminster, 1987).

Chapter 27

Hebrews
Sakae Kubo

"Since, then, we have a great high priest who has passed through the heavens, Jesus, the Son of God, let us hold fast to our confession. For we do not have a high priest who is unable to sympathize with our weaknesses, but we have on who in every respect has been tested as we are, yet without sin. Let us therefore approach the throne of grace with boldness, so that we may receive mercy and find grace to help in time of need."

BRIEF OVERVIEW OF THE BOOK

This anonymous letter of the New Testament is usually grouped with Paul's letters, although Paul is not named as the author. However, because early tradition connects it with Paul, because of the mention of Timothy (13:23), who definitely was connected with Paul, and because of other similarities in the letter, it came to be connected with Paul's letters.

Hebrews does not begin like a letter. If we compare it with one of Paul's letters, say 1 Corinthians, we see immediately that the writer's name and title are not mentioned, nor is the destination or name of the church to which the letter is addressed, and the salutation and greetings are not present. However, Hebrews does close more or less in a way that reminds us of Paul's letters. It is obviously directed to a group of people who have a common background and experience. But because specific names are not mentioned, this book raises many questions, regarding not only authorship and place of writing, but destination, the people addressed, and the date of the letter.

BACKGROUND CONCERNS

The early tradition (Pantaenus, 180 C.E.; Clement of Alexandria, 200 C.E.; Origen, 225 C.E.) connected Hebrews with Paul, but not without some reservations. They could not say straight out that Paul actually wrote it the way we have it. One writer said he wrote it in Hebrew, and Luke translated it into

Greek; another said that the thought was his, but "the diction and phraseology" were someone else's. They saw that the Greek of Hebrews was quite unlike that of Paul. Others (Tertullian, Cyprian and Hippolytus) denied Pauline authorship, one ascribing it to Barnabas.

Doubts about Pauline authorship were raised during the Reformation period also. Luther considered Apollos the author. Calvin could not be convinced that Paul wrote it, but does not question its apostolic origin or canonical authority. Later, Hebrews was subjected to thorough scrutiny in regard to its vocabulary, style and theology, and these were compared with Paul's writings. There is a consensus that the writing could not have been Paul's direct work, although many feel that someone connected with Paul and who knew some of Paul's teachings was the actual writer.

The traditional view is that the letter is addressed to Jewish Christians in Palestine. Those who hold this view point to the fact that the Old Testament and the ceremonial system play such a dominant part in the lives of the recipients, and the fact that the book makes comparisons and contrasts between Moses and Christ, Melchizedek and Christ, the Levitical priesthood and Christ's high priesthood, and conclude that the book must be directed to former Jews.

The place where the Temple played a dominant part in the life of the people was Palestine. Some have sought to be more specific by referring to the recipients as converted Jewish priests or Christian Essenes, some of whom would be ex-Qumranians.

Some see the recipients as the Jewish Christians in Rome because of Heb 13:24. Since the greetings are being sent by "those who come from Italy," it could very well be that the author is addressing those in Italy. Other arguments for this position include the fact that the earliest attestations of the letter come from Rome (*1 Clement* and *Shepherd of Hermas*) and that the allusions to the past history of the community have things in common with Rome. Other places have been suggested such as Cyprus and the Lycus Valley in Asia Minor. Some have even suggested that the recipients of this letter were Gentile Christians, but the argument for this position seems strained.

The dating of the letter focuses on the issue of whether it was written before or after the destruction of Jerusalem. The reason for this is that the letter puts so much emphasis on the priestly ministry and the sacrificial services. Would the author have put so much stress on these later if they, in fact, were no longer relevant because the Temple had been destroyed? Others say that the destruction of the Temple is irrelevant, since the author is focusing on the Levitical system in the Pentateuch, not on what is actually going on in their present situation and circumstances.

Some of these questions cannot be answered in a definitive way, but the working hypothesis in this section is that the author was not Paul, though acquainted with him, and that he was writing to Jewish Christians in Palestine before the destruction of the Temple.

LITERARY CONSIDERATIONS

As we have already mentioned, Hebrews does not begin like a letter, though it ends like one. It is different from Paul's letters also in the fact that it carries *homily* on a common theme throughout the letter. Some have described it as a homily rather than a letter, and some as a combination of both. Some have described it as a literary epistle directed to the general public in opposition to a letter which is nonliterary, more conversational and directed to an individual or a particular community. The author also uses literary devices which are lost in a translation.

An interesting literary feature is the juxtaposition of argument and *argument* application throughout the book.[1] The arguments are presented more theoretically, but are then followed by practical application and admonition. *application* Arguments appear in 1:1-14, 2:5-3:6a, 5:1-10, and 7:1-10:18. Applications appear in 2:1-4, 3:6b-4:13, 5:11-6:20, and 10:19-13:25.

THE MESSAGE
Outline

The content of Hebrews may be outlined as follows:

Survey of contents

The author is trying to bolster up the faith of those who are beginning to lose their new-found faith in Christ and fall back into their traditional patterns of belief. He, therefore, seeks to show how the "new and living way" is so much superior to the old. The old came in bits and pieces by various prophets; the new in a final and ultimate sense in Jesus Christ. Christ is so much superior to the angels through whom the former message came. He is superior to Moses and Joshua, their leaders; he will bring them the true rest which they did not obtain in entering Canaan. His priesthood fulfills perfectly the role of representing God to man and man to God because he was both. It is also an eternal priesthood like that of Melchizedek, rather than a succession of mortal priests, like those of the Aaronic priesthood. Above all, his sacrifice cannot be compared to those of the bulls and goats. It is once and for all; the others were continual, indicating that they did not remove sins, but only reminded one of their inefficacy. It purified the conscience; they only the flesh. With a better founder, better leader, better priest, and better sacrifice, how can they fall back into their former ways which really only feebly pointed forward to Jesus Christ. "Let us hold fast the confession of our hope without wavering ..." (Heb 10:23).

This emphasis on holding fast seems to suggest that the recipients of Hebrews were not only tempted to fall back into old patterns of thinking, but also to become apathetic. This is why the author admonishes them to be alert (2:1) and earnest (4:11; 6:11).

Finally, the emphasis of the book is on confidence and assurance in Christ. *(handwritten: confidence + assurance in X)* Because of Christ's superiority as high priest, Christians who put their confidence in him have nothing to fear. The entire central section of the letter, which focuses on the Old Testament temple services, begins and ends with this emphasis. In Heb 4:16 we read that because Christ was tempted in all points as we have been, he can sympathize with our weaknesses, and therefore we can have confidence to receive mercy and find grace to help us in our need. Hebrews 10:19 concludes the emphasis on the sanctuary serves by emphasizing that because Christ opened the way into the holy place for Christians they can have confidence. This focus on confidence and assurance in Christ is part of the central message of Hebrews.

RELEVANCE FOR TODAY

What Hebrews is trying to show is the centrality and cruciality of faith in Jesus Christ. While the arguments for showing this are definitely connected with the thinking of the people of that day, the point at issue is always relevant. Jesus Christ is the same yesterday, today and forever. Other issues may compete with loyalty to Jesus, but the truth of Jesus' supremacy remains true today as ever.

Hebrews also shows us that Jesus is not a priest who is aloof from us, but *(handwritten: Jesus has walked in our skin)* one who was tempted in all points and yet overcame. We have a priest who knows how to sympathize and help us overcome, because he has walked in our skin.

Christians continue to struggle with apathy and discouragement. Hebrews not only addresses these issues, but offers a theological basis for overcoming these temptations. The author obviously believed in a close connection between theology and Christian experience. Understanding of Christ's work can help us keep our confidence as Christians.

ISSUES FOR DISCUSSION AND REFLECTION

1. How can what appears alien to us (the ceremonial system, sacrifice, priesthood) have relevance to us today? To say that Christ is the fulfillment of these may have had meaning to the Jewish Christians back then, but what meaning would it have for us today?
2. If the author were writing to us, in what ways would he say that Jesus is superior to the things that men hold dear today? If Jesus is "the same, yesterday, today, and forever," his relevance must continue to this day.
3. How was Jesus tempted in all points like we are, when he was born at a certain time and place?
4. What does Hebrews teach about the sanctuary in heaven?
5. How would you characterize the use of Scripture in Hebrews and how you use Scripture today?

6. Does Hebrews teach that once you apostatize, there is no hope for you to return? (See 6:4-6.)
7. What does "perfect the conscience" (9:9) mean? And how is Christ made "perfect through suffering" (2:10)?
8. What is the difference between the old covenant and the new in Hebrews? Was there no forgiveness in the Old Testament if the blood of bulls and goats were not efficacious?

FURTHER READING
Bruce, Frederick F.
    1990   *The Epistle to the Hebrews, rev ed.* (New International). Grand Rapids, MI: Eerdmans.
Johnsson, William G.
    1994   *Hebrews: Full Assurance for Christians Today.* (Abundant Life Bible Amplifier). Boise: Pacific.
    1979   *In Absolute Confidence.* Washington, DC: Review and Herald.
Montefiore, Hugh
    1964   *A Commentary on the Epistle to the Hebrews.* (Harper). San Francisco: Harper and Row.

ENDNOTES
1. See William Johnsson, *Hebrews*, p 18-19.

Chapter 28

James
Pedrito U. Maynard-Reid

> *"Religion that is pure and undefiled before God, the Father, is this: to care for orphans and widows in their distress, and to keep oneself unstained by the world."*

BRIEF OVERVIEW OF THE BOOK

[margin note: most concentrated ethics]

James is the most concentrated ethical document in the New Testament which speaks directly to the practical, social issues of the first century society as well as today's—issues which transcend local concerns and can serve as guidelines even between the rich Developed World and the poor Two-Thirds World. And yet the concerns are personal and spiritual, speaking to the Christian in his or her daily piety.

BACKGROUND CONCERNS

The Epistle of James has never enjoyed pride of place among the New Testament documents. This is due to a number of factors. First, Protestants' view of the book has been influenced by Martin Luther, the sixteenth century Reformer, who dubbed it "the Epistle of Straw." Luther's preoccupation with the Pauline teaching of justification by faith in Jesus Christ led him to judge all other New Testament (as well as Old Testament) books against the criterion that those that demonstrate Christ are superior to those that don't. For Luther, even though James has many good sayings in it, it along with Hebrews, Jude, and Revelation, were relegated to the back of his German translation of the New Testament. *[margin note: our view influenced by Luther]*

The second and subsequent factors pre-date Luther and explain why the epistle had such a difficult time achieving canonical status. Of all the New Testament writings James seem to have a stronger Jewish orientation than a Christian one. Third, many early church Fathers questioned the apostolic authorship of the epistle—an important factor in the canonization process. And fourth, its strong language against the rich was offensive during the early centuries when overtures were being made to attract the wealthy to Christianity. *[margin note: a strong Jewish orientation]* *[margin note: strong language against rich offensive]*

291

The issues of the authorship, date and setting of James have hardly been challenged since the epistle achieved canonical status. The book states that James is the author. He has been identified as the brother of Jesus and leader of the early Jerusalem church. A date prior to 50 C.E., therefore, has been the traditional date of preference. Besides, the Jewishness of its tone and the absence of any controversy between Jew and Gentile as is found in Paul or Acts 15 at the time of the Jerusalem Council, all presuppose an early date. In recent times, note has also been taken of the economic, social, political, and religious upheavals of that decade, and parallels have been drawn with the concerns of the Epistle.

With the rise of more careful, critical, and in depth literary and historical studies of the New Testament since the eighteenth century, the above view has been challenged. The author is pseudonymous or anonymous, the date is late first century or early second century, and the setting is in the Greco-Roman world outside of Palestine—probably a Roman Christian community. The strongest evidence in favor of this position is the language of the epistle. The Greek of James is among the best Greek styles in the New Testament. An argument thus can be made that it is doubtful that a Galilean carpenter's son could write such eloquent Greek.

The argument of style seems to be an unassailable one. Yet the traditional positions, particularly the arguments regarding content and setting are equally strong. It is possible that a solution to the impasse would be to suggest that the document was originally written at a very early period—before there was a clear break between Judaism and Christianity, and the social issues of society were part and parcel of James' community. However, some decades later an editor improved the document (allowing it to speak clearly to a later Hellenistic world/culture in their lingua franca) without obscuring the message of the original author.

LITERARY CONSIDERATIONS

The document as we have it is not only excellent in its use of the Greek language, but in its freshness, variety, and vividness. The author has a penchant for creating new words. At least ten words are used for the first time in this small epistle. But even more outstanding is his style of address. Although it is structured like a letter, it reads more like a homily. (Possibly it was originally a sermon, and the later editor gave it an epistolary format in order to circulate it widely to the Christian churches). It also has a vivid prophetic style, particularly in the harshness of its language—reminiscent of the eighth century Hebrew Scriptures prophets: the rich, in quite brusque fashion are told to weep and wail for the miseries coming upon them (5:1); those engaging in disputes are called "adulterers" (4:4), etc. On the other hand, the document exudes a familial and pastoral tone: fifteen times the readers are addressed as brothers and sisters, or beloved brothers and sisters (just as Peter addressed the Jews [Acts 2:29], and Paul the Christians throughout his letters).

The epistle of James should take pride of place in the New Testament as one of the most, if not the most, concentrated prophetic, pastoral, relevant ethical document which spoke to the felt needs of early communities, Jewish and Christian; and continues to address the pressing needs of Christian and non-Christians in our contemporary society.

THE MESSAGE
Outline
The contents of James may be outlined as follows:

Survey of contents

Up until very recently careful students of James have accepted the view that the epistle of James is simply a loosely constructed group of sayings without any cohesion, thought or design. This view is being challenged. James has a central focus and is theologically united (even though, like in a sermon, tangential points crop up while a particular issue is being presented). The theme which seems to dominate is that of suffering.

That suffering is the focus of the epistle is seen in the fact that the letter begins with a treatment of this concern ("my brothers and sisters whenever you face *trials of any kind* ..." [1:2]), and ends with it ("Are any among you suffering? [5:13]), forming an inclusio in which the message is framed.

The main treatment of the subject is in 1:2-18. Here he makes three points: 1) trials should be endured with joy; 2) there will be a great reversal between the poor and the rich; 3) it is not God who brings on trials. In the first place James calls for unconditional joy in the face of trials of any kind, because such testing of one's faith produces endurance, which is an evidence of maturity (1:2-4). If one lacks this maturity it takes wisdom to obtain it. This only comes from God who gives to whoever asks (1:5-7).

In the second place the person who is lowly and poor (1:9) is the one who is meeting various trials; in contrast to the rich who has the best of this life. The suffering poor are given the assurance that there will be a great reversal when they will be raised up while the rich will be brought low and perish like vegetation under the effect of the scorching Middle Eastern desert wind (the sirocco).

The question now arises: Does God bring on trials? Here James addresses his third point, which also brings up the issue of the relation of trials to temptation (the same word in the Greek for both ideas). James follows the position of the late Hebrew Scriptures and later Judaism that it is not God who sends tests, trials and temptations. But suffering is a test of human's faith because of the evil internal desires (1:12-16). In this complex passage James offers a theodicy; seeking to explain the suffering and trials that his community is undergoing.

The most intense suffering and trials are borne by the poor. It is to this issue that James devotes more attention than any other in the epistle. He opposes whoever is not willing to be on the side of these marginal ones; whether it is those who profess to be "hearers of the word" but don't act (1:22-26); or those who claim to have "faith," but have no "works" (2:14-26). In both instances the "doing" and the "works" are care for the poor and needy. In the first instance he explains that a person who does not "do," that one's religion is worthless. Pure and undefiled religion is "care for orphans and widows in their distress" (1:27). In the second instance, "works" is taking care of a person who is naked and lacks daily food (2:15-16).

We totally misread James, when we like Martin Luther compare his use of the term "works" with Paul's use of the term in the latter's discussion of legalism in Romans, Galatians, and Ephesians. James is clearly here dealing with a social ethical issue, viz. social justice for the poor. Paul on the other hand is addressing a theological dispute with Jewish Christians who were arguing that one had to follow Jewish laws (e.g. circumcision) in order to be saved. The issues in James and Paul are different; each must be independently read in their context. One, however, cannot ignore the issue of faith and works in James when placed in the context of the entire New Testament. If this is done and comparisons are made with Paul's theological structure, it must be admitted that the works which James argues for would be performed after the initial act of Justification according to Paul's definition.

James is concerned that his audience is not identifying with the poor. On the contrary they are showing partiality to the rich. This attitude he addresses in 2:1-13. For him favoritism to the rich at the expense of the poor is clearly a sin equal to adultery and murder. And even if one keeps the entire law but shows partiality to the rich while ignoring the poor, that person has broken the entire law. James feels very strongly regarding this issue because of two reasons: first, because God has chosen the poor in a special way (2:5); and second, because of the actions of the rich. These wealthy individuals are the financiers, merchants, and landed proprietors of James' times (see 1:9-11; 2:2-7; 4:13-17; 5:1-6). These are condemned because they oppress the poor in their legal dealings with them, by their trading systems, and in labor disputes. For James their actions to the suffering poor makes them blasphemers (2:7), and judgment is all that they can hope for (1:11; 4:14).

James recognizes that for the one going through trial he or she needs the gift of wisdom to endure (1:5) and wisdom as well to do the works which are essential to the well-being of the poor (3:13). It is possible for this reason that he chooses the wisdom genre of literature to express himself. Throughout the document one finds numerous parallels to the wisdom literature of the Hebrew Scriptures and the intertestamental writings. An extended case in point is his discussion on the taming of the tongue, in which he uses numerous well chosen metaphors to portray the influence of the tongue (e.g. bridle and horse, ship and rudder—3:2-4). James, however, finds it necessary to make it clear that there is false wisdom and there is true wisdom. The false is earthly, unspiritual and demonic (3:15). The true is from above, is pure, peaceable, gentle, willing to yield, full of mercy and good fruits, and without partiality and hypocrisy (3:17).

The community of James was to a large degree not exhibiting true wisdom. This is evidenced in their conflicts, disputes, and wars. This violence was personal and social. It is a fact that a community under pressure tends to split into factions and bicker and fight. Possibly the stress of suffering triggered this type of behavior among the readers of the epistle. But the conflict in this historical context seems to have also political overtones. The nationalistic controversies between the Jewish Palestinians and Rome led the Zealot party to take up arms against their oppressors; much of this was in defense of the poor. The Zealots used banditry, coercion, kidnapping, and murder in their war against their oppressors. James opposed that. James, with just as much vigor opposed the powerful wealthy who controlled the government and economy and told them that they were violent murderers and God would oppose them (5:6).

In response to this violent suffering James calls for patience by the oppressed (5:7). For James violence should not be met with violence. One should leave retribution to God at his coming (5:7-9). James hoped that this would be a source of solace to his hearers who were facing all types of trials. But he would not stop at that, he drew from the experience of Job to exhort the sufferers. And he finally concludes by urging them to utilize the mode of prayer to alleviate suffering (5:13) whether in sickness or otherwise.

VALUE/RELEVANCE FOR TODAY

The homily speaks directly to the world of the twentieth and twenty-first centuries—both in the Christian church and outside in the political arena. Within the church there is suffering, conflicts and disputes. The issue of righteousness by faith versus whether one needs to keep the ten commandments to be saved divides communities of faith while the poor go hungry and naked. In the world the economic giants, both individual and corporate, control the engines of the economy while the poor go hungry and naked. Conflicts and wars are considered the norm to settle disputes. The language of James might have been stronger if he had been writing today than it was in the first century.

ISSUES FOR DISCUSSION AND REFLECTION

1. How would James answer the question: "Why do bad things happen to good people?"
2. How does James describe the tongue as an instrument of conflict and disputes?
3. Do you agree that God has a preferential option for the poor?
4. In what ways can you be sensitive to all persons and still condemn the economic and social inequities in society and the church? How political should be your denunciation?

FURTHER READING

Adason, James B.
    1989   *James: The Man and His Message.* Grand Rapids, MI: Eerdmans.

Davids, Peter H.
    1989   *James.* (New International). Peabody, MA: Hendrickson.

Dibelius, Martin
    1976   *James: A Commentary on the Epistle of James.* (Hermenia). Philadelphia: Fortress.

Laws, Sophie
    1980   *A Commentary on the Epistle of James.* San Francisco: Harper and Row.

Martin, Ralph P.
    1988   *James.* Waco, TX: Word.

Maynard-Reid, Pedrito U.
    1987   *Poverty and Wealth in James.* New York: Orbis.

Moo, Douglas J.
    1985   *James.* (Tyndale). Grand Rapids, MI: Eerdmans.

Chapter 29

1 Peter

Bruce C. Johanson

"He himself bore our sins in his body on the cross, so that, free from sins, we might live for righteousness; by his wounds you have been healed."

BRIEF OVERVIEW OF THE BOOK

First Peter was sent to Christians scattered in the Northwestern provinces of Asia Minor to instruct, encourage and comfort them as they suffered under an outbreak of persecution. It testifies to the certainty of the salvation they had accepted and exhorts them to genuine and proper behavior, both among themselves and among surrounding unbelievers. Above all, it encourages them to remain faithful to Christ and steadfast like Christ. Especially so, since Christ also suffered unjustly and offered the hope of sharing his glory.

BACKGROUND CONCERNS

Peter is presented as the author of the letter. This is done explicitly in the prescript (1:1) and implicitly in 5:1 as "a witness of the sufferings of Christ." Commentators are divided on whether Peter wrote or sent the letter himself or whether it was written in his name by someone else in the late first century or early second century. The following are a few of the more important objections and counter arguments:[1]

1) Many have seriously questioned whether the elegant and sophisticated Greek style of the letter could have been produced by a Jewish Galilean fisherman, even if Peter may have known some Greek as a Galilean. Against this, others have observed that according to 5:12 a certain Silvanus was most likely the secretary and not just the carrier of the letter. Furthermore, a secretary at that time could be given a great deal of freedom in the composition of a letter, even to the point of composing it entirely. This would be subject, of course, to the final approval of the sender who would often pen a postscript at the end. The closing in 5:12-14 may be an example of this (cf. Gal 6:11ff.).

299

[margin note: uses phrases close to Paul's]

2) It has been questioned whether Peter would have used so many expressions that suggest a close dependence on Paul's letters and theology, e.g., "Do not be conformed" (1:14, cf. Rom 12:1), "destined before the foundation of the world" (1:20, cf. Eph 1:4), "died to sin" (2:24 [RSV], cf. Rom 6:2, 10), "in Christ" (3:16, 5:10, 14, often in Paul's letters). However, it has been shown that in the case of theological content there really is not any direct literary dependence by 1 Peter. Instead, both Paul and 1 Peter most likely make independent use of traditional materials common to early Christianity in general.[2] The formal similarities in epistolary style and certain verbal expressions find a natural explanation, if Silvanus was Paul's missionary companion.

[margin note: which persecution is described?]

3) Finally, it is objected that the persecution described, especially in 4:12-13, finds its most likely setting long after Peter's martyrdom (ca. 64-68 C.E.) either during the reign of Domitian (81-96 C.E.) or the reign of Trajan (98-117 C.E.). Many favor the latter, since our earliest documented evidence of persecution in Bithynia and Pontus is found in a letter from the governor Pliny the Younger to Trajan (Pliny, *Epist.* 10.96). Against this, many argue that persecution of Christians appears to have been an ever present threat with many local, popularly instigated outbreaks (see, e.g., Acts 13:50, 1 Thess 1:6, 2 Thess 1:4, Rom 8:35; 12:14). Due to their frequency, such events soon came to be seen as inevitable (2 Tim 3:12). Consequently, one does not need to look for an official persecution behind 4:12-13.

[margin note: if Peter, Silvanus as secretary is a must]

What can we make of all this? Given the slight evidence with which we have to work, one cannot realistically hope to "prove" that this letter did not come from Peter any more than to "prove" that it did. For those who lean toward Petrine authorship, the Silvanus secretary hypothesis is very important.[3] It is entirely possible that the secretary Silvanus is the same person who accompanied Paul (1 Thess 1:1, 2 Thess 1:1, 2 Cor 1:19). Luke uses the Semitic form of his name "Silas" (Acts 15:40), while the Latin name "Silvanus" is used by Paul. It may be significant that Acts 16:37-39 includes him with Paul as possessing Roman citizenship. Roman citizenship for a Jew suggests a family background of some status and perhaps wealth as well. While this does not prove he had the level of education suggested by the letter's literary style, it certainly makes it a reasonable possibility.

[margin note: if not, one close to Peter]

On the other hand, if direct Petrine authorship appears too problematic, it could quite likely have been the idea and work of a person who was close to Peter. He could have preserved those elements of Peter's preaching and teaching that he and his community held in esteem.[4] Thus, in applying what he had learned from the apostle to a new and pressing situation, the letter would have properly been written as coming from Peter. As we will see below, a good portion of 1 Peter may have originally been a baptismal exhortation, possibly given on one or more occasions by Peter and subsequently incorporated into this letter. Outright pseudepigraphy (attribution of authorship to a previous author by a later author) by some unknown author without any special connection to Peter seems unlikely, primarily because such pseudepigraphy usually had a special theological axe to grind, e.g., the spurious *Gospel of Peter* with its gnostic tendency. First Peter does not.

Later tradition places Peter's martyrdom in Rome during Nero's persecution.[5] If this is reliable and if the letter comes directly from Peter, a likely date for it would fall sometime during 64-68 C.E. If it was composed later by one of Peter's close associates, a date sometime in the last quarter of the first century *Rome* is a fair guess. Rome would be the most likely place of origin. This is indicated *as* in the closing greetings (5:13): "Your sister church in Babylon, chosen together *origin (5:13)* with you, sends you greetings." "Babylon" is obviously a pejorative cryptogram for Rome, a natural reaction, if persecution by Nero or possibly Domitian was a present or recent event.

As for the addressees, they were Christians scattered in Pontus, Galatia, *Xians in* Cappadocia, Asia, and Bithynia in Northwestern Asia Minor (1:1). The multiple *area* areas suggest that the letter was intended to be a circular one.[6] Its primary *Minor:* occasion must have been a report of persecution from that region. This is more *a circular* likely than any close connection with a presumed ministry by Peter, since he is *letter* not included among those who brought them the gospel (1:12). Although the Jewish designation "dispersion" is used to address them (1:1), they were *mostly* obviously of predominantly Gentile background. Several times the author refers *Gentiles* to their pre-Christian background in terms that fit Gentiles rather than Jews (1:14, 18; 2:10). We find the clearest expression of this in 4:3-4: "You have already spent enough time doing what the Gentiles like to do, living in licentiousness, passions, drunkenness, revels, carousing, and lawless idolatry. They are surprised that you no longer join them in the same excesses of dissipation, and so they blaspheme." When the author describes them with terminology that was typically applied to Israel in the Old Testament (1:1; 2:4-9, 12), it only indicates that he regards Christians as the new Israel.

While there are instances of language usage similar to 1 Peter in later literature such as *1 Clement* (ca. 96 C.E.) and clear quotations in Polycarp's *Letter to the Philippians* (ca. 135 C.E.), Irenaeus is the first to attribute the letter to Peter explicitly by name late in the second century. After that, there is widespread evidence of its general acceptance as authentic and authoritative by Christian writers.

LITERARY CONSIDERATIONS

Unified?

The letter's unity has come in for a fair amount of debate.[7] Some have seen 1:3-4:11 as somehow originally connected with the occasion of baptism, with 1:1-2 and 4:12-5:14 added later, or some variation of this. One view takes 1:3-

4:11 as a baptismal liturgy. According to this, the baptism takes place between 1:21 and 1:22, and 4:12-5:11 follows as a sermon to the rest of the congregation.[8] Building on this, another view sees 1:2-4:11 as the celebrant's part in a "paschal" liturgy at the baptismal rite that takes place at Easter.[9] Both of these views are too inventive to have found any substantial acceptance.

However, the idea that 1:3-4:11 may have originally been a post baptismal exhortation incorporated into a letter (1:1-2 and 4:12-5:14) merits serious consideration.[10] The following is a summary of the more viable observations that support this view:

[handwritten margin note: a post baptismal sermon incorporated into a letter]

1. The association of 1:3-4:11 with baptism is due to the following features: references to rebirth (1:3, 23; 2:2) and purification (1:22), the creedal material in 3:18-22 which incorporates an explicit definition of baptism (3:21), and references to the recently abandoned pagan life (1:14, 18; 4:3-5).

2. In 1:3-4:11 Christian suffering is expressed in terms of only a threatening possibility (1:6; 2:18-20; 3:13-14, 17), whereas in 4:12-5:11 it is spoken of as a present ongoing fiery ordeal (4:12-13; 5:9). Particularly in 4:12 we should translate: "Beloved, do not be surprised at the fiery ordeal which *is taking place* to test you as something strange that *is happening to you*." This simply does not fit with what is written in 3:13-14: "Now *who is going to harm you* if you are eager for what is right? But *even if you should possibly suffer for righteousness' sake*, you would be blessed." The Greek language used here is such that one simply cannot gloss over the differences.

[handwritten margin note: persecution a threat or reality?]

3. Of lesser importance, but still significant is another shift of view that can be seen to fit in with the different references to suffering in the two passages. In 2:13-17, the author speaks positively of the emperor and his governors as appointed by God to keep order. Also, special emphasis is given to honoring the emperor. This echoes the positive attitude that Paul also expressed in Rom 13:1-7. By contrast, the pejorative cryptogram "Babylon" used in 5:13 expresses the negative attitude we find in Rev 13. Has the arrival of persecution colored the perspective?

[handwritten margin note: 2 perspectives on Rome]

4. It has been observed that 1:3-4:11 is composed of intricately constructed passages with balanced rhythms, parallelisms and antitheses. In 4:12-5:11, however, the style is more direct and simple.[11] This is especially true when we compare 4:12-5:11 with 3:13-4:6, both of which particularly focus on the question of suffering.

5. Finally, try reading 1:3-4:10 aloud with a hortatory sermon to the recently baptized in mind! There simply is a natural fit. The newly baptized are reminded of the hope of salvation into which they are born anew by God's mercy (1:3-12). Because of this hope, they are admonished to relate to God and one another in terms of holiness, earnest love and spiritual growth (1:13-2:8). Another reminder of their very special status based on God's mercy

(2:9-10) closes the section. Then turning from this focus on life in the community of faith, the next most relevant question is how to live in a world where misunderstanding, suspicion and hostility will now threaten them at every turn. The admonitions focus on Gentile society in general, both at the beginning (2:11-12) and at the close (3:13-4:11). In between, attention turns to the civil arena (2:13-17) and domestic contexts (2:18-3:7). At a couple of intervals, there are two shorter units (3:8-12, 4:7-11) which appropriately exhort to behavior that preserves unity and goodwill among the believers themselves. Unity was vital for survival in a capriciously hostile world. When we come to 4:7-11, we find all the features typical of a conclusion: a series of short general exhortations (cf. 1 Thess 5:12-22), a doxology and a closing "amen."

These observations make it plausible that a baptismal exhortation was later incorporated into the letter. It may have been given on one or more occasions by Peter and captured in elegant Greek by Silvanus. As coming from Peter, a reputed pillar of the church (Gal 2:9), it would particularly serve to comfort and encourage suffering Christians. At the same time, by preserving his rich theology for subsequent Christian generations, the letter would stand as a tribute to a great disciple who had honored his Lord in life, suffering, and death.

Alternatively, the differences between the two passages have also been explained by the observations that, since 2:11-4:11 and 4:12-5:11 each have an independent unity of their own, the former may have been sent in a letter to Christians not under persecution and the latter sent in a parallel letter to those who were actually suffering.[12] In that case, the baptismal references and motifs would be taken simply as part of the exhortation that reminds the addressees of their initial commitment. This, however, is a less plausible solution, since it is difficult to explain how the letter got into the shape in which we have received it.

Regarding form, Paul's letters have clearly made an impact on 1 Peter. In the letter opening (1:1-2), Peter is introduced as "an apostle of Jesus Christ" as Paul is regularly introduced (contrast Jas 1:1). There is a theological expansion attached to the identification of sender and addressee (cf. 1 Cor 1:1), followed by a greeting of "Grace and peace." Paul used this to replace the more neutral "Greetings" found in Hellenistic letters (compare Jas 1:1). The letter opens with a blessing formula in 1:3 (cf. 2 Cor 1:3, Eph 1:3). Doxologies followed by "amen" are used to conclude discrete sections of text in 4:11 and 5:11 (cf. Rom 11:36, Gal 1:5). The *parakalo* (the Greek word for "I appeal") formula is used to introduce sections of moral exhortation in 2:11 and 5:1 (cf. 1 Thess 4:1, Rom 12:1), and use is made of social codes that address admonitions variously to slaves, spouses, etc., in 2:18-3:7 (cf. Eph 5:22-6:9, Col 3:18-4:1).

[handwritten margin note: draws on traditional materials]

First Peter also draws on a variety of traditional materials. There is the use of traditional forms of moral exhortation, i.e., the social codes just mentioned, catalogues of vices (2:1; 4:3) and an instructional persecution form (4:13, cf. Matt 5:11-12). As for liturgical materials, the use of early creeds has been claimed for 1:18-21 and 3:18-22, a hymn in 2:6-10, and baptismal hymns in 1:3-5, 2:22-25, 3:18-22, and 5:5-9. Although baptismal hymns may be possible in the first three instances, the last one is hardly likely, since right in the middle of it the author divides the passage by a change of address from "you who are younger" to "all of you." More generally, the influence of the language of worship is reflected in such expressions as "Blessed be" (1:3) and the doxologies concluded by "amen" (4:11; 5:11).

[handwritten margin note: language of worship]

In relation to length, no other New Testament books, apart from Hebrews and Revelation, use the Old Testament so extensively as 1 Peter. There are many explicit quotations (1:16, 24-25; 2:6, 7, 8, 9; 3:10-12; 4:8b, 18; 5:5), almost entirely from the Septuagint (Greek Old Testament), which the author uses like a preacher to support the points that he makes. There also are many Old Testament allusions that he weaves into his text, while keeping his own very distinctive Greek style.

[handwritten margin note: extensively uses OT]

THE MESSAGE
Outline

This breakdown of the contents and structure may be summarized by the following general outline:

I. Letter opening 1:1-2
II. Letter body 1:3-5:11
   A. Living in the hope of salvation 1:3-2:10
     1. God is blessed for the hope of salvation his mercy provides in Jesus Christ 1:3-12
     2. Exhortation to hope and to obedient behavior that seeks holiness and earnest mutual love 1:13-25
     3. Exhortation to spiritual growth and worship of God who chose them in mercy 2:1-10
   B. Living in the world of unbelievers 2:11-4:11
     1. Exhortation to abstain from fleshly lusts and to behave well among the "gentiles" 2:11-12
     2. Exhortation to be subject to and to honor civic authorities in order to silence ignorant misunderstandings 2:13-17
     3. Exhortation to (Christian) domestic servants to be subject to masters, even in unjust suffering, according to the example of Jesus Christ 2:18-25

Survey of contents

The practical, hortatory character of the letter is explicitly expressed in the closing: "I have written this short letter to encourage you and to testify that this is the true grace of God" (5:12). This description is appropriate. After the introductory summary of the salvation experience in 1:3-12, the rest of the letter, as we have it, consists of spiritual and moral exhortations. They are variously expanded by theological and practical motivations, all intended to instruct, encourage and comfort. *[handwritten margin note: spiritual + moral exhortation]*

Such a general outline, however, does not do justice to the carefully crafted structure of the materials in the letter. This may be done by attending to the following indicators: thematic transitions and expansions; opening and transitional markers such as "Blessed be" (1:3), "Beloved" (2:11; 4:12), "Slaves" (2:18), "all of you" (3:8; 5:5b), etc.; connectors like "Therefore" (1:13; 4:1), "So" (2:1; 5:1 [RSV]), "Finally" (3:8), etc.; and terminating markers such as doxologies concluded by an "Amen" (4:11; 5:11).

In *1:1-12* the letter opens with the conventional identification of the sender and the recipients. This is extended with a Trinitarian elaboration that refers to

God's election, the Holy Spirit's sanctification and blood sprinkled obedience to Jesus Christ. A greeting of grace and peace ends the prescript.

The body of the letter is opened by a solemn blessing of God for the believers' new birth to a living hope by his mercy (1:3-11). God's salvation is kept in heaven for them. If they have to suffer, this will be a purifying process and their faith in Jesus will carry them through. It is a salvation made available by the suffering and glorification of Jesus Christ. It was searched for by the prophets and has now been preached to the addressees, a salvation into which angels long to peek.

In *1:13-25* the author connects the subsequent exhortations to the thought in 1:3-12 by the connector "Therefore." He opens the exhortation by urging the addressees to fasten their hope on the grace of salvation coming at the revelation of Jesus Christ. Then he develops the topic of obedience by exhorting them to be holy, because God is holy. Their behavior must be reverent, because they have been ransomed by the precious blood of Christ. Since they have been born anew by God's abiding word, they are to purify themselves by obedience to the truth as expressed in earnest mutual love. His eternal word is the gospel that was preached to them.

In *2:1-10* "therefore" ("So," RSV) is again used to connect with the previous thought. Following a brief catalogue of vices to be avoided, the author shifts his exhortation to the theme of spiritual growth. The initial growth metaphor is that of babes longing for spiritual milk (2:2-3). Then it suddenly shifts to a building metaphor (2:4-8). Finally, a rich array of designations, typically applied to Israel, is applied to the addressees, who have become God's people by his mercy.

This ends the first major section of the body of the letter (1:3-2:10) which views Christian status and behavior in the hope of salvation. The next major section (2:11-4:11) views Christian life and behavior in the midst of nonbelievers. This thematic focus is expressed in the opening section *2:11-12*. After exhorting abstinence from fleshly lusts, the author calls on the addressees to behave well among the "Gentiles" in general. Such good behavior will vindicate them on the day of visitation.

In *2:13-17* the exhortation shifts to the subordinate theme of subjection to those in civic authority, since their divinely appointed task is to keep good social order. The emperor especially is to be honored.

In *2:18-25* the focus turns to slaves. The Greek word used specifies them as "domestic servants." They are to be subject to their masters, both the gentle and the overbearing ones. The particular circumstances in view here are those of Christian servants in relation to non-Christian masters. If they should suffer unjustly, they have Jesus Christ as an example. He never retaliated under unjust suffering, but trusted in the just judgment of God. It was his wounds that brought them healing.

In *3:1-7* the focus changes to wives and husbands. Christian spouses are viewed in relation to their partners, some of whom are non-Christians. Christian wives should be subject and behave so that they may win over their spouses to the faith. Christian husbands are to treat their wives considerately and with honor as co-heirs of the "grace of life."

In *3:8-12* the connecting expression "finally" and the address "all of you" signals a shift of focus back to the audience at large. The opening exhortations (3:8) enumerate a catalogue of virtues to be pursued, followed by the vices of retaliation to be avoided, in order to be blessed (3:9). This is proved by a lengthy quotation from Ps 34:12-16 in 3:10-12. The first line in 3:11 of the quotation captures the basic theme of the paragraph, namely, to "turn away from evil and do good."

A rhetorical question opens the unit *3:13-4:6*. The theme returns to the relationship of Christians to nonbelievers with a special focus on the question of suffering: "Now who will harm you if you are eager to do what is good?" Although harm from unbelievers is only potential, in case it happens, believers are given the following exhortations: They should regard this as a blessing; they should reverence Christ as Lord; they are to be ready with a defense for the hope in them, and to have the same mind as Christ with regard to suffering. The primary motivation for accepting suffering is presented in 3:18-22. The flow of thought here takes some gigantic leaps. It moves from Christ's death and resurrection, to making a proclamation to spirits in prison that were formerly disobedient in Noah's time. At that time eight people were saved by the ark through water. Their salvation through water is taken as a symbol of baptism that now saves "as an appeal to God for a good conscience" (3:21). This appeal is made through the resurrection of Christ who sits at God's right hand with all angels, powers and authorities subject to him. The connection of their baptism to Christ's passage from suffering to heavenly dominion offers them comfort, hope and an example. Like Christ, to suffer unjustly brings triumph over sin and gives life in the spirit.

The unit *4:7-11* brings things to a close. After a reminder that the end is near, a series of shorter, general exhortations is given. The addressees are admonished to mutual love, hospitality and service. Then there is a brief doxology concluded by "amen."

The conclusion of the letter, however, is not reached yet. The last major section (*4:12-5:11*) now turns to focus on Christian suffering, not as a potentiality, but as something that is actually happening to the addressees. The initial subsection is 4:12-19. Here the author exhorts the recipients not to be surprised at the fiery ordeal that is taking place, but to rejoice in so far as they are sharing in Christ's sufferings. They should avoid suffering for doing wrong, but suffering for being a Christian brings a blessing and glorifies God.

In *5:1-5a* the author turns to address elders and young men. As one who witnessed the sufferings of Christ, he exhorts the elders to be good shepherds. They are not to serve under constraint, or because of financial gain, or in a domineering way. Young men, in turn, are to be subject to the elders.

In *5:5b-11* the address reverts to "all of you." They are exhorted to humility and to steadfastness in the knowledge of other Christians having the same experience of suffering. They are warned of the Devil's activity and comforted by God's present care and future restoration. This closes with a doxology and "amen."

Silvanus as secretary 5:12-14

Finally, in the letter closing, *5:12-14*, Silvanus is identified as the secretary. The letter is referred to as an exhortation and declaration of God's grace. Greetings are sent from the church in "Babylon" and from Mark and a final blessing is given.

It has been observed that in 1 Peter the theology is not argued, but declared. There is no agony over the Old Testament, as we find in Paul, who struggles with what still applies and what is to be left behind (e.g., Rom 3-8). Instead, 1

broad view of OT

Peter's allusive use of the Old Testament provides a fluidity that moves easily between the old and the new. This is possible, because it does not get bogged down in the details of regulations and applications. Instead, it soars with the overarching concepts of God's great mercy, election, and salvation and the human responses of faith and obedience. Along with Romans and 1 John, this letter has more references to God relative to length than any of the other New

concentrated on God who made all possible

Testament writings. It is primarily theocentric, rather than christocentric. As important as the work of Christ is, the concentration is on God who makes it possible. The addressees are called to a relationship, not so much to Jesus Christ as to God through Jesus Christ.

As mentioned previously, 1 Peter makes extensive use of the Old Testament With regard to Old Testament allusions, he uses them in such a way that the resonances bring out a rich theology of the continuity of God's purpose of

OT quotes
God's continuing purpose

salvation for and through a chosen people. For example, we find words like "exile" (1:1, 17; 2:11), "chosen" (1:2; 2:9), "obedience" (1:2, 14, 22), "sprinkled with ... blood" (1:2), "inheritance" (1:4), being "holy" (1:15-16; 2:5, 9), the string of designations "a chosen race, a royal priesthood, a holy nation, God's own special possession, ... God's people" (2:9-10 [RSV]), and "his wonderful deeds" (2:9). These all resonate together to recall and connect with the Old Testament God of the covenant who continues to select a special people whom he calls into covenant obedience and holiness, who declare his wonderful deeds, and for whom he will provide the promised inheritance when their exile is over at last.

Mingled with allusions to the Israel of wilderness exile and sojourn are other allusions to Israel as established, temple community. They are called to the "*living* stone" Jesus and are themselves to become "*living* stones" (2:4-5). The imagery is fluid, almost surrealistic. As living stones, they are to be built into a "spiritual house." Simultaneously, they are a "holy priesthood" who offer "spiritual sacrifices" to God, made acceptable through Jesus Christ. Christians are thus regarded as the new and true Israel.

The assurance and the permanence of life that God's salvation brings are emphasized by such vivid expressions in 1:3-4 of the addressees having been born anew to "a *living* hope" and to an inheritance that is "*imperishable, undefiled and unfading.*" Again in 1:23, the new birth is said to be of "*imperishable* seed" by the "*living* and enduring word of God." The certainty of salvation is grounded in God's mercy. It was predestined from the foundation of the world and manifested in the ransoming blood and triumphal resurrection of Jesus Christ (1:18-21).

In the difficult passage of 3:18-22, the suffering of Christ (3:18) and the subsequent triumph of his resurrection and exaltation over all angelic hosts (3:22) frame a strange concatenation of references to disobedient spirits, Noah's flood, and baptism. A pseudepigraphal book called *1 Enoch*, widely read and even quoted in Jude 14-15 (cf. 2 Pet 2), is the probable background behind much of the thought here. The key idea in this highly structured and densely imaged passage is the assurance that those who have been baptized serve a Master who through suffering, death, resurrection and exaltation has conquered the powers of evil.[13]

There is a distinct eschatological focus throughout the work. In some passages it is expressed in subdued tones (1:4-7, 13; 2:12; 4:5; 5:10) and more urgently in others (4:7, 17). It is also evident in the repeated motif of past or present suffering and future glory (1:6-7, 11, 21; 4:13; 5:10). Thus, hope not only looks back on what Christ has accomplished (1:3, 21), but especially forward to the "grace" that his coming will bring (1:13).

Contrary to much pastoral use of 1 Peter in comforting those who struggle with the personal tragedies common to all of human life, it must be honestly contended that it was not that kind of suffering the author had in mind when he wrote. While a faulty exegesis may not hinder good pastoral care, the latter should look for more appropriate texts elsewhere in the New Testament. Suffering in 1 Peter is primarily about the kind of persecution aroused by the very goodness of Christians (3:16). It is the mysterious and irrational reaction of evil against goodness that was particularly associated with the time of the end (4:7). In as far as Christians undergo this suffering, they are sharing in the sufferings of Christ and may rejoice when his glory is revealed (4:13).[14]

The nearness of the end of time in 1 Peter does not give rise to frantic exhortations about superhuman perfection. Instead we find calm and levelheaded admonitions to behave with holiness in the presence of God, with love toward one another, and with honor, respect, and prudence among nonbelievers. In the case of unjust suffering for being a Christian, they were to submit without retaliation. Whatever happened, God would see them through and eternal glory would bring relief and restoration (5:10), a homecoming from exile.

RELEVANCE FOR TODAY

The more isolated Christianity becomes in an increasingly secular, permissive and even hostile society, the more germane the messages of 1 Peter become. First, no matter what the situation, all Christians stand in need of repeated reminders of the fundamental assurance of salvation and the greatness of God's mercy, but especially so when the walls of faith are being shaken.

Second, there are several developments making devastating inroads on the values and spirituality needed to preserve and enrich both the external relations of society and the inner life of the individual today. We can name the social dissonance set up by increasingly divergent lifestyles, the pressure to conform to sexual permissiveness, indulgence in materialistic excess, and lax ethical norms. Peter's call to holiness, as expressed in genuine Christian love and generosity and in decent social behavior, is a voice that needs to be heard. At the same time, he is sensitive to the pain from ridicule inflicted by former associates on those who have recently decided to follow Christ. This is especially relevant to young people in the process of finding and establishing their personal identity and values.

Finally, the promised relief of eschatology in the face of suffering still tempts Christians to isolate and lose themselves in an escapist theology and lifestyle. Against this tendency, 1 Peter strikes a fine balance of responsible life in this world, while repeatedly reminding Christians that this world is only a place of sojourn; heaven is their home.

ISSUES FOR DISCUSSION AND REFLECTION

1. When 1 Peter describes the experience of salvation in 1:3-2:10, what does he have primarily in view, a collective or individual experience? How is the one important in relation to the other?

2. Is the author's call for submission without retaliation still relevant in our time and culture for Christian's who are suffering unjustly?

3. Peter calls Christians to follow Christ's example in suffering. Would it be legitimate to take this beyond the application to suffering? How can this idea be theologically abused?

4. Survey several commentaries with differing interpretations of 3:18-22. How many distinct types can you find? What are the strong and weak points in each? Which do you find the most satisfying in terms of doing reasonable justice to all the different features in the text?

5. Survey several commentaries with differing interpretations of 4:6. What do you think the most reasonable interpretation is in view of the immediately preceding context? Is there any connection with the thought in 3:19? How would you explain this?

6. What do you think the author means in 4:1, when he writes that "whoever has suffered in the flesh has finished with sin"? Does the subsequent context help?

7. What does the author mean when he admonishes them to "*good* conduct" (or "behavior," 2:12; 3:16)? Does he explain in any detail what "good" entails? Can a Christian view of "good conduct" overlap at all with a pagan view of "good conduct"? If so, what would be the same, what would be different, and how would you be able to recognize the difference?

FURTHER READING

Barr, David L.
    1995   *New Testament Story.* Second ed. Belmont: Wadsworth.
Beare, Francis W.
    1970   *The First Epistle of Peter.* (First ed., 1945) Third ed., revised and enlarged. Oxford: Basil Blackwell.
Best, Ernest
    1971   *1 Peter.* (New Century). London: Oliphants.
Brunt, John
    1988   "Christ and the Imprisoned Spirits," *Ministry* (April 1988) 15-17.
Cross, Frank L.
    1954   *1 Peter: A Paschal Liturgy.* London: Mowbray.
Davids, Peter H.
    1990   *The First Epistle of Peter.* (New International). Grand Rapids, MI: Zondervan.
Goppelt, Leonhard
    1993   *A Commentary on 1 Peter.* Ed. by F. Hahn, trans. and aug. by J.E. Alsup. Grand Rapids, MI: Eerdmans.
Moule, Charles Francis D.
    1957   "The Nature and Purpose of 1 Peter," *New Testament Studies* 3, 1-11.
Reike, Bo Ivar
    1946   *The Disobedient Spirits and Christian Baptism: A Study of 1 Pet. iii.19 and its context* (Acta Seminarii Neotestamentici Upsaliensis, 13). Copenhagen: Munksgaard.
Selwyn, Edward G.
    1947   *The First Epistle of St. Peter.* Second ed. London: Macmillan.
Streeter, Burnett H.
    1929   *The Primitive Church.* New York: Macmillan.

ENDNOTES

1. Two classic commentaries are representative of the opposing positions on Peter's authorship. One is by E.G. Selwyn, *The First Epistle of St. Peter*, second ed., London: Macmillan, 1947, 7-17, who supports Petrine authorship, and the other by F.W. Beare, *The First Epistle of Peter*, (first ed., 1945) third ed., revised and enlarged, Oxford: Basil Blackwell, 1970, 43-50, who rejects Petrine authorship.

2. See L. Goppelt, *A Commentary on 1 Peter*, Ed. by F. Hahn, trans. and aug. by J.E. Alsup, Grand Rapids, MI: Eerdmans, 1993, 28-29.

3. Recently in favor of this, see P.H. Davids, *The First Epistle of Peter*, (New International). Grand Rapids, MI: Zondervan, 1990, 6-7.

4. See, e.g., D.L. Barr, *New Testament Story*, second ed., Belmont, etc.: Wadsworth., 1995, 442-43.

5. See e.g., *1 Clement* 5:2-4 and Eusebius' *H.E.* 2.25.8.

6. See *II Baruch* 78-86 as a striking example of such a circular letter in Jewish literature. It refers to the addresses as the "dispersed," exhorts them to solidarity in the midst of suffering and gives an interpretation of suffering quite similar to that in 1 Peter. See Goppelt, *1 Peter*, 24.

7. For a clear, more detailed account see E. Best, *1 Peter*, New Century Bible, London: Oliphants, 1971, 20-27.

8. This was developed initially by German scholars, and accepted by B.H. Streeter, *The Primitive Church*, New York: Macmillan, 1929, 115ff., 129ff.

9. See F.L. Cross, *1 Peter: A Paschal Liturgy*, London: Mowbray, 1954.

10. For proponents of this view see Beare, *1 Peter*, 25-28, and most recently, D.L. Barr, *Story*, 439-40, 442-43.

11. Thus, Beare, 26-27.

12. So, C.F.D. Moule, "The Nature and Purpose of 1 Peter," *New Testament Studies* 3 (1956-57), 1-11.

13. See B. Reike, *The Disobedient Spirits and Christian Baptism: A Study of 1 Pet. iii.19 and its context*, (Acta seminarii neotestamentici uppsaliensis, 13) Copenhagen: Munksgaard, 1946. For a short, well-expressed view on this, see J. Brunt, "Christ and the Imprisoned Spirits," *Ministry* (April, 1988) 15-17.

14. See Davids, *Peter*, 30-44, for an especially excellent outline of the development of the concept of suffering in the Bible and where 1 Peter stands in relation to this.

Chapter 30

2 Peter
Ronald L. Jolliffe

*"But the day of the Lord will come like a thief, and then the heavens will pass away
with a loud noise, and the elements will be dissolved with fire, and the earth and
everything that is done on it will be disclosed."*

BRIEF OVERVIEW OF THE BOOK

Second Peter is a short letter written to admonish Christians to live in ways
pleasing to God and warning them of temptations to sin. The 965 words (in the
Greek text) make up the 61 verses of this book. For such a few number of
words, the text contains an amazing array of biblical illustrations which focus on
the problem of living as spiritual people while being physical bodies. The book
draws heavily on earlier texts to describe the dangers of the sins of the flesh by
telling famous stories from the past that describe the destruction which can be
expected from God for licentious behavior. These illustrations include the angels
who sinned, the cities of Sodom and Gomorrah and the experience of "righteous"
Lot. The book concludes with an apocalyptic warning of the kind of people who
will live in the last days and the kinds of sins they will promulgate. This
warning is followed by the promise that the Lord will come and dissolve
everything with fire, but not before first allowing time for those who will repent
to do so. The book reminds its readers that Christians are to live without spot
or blemish as they watch and wait for these things to take place.

BACKGROUND CONCERNS

The petrine authorship of 2 Peter has been a source of serious contention
since the time of the early church fathers of the second and third centuries. In
fact, no other book in the New Testament had such a difficult time being
accepted into the canon. The first clear reference to 2 Peter in early Christian
writings is found in Origen (185-254 C.E.), who mentions 2 Peter for the
purpose of disputing its validity. In the fourth century Eusebius (260-340 C.E.)

disputed validity

writes, "As for the current second epistle [of Peter], it has not come down to us as canonical, though it has been studied long with the rest of the scriptures, since it has seemed useful to many people."

In spite of these difficulties, some argue, based on the following statements from the book itself, that the letter was written by Peter, the brother of Andrew and disciple of Jesus. They note that the letter says it is from "Simeon Peter" (1:1), an "apostle" (1:1). It claims to record the observations of an eyewitness: "We had been eyewitnesses of his majesty" (1:16); "We ourselves heard this voice come from heaven, while we were with him on the holy mountain" (a reference to the Mount of Transfiguration, Mark 9:2-8) (1:18). Second Peter 1:13-14 makes reference to a revelation from Jesus' of the author's death. Additionally there is the reference to this letter (2 Peter) being "the second letter I am writing to you" (apparently reminding the reader of 1 Peter). And the letter mentions Paul as "our beloved brother Paul" (3:15).

Those who argue against the petrine authorship feel the arguments against petrine authorship are so strong and serious they require reevaluating the claims the book makes for itself regarding authorship. These observations fall into three major categories. First, the problem of the severe asceticism of the letter, which became an issue for the church during the second and third centuries. The letter warns of "the corruption that is in the world because of lust" (1:4); of "licentious ways" (2:2). The text has an extended quotation from the pseudepigraphical book of *Enoch* concerning the angels who were cast out of heaven because of their illicit sexual affairs with human women (2:4), and "the licentiousness of the lawless" in reference to Sodom and Gomorrah (2:6-8). Second Peter 2:9-10 warns that "the Lord knows how ... to keep the unrighteous under punishment until the day of judgment—especially those who indulge their flesh in depraved lust." It warns of people who "have eyes full of adultery, insatiable for sin" (2:14). These people entice others "with licentious desires of the flesh" (2:18). In the last days scoffers will be "indulging their own lusts" (3:3).

While these repeated references against sexual lust warn Christians of the dangers of illicit sexuality, some are surprised that 2 Peter does not call Christians to marry and lead lives of purity with their spouses. Instead they are called to lead lives free from desire. Note the repeated appeals made in this letter "to purity and godliness" (1:3); to being "participants of the divine nature," (1:4); to having "self-control with endurance" (1:6). To lack these things is to be "forgetful of the cleansing of past sins" (1:9). True Christians are to lead "lives of holiness and godliness" (3:11) and to strive to be "without spot or blemish" (3:14).

While it is not surprising that an apostle would have been concerned and taught against sexual infidelity (as did Jesus himself, Mark 10:2-12), it is difficult for some to understand why an apostle would make this radical shift away from Jesus' powerful focus on justice to a pietistic concern for asceticism as the definition of what it means to properly wait for the new heavens and the new earth where righteousness is at home. This is a shift in focus from an altruistic concern to a pietistic concern. Those who argue for petrine authorship doubt that the text endorses asceticism and point out that this is merely an argument from silence.

shift from altruism to pietism [margin note]

The second argument against petrine authorship is the view of scripture in 2 Peter. While the Hebrew scriptures were the scriptures of the early church, the "New Testament" writings were not considered scripture until long after the end of the first century. Yet 2 Peter appears to have been written at a time when the writings of Paul were considered scripture. Second Peter 3:15-16 says there are things in Paul's letters which people twist to their own destruction "as they do the other scriptures." Such a sentence would only be written at a time when Paul's letters were considered to be part of scripture. Additionally, the reference in 3:2 appears to consider some Christian writings as scripture, "that you should remember the predictions of the holy prophets and the commandment of the Lord and Savior through your apostles." Those who argue for Petrine authority suggest this is making too much out of these words, since "the other scriptures" of 3:16 is literally "the other writings" and may not be referring to scripture at all. Furthermore, some maintain that the 3:2 reference to predictions is hardly a reference to all of the Jewish scriptures any more than the "commandment of the Lord and Savior" is a reference to the New Testament.

2) view of scripture [margin note]

A third argument raised against petrine authorship is that the letter is heavily dependent upon several (readily identifiable) sources, and these sources provide the major factual content of the book. The book offers no teaching or information concerning Jesus that is not readily available to anyone with a basic knowledge of the synoptics and the tradition of the death of Peter recorded in the addendum to the Gospel of John (21:18) and the book of Jude upon which the central section of 2 Peter is dependent. Compare the accompanying parallel chart which displays the texts of 2 Peter and Jude side by side. Such heavy reliance on the work of others is seen as strange behavior for an apostle who walked and talked with Jesus. Of course, one might object that this is a type of argument from silence and that an apostle does not have to be always saying something new in order to continue to be an apostle. But it is difficult to imagine an apostle feeling the need to copy the works of others so extensively.

3) dependent on other sources [margin note]

A fourth argument is more difficult for the student who reads English, but not Greek to verify, though it is not difficult to understand. Second Peter is notorious for being written in a Greek very much unlike most of the rest of the New Testament, certainly very different from the Greek of 1 Peter. Instead of being written in the Koine, or common street-language of the uneducated, it is

4) literary Atticizing Greek [margin note]

written in the literary Greek of an author who chose to write in what was a literary fashion that mimicked an earlier stage of Greek, coming out of the Attic period and dialect. It is analogous to someone today choosing to write in Elizabethan English. Those who hold it was written by Peter suggest that he simply used different amanuenses (scribes) for the two epistles.

Nevertheless, in view of the weight of these arguments, it seems necessary to avoid assuming the book was written by the disciple whom Jesus called Cephas. Such an assumption naturally leads to the danger of letting what we know (or think we know) about Peter influence how we interpret this epistle. In other words, 2 Peter is part of the accepted New Testament canon, and appropriate for serious investigation on its own merits.

LITERARY CONSIDERATIONS

Second Peter is written in the form of an epistle (letter). Letters in antiquity fell into two basic categories, personal or private letters sent to an individual or group concerning some particular circumstance, and more general correspondence, frequently referred to as epistles, which were of a more general nature concerning moral teaching, ethical guidance, etc. Most letter writers employed an amanuensis to write their letters. Normally, only the final greeting would be written by the sender in his/her own hand. Consider Gal 6:11-18 where Paul adds his final words in his own hand.

Correspondence in antiquity, whether written by Jews, Christians, or any one else, utilized a conventional three-part form: the opening, the body, and the closing. The opening of a letter itself contained three sub-parts: a) the name of the sender, in this letter "Simeon Peter"; b) the person(s) to whom the letter is being sent, in this letter there is no named recipient, nor even any indication of where the recipients live, in contrast to 1 Pet 1:1-2, but simply, "to those who have obtained a faith of equal standing with ours ..."; c) a prayer of blessing upon the receiver. In this letter the prayer of blessing is "May grace and peace be multiplied to you" (1:2b).

The body of the letter contains the message of the letter. It is the reason the letter was written. The body of a letter can be very short, containing no more than a few words, or quite extensive, running on for pages. The contents of the body of 2 Peter extend from 1:3-3:16.

As noted above, the Closing of the letter was usually written by the sender in his/her own hand, in 2 Peter the final two verses constitute the closing, 3:17-18.

Second Peter contains a very long quotation that is also found in the epistle of Jude. It is somewhat adapted to fit the flow of the argument in this epistle from the form that appears in Jude. It is instructive to see the parallels between Jude and 2 Peter. They are printed in parallel columns on pp 327-333. Most *from Enoch*

scholars assume that 2 Peter copied the text from the epistle of Jude who copied it from the book of *Enoch*, which belongs to the pseudepigrapha.

THE MESSAGE
Outline
The three chapters of this short epistle can be outlined as follows:

Survey of contents

The primary message of 2 Peter concerns how to live as spiritual people *how to live spiritually in body* while being a physical body. The people to whom the letter is sent have been tempted to abandon their faith when they are confronted by teachers who appear to have a winsome theory which leads to violations of the basic principles of Peter's earlier instruction to them. No text exists, aside from the letter itself, to inform us what these false teachers were saying or doing, though the basic result of their teaching leads to the indulgence of licentious passion.

This false teaching has led the author to formulate a clear plan of attack which first requires the establishment of the authority of church leadership. The work of the "false teachers" (2:1) has diminished the authority of the author because it has led these Christians to set aside the practice of Christianity which they had originally been taught. The issue of authority clearly surfaces in numerous places throughout the book, beginning with the very first words of the greeting which affirm that Simeon Peter is "a servant and apostle of Jesus Christ."

It is essential that the recipients of this letter clearly understand the authority of the author, because there are false teachers who have been leading people away from the truth. It is important for the author to establish his credentials as impeccable in order that the recipients will accept the authority of his letter. Therefore the first order of business is to establish the basis for the writer's authority. [It will be helpful to the student to look at the text of 2 Pet 1:12-19 while reading the following paragraph.]

This authority is based on the author's personal contact with Jesus Christ. In 1:12-19, the author claims a direct, personal revelation from Jesus concerning his own death (1:13-14). The value of the author's teaching is so important that it will be provided in written form (1:15) so that it can be consulted even after he dies. The author affirms that his teachings are those of an eyewitness, and not (as he here implicitly alleges of the false teachers) cleverly devised myths (1:16). In order that the readers of the letter not assume this authority is based on some kind of vision or dream or other ethereal idea, he continues by stating that he had been with Jesus "on the holy mountain" when the voice said, "This is my beloved Son ..." (1:17-18). But not only is the author one who has seen and heard, he also understands the true meaning of the Hebrew Scriptures, because of his time with Jesus Christ (1:19). To be sure there is no misunderstanding about the authority these experiences confer, he writes in 1:19b, "You will do well to pay attention to this ...."

The beginning of ch 2 attempts to clarify for the reader why the authority of church leadership is so important to understand; there are not only the true leaders, there are also false prophets who sound authoritative, but the result of what they teach is destruction (2:1-3). This is no new phenomenon (2:3), evil has always brought destruction. Consider the destructiveness of heresy as seen in many examples from the past: the angels who sinned were not spared, but sent to pits of nether gloom to await punishment (2:4); the antediluvians in the days of Noah were destroyed (2:5); and the residents of Sodom and Gomorrah were turned to ashes (2:6). Neglecting God's guidance leads to destruction.

But that is only half of the story. The Lord also knows how to rescue the righteous (2:9). The Lord has demonstrated this by rescuing people who have lived right in the midst of evil. God preserved Noah, who was a herald of righteousness (2:5). He also rescued Lot, who was greatly distressed by the evil surrounding him (2:7). But even though the Lord knows how to rescue, he keeps the unrighteous under punishment, and "especially those who indulge in the lust of defiling passion" and those who "despise authority" (2:10).

Those who despise authority are an especially despicable lot. "Bold and wilful, they are not afraid to revile the glorious ones" (2:10b). They are "like irrational animals, creatures of instinct ... reviling in matters of which they are ignorant" (2:12). "They count it pleasure to revel in the daytime. They are blots and blemishes, reveling in their dissipation, carousing with you. They have eyes full of adultery, insatiable for sin" (2:10b-14a). This set of reflections leads the author next to the story of a prophet, Balaam, (2:15-16) who led Israel into false doctrine and licentious practices (Num 22). Then follows an extended quotation from the pseudepigraphical book of *Enoch* concerning the nature of evil persons (2:17-19), followed by the comment that it would be better never to have heard of the Lord than to hear and then fall back again into sin.

description of false teachers

The final chapter warns readers not to be lead astray by the scoffers who will come in the last days, denying the doctrines and practices which they have been taught. The readers are cautioned that, although the Lord is patient, he will not wait forever to bring the final destruction of evil that precedes the promised new heavens and new earth.

In the discussion of authorship above, the attention this epistle gives to lust was itemized at some length. This is clearly a matter of urgent concern for the author. It is part of the focal point of the book. Most assume that the false teachers were some type of gnostics who sharply divided reality into the sphere of good (also known as the sphere of the spirit), and the sphere of evil (also known as the sphere of matter). Matter was considered to be thoroughly evil and not redeemable. Spirit was absolutely pure and could not be defiled. Human beings were caught in this struggle between good and evil, with their evil bodies warring against their pure spirits.

a view: matter, evil; spirit, good

The early church fathers tell us that this theological construct led to two quite different understandings of how to live. One way may be that of the false teachers of 2 Peter who apparently believed and taught that since spirit is good and cannot be contaminated with evil, what one does with one's body is irrelevant to the spiritual life. This false teaching seems to be of a "spiritual" kind that either treats the physical as irrelevant, or ignores it completely. Whichever, it has led to serious moral problems that dominate the content as well as the tone of this epistle.

The epistle seems to agree, in part with the premise of the false teachers, that the body is problematic. It needs to be subdued and denied, and brought under the control of the spirit. However, 2 Peter stops short of a full-fledged dualism, for the epistle clearly looks forward to a new heavens and a new earth. For those whose dualism was full-fledged, the future hope involved escape from the material world, including a new heaven and a new earth.

2 Peter avoids full-fledged dualism

The imminent return of the Lord mandates a life characterized as spotless and without blemish. In the face of a judgment that is in the immediate future, one dare not ignore the examples all around of people who have already suffered the judgment of God. This apocalyptic message requires that true Christians live lives of purity and godliness, without any taint of the desires of the flesh.

RELEVANCE FOR TODAY

The modern world faces apocalyptic warnings as threatening as those found in 2 Peter. Apocalyptic-style warnings come at modern people from secular, as well as religious, sources. For example, both religious and secular sources warn of the seriousness of the threat to everyone of the AIDS epidemic which has already become the foremost killer of the young in the United States. Second Peter's warnings about the serious consequences of carousing, dissipation, lawless deeds, and licentious passions of the flesh is certainly timely!

The idea of living mindful of having to answer for one's actions is an art that seems to have been lost by many in today's world. If every decision were made with the assumption that one would be required to defend that decision before a fair and honest judge, the world would be a far safer and saner place in which to live. When one chooses to live so that one only answers to oneself, the most atrocious of crimes result.

ISSUES FOR DISCUSSION AND REFLECTION

1. Given the problems of sexually transmitted diseases, including HIV and AIDS, what would be the message of this epistle to society? Should the message include sex education? Given the rapidly developing epidemic of AIDS, would the message based on this epistle include education concerning how to reduce the risk of contracting sexually transmitted diseases in casual sexual encounters?

2. Clearly, the author of this epistle assumed Jesus would return in his and his original readers' day (3:11-14, etc). Does the fact that Jesus did *not* affect the validity of the argument of the epistle that people should live blameless lives?

3. How does one evaluate the reliability of an authority? In the media we are constantly bombarded with advertising designed to win our trust, or at least our money. What constitute valid grounds for trusting an authority?

4. Some Christians maintain a clear dualism in their view of the human being, which understands a person to be part matter and part spirit, while others adopt an organic model of the person as a living, thinking body. What differences do these two views entail in their understandings of human sexuality with regard to sex partner, birth control, conception, abortion, purpose of human sexuality (pleasure, producing children, etc.), uses of fetal tissue (such as organ transplants), etc.?

FURTHER READING
Arichea, Daniel C. and Howard A. Hatton
   1993   *A Handbook on Jude and Second Peter.* New York: United Bible Society.
Charlesworth, James H., Ed.
   1983   *The Old Testament Pseudepigrapha. Volume 1: Apocalyptic Literature and Testaments.* Garden City, NY: Doubleday.

Chapter 31

Jude
Ronald L. Jolliffe

"Now I desire to remind you, though you are fully informed, that the Lord, who once for all saved a people out of the land of Egypt, afterward destroyed those who did not believe."

BRIEF OVERVIEW OF THE BOOK

Jude, with only 361 words (in Greek), is the shortest book in the New Testament, so short that it has only verse divisions. Even though the epistle was written because ungodly people had gained admission into the congregation and were leading believers away from the original faith, the epistle was not written as a condemnation of the evil ones, but as an encouragement to the faithful to continue to struggle for the faith. The epistle warns its readers of the dangers of assuming that persons who belong to the community are safe from God's destruction and reinforces this warning with examples from the past. The letter notes that the presence of ungodly persons in the congregation is what was prophesied by the (pseudepigraphal) book of *Enoch* and the apostles. The book then counsels the faithful to strengthen themselves and to rescue the ones being taken in by evil. The book ends with a lyrical doxology.

BACKGROUND CONCERNS

Jude is the same name as Judah, the son of Jacob, whose family became the tribe of Judah. In addition to being the name of the land which had Jerusalem as its main city, it was a common name in the New Testament including an otherwise unknown ancestor of Jesus mentioned in Luke's genealogy (Luke 3:30); two disciples of Jesus, (1) Judas, son of Jacob (or James), and (2) Judas Iscariot (Luke 6:16), who betrayed Jesus; Judas, the Galilean, a famous revolutionary (Acts 5:37); Judas Barsabbas (Acts 15:22, 27, 32); and others. The tradition of spelling the name of this book as "Jude" in English probably arose in order to avoid confusion with the Judas who betrayed Jesus, though there is no difference in the spelling of the names in the original Greek.

"Jude" to distinguish from Iscariot

323

Since Jude 1 calls Jude a "brother of James," Christian tradition considers Jude to be one of the four brothers of Jesus (with James, Joses and Simon; Mark 6:3), who became a disciple only after Calvary (Acts 1:14). The fact that Jude does not claim to be an apostle, but simply a "servant of Jesus Christ" (Jude 1), and that he does not include himself among the apostles (Jude 17) is thought to confirm this tradition.

Against this identification of Jude as the brother of Jesus, the following arguments are brought: the book looks back to former days when it speaks of "the faith once delivered to the saints" (Jude 3) and treats Christianity as a well-established doctrine, with the term "your most holy faith" (Jude 20). This sounds like the language of later generations of Christians. Additionally, the book suffered difficulty being included within the canon of the New Testament in some areas, especially in the region of Antioch where it was included in a list of heretical books. Additionally, Jude indicates no personal knowledge of Jesus nor awareness of any of Jesus' characteristic teachings.

not written during 1st gen. of Xians

Many things in the book indicate it was not written during the first generation of Christians, when beliefs were still in a state of development and growth. The language of this book looks back at the time when the apostles were leading the church and beliefs were being formalized. The language of Jude reflects a more settled and institutional community. "Faith" has become "the faith." A commitment to follow Jesus has become an allegiance to a set of beliefs. While it is not possible to date this development precisely, these kinds of qualities place this book among the later books of the New Testament, perhaps, along with the pastorals and general epistles. The language is certainly more like the pastorals and general epistles than Paul and Mark. Examples include "our common salvation" (3); "contend for the faith once delivered to the saints" (3); "our only Master and Lord, Jesus Christ" (4); "remember the predictions of the apostles of our Lord" (17).

attention to problem of lust

One also notes the attention given to the problem of lust and passion. This is characteristic of a developing struggle with gnosticism in the church after the days of the apostles. It is seen in phrases such as "ungodly persons who pervert the grace of our God into licentiousness" (4); "indulged in unnatural lust" (7); "defile the flesh" (8); "by those things that they know by instinct as irrational animals do" (10); "they boldly carouse together" (12); "casting up the foam of their own shame" (13); "following their own passions" (16, also 18); "hating even the garment spotted by the flesh" (23).

The book provides little internal evidence suggesting its provenance or destination. The opening verses, where epistles normally indicate the addressees, speak only of "those who are called, beloved in God the Father and kept for

Jesus Christ." The book has to have been written where strong Jewish traditions existed, probably in Palestine or Syria.

LITERARY CONSIDERATIONS

Jude contains the only explicitly cited quotations from the Pseudepigrapha in the New Testament. Jude quotes by name and verbatim from *1 Enoch* 1:9, and also paraphrases other sections of *1 Enoch*, and many think the book also utilizes sections from now lost portions of the *Assumption of Moses* or the *Testament of Moses*. Jude is one of the literary sources of 2 Peter (see the accompanying parallel texts). It seems easier to explain 2 Peter as copied from Jude, than vice versa, because of Jude's direct citation of *Enoch*. It seems easier to understand why the author of 2 Peter felt uncomfortable with, and therefore omitted, references to a work which was not widely accepted as authoritative. On the other hand it is more difficult to understand why Jude would insert a reference to *Enoch*, if he were using 2 Peter as his primary text.

THE MESSAGE
Outline

Survey of contents

Immediately following the opening of the letter, the author introduces the problem that has prompted it. Certain "ungodly persons" have managed to find their way, unnoticed, into the community. While there is not much information about who these troubling people are, it is clear that the author is concerned that they are leading some of the believers away from the faith they have been taught. Although the entire book interfaces descriptions of the problems of these evil people with comparisons and prophecies out of Jewish history, the information is generic rather than specific. Jude 4 indicates that these ungodly ones "pervert the grace of God into licentiousness" and deny "our only Master and Lord, Jesus Christ." Jude 8 further describes these evil ones as defiling the flesh, rejecting authority, and reviling the glories. Jude 10 alleges that these men lack understanding and therefore act irrationally in reviling things they shouldn't. They participate in the community's love feasts, though their participation involves boldly carousing together (12). They are vocal about their misgivings, their own qualities, and shamelessly manipulate people for their own ends (16). They are "worldly people, devoid of the Spirit" (19). All of these descriptions provide little concrete information that can be utilized to identify the beliefs or allegiances of these intruders. It is also clear that it is not so simple a matter as throwing them out of the congregation, since some of them are not sure of their way and can still be restored to the community and others can be spared from the fire, and a few deserve cautious mercy (22, 23).

In order to encourage believers to be faithful to God, Jude refers to the experiences of people in the past. The book uses the stories of the Exodus, the fall of the angels, the cities of the plain, the dispute over the body of Moses, the experience of Balaam, and of Korah to warn that it is not enough merely to belong to a community of believers. They must fortify themselves in their faith.

Two of the quotations in this book were derived from books which are not part of the Hebrew Bible. Jude 8-9 seems to be taken from now lost portions of either the *Assumption of Moses* or the *Testament of Moses* (both known today as works from the Pseudepigrapha) and 14-16 comes from *1 Enoch 1:9*.

RELEVANCE FOR TODAY

Jude, with its clear affinities to, as well as quotations from, *1 Enoch*, provides an informative window of insight into the apocalyptic world views of *a Jewish-* early Judaism. Jude clearly shares in, and has been shaped by the Jewish- *Xian* Christian milieu in which it was produced. Perhaps, in addition to hearing the *apocalyptic* explicit warnings of the book, there are also unintended, but important, lessons *worldview* to be learned about the way world views, and religious views are shaped by culture and society.

In the age of AIDS, Jude's warnings about the dangers of promiscuity take on an additional tone of urgency. Jude not only appeals to this congregation to be wary of the dangers that promiscuity creates, but also appeals to the congregation to be a source of caring and redemption to those afflicted in their community.

ISSUES FOR DISCUSSION AND REFLECTION

1. Read (sections from) the book of *1 Enoch* and compare the content and conceptual world of Jude with that of *Enoch*. In what ways does Jude differ from *Enoch*? In what ways are they alike?
2. Discuss the use of an apocryphal book as an authority by this canonical writer. Are there inspired, but not canonical, texts? Does a text have to be inspired to be used by an inspired writer? What does inspiration mean?
3. Make a list of the problems of those who disturb the community in Jude. How serious is this threat to the health of this church?
4. Carefully read the epistle through and make note of how the epistle has used the verb "keep" (both active and passive voice, and in present and past tense) to provide structure to the book.

FURTHER READING

Arichea, Daniel C. and Howard A. Hatton
    1993   *A Handbook on Jude and Second Peter*. New York: United Bible Society.
Bauckham, Richard
    1990   *Jude and the Relatives of Jesus in the Early Church*. Edinburgh: T & T Clark.

Bigg, Charles
  1901   *A Critical and Exegetical Commentary on the Epistles of St. Peter and St. Jude.* (International). Edinburgh: T & T Clark.
Charlesworth, James H., Ed.
  1983   *The Old Testament Pseudepigrapha. Volume 1: Apocalyptic Literature and Testaments.* Garden City, NY: Doubleday.
Elliott, John H.
  1982   *I-II Peter/Jude.* Minneapolis: Augsburg.
Kelly, John Norman D.
  1969   *The Epistles of Peter and of Jude.* London: Adam and Charles Black.
Krodel, Gerhard
  1977   *Hebrews, James, 1 and 2 Peter, Jude, Revelation.* Philadelphia: Fortress.
Neyrey, Jerome H.
  1993   *2 Peter, Jude: A New Translation With Introduction and Commentary.* (Anchor). Vol. 37c. New York: Doubleday.
Reicke, Bo Ivar
  1964   *The Epistles of James, Peter and Jude.* (Anchor). Volume 37. New York: Doubleday.
Sidebottom, E.M.
  1967   *James, Jude and 2 Peter.* London: Thomas Nelson.

1 Enoch	Jude 4-24	2 Peter 2:1-3:7
		1But false prophets also arose among the people, just as there will be false teachers among you, who will <u>secretly</u> *bring in* destructive heresies, even <u>deny</u>ing the <u>Master</u> who bought them, bringing upon themselves swift destruction. 2And many will follow their <u>licentiousness</u>, and because of them the way of truth will be reviled. 3And in their greed they will exploit you with false words; *from of old* their <u>condemnation</u> has not been idle, and their destruction has not been asleep.
	4For admission has been <u>secretly</u> *gained by* some who *long ago* were designated for this <u>condemnation,</u> ungodly persons who pervert the grace of our God into <u>licentiousness</u> and <u>deny</u> our only <u>Master</u> and Lord, Jesus Christ.	
	5Now I desire to remind you, though you were once for all fully informed, that he who saved a people out of the land of Egypt, afterward destroyed those who did not believe.	
10:5-7 the Lord said to Raphael: "*Bind* Azazel hand and foot, and **cast** him into the **darkness**: and make an *opening* in the desert, which is in Dudael, and **cast** him therein. And place upon him rough and jagged rocks, and cover him with **darkness**, and let him abide there for ever, and	6And <u>the angels</u> that did not keep their own position but left their proper dwelling have been <u>kept</u> by him in eternal chains in the <u>nether gloom</u> until **the judgment of the great day**;	4For if God did not spare <u>the angels</u> when they sinned, but **cast** them **into** *hell* and committed them to *pits* of <u>nether gloom</u> *to be* <u>kept</u> **until the judgment**; 5if he

cover his face that he may not see light. And on **the day of the great judgment** he shall be *cast* into *the fire*.

7just as <u>Sodom and Gomorrah</u> and the surrounding cities, which likewise acted immorally and indulged in unnatural lust, serve as an <u>example</u> by undergoing a <u>punishment</u> of *eternal fire*.

did not spare the ancient world, but preserved Noah, a herald of righteousness, with seven other persons, when he brought a flood upon the world of the ungodly; 6if by turning the cities of <u>Sodom and Gomorrah</u> to *ashes* he condemned them to extinction and made

them an <u>example</u> to those who were to be ungodly; 7and if he rescued righteous Lot, greatly distressed by the licentiousness of the wicked 8(for by what that righteous man saw and heard as he lived among them, he was vexed in his righteous soul day after day with their lawless deeds), 9then the Lord knows how to rescue the godly from trial, and to keep the unrighteous under <u>punishment</u> until **the day of judgment**, 10and especially those

8Yet in like manner these men in their dreamings <u>defile</u> the flesh, *reject* <u>authority</u>, and

revile the glorious <u>ones</u>. 9But when the arch<u>angel</u> Michael, contending with the devil, disputed about the body of Moses, he *did* not presume to pronounce a reviling judgment upon him, but said, "The Lord rebuke you."

10But these men revile *whatever they do not understand,* and by those things that they know by instinct as irrational animals do, they are destroyed. 11Woe to them! For they walk in the way of Cain, and *abandon* themselves for the sake of gain to Balaam's error, and perish in Korah's rebellion. 12These are blemishes on your love feasts, as they boldly carouse together, looking after

Enoch 80:2-8 In respect to their days ... He will turn and appear in their time, and *withhold rain*; ...the fruit *shall not be born* in its (proper) season.... Many of the chiefs of the stars shall make errors ... and plagues shall come upon them, so as to destroy them. **Enoch 88:1** I then saw one of those

who indulge in the lust of defiling passion and *despise* authority. Bold and wilful, they are not afraid to revile the glorious ones, 11whereas angels, though greater in might and power,

do not pronounce a reviling judgment upon them before the Lord.

12But these, like irrational animals, creatures of instinct, born to be caught and killed, reviling *in matters of which they are ignorant,* will be destroyed in the same destruction with them, 13suffering wrong for their wrongdoing. They count it pleasure to revel in the daytime. They are blots and blemished, reveling in their dissipation, carousing with you. 14They have eyes full of adultery,

four who had come.
out earlier seizing
that first star,
binding his hands
and feet, and
throwing him into
an abyss—this abyss
was narrow and
deep, empty and
dark.

1:9 And **behold!**
He *cometh* **with ten
thousands** of **His
holy** ones **to
execute judgment**
upon **all** and to
destroy all **the
ungodly: and to
convict all** *flesh* **of
all** the *works* **of
their ungodliness
which they have
ungodly
committed, and of
all the**
hard **things which
ungodly sinners
have spoken
against Him.**

themselves;
*waterless clouds,
carried along by
winds*; fruit*less* trees
in late autumn,
twice dead,
uprooted; 13wild
waves of the sea,
casting up the foam
of their own shame;
wandering stars for
whom the nether
gloom of darkness
has been reserved
for ever.

14It was of
these also that
Enoch in the
seventh generation
from Adam
prophesied, saying,
"**Behold**, *the Lord*
**came with his holy
myriads, 15to
execute judgment
on all, and to
convict all the
ungodly of all their**
deeds **of
ungodliness which
they have
committed** in such
an **ungodly** way,
and of all the
harsh **things which
ungodly sinners
have spoken
against him.**"

insatiable for sin.
They entice
unsteady souls.
They have hearts
trained in greed.
Accursed children!
15*Forsaking* the
right way they have
gone astray; they
have followed the
way of Balaam, the
son of Beor, who
loved gain from
wrong-doing, 16but
was rebuked for his
own transgression; a
dumb ass spoke
with human voice
and restrained the
prophet's madness.

17These are
waterless springs
and *mists driven by
a storm*;

for them the
nether gloom of
darkness has been
reserved.

16These are grumblers, malcontents, following their own passions, loud-mouthed <u>boasters</u>, flattering people to gain advantage.

18For, uttering loud <u>boasts</u> of folly, they entice with licentious passions of the flesh men who have barely escaped from those who live in error. 19They promise them freedom, but they themselves are slaves of corruption; for whatever overcomes a man, to that he is enslaved. 20For if, after they have escaped the defilements of the world through the knowledge of our Lord and Savior Jesus Christ, they are again entangled in them and overpowered, the last state has become worse for them than the first. 21For it would have been better for them never to have known the way of righteousness than after knowing it to turn back from the holy commandment

17*But you must
remember*, beloved,
the predictions of
the apostles

*of our Lord Jesus
Christ*; 18they said
to you,

"In the last *time*
there *will be*
scoffers, following
their own ungodly
passions." 19It is
these who set up
divisions, worldly
people, devoid of
the Spirit. 20But
you, beloved, build
yourselves up on
your most holy
faith; pray in the
Holy Spirit; 21keep
yourselves in the
love of God; wait
for the mercy of our
Lord Jesus Christ
unto eternal life.
22And convince
some, who doubt;
23save some, by
snatching them out

of the fire; on some
have mercy with

delivered to them.
22It has happened
to them according
to the true proverb.
The dog turns back
to his own vomit,
and the sow is
washed only to
wallow in the mire.

1This is now
the second letter
that I have written
to you, beloved, and
in both of them I
have aroused your
sincere mind by
way of reminder;
2*that you should
remember* the
predictions of the
holy prophets and
the commandment
*of the Lord and
Savior* through your
apostles. 3First of
all you must
understand this, that
scoffers *will come*
in the last *days* with
scoffing, following
their own passions
4and saying,
"Where is the
promise of his
coming? For ever
since the fathers fell
asleep, all things
have continued as
they were from the
beginning of

fear, hating even
the garment spotted
by the flesh.

creation." 5They
deliberately ignore
this fact, that by the
word of God
heavens existed
long ago, and an
earth formed out of
water and by means
of water, 6through
which the world
that then existed
was deluged with
water and perished.
7But by the same
word the heavens
and earth that now
exist have been
stored up for fire,
being kept until the
day of judgement
and destruction of
ungodly men.

Chapter 32

The Authority and Use of the Bible
Glen G. Greenwalt

THE QUESTION OF AUTHORITY ITSELF
The ambiguity of authority

Any discussion of the authority and use of the Bible must first confront the larger issue that in our modern world the role of authority is itself ambiguous. Whereas certain persons, institutions and ideas once held respect and the sway of opinion by the simple fact of their position, role or place in society, this very understanding of authority is questioned within modern societies. While authorities still exist, they are not ends in themselves. Authority is rather something acquired by perfecting skills, amassing and handling exponentially expanding mounds of information, by controlling and allocating scarce resources, and by serving the public interest.

So, for example, parents no longer possess authority over their children by the mere fact of parentage. Parents who fail to safeguard the interest of a child jeopardize their right to the child. Likewise, statecraft no longer belongs to the domain of sovereign rights, but to the political satisfaction of the collective interests of individual citizens. And so the list goes on and on. While industry, the courts, news organizations, and even academic communities still appeal to noted authorities, the status of authorities is measured by the skills, information, or the threat or accommodation of interests they bring to a particular issue or conversation. Thus in our modern world belief, respect, obligation, and even obedience are seldom evoked by appeal to authority alone. Even the use of the threat of force is couched in terms of some broader need, interest or reason.

Analysts of the modern world often point to the world's loss of unconditional authorities as a major cause of most of the ills that beset modern societies. Wherever modernity makes inroads into a society an erosion of established institutions follows that can be measured by the fragmentation of the society at large. The irony, however, is that the modern world with its flight from

337

authority first arose as an attempt to overcome the fragmentation of an earlier world torn apart by religious and national strife. It is this story that must be remembered in any attempt to retrieve an authoritative role for the Bible in the life of the individual or of the wider community.

Modernity's flight from authority

As in any story, the actual causes of modernity's flight from authority are complex, but most scholars agree on the major events in the story. The first major challenge to the conception of a world ruled by established authority took place in that flowering of human knowledge known as the Renaissance. While the Renaissance is usually remembered for its works of art and its nascent science, the discoveries made regarding the literary process of constructing texts was no less significant as a factor in creating the world we now assume as our everyday world. Court scholars, and particularly monastery monks, pouring over recently discovered texts from the ancient world, greatly expanded their knowledge of the historical origins and backgrounds of available texts. As a consequence of this study, claims to the right of dominion by both the nobility and the clergy could be tested for their authenticity against the records of other ancient texts. The result was a certain loss of authority for both regal and religious texts, as it was demonstrated that these texts possessed the same human characteristics as other texts. The seal of a king or bishop was not a guarantee of the authenticity of a text. Texts were open to outside critique.

Without question, much of the criticism that is directed toward authorities is produced by the antics of authorities themselves. Our age is not the first to become disillusioned by the ineptitude, not to mention, scandalous immorality and blind ambition of its religious and political leaders. When authorities behave like other mere mortals, any transcendence of status is obliterated. As a matter of historical record, long before Protestants split with the Roman church and hurled epithets of Babylon against its leadership, battling popes who resided both in Rome and Avignon France, not only hurled apocalyptic curses at each other, but mustered their armies as well. In such situations, where there exist not only corrupt, but conflicting authorities, the first casualty is often authority itself, since right of rule is now determined not by divine right or title but by strength of arms. In such a situation the strongest brute becomes lord and master.

Still, Martin Luther and his appeal to the Bible and the Bible alone as the founding authority of life is perhaps the major cause of modernity's suspicion of authority. Luther certainly never intended to set the individual over against established authority, but the effect of his famous stand against the medieval church at the Diet of Worms was no less the same. Once authority becomes internalized as a matter of conscience, then no external authority can hold ultimate sway. Not surprisingly, Luther and the other Reformers sought to stifle the spirit of anarchical individualism by the establishment of church creeds that defined the proper meaning of the Bible, but once the Bible became the property of the individual interpreter, individual conscience became the final authority of all beliefs and practices. The consequence was a clash of authorities that has never since been quelled. The two hundred years following the Reformation were years of almost unremitting warfare that left Europe impoverished and war-weary.

It is against this backdrop of the fagot, the guillotine and endless religious and political warfare that modernity's flight from authority must be measured.[1] What modernity offered was a way of thinking that promised to restore order to the religious and political bedlam that threatened to disintegrate Europe in the clash between its warring factions. The scientific writings of Bacon, and Newton in particular, offered a process of thinking whereby, by means of a few fundamental laws and with a degree of precision and simplicity previously not imagined, the properties and behavior of every particle of every material body in the universe might be explained. Order and clarity now reigned in the realm of physical science in a way that could only be hoped for in the social sciences. It is hardly surprising, therefore, that thinkers involved in the areas of logic, ethics and theology would seek to duplicate the success of the natural sciences in the realms of philosophy, psychology, sociology and even religious studies. The hope was that in this way those areas of human life most plagued by ignorance, superstition and idle conjecture might be governed by clear, exact methods.

The recovery of authority's wider meaning

The crisis of authority now confronting human civilization is more daunting than that faced by any previous generation. Not only do we possess the capacity to destroy ourselves with weapons of mass death, but our world has become a global village where we simply cannot live apart from each other any longer. As a result of our global communications and our rapid forms of transportation, what happens in any isolated corner of the world almost immediately affects what is happening in the rest of the world. This means that Christians cannot work out an understanding of the authority of the Bible outside other claims to authority be they secular or those of other religious faiths.

How then can the Bible function as an authority today, given the history of conflict and suspicion that now greets any claim to authority? Perhaps the answer lies in recovering the original, wider meanings of authority itself. Our English word for authority is derived from the Latin *auctoritas* (opinion, decision, power), the root of which is *auctor* (cause, sponsor, promoter, surety), which in turn is traced to *augere* (to increase, to enrich). Thus the concept of authority is a rich one that entails elements of generating, enriching, causing something to increase and thus to become established and certain. Only in a derived sense is authority a matter of power, since force may exist without proper authorization.

Unfortunately, this distinction between power and authority is often glaringly absent in the actual annals of church history. Far too often the church, both Catholic and Protestant, has resorted to the power of its tribunals and armies to do what the Bible itself can never do, namely, coerce by means of force those who hold some opinion differing from that of the divines or the church councils. If the notion of Bible authority can be recovered, it will be in the sense of something that engenders, secures, enriches and fosters the well-being of human communities. No one of these facets of authority can be eliminated without severely undermining the Bible's authority, as we will now see.

MODELS OF BIBLICAL AUTHORITY
Authority located IN the biblical text

In its classical formulation, the authority of the Bible is located in its divine infallibility. On this view, the Bible is regarded as the final authority for faith and practice in the church because it is believed that while God did not write the actual words of the Bible, God so stimulated and moved the human authors to write, and assisted them while they were writing, that the ideas conceived in their minds and expressed in their words are the infallible truths God meant to convey to human beings.

So understood, the authority of the Bible is founded upon an act of divine intervention that assures an infallible and inerrant written revelation. Utilizing what might be called the logic of divine sovereignty,[2] defenders of the classical formulation assume that since the qualities of inerrancy, infallibility, and absolute truthfulness belong properly to divine knowledge and since God has communicated the contents of the Bible to human beings, then the Bible, along with the laws, doctrines, and teaching authority pursuant to it, must share the same divine status. A synthesis is thus assumed between the divine communicator and human recipients. The one receiving the divine revelation cannot be merely God's messenger or representative if that means the recipient possesses autonomy enough to block or distort the message.

Clearly, on this view, it is the model of authority as authorship that serves as the reigning metaphor. As a matter of fact, both Jewish and Christian exegetes have long understood the limitations of the metaphor of authorship as the foundation for biblical authority. The Old and New Testaments alike bear witness to the fact that they were not the product of an author simply sitting down to write, or even of a scribe taking notation. The Bible contains a rich mixture of literature that is distorted if it is read as if it were only the product of divine authorship or dictation. Parts of the Bible are collections of earlier remembrances that have been collected by redactors, as is evident in the conclusion of Deuteronomy, where an editor tells of Moses' death. Other parts of the Bible are comprised of hymns and praises *to* God, which would lose their very intention if they were authored *by* God. Furthermore, half of the Psalms are laments and some are even curses *against* God, which make no sense at all if they are thought to be inspired by God. Still other sections of the Bible are historical records of God's dealings *with* human beings and human beings' dealings with God.

Because of the inherent diversity in the Bible, both Jewish and Christian interpreters long favored allegorical and typological interpretations of the Bible to literal ones. The earliest existing commentaries on the Bible were written in the form of glosses between the texts (*glossa interlinearis*) or in the margins surrounding the text (*glossa marginalis*), which were comprised of allusions to other texts, collected bits of wisdom, and allegorical and typological re-presentations of the text. With the arrival of the Renaissance and particularly the Reformation, biblical commentators began abandoning allegorizing readings of the text. In the interest of substantiating church doctrine in the face of religious controversy and the historical knowledge that the humanists brought to the biblical text, they began interpreting the Bible primarily as the foundation for dogmatic theology, apologetics, and sectarian polemics. Luther, for example, distinguished only between the Christological and the literal sense of the text. Ironically, it was in the very attempt to use the Bible as a theological weapon, that the original sense of the Bible's authority as the Word of God was threatened. Whereas prior to the Renaissance and the Reformation, exegetes possessed a great deal of latitude in interpreting the biblical text, the existence of theological controversy within the church moved them toward apologetic readings of the Bible. The result was a loss of the original diversity of readings that surrounded the biblical text. Under the pressure to substantiate competing theological claims, the Bible became a book of dogmatic law.

The facts are that the Bible itself testifies otherwise to its identity. The model of the Bible as a book of canon law or as an address sent by God is but one of many images the Bible contains of itself. In reality, the Bible (Old Testament) never existed as a book until the second century of the Christian era, and even then its origin as book arose out of the controversies between Jews and Christians over issues of authority. For most of Jewish history, the texts that comprise the Old Testament were a loose collection of laws, histories, songs used in dance, moral sayings, prophecies, and even legends and fables that were used in multiple fashions. The texts of the tradition were sewn into garments, chanted, recalled in times of crisis and joy, appealed to in legal disputes, recited in prayers, and so on. What we now call the Old Testament was in fact the heritage of a faith that kept alive Yahweh's relationship with the Jews. Thus the model of the Bible as canon law or oracle fails to do justice to the texts of the

Bible itself. Inspiration in the Old Testament and the New Testament is an aspect of the overall guidance of God by the divine Spirit.

The practical matter of the case, however, is that appeals to the Bible's inspiration never resolve questions of its authority or use. The unbeliever asks for confirmation of the Bible's teaching on some other basis than the Bible's own claim to authority. And as for believers, it is often precisely those who insist most strongly upon the Bible's inspiration that often disagree as to the meaning of what the Bible says. In today's climate the metaphor of authorship functions more to legitimate apologetic stances than it does to help explain how God's voice yet speaks to men and women in a way that can be distinguished from all the conflicting voices that clamor for attention around them. In order to retrieve the metaphor of authorship, the church must do a better job of showing how all that we know and perceive comes as an original revelation that addresses human beings. Originally, both Jews and Christians believed that the Bible was only one of the means by which God addresses human beings. Nature, history, and human consciousness were also the books upon which God wrote. By again making this point clear, the Bible can be better appreciated as the voice of God.

Authority located BEHIND the biblical text

In their attempt to locate the authority of the Bible in a way that escaped controversy, many biblical scholars in the past two hundred years have attempted to locate the Bible's authority behind the text, rather than in the divine infallibility of the text itself. Here authority assumes the role of providing the warrant or justification of a claim by means of its witness to the founding moments of Jewish and Christian faith. Thus the authority of the Bible rests not upon what it says, or how it was written, but on the adequacy of its witness to God's saving action within a historical community. The true authority in the Christian faith is the redemptive power of God that is yet luring and shaping history in the direction of the redemptive ends God has established for creation. The Bible, then, is authoritative not because it comprises a unique category of human literature. Its authority resides rather in the quality of its moral and religious insights, and in the fact that it is an indispensable source for understanding the historical roots of Jewish and Christian faith. The metaphor of authority here employed is that of the expert witness.

On this understanding of the Bible's authority, biblical exegesis and theological inquiry are directed not so much to the text of the Bible itself, but rather to the events that stand behind the text and its production. As a consequence, the last two hundred years of biblical research have been directed toward the development of methodologies that distinguish within the text its true witness to God's revelatory activity. The primary methods of research scholars have employed in this task include source criticism (examines a text for its literary unity), form criticism (seeks to determine the nature of the literary forms or units that comprise a text and thereby the *Sitz im Leben* or actual situation out of which it arose), tradition criticism (explores sacred concepts handed down from generation to generation), redaction criticism (seeks to recover the various stages through which the text was produced), and social criticism (seeks to understand social realities out of which the text emerged).

The great strength of this position is that it has focused attention on the notion that the strength of Jewish and Christian claims is not based on any sort of special pleading to the doctrine of inspiration, but on the reality that God has indeed acted in history. This view is further enhanced by the fact that it has greatly enriched our understanding of the biblical texts and the historical contexts that stand behind them.

Still, taken in isolation, this metaphor for authority as that which legitimates or provides warrant is not without its limitations. In the first place, scholars have become increasingly wary of crediting the biblical witnesses with historical objectivity in the modern sense. The documents of the Bible arose out of the confessions and proclamations of particular communities of faith, so that the line between their faith and the exact facts of history was one they seldom if ever maintained. The writers of the Bible would have been surprised by the demands of being disinterested observers. They were passionately committed to their faith. Second, since the revelation of God in history is never one among other mundane objects within history, however far down one digs through layers of cultural accretions, the divine is never immediately grasped. Because the referent of faith lies not only outside of the text itself, but outside of history as well, historical investigation tends to confirm the suspicion that faith lacks realities. So one method of historical-critical procedure after another has been proposed— literary criticism, form criticism, etc.—all of which have failed to disclose the divine source of the Bible's authority.

Third, and perhaps most significant, the actual role the Bible serves within the church has changed. The critical methods of Bible study that have been developed during the past two hundred years, while they have provided a rich treasure trove of information about the Bible, have tended, inexorably, to distance the text from the average reader. Even an introduction to the Bible that is intentionally reader-friendly, as is this present one, distances the Bible from those who lack the time or the literary inclination or ability to read a text like this. The reality in the church today is that while more information about the Bible is now available than at any other point of the church's history, the actual impact of the Bible on the daily life of Christians appears to be at an all-time low. The daily discourse of Christians is simply not enriched with the language of the Bible in the way it once was. If the Bible is again to *function* in an authoritative way within the *daily life* of the church, the actual reading of the Bible must again take place at all levels.

Authority located *IN FRONT OF* the biblical text

In an attempt to move beyond the limitations imposed by the first two understandings of the Bible's authority, Karl Barth and many of those who trace their theological identity to Barth have sought to locate the identity of the Bible's authority in the aura of authority that surrounds the Bible. For Barth and his followers, God is a living God who cannot be confined either to the pages of a text or to the archaeological ruins of history. It is the Bible's capacity to provide a place of encounter between God and humanity that makes it authoritative. The metaphor of authority that overrides this position is that of an august presence that evokes a response of awe and wonder.

Central to Barth's understanding of the Bible was his claim that we know things and people in very different ways. To know things we observe them and perhaps do experiments on them. But to know a person one must enter into some sort of communication in which there is give and take. The purpose of the Bible, then, is not to tell us things about God, however true or helpful. Christian faith is not a matter of submission to various propositions that must be believed and acted upon. Faith is rather a matter of commitment of the self in trust to the God who is encountered in a personal way through the texts of the Bible.

In Barth's words, the Bible "renders God as an agent." In everyday words, the Bible is the place where God comes alive for the reader. From this perspective, the Bible's authority is dependent not on its facticity in every detail, nor is it dependent on the breadth of its scientific knowledge or the depth of its philosophical acumen. What matters is that through its symbols, poetry, narratives, epistles, and so on, we come to *know God*, rather than *many things about God*. Even as a historical novel often better captures the personality and importance of a historical figure than the biographical details in a historical text, so the Bible is a history-like story of God's action in history. The Bible's authority, then, is located in the power of its proclamation and hearing. When people approach the Bible with the expectation of hearing God, God does not disappoint them, but meets them in the foolishness of preaching and listening.

On this view, the primary mode of studying the Bible is that of hearing. While Barth was himself an accomplished practitioner of historical-critical methods of textual exegesis, he subordinates such exegesis to the bottom of his list. Barth was above all else a preacher, who believed that through the foolishness of preaching, the Word of God is made ever alive. In this sense, Barth's use of the Bible most closely approximates that of the Bible's earliest exegetes. The only difference is that Barth's glosses have passed through the fire of critical inquiry—a demand that Barth imposed upon all of his students.

The magisterial power of Barth's understanding of the Bible is seldom denied, even by Barth's staunchest critics. The strength of Barth's position is located in the fact that the Bible's authority is recognized despite the historical limits of both the text and the hearer. Revelation is always God's responsibility, rather than a human responsibility. God is always free, ever and again, to make the divine will and presence known.

Still, for all its power, Barth's way of encounter never fully escaped the limits imposed by the critical outlook. Critics often push those who follow Barth to make more explicit how it is that God meets us in the reading and preaching of the Bible. Is God simply an agent created by the narrative in the way that any character "comes alive" in a story, or is God an agent outside of the text? If the latter is the case, then questions must be asked why the Bible is the primary place where we encounter God. And questions must also be asked whether all encounters with the Bible truly evoke the presence of God. Thus the critical questions Barth wished to escape remain in place at the end of the day. For Barth's position to recover the place of dominance it held during the middle decades of this century it would have to be enriched by the more dialogical methods of inquiry and confession that our ever shrinking world demands. While the days of proclamation are certainly not over, the dangers and smallness of our world demand that we listen more than we speak—even to those we deem our opponents.

Authority located THROUGH the biblical text

Among biblical scholars and theologians of the church, one can detect the emergence of a new consensus regarding the Bible's authority that draws together positive claims of each of the earlier models. On this view, the Bible, as a gathering of texts that took place over several millennia, is viewed as an integral part of the process by which the Spirit of God is ever luring and drawing human beings in the direction of redemption. The inspiration of texts is but a part of the much larger work of the Spirit that is described in the Bible, for it was by the Spirit that the heavens and earth were formed, and it was the Spirit that inspired the artisans who constructed the Hebrew tabernacle in the wilderness, and it was by the Spirit that Samson and the other Judges performed mighty deeds, and it was the Spirit that Jesus promised to guide human beings into all truth. The canon of the Bible is closed, on this view, only in the sense that the Bible bears unrepeatable witness to the founding moments of faith. No later witness of the Spirit can make similar claims.

The authority of the Bible, then, while it includes the previous definitions of authority, focuses the seminal meaning of authority on that which causes something to increase or be enriched. The authority of the Bible is located in the role that the Bible plays in shaping and molding a redemptive form of life.

Simple recognition of the Bible's inspiration is not sufficient to define the Bible's authority. Nor is the amassing of technical knowledge about the Bible's situation of origin or its literary production essential for the Bible to possess authority. The metaphor here is that of a fount of life. For the Bible to possess authority over peoples' lives, they must be exposed to the same questions and difficulties and carry on the same conversations that mark the boundaries of the biblical community. Simply put, authority is a creative force within the life of a person or a community. For those whose lives and speech are shaped by a particular way of life, they cannot escape the authority of that way of life even when they protest against it; for even their protest takes place within the language and concepts that have already shaped them.

On this view, the Bible is not simply a letter from God (although it may include letters from God), or a history of God's activity in history (although it certainly contains historical records), or even the place where God's Word is yet heard. It is more the place where God's people continue their conversation of what it means to live faithfully to God. The Bible in W.G. Chesterton's famous turn of a phrase, is a truly democratic process that gives a vote even to the dead. It is the place where God's people from all ages meet together in council to determine what is the will of God for our present situation.

The discovery of God's will is understood, therefore, according to this emerging view, as a dialectical process. The authority of the Bible rests as much in the tension between its many stories, admonitions and principles as in its content. Stories are clarified through admonitions and principles, and in turn, principles and admonitions are enriched and take on life through examples and stories. During this process of achieved synthesis, both rational and experimental, patterns and shapes of God's redemptive leading emerge. This is not a license for Christian arrogance. Although Christians must answer all questions from within the bounds of the world of Scripture, that world is not a closed one. It is open to all voices of hurt and anguish. At the heart of Christian faith is what Peter Hodgson has called "a sober, almost defiant hope" that impels Christians beyond every present achievement, however good, into an ongoing "emancipatory project that will never be finished in history."[3] The critical credibility of the Christian arises then only in the embrace and liberation of all who are hurting and oppressed—whatever their language, color, gender or race. Only in this way can the Christian story, the story of the redeeming God, become the story of all peoples.

In the end, what matters in reading the Bible is not that one possess the skills of a legal jurist or the learning of a biblical scholar, although these may prove helpful, but that one seeks to live life in accordance with the best available understandings of God's unfolding story. To read the Bible faithfully requires the analogical imagination of a novelist, or better yet, the empathic sensitivities of a family member. Skills in Christian faith are best acquired by imitation and habit. In the final analysis, authority is located in the Christian community not by force of legislation or by wealth of knowledge, but by the redemptive shaping of God's inbreaking kingdom. In a word, the Bible, much like a family scrapbook, is the collective memory over time of what it means to live faithfully to the ongoing call of God. The Bible is authoritative not because it is inerrant, or even because everything in it came by way of direct revelation. Rather, it is authoritative because it is via these stories, aphorisms, rules, histories, and witnesses that God's people continue to be inspired in their following after God.

FURTHER READING

Barr, James
   1973   *The Bible in the Modern World.* London: SCM.
Barth, Karl
   1957   *The Word of God and the Word of Man.* New York: Harper.
Blaisdell, Charles R., Ed.
   1990   *Conservative, Moderate, Liberal: The Biblical Tradition.* St Louis: CBP.
Farley, Edward
   1982   *Ecclesial Reflection: An Anatomy of Theological Method.* Philadelphia: Fortress.

ENDNOTES

1. See Farley pp 27-82.
2. Jeffrey Stout, *Flight from Authority: Religion, Morality, and the Quest for Autonomy.* (Notre Dame: University of Notre Dame Press, 1981).
3. *God in History: Shapes of Freedom* (Nashville: Abingdon, 1989), pp 182, 183, 222.

Am-ha-Aretz	Literally, "people of the land" (Hebrew). The common people of first-century Palestine who were not members of the so-called parties described by Josephus.
Alexandrinus, codex	A fourth-century manuscript of the New Testament symbolized by the letter *A*.
chiasm	A literary device where the author uses a pattern such as A, B, B′, A′, where there is correspondence between the first and last item, the second and next-to-last item, etc.
diaspora	The dispersion of Jews from Palestine throughout the entire Mediterranean world during the Hellenistic era. By the time of Jesus, more Jews lived outside of Palestine than within it.
Essenes	One of the parties of Jews that Josephus describes. They are often identified with the community that produced the Dead Sea Scrolls.
God-fearers	Gentiles who were attracted to the Jewish religion and worshiped with Jews, but did not take the full step of converting to Judaism and being circumcised.
Hellenism	The spread of Greek culture, languages and customs throughout the Mediterranean world after the time of Alexander the Great in the fourth century B.C.E.
inclusio	A literary device where the author begins and ends a segment of material with the same idea, concept or terminology.
Koine	A form of the Greek language that was spoken by common people in the first century, and in which most of the New Testament is written.

minuscule	The cursive form of Greek writing found in later manuscripts.
mystery religions	Religions in the Greco-Roman world which were often traced back to foreign deities and usually included initiation rites that were known only to those who joined the religion. One of the most popular in New Testament times was the cult of Isis.
palimpsest	A manuscript that has been written over by a subsequent scribe.
papyrus	The form of paper made from the papyrus reed that was used for the earliest New Testament manuscripts.
paraenesis	Short segments of moral and ethical instruction included in Greco-Roman writings, including letters of the New Testament.
pericope	A segment of literary material that was probably an individual unit or story later included in a larger writing.
Pharisees	One of the so-called parties of Jews that Josephus describes. Their life centered around the synagogue and the oral tradition. They believed in the resurrection and accepted the law, prophets and writings.
Q	A name scholars gave to the sayings of Jesus material that is found in both Matthew and Luke.
Sadducees	One of the so-called parties of Jews that Josephus describes. They were priestly, centered around the temple, did not believe in the resurrection, and accepted only the five books of Moses.
Septuagint	The Greek translation of the Hebrew Old Testament made in inter-testamental times. It is abbreviated LXX.
Sinaiticus, codex	An early fourth-century manuscript of the New Testament found in a monastery on Mount Sinai. It is one of the oldest complete New Testament manuscripts and is designated by the symbol ℵ.
sondergut	Unique material found in an individual gospel which is not included in any other.
stoicism	One of the most popular philosophies of the first-century Greco-Roman world. Although it had earlier emphasized cosmology, by the first century the emphasis was on morality, including an emotional

detachment that enabled a person to accept whatever circumstances life brought.

synagogue
Jewish place of worship which by the first century had spread throughout Palestine and the Diaspora. Jews met in the synagogue for Sabbath worship, where reading of the Torah was emphasized. It also served as a school for Jewish boys.

syncretism
The practice of combining elements from various traditions and religions into a new system.

synoptic
Literally, with the same view. It refers to the three gospels Matthew, Mark, and Luke. Each view the story of Jesus from a common perspective that includes literary dependence.

temple
The Jewish worship place in Jerusalem where sacrifices were carried out. It served as the center for the Jewish religion in Palestine, and was destroyed by the Romans in 70 C.E.

textus receptus
The common textual tradition of the Greek New Testament based on later minuscule manuscripts.

uncial
A type of writing in which all letters are capitals and there are no divisions between words. The early manuscripts of the New Testament were written in this form.

Vaticanus, codex
An early fourth-century manuscript of the New Testament. It is one of the earliest manuscripts of the entire New Testament. It is designated with the symbol *B*.

Zealots
One of the groups that Josephus describes in first-century Judaism. These were the revolutionaries who wished to overturn Roman rule.

Index of Subjects

357

Index of Biblical References

362

363

366

367

371

374

Contributors

John C. Brunt, Ph.D. (Emory University) Vice-President for Academic Administration and Professor of Biblical Studies at Walla Walla College.

Ernest J. Bursey, Ph.D. (Yale University) Professor of Biblical Studies at Walla Walla College.

Douglas R. Clark, Ph.D. (Vanderbilt University) Dean of the School of Theology and Professor of Biblical Studies at Walla Walla College; Consortium Director, Madaba Plains Project.

Glen G. Greenwalt, Ph.D. (Vanderbilt University) Professor of Theology at Walla Walla College.

Bruce C. Johanson, D.Th. (University of Uppsala) Professor of Biblical Studies at Walla Walla College.

Ronald L. Jolliffe, Ph.D. (Claremont Graduate School) Professor of Biblical Studies at Walla Walla College.

Sakae Kubo, Ph.D. (Chicago University) Former Dean of the School of Theology at Walla Walla College, Former President of Newbold College, Former Academic Vice-President at Atlantic Union College.

Pedrito U. Maynard-Reid, Th.D. (Andrews University) Professor of Biblical Studies at Walla Walla College.